Great Civil War Heroes and Their Battles

Great Civil War Heroes

and Their Battles

EDITED AND WITH AN INTRODUCTION BY WALTON RAWLS

ABBEVILLE PRESS · PUBLISHERS · NEW YORK

For B.H.R.

Editor: Walton Rawls

Designer: Jack Golden

Library of Congress Cataloging in Publication Data

Main entry under title:

Great Civil War heroes and their battles.

1. United States – History – Civil War, 1861-1865 –
Biography. 2. Generals – United States – Biography.
3. Admirals – United States – Biography. 4. United
States – History – Civil War, 1861-1865 – Campaigns.
5. United States – History – Civil War, 1861-1865 –
Personal narratives. I. Rawls, Walton H.
E467.G77 1985   973.7'092'2 [B]   85-1404
ISBN 0-89659-522-6

About the Illustrations:
Most of the decorative and patriotic engraving
used throughout the book come from rare
envelopes prepared for the benefit of both Union
and Confederate soldiers – to bolster their resolve
and to encourage them to write home regularly.
The weapons illustrated are taken from U.S.
Ordnance manuals of the period and from *The Atlas
to Accompany the Official Records of the Union and
Confederate Armies.* The portraits and vignettes, as
well as many of the battle scenes, come from two
rare books, *The Heroes of the Civil War* and *Generals
and Battles of the Civil War,* discussed at length in
the Introduction. Other rare items have been
supplied by private collectors and public
institutions, including the Museum of the City of
New York, which permitted us to use Currier &
Ives prints from the Harry T. Peters Collection.

CONTENTS

LIST OF BATTLES ILLLUSTRATED

The Commanders in Chief

Gen. U.S. Grant.

Gen. Robt. E. Lee.

INTRODUCTION

The fifty valiant men featured in this book were selected by an anonymous compiler of a nineteenth-century volume called *The Heroes of the Civil War*. The book's individual leaves apparently first had been issued serially as sales-promotion premiums by a tobacco manufacturer late in the last century, one of numerous similar series, judging from the volume's introduction: "The albums previously published by us, interesting and instructive as they are, have been quite as much devoted to the world at large as to our own country. We have now decided to issue an Album pertaining entirely to the United States. Looking around for a suitable subject, what could we find more appropriate than a History of the Heroes of the Civil War—a strife so full of deeds of valor on both sides that one would fain pass by the cause of the strife and admire the individual. We find numberless heroes, fighting on their respective sides, leaving behind them reputations and characters that will challenge the attention of the world for all time. Much care has been taken to have the sketches and histories accurate; and we offer this Album to our patrons with full confidence, believing that all will enjoy it, and, while doing so, will have a kindly feeling for W. Duke, Sons & Co."

W. Duke was Washington Duke, a Confederate veteran who returned to his small farm near Durham Station, North Carolina, after the war. He had few assets to his name besides two young sons, Benjamin and James, and a barn full of locally grown tobacco. General William T. Sherman's Union army was still quartered nearby, and he began to make a living by selling his former enemies the "makin's" of Bull Durham cigarettes in little cloth bags closed by a drawstring. By the time the Duke Company's Civil War album was published, Washington's sons were producing more than half of the cigarettes in the country, and James eventually monopolized the U.S. retail tobacco trade through his American Tobacco Company. Although the monopoly was dissolved by the Supreme Court in 1911, the company has survived to the present.

There is no direct indication of when this album was published, but judging from the latest dates mentioned in the biographies and the fact that fifteen of the heroes covered were still alive at publication, it is clear that the book was issued no earlier than 1888 and no later than 1890. The most remarkable aspect of this publication was its set of fifty color portraits of leading generals and admirals, both Union and Confederate. One had seen old photographs and steel engravings, and occasional hand-colored lithograph portraits among the Currier & Ives prints, but never before so complete a coverage of Civil War notables in chromolithographs this vibrant and lifelike. In most cases the source of the portrait from life is readily identifiable, but, of course, some now-unknown lithographer was given the difficult task of reconstituting the monochrome portrait into color for "chromo" printing—through his own innate or carefully trained sense of what hues to combine in the plates to produce such a splendid result. Several of the Confederates' likenesses match those in a set of engravings made in 1865, among them the ones of Beauregard, Hardee, Joe Johnston, Bragg, and Hampton, while portraits of others, such as Halleck, Hood, and Breckinridge, closely resemble well-known photographs. The picture of Sherman comes from a portrait made in 1888, when he was sixty-eight years old, and shows him with a white beard and bereft of the unruly shock of hair so characteristic of his Civil War photographs.

Each portrait was issued with a concise biography (or "Short History of . . .") printed in a virtually unreadable type size. The letters are so small that two lines of type could almost fit in the white space between these lines. It would seem that the publishers valued the portraits more highly than the biographies, or they were determined to get as much information as possible onto two pages. Nevertheless, the biographies are, as the Duke Company assured us, "accurate," and so carefully typeset that only a handful of typographical errors could be found in what turned out to be a total of nearly 100,000 words. Despite a few nineteenth-century flourishes, the text is admirably informative and remarkably well-written. There is no clue to the identity of the author, or authors; and, even though there is some repetition in the re-describing of the same battle for several generals, care obviously has been taken to vary the telling. The text makes use of numerous quotations from contemporary sources, but relatively few are identifiable. Some are clearly from autobiographies and memoirs, and others are said to come from the works of a "well-known historian" or "competent military authority," or from magazine articles and newspapers of the period. There is even one reference to a pe-

The Irrepressible Conflict.

scnal interview, so it is very likely that many a bit of information about Civil War times is captured here that might otherwise have been lost to posterity. It is in this hope that the material is now republished.

Another important feature in the makeup of the present volume is a small souvenir album called *Generals and Battles of the Civil War*, which bears a sticker with the notation, "Copyrighted Feb. 2nd, 1891, by A. W. Bomberger, Canton, Ohio." However, the original date of conception (and, possibly, execution) is certainly much earlier, since the latest illustration is dated May 21, 1864—nearly a year short of the end of the war. The picture in question, of General Grant's council of war at Massaponax, Virginia, is clearly based on a well-known photograph by Timothy H. O'Sullivan, who learned photography from Mathew Brady in New York and worked for Alexander Gardner in photographing Union army camps, fortifications, and the ghastly aftermath of battles for Northern publications. The spectacular thing about all the sepia-toned lithographs in this small book is that they strongly resemble good-quality photographs, except that in contrast to the posed, rather static Civil War pictures of Brady, O'Sullivan, Gardner, and others, these mostly are like snapshots taken at the height of battle—something not then possible photographically because of the long exposures and bright illumination required. Anything that moved during exposure would be either a blur on the glass plate negative or would not register at all on the very slow emulsions of the period.

Chances are both books were conceived during the late 1880s—as was the famous Kurz and Allison series of battle scenes also included in this volume—a period twenty years after Appomattox, ten years after the last former Confederate state had been "reconstructed," and when time enough had passed for the hatred and bitterness to have mellowed somewhat. Union General William Tecumseh Sherman commented on this change in a March 8, 1876, interview with the *New York Herald*: "I feel kindly toward all Southern Generals. I think people of the West and North cherish no bad feelings except toward Jeff. Davis. He did no worse than anybody else but people seem bound to have somebody to hate. For instance the Southern people hate Butler." Sherman's

1875 *Memoirs* was the first book by an important Civil War figure to appear, and it definitely stirred up bitter memories and recriminations for a period, but by the time Grant's volumes were published in 1885 and 1886 a friendly truce seemed to be in effect. Southerners were again in the president's cabinet, and Radical Republican control of the House and Senate, with its vindictive program against the South, had been broken. The former ruling class of the South was once more in power, having displaced the carpetbaggers and the scalawags, recovered the state legislatures and governorships, and begun a new relationship with its former slaves. In the fall of 1880, the United States Government had issued the first of 128 volumes in its evenhanded series *War of the Rebellion: A Compilation of the Official Records of the Union and Confederate Armies*, and in the years 1891 to 1895 the War Department was to follow that with the fascicles of *The Atlas to Accompany the Official Records of the Union and Confederate Armies*, which basically reproduced battle maps of both sides.

For many, it was a melancholy reflection that brother had been pitted against brother in the late War between the States, and the time had come for family bonds to be reunited for the country's sake. There had been many instances of divided families. Major General Thomas L. Crittenden of the United States Army was the brother of former Brigadier General George B. Crittenden of the Confederate States Army. Confederate General Edmund Kirby Smith had planned an attack on a Union position that his own younger brother was killed in opposing. Also, friend had fought friend. Union generals Hooker, Sedgwick, Townsend, and Besham had been West Point classmates of Confederate generals Bragg, Early, and Pemberton. Generals Pope and Longstreet, both in the West Point class of 1842, found themselves battling each other all through the war. And as a young officer, Robert E. Lee had served together with Ulysses S. Grant on General Winfield Scott's staff in the Mexican War, along with future Union generals Sheridan, Hancock, Lyon, Kearny, and Sedgwick.

Late in the nineteenth century the feeling spread that all the old Civil War soldiers had conducted themselves both bravely and honorably in the great battles of their prime. As former Captain Oliver Wendell Holmes, Jr.—who had been wounded three times—ex-

Now, boasting Southron, hold thine own,
No maiden's arms are round thee thrown!
A Northern Freeman holds thee fast—
Yield! or this moment is thy last!

pressed it twenty years after the war: "Through our great good fortune, in our youth our hearts were touched with fire." Old enemies were no longer still enemies. Eighty-two-year-old Confederate General Joe Johnston stood bareheaded in New York on a raw, cold mid-February day in 1891 throughout the long funeral of General William T. Sherman, the man to whom he had finally surrendered his Rebel forces in late April, 1865. Although repeatedly urged, Johnston refused to cover his aged head, saying "If I were in his place and he were standing here in mine, he would not put on his hat." This gesture of respect cost him his life from pneumonia ten days later.

By this time, all restrictions had been lifted on the restoration of citizenship and rights to former Confederate leaders, but full restitution still required an oath of allegiance to the Union that a few diehards would not make, preferring to enter the grave as unreconstructed rebels. Characteristically, General Lee had been among the first to ask for a presidential pardon after all general officers and civil officials of the Confederacy were denied the vote unless they sought pardon and swore allegiance. Later, in 1868, President Andrew Johnson had issued a "universal proclamation" of pardon at Christmas, but it still excluded about 300 Confederate veterans from full rights.

Just after the war ended, the national trauma of Lincoln's tragic assassination spurred wild demands for vengeance against the Southern leaders, and only Grant's intervention prevented the arrest of General Lee and other Confederate generals as "conspirators." Nevertheless, "Hang Jeff Davis" persisted as a popular cry of the time—backed up with large rewards on his head—and when captured he was incarcerated in Fortress Monroe for two years. A few other Southern officials were imprisoned for shorter terms, but only one man was executed as a war criminal: Confederate Captain Henry Wirz, the commander of the infamous Andersonville prison. The swift capture and expeditious hanging of the Lincoln conspirators seems to have slaked public hunger for revenge.

The ready acceptance by most Southerners of the outcome of this bloody affair of honor spawned no bands of Rebel guerrillas holding out in mountain keeps or fervent attempts to establish a Confederate government in exile (an acquiescence perhaps re-

lated to a tradition of duelling; the American *code duello* was formulated and published in Charleston in 1838 by John Lyde Wilson). But failure to acknowledge their cause as lost did lead some hotheads to offer their well-honed military skills to the hard-pressed Archduke Maximilian, Emperor of Mexico, whose own cause was lost in front of a firing squad ordered by Benito Juarez in 1867. Others—in the American tradition—headed west for a new start on the frontier, while some of the still-wealthy went to Europe, and one group of Southern families even colonized a part of Brazil. The vast majority of footsore and ragged Confederate veterans headed home, where there was still just about time to plant and harvest a few vegetables and fatten a pig for the family before winter set in. With no need for a mopping-up campaign or an army of occupation, the Union volunteer army was quickly demobilized, and of the million men in blue at the time of Appomattox only 183,000 were on the active rolls in November, 1865. By the end of 1866, the regular army was down to its prewar assigned strength of 25,000, a figure it was nearly 10,000 shy of in 1860.

The choices of the fifty heroes whose biographies appear in this volume probably will not satisfy everyone. However, this nineteenth-century selection necessarily reflects the popular estimation of reputations at the time. Immediately one might question the absence from the list of General George H. Thomas, "The Rock of Chickamauga," or of General John Pope, the hero of Island No. 10 and of Corinth. In the case of Pope, this slight probably is embedded in his total failure at the Second Battle of Bull Run and his subsequent resignation as commander of the Army of the Potomac. The case of General Thomas is more problematical; his qualifications as a hero far exceed those of many listed generals. Not only did General Thomas earn his sobriquet by holding his position on the field at Chickamauga long after the rest of the Union army had been swept away, but on December 16, 1864, at Nashville, he inflicted on General John B. Hood's army the greatest defeat of the war, capturing over 10,000 men and 72 field guns. The failure to include Thomas on this list may stem from residual feelings of ambivalence toward him—by Southerners and Northerners alike—as a native-born Virginian who chose to ignore the call of his home state and remain in the Union army.

AS IT IS.

"GOD WATCHES OVER THEM."

AS IT WILL BE.

nother Virginian who wore the Federal blue uniform in 1861 (and made the list) was General Winfield Scott, and since he never took part in any Civil War battle one might question his inclusion among the heroes of this war. It is not that Scott lacked ample claims to being a hero, he fought bravely in the War of 1812, the Indian wars of the 1830s, and, finally, in the Mexican War. However, at the beginning of the Civil War he was seventy-five years old, weighed 300 pounds, suffered from dropsy, was unable to leave his chair unaided, and, hence, could not take the field. He was, nevertheless, general-in-chief of the U.S. Army, and had been since 1841. His venerability was not all that unusual in military service at the time: the average age of department heads in the army establishment was seventy-four, and the commander of the commissary department was seventy-eight. One of Scott's three brigadier generals in the field, John E. Wool, was seventy-seven and would not retire from active service until he was seventy-nine! Although infirm physically, General Scott retained his strategic faculties and set about crafting an overall plan for Union victory. He called for a complete blockade of Southern seaports, a splitting of the Confederacy along the Mississippi River, and a gradual closing in on the Southern armies. Derisively called the "Anaconda" plan by opponents who thought it would take only ninety days to demolish the Southern armies, Scott's scheme estimated a need for at least 300,000 men and three years to conquer the South. Younger strategists scoffed, urging quick retirement for Scott, and, on April 15, 1861, President Lincoln called for 75,000 volunteers to serve a period of three months.

Although not literally a hero of the Civil War, General Scott certainly was an important factor in the make-up of the list of luminaries in this book, for he had trained or commanded many of them at one time. A pompous and exacting Virginia aristocrat—nicknamed "Old Fuss and Feathers"—he had favored the advancement of Southern officers in his military organization: "If the Southern rascals have so much merit, how are we to deny them?" Partly as a result of his predilection, many promising Northern-born officers had resigned their commissions in the years following the Mexican War, hoping for faster advancement and better futures in civilian life—among them McClellan, Halleck, Hooker, Burnside, Sherman, Slocum, Rosecrans, and Grant.

In fact, Scott's staff was all Southern except for one man, but after South Carolina and ten other Southern states seceded, a movement Scott emphatically opposed, three of his most-valued officers—Albert Sidney Johnston, Joseph Johnston, and Robert E. Lee—departed for positions in the Confederacy. General Scott even had offered Lee the job of commander of the U.S. Army, but when Virginia left the Union Lee felt compelled to follow.

In the two administrations prior to Lincoln's, the secretary of war had been a Southerner: Jefferson Davis under Franklin Pierce, and John B. Floyd under James Buchanan. Davis returned to the Senate at the end of Pierce's term, and when his native state Mississippi seceded in January of 1861 he had resigned, expecting to be named commander of the Confederate armies, for he was a West Point graduate and had commanded a volunteer regiment in the Mexican War. His successor at the War Department, who became a Confederate general, resigned his post (or was dismissed) on December 29, 1860, over President Buchanan's refusal to evacuate the Federal garrison at Fort Sumter in Charleston harbor. General Scott had pleaded in vain with Buchanan during the final months of 1860 to reinforce the forts in Southern states against possible seizure in the event of rebellion.

Three of the Southern generals in this volume had commanded the U.S. Military Academy at West Point in the eight years prior to the outbreak of war—one of them for only 48 hours. Robert E. Lee and William J. Hardee served normal tenures, but Pierre G. T. Beauregard was abruptly relieved by President Buchanan following the secession speech of Louisiana Senator John Slidell, Beauregard's brother-in-law. Among the forty-six generals whose biographies appear in this volume (four of the fifty are admirals), thirty-four were West Point graduates. Of the 387 U.S. Army officers who resigned their commissions to join the Confederacy (out of a total of 1,108 regular army officers in 1861), 288 of them were West Pointers, including nineteen graduates born in the North—among them John C. Pemberton of Pennsylvania, the man who was to surrender Vicksburg. Twelve of these Northerners reached the rank of brigadier general or higher in the Confederate army. Of the men still active in General William T. Sherman's West Point class of 1840, eight would fight for the Confederacy while twenty-eight remained loyal to the Union. Public awareness of this anoma-

The WRONG Man in the RIGHT Place.

lous situation led the Northern press to wildly brand West Point as a training ground for traitors. On the other hand, 162 West Pointers of Southern birth remained with the Union army, including Virginian George H. Thomas, the Rock of Chickamauga. Despite his numerous military victories over Confederate armies, Thomas was never to be quite free of the taint of Southern sympathizer, for he had been on leave in New York when, in February, 1861, General David E. Twiggs surrendered his regiment, the Second Cavalry, to Texas authorities; speculation simmered about what direction Thomas's loyalty might have taken had he been in San Antonio. The crack Second Cavalry was formed in 1855, and thirty-one of its fifty officers were from slave states, among them Robert E. Lee, Albert Sidney Johnston, William J. Hardee, Earl Van Dorn, Edmund Kirby Smith, John B. Hood, and Fitzhugh Lee—all to become general officers in the Confederate army.

So this was the military leadership situation following the secession of eleven Southern states in a matter of months: about one-third of the officers of the regular U.S. Army and one-quarter of the U.S. Navy had resigned to take up equivalent posts in the Confederacy. There seems to have been no similar outflux among the enlisted grades, for privates could not simply resign; they had to desert—and face the possibility of execution if caught.

Except for occasional skirmishes, and the bombardment and surrender of Fort Sumter, there had been no major encounters between North and South in the six months following South Carolina's secession. Radical Republican politicians and the Northern press were eager for some real action—as were Lincoln's three-month recruits, nearing the end of their enlistments—but Union General Irvin McDowell, commander of the Army of the Potomac, was in no hurry to test his raw recruits in battle until they were better trained. By the beginning of July, 1861, the Confederacy had nearly 60,000 men under arms in Virginia—22,000 under General P. G. T. Beauregard near Centreville, and another force under General Joseph Johnston at Harper's Ferry.

Under severe pressure from his party and with the Northern press daily crying "On to Richmond, On to Richmond," Lincoln finally yielded and directed the reluctant General McDowell to cross the Potomac with his 25,000 troops (no more than 800 of

SCOTT'S HOLD ON THE SECESSIONISTS

them regulars) and to seek confrontation with General Beauregard some twenty-four miles south of Washington, near Manassas Junction. General McDowell's prior service had been on headquarters staff duty, and he never had held a command of his own, not even of a company, when General Scott promoted him to brigadier general and named him commander of the Army of the Potomac.

President Lincoln was well aware that his troops were inexperienced, but he felt that the Rebels must be equally green. What he had not taken into account was the difference between the leaders of the two armies. Of the thirteen senior Union commanders sent south, eight had never been in a battle. Not one had ever maneuvered a unit as large as a brigade through the dispositions and tactics of warfare. Only one of the three division commanders had even seen a battle; another had not been on active duty since 1854; and the third previously had been just a paymaster. The nine brigade commanders were hardly any better schooled or blooded, for six of them had never faced an enemy's cannon, and one—a Lincoln appointee—had never even worn a uniform before.

Of the fifteen commanders on the Southern side of Bull Run, thirteen were West Pointers, and twelve of them were well acquainted with the smell of black powder exploding behind an enemy projectile: Beauregard, Longstreet, Cocke, Jones, Early, Evans, Jackson, Bee, Stuart, Kirby Smith, Joe Johnston, and Lee. Nevertheless, their troops were indeed as green as Lincoln's. Given these circumstances, the Battle of Bull Run—as you will learn in reading the several individual accounts in this volume—was necessarily a scene of wild confusion, with General McDowell racing around the battlefield in a carriage, personally trying to make up for a lack of staff organization and communication. Nonetheless, he never managed to get more than half his army into the battle. In "Stonewall" Jackson's account (he earned his nom de guerre in this conflict), we read that the fighting raged back and forth for several hours—often anyone's battle—with one central hilltop taken and lost three times. As General Joe Johnston said of Bull Run, "whichever army had stood a while longer on that day, the other would have given way."

As we discover in the McDowell biography, the key to the outcome of the battle was the sudden appearance—at three in the afternoon—of a unit of Joe Johnston's Confederates supposedly held at bay by General Robert Patterson near Harper's Ferry. The sight of fresh troops entering the fray was too much for the Union soldiers, and they departed the field in haste, streaming back to Washington in disorder. As described in Johnston's account: "Soldiers in every style of costume, ladies who came with opera glasses to survey the battle, members of congress and governors of States who had come with champagne and after-dinner speeches to celebrate a great Federal victory, editors, correspondents, telegraph operators, surgeons, paymasters, parsons—all were running for dear life—disordered, dusty, powder-blackened, screaming, or breathless in the almost mortal agonies of terror." As is typical of Civil War histories, the casualty count varies with the source. The author of the Johnston biography tells us that the Confederates' entire loss in killed and wounded was 1852, while the Federals lost 4500 in killed, wounded, and prisoners. Current estimates for the day's fighting are about 500 killed, 1000 wounded, and 1200 missing on the Federal side; 400 killed, 1600 wounded, and 13 missing for the Confederates. General Sherman said of Bull Run that it was "one of the best planned battles, and one of the worst fought."

The biographies, of course, do not tell a chronological story of the Civil War—only in terms of the participation of each individual, and the battles he engaged in. Nevertheless, the effect of reading these accounts is cumulative and in many ways richer than a straight history might be—something akin to the development of the central event in Akutagawa's novel *Rashomon*. Every general's role in a battle is different from those of the other participants, and, as we have seen in relation to the Battle of Bull Run, each account—those of McDowell, Howard, Johnston, Jackson, and others—adds exciting details to a growing and deepening perception of what actually happened.

All of the famous stories of the Civil War are related in these pages—Pickett's Charge, Sheridan's Ride, the Crater, the accidental shooting of "Stonewall" Jackson, the sinking of the CSS *Alabama*, the Fort Pillow Massacre—along with many lesser-known episodes, including the mystery of John Hunt Morgan's death, the blunder that cost Phil Kearny his life one rainy after-

noon, and James Longstreet's own tale of the last silk dress in the Confederacy.

For the reader not thoroughly versed in the history of the Civil War, a chronology is provided to detail the sequence and dates of significant events. The illustrations, arranged in strict chronological order, serve as a guide to the high points of the war, and two accurate maps indicate where every important engagement took place. If one is not completely conversant with which general was on whose side, the contents page can serve as a handy reference, listing the generals of the two armies separately and alphabetically, following their respective leaders. A roster of each general's major battles is to be found in the margins of his biography, along with such other information as his class at West Point (if applicable), his dates of rank (brigadier general and above), and his independent commands.

Everything in the core of this book—with very few exceptions—is authentically nineteenth-century in origin. Both the biographies and the captions to the monochrome illustrations are reprinted as originally published, except for occasional punctuation marks and the rare correction of a date or the clearer identification of a battle the writer assumes we recognize or refers to by an uncommon name. Spelling and capitalization follow the original form except in a few cases where the writers were inadvertently inconsistent in following their own style. Since fifteen of the heroes were still active when their biographies were published, their stories treat them as living; we have not altered these references but supply a death date at the end of the account.

Basically, this captivating book combines the color portraits and biographies found in one very scarce volume with the monochrome illustrations and captions from another even rarer one. These are supplemented with the avidly collected Kurz and Allison battle series and a few choice Currier & Ives prints to bring the total of battles illustrated to nearly seventy, and we also include period engravings of the uniforms, insignia, and major weapons used in the war. The result is a unique and enriching introduction to this ever-fascinating conflict, presented in the evocative words and pictures of the generation that experienced it.

OLD ABE.

He will steer the old Ship of State safely through the breakers of Secession and Disunion.

13

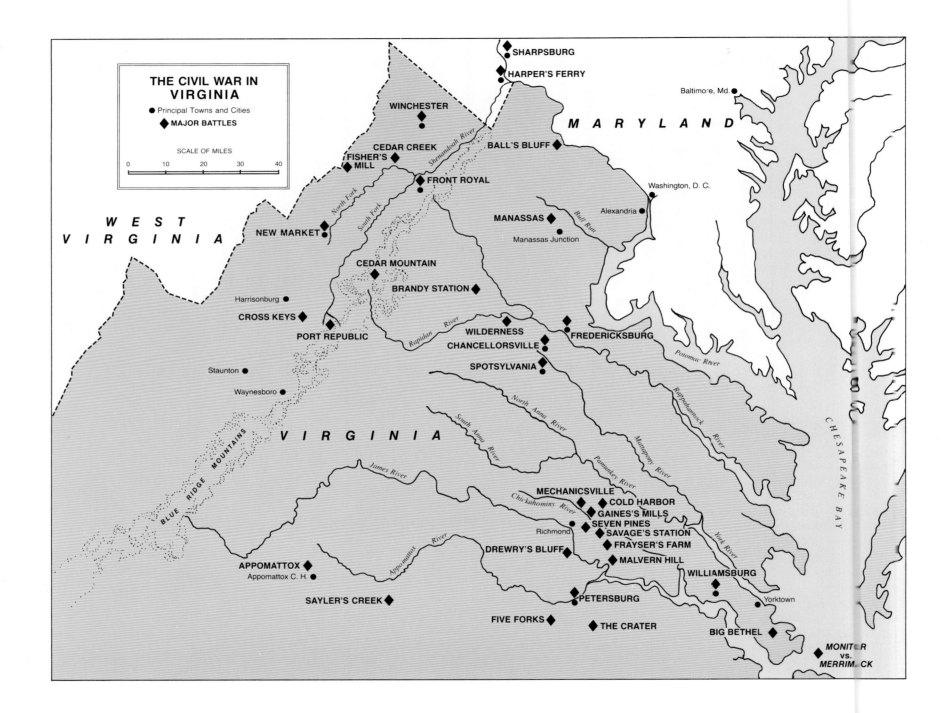

THE CIVIL WAR IN
VIRGINIA

● Principal Towns and Cities
◆ MAJOR BATTLES

SCALE OF MILES

0   10   20   30   40

MARYLAND

WEST VIRGINIA

VIRGINIA

BLUE RIDGE MOUNTAINS

CHESAPEAKE BAY

◆ SHARPSBURG
◆ HARPER'S FERRY
● Baltimore, Md.

WINCHESTER ◆

CEDAR CREEK ◆
FISHER'S ◆
MILL
◆ BALL'S BLUFF
● Washington, D. C.
◆ FRONT ROYAL
● Alexandria

NEW MARKET ◆
MANASSAS ◆
● Manassas Junction

CEDAR MOUNTAIN ◆

BRANDY STATION ◆

● Harrisonburg
CROSS KEYS ◆
◆ WILDERNESS
◆ FREDERICKSBURG
PORT REPUBLIC ◆
CHANCELLORSVILLE ◆
● Staunton
SPOTSYLVANIA ◆
● Waynesboro

James River
North Anna River
South Anna River

Rapidan River
Shenandoah River
North Fork
South Fork
Bull Run
Potomac River
Rappahannock River
Pamunkey River
Mattapony River
Chickahominy River
Appomattox River
York River

MECHANICSVILLE ◆
◆ COLD HARBOR
◆ GAINES'S MILLS
SEVEN PINES ◆
● Richmond
◆ SAVAGE'S STATION
DREWRY'S BLUFF ◆
◆ FRAYSER'S FARM
APPOMATTOX ◆
◆ MALVERN HILL
● Appomattox C. H.
WILLIAMSBURG ◆
SAYLER'S CREEK ◆
● Yorktown
◆ PETERSBURG
FIVE FORKS ◆
◆ THE CRATER
BIG BETHEL ◆
◆ MONITOR vs. MERRIMACK

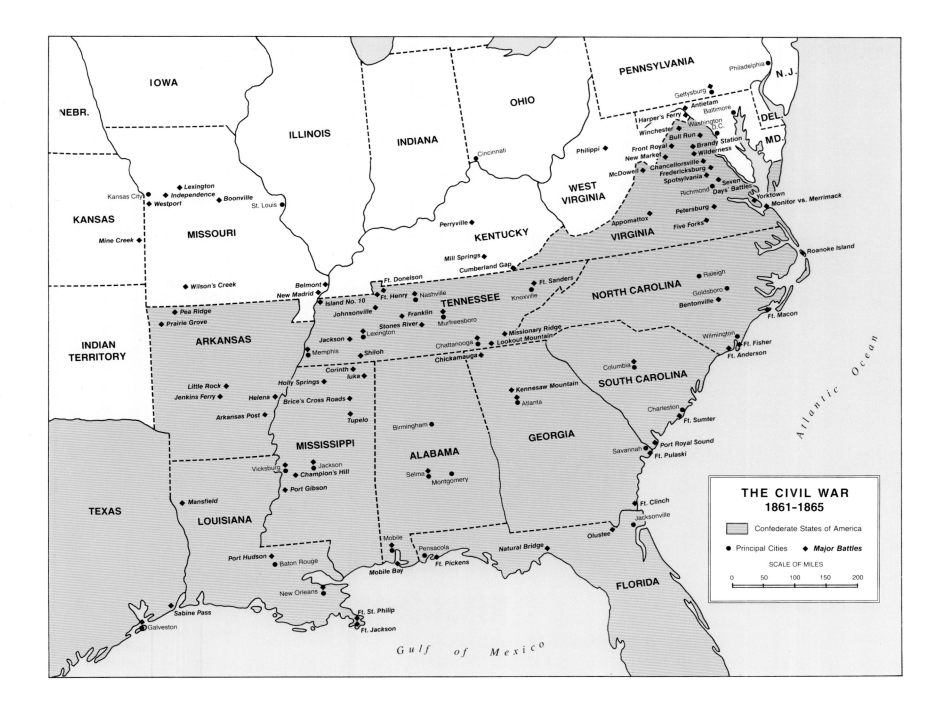

THE CIVIL WAR
1861-1865

Confederate States of America

● Principal Cities

◆ Major Battles

SCALE OF MILES

0   50   100   150   200

CHRONOLOGY

1860

6 Nov. – Abraham Lincoln elected President of the United States on the antislavery Republican ticket

20 Dec. – South Carolina secedes from the Union

*26 Dec. – Major Robert Anderson removes Federal garrison from Fort Moultrie to less-vulnerable Fort Sumter in Charleston harbor

*30 Dec. – South Carolina seizes U.S. Arsenal at Charleston; other Southern states take over Federal facilities as they secede

1861

9 Jan. – USS *Star of the West* is repulsed by South Carolina shore batteries in an attempt to reinforce and provison Federal garrison at Fort Sumter

9 Jan. – Mississippi secedes from the Union

10 Jan. – Florida secedes from the Union

11 Jan. – Alabama secedes from the Union

19 Jan. – Georgia secedes from the Union

26 Jan. – Louisiana secedes from the Union

1 Feb. – Texas secedes from the Union

4 Feb. – Representatives of seceding states convene in Montgomery, Alabama, to plan united action

4 Feb. – Peace convention is held in Washington, D.C., at urging of Virginia Assembly—attempts to find ways to restore Union

8 Feb. – Constitution and provisional government established for Confederate States of America

9 Feb. – Jefferson Davis elected President of the Confederacy

18 Feb. – General David E. Twiggs surrenders all U.S. military posts in Texas to state authorities, including, at San Antonio, the 2nd Cavalry Regiment, with Albert Sidney Johnston, colonel, Robert E. Lee, lieutenant colonel, and William J. Hardee, Earl Van Dorn, Edmund Kirby Smith, John B. Hood, and Fitzhugh Lee—all future Confederate generals

23 Feb. – President-elect Lincoln arrives unannounced in Washington aboard special train, fearing assassination attempt

4 Mar. – Lincoln inaugurated: "No State, upon its own mere action, can lawfully get out of the Union."

6 Mar. – Confederate President Davis calls for 100,000 one-year volunteers for the army

6 Apr. – Lincoln notifies Confederacy he will attempt to provision Fort Sumter

REMEMBER FORT SUMTER

11 Apr. – South Carolina demands surrender of Fort Sumter; Major Anderson asks for more time

*12 Apr. – Bombardment of Fort Sumter begins at 4:30 A.M.

13 Apr. – Fort Sumter surrenders at 2:30 P.M.

15 Apr. – Lincoln declares "insurrection" exists and calls for 75,000 three-month volunteers

17 Apr. – Virginia secedes from the Union

*19 Apr. – 6th Massachusetts Regiment, on the way to Washington, attacked by pro-Southern mob as it passes through Baltimore

19 Apr. – Federal blockade of Southern ports proclaimed

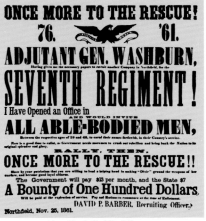

3 May—Lincoln calls for forty more volunteer regiments from Northern states and 40,000 three-year enlistees

6 May—Arkansas secedes from the Union

7 May—Tennessee secedes from the Union

13 May—Britain proclaims neutrality in American crisis

20 May—North Carolina secedes from the Union

2_ May—Richmond, Virginia, chosen as Confederate capital

29 May—General Irvin McDowell named commander of the U.S. Army of the Potomac

*10 June—Battle of Big Bethel, Virginia; first sizable clash between Union and Confederate troops

*12 July—Battle of Rich Mountain, West Virginia; General William S. Rosecrans routs Confederate forces

*21 July—Battle of Bull Run, or Manassas, Virginia; Federal forces retreat in disarray to Washington

*21 July—Richmond celebrates Confederate victory at Bull Run with 100 gun salute

24 July—General George B. McClellan replaces McDowell in command of the Army of the Potomac

*10 Aug.—Battle of Wilson's Creek, or Oak Hill, Missouri; first Confederate success in the West

*17–20 Sept.—Siege of Lexington, Missouri; Union forces surrender to General Sterling Price

31 Oct.—General Winfield Scott retires as general-in-chief of the United States Army

1 Nov.—General McClellan is named general-in-chief of the U.S. Army

8 Nov.—U.S. Navy removes Confederate commissioners Mason and Slidell from British steamer *Trent* en route to England; provokes intervention fever in England

20 Dec.—Congressional Joint Committee on the Conduct of the War challenges Lincoln's leadership; dominated by Radical Republicans

---

1862

*19–20 Jan.—Battle of Mill Springs, or Logan's Crossroads, Kentucky; General George H. Thomas defeats larger force of Confederates

27 Jan.—Impatient with McClellan's inaction, Lincoln issues War Order No. 1, which calls for general Union offensive against Confederate forces to commence 22 Feb.

6 Feb.—Union troops, under General Ulysses S. Grant, capture Fort Henry, on the Tennessee River, in Tennessee

HAVING BEEN SOLICITED BY MANY GENTLE-MEN to raise an ARTILLERY COMPANY for the Confederate service, during the War, any Volunteer wishing to join will find an opportunity by applying at 89 Church-street. Equipments and rations furnished.
August 26   CHARLES E. KANAPAUX.

*8 Feb.—Federals seize Roanoke Island, North Carolina

*12–16 Feb.—General Grant besieges and takes Fort Donelson, on the Cumberland River, in Tennessee

*6–8 Mar.—Battle of Pea Ridge, or Elkhorn Tavern, Arkansas

*9 Mar.—Battle of the USS *Monitor* versus the CSS *Merrimack* off Hampton Roads, Virginia; first encounter between ironclads

11 Mar.—General McClellan is relieved of supreme command, but retains leadership of Army of the Potomac

13 Mar.—General Robert E. Lee is "charged with the conduct of military operations in the armies of the Confederacy"—under direction of President Davis

16 Mar.–7 Apr.—Federal siege under General John Pope leads to surrender of Island No. 10 in the Mississippi River

*17 Mar.–2 July—Peninsula campaign; McClellan launches his drive on Richmond by advancing between the York and James rivers

23 Mar.–31 May—Shenandoah Valley campaign; General Thomas J. "Stonewall" Jackson harasses and routs Union armies from the valley

5 Apr.–4 May—McClellan lays siege and occupies Yorktown, Virginia

*6–7 Apr.—Battle of Shiloh, or Pittsburg Landing, Tennessee; reinforcements save General Grant from defeat

*11 Apr.–Fort Pulaski falls to Federal bombardment; commanded approaches to Savannah, Georgia

16 Apr.–First Confederate conscription act passed

*24 Apr.–Battle of the USS *Varuna* versus the CSS *Breckinridge*, in the Mississippi River below New Orleans

*25–26 Apr.–Surrender and occupation of New Orleans

*5 May–Battle of Williamsburg, Virginia

25 May–First battle of Winchester, Virginia

*31 May–Battle of Fair Oaks, or Seven Pines, Virginia

1 June–General Lee replaces General Joseph E. Johnston in command of Confederate forces in Virginia; reorganizes them as the Army of Northern Virginia

*6 June–Battle of Harrisonburg, Virginia

*8 June–Battle of Cross Keys, Virginia

MAJ. GEN'L McCLELLAN,

Our Napoleon.

GENERAL ORDER.

New York Public Library

25 June–Confederate council of war held at Richmond; Generals Lee, Jackson, James Longstreet, and A. P. Hill present

26 June–2 July–Seven Days' battles around Richmond; McClellan forced to abandon campaign against Confederate capital

26–27 June–Battle of Mechanicsville, Virginia

27 June–Battle of Gaines's Mill, Virginia

29 June–Battle of Savage's Station, Virginia

30 June–Battle of Frayser's Farm, or Glendale, Virginia

*30 June–Battle of White Oak Swamp, Virginia

*1 July–Battle of Malvern Hill, Virginia; Confederates lose 20,000 men in repeated failure to gain crest of hill

2 July–Lee withdraws toward Richmond

*8 July–Lincoln meets with McClellan at Harrison's Landing, on the James River, after the Seven Day's battles around Richmond

11 July–General Henry W. Halleck named general-in-chief of the U.S. Army; he replaces McClellan with General John Pope

11 July–General Grant becomes commander of the Army of West Tennessee

*9 Aug.–Battle of Cedar Mountain, Virginia

*29–30 Aug.–Second Battle of Bull Run, or Manassas, Virginia; Federals, under General Pope, defeated there once more

5 Sept.–General Pope resigns and McClellan is restored to command of the Army of the Potomac

---

14 Sept.–Lee crosses the Potomac and invades Maryland; carries the war into Northern territory

*14 Sept.–Battle of South Mountain, Maryland

*14–15 Sept.–Confederate General Jackson captures U.S. Arsenal at Harper's Ferry, Virginia

*17 Sept.–Battle of Antietam, or Sharpsburg, Maryland; bloodiest day in the war: 12,400 dead and wounded on the Union side; 13,700 on the Confederate

18 Sept.–Lee returns to Virginia

19 Sept.–Battle of Iuka, Mississippi

Excerpt from Lincoln's original draft of the Emancipation Proclamation

22 Sept.–Lincoln issues his Preliminary Emancipation Proclamation

*3–4 Oct.–Battle of Corinth, Mississippi

8 Oct.–Battle of Perryville, Kentucky

10–12 Oct.–Confederate General James Ewell Brown Stuart executes cavalry raid around McClellan's army and into Pennsylvania

7 Nov.–General Ambrose E. Burnside replaces McClellan in command of the Army of the Potomac

*13 Dec.–Battle of Fredericksburg, Virginia; General Burnside loses more than 12,000 men in futile attack on Confederate position

31 Dec.–Battle of Stones River, Tennessee

31 Dec.–3 Jan.–Battle of Murfreesboro, Tennessee

1863

1 Jan. – Lincoln's Emancipation Proclamation

25 Jan. – General Joseph Hooker replaces Burnside as commander of the Army of the Potomac

3 Mar. – First U.S. conscription act passed

Avoid the Draft!

HEADQUARTERS PROVOST MARSHAL, SIXTH DISTRICT, No. 6 Union Buildings, Main street, below De Kalb, NORRISTOWN, June 2, 1863.

PUBLIC attention is solicited to the subjoined circular from the Provost Marshal General. All persons wishing to join any of the Regiments here referred to, will make application to these Headquarters within the next thirty days.

JOHN J. FREEDLEY, CAPTAIN.
Provost Marshal, Sixth District.

PROVOST MARSHAL GENERAL'S OFFICE, WASHINGTON, D. C., May 22, 1863.

All men who desire to join any particular regiment of

CAVALRY

Now in the field, are hereby authorized to present themselves at any time during the next thirty days to the Board of Enrolment, in their respective Districts. The Board shall examine them and determine upon their fitness for the service, and if found to be fit, the Provost Marshal of the District shall give them transportation tickets to the general rendezvous, at the Headquarters of the A. A. Provost Marshal General of the State. As soon as they present themselves at this general Rendezvous they shall be duly mustered by a mustering and disbursing officer, and paid by him the bounty allowed by law.

JAMES B. FRY,

PROVOST MARSHAL GENERAL.

June 2, 1863.

Herald and Free Press Print, Norristown, Pa. All kinds of Job Work done to order.

Library of Congress

1 May – Battle of Port Gibson, Mississippi

*2–4 May – Battle of Chancellorsville, Virginia; General "Stonewall" Jackson accidentally shot by his own men; South's costliest victory

*16 May – Battle of Champion's Hill, Mississippi

17 May – Battle of Big Black River, Mississippi

Mid-May – Occupation of Baton Rouge, Louisiana

18 May – 4 July – Siege of Vicksburg, Mississippi

3 June – General Lee invades Pennsylvania

*9 June – Battle of Brandy Station, Virginia; biggest cavalry clash of the war, between Union General Alfred Pleasonton and Confederate General J. E. B. Stuart

13–15 June – Second battle of Winchester, Virginia; Confederate General Richard S. Ewell smashes Union garrison

15 June – Lincoln calls for 100,000 six-month volunteers

28 June – General George G. Meade replaces Hooker as commander of the Army of the Potomac — fifth commander in ten months

*1–3 July – Battle of Gettysburg, Pennsylvania; "highwater mark" for the Confederacy; Union losses 23,049, Confederate 28,063

*4 July – Confederate General John C. Pemberton surrenders Vicksburg; Grant's terms: "unconditional surrender"

9 July – Capture of Port Hudson, Louisiana; last Confederate stronghold on the Mississippi; "The Father of Waters again goes unvexed to the sea"

ATTENTION!

MERCHANTS, BANKERS AND MERCHANTS' CLERKS AND OTHERS

Meet for Organization and Enrolment

At Two O'clock

AT THE MERCHANTS' EXCHANGE,

111 *Broadway,*

To take immediate action in the present crisis. Military now engaged with the Mob. The Mayor's House being Sacked and Torn Down!!

New York Public Library

13–16 July – Draft riots in New York; several hundred killed and wounded in protest against conscription

*18 July – Battle of Fort Wagner, South Carolina

*19–20 Sept. – Battle of Chickamauga, Tennessee; Union forces retire into Chattanooga

16 Oct. – Lincoln names General Grant commander of most Union armies in the West

19 Nov. – Lincoln delivers Gettysburg Address at dedication of military cemetery

*22–25 Nov. – Battle of Chattanooga, Tennessee

*24 Nov. – Battle of Lookout Mountain, Tennessee

*24–25 Nov. – Battle of Missionary Ridge, Tennessee; Confederate General Braxton Bragg routed by General Thomas

*29 Nov. – Battle of Fort Sanders, Knoxville, Tennessee; state cleared of Confederate forces

1864

*20 Feb. – Battle of Olustee, or Ocean Pond, Florida; Union troops repulsed in move on Florida

9 Mar. – Grant promoted to lieutenant general and replaces Halleck as general-in-chief of the Union armies

*12–13 Apr. – Battle of Fort Pillow, Tennessee

*5–6 May – Battle of the Wilderness, Virginia; General Lee outmaneuvers Grant and Meade

7 May – 2 Sept. – General William T. Sherman marchs through Georgia to split upper and lower South

*8–12 May – Battle of Spotsylvania, Virginia; General Grant fails to outflank Lee's army

10 May – Battle of Yellow Tavern; General "Jeb" Stuart mortally wounded

*13–16 May – Battle of Resaca, Georgia

*21 May – Grant calls council of war at Massaponax, Virginia

25–28 May – Battle of New Hope Church, Georgia

*1–3 June – Battle of Cold Harbor, Virginia; General Grant loses 12,000 men on final day alone — lost nearly 60,000 in preceding month

15–18 June – Battle before Petersburg, Virginia

19 June – 2 Apr. – General Grant lays siege to Petersburg; longest of the war

19 June–Confederate raider CSS *Alabama*, after 64 victories, sunk by USS *Kearsarge* off Cherbourg, France

*27 June–Battle of Kennesaw Mountain, Georgia; General Sherman is repulsed with heavy losses in attack on General Johnston

2–13 July–Confederate General Jubal A. Early strikes into Maryland and reaches within five miles of Washington, D.C.

*17 July–1 Sept.–Battle of Atlanta campaign, Georgia

30 July–Battle of the Crater, Petersburg, Virginia; Grant loses 4,400 men when scheme to mine Confederate fortifications backfires

5 Aug.–Battle of Mobile Bay; Admiral David G. Farragut defeats Confederate ironclad CSS *Tennessee* and seals off city of Mobile from blockade-runners

29 Aug.–Democratic National Convention nominates Union General George B. McClellan for president on platform of immediate cessation of hostilities

*1 Sept.–Battle of Jonesboro, Georgia

*19 Sept.–Battle of Opequon, or third battle of Winchester, Virginia; Union General Philip H. Sheridan turns back General Early

IN UNION THERE IS STRENGTH.

22 Sept.–Battle of Fisher's Hill, Virginia; General Sheridan defeats General Early and begins devastation of Shenandoah Valley

*19 Oct.–Battle of Cedar Creek, Virginia; "Sheridan's Ride" from Winchester rallies retreating Union army and turns rout by General Early into victory

19 Oct.–Confederate force stages surprise raid on St. Albans, Vermont, from Canada

8 Nov.–Lincoln reelected president of the U.S.

14 Nov.–22 Dec.–Sherman's March to the Sea

*30 Nov.–Battle of Franklin, Tennessee

*15–16 Dec.–Battle of Nashville, Tennessee; Union General Thomas crushes Confederate army of General John B. Hood

1865

*15 Jan.–Capture of Fort Fisher, North Carolina; closes Wilmington, last open Confederate port

16 Jan.–21 Mar.–Sherman's drive through the Carolinas

3 Feb.–Hampton Roads Conference, between Lincoln and Confederate Vice President Alexander H. Stephens, fails

9 Feb.–General Lee named commander-in-chief of all Southern armies

17 Feb.–General Sherman burns Columbia, South Carolina

18 Feb.–Confederates evacuate Charleston, South Carolina

4 Mar.–Lincoln's second inaugural: "With malice toward none; with charity for all. . . ."

19–20 Mar.–Battle of Bentonville, North Carolina; General Johnston clashes with General Sherman for last time

*1 Apr.–Battle of Five Forks, Virginia; Lee's last assault

*2 Apr.–Fall of Petersburg, Virginia

*2 Apr.–Evacuation of Richmond, Virginia

9 Apr.–Lee surrenders to Grant at Appomattox Courthouse, Virginia

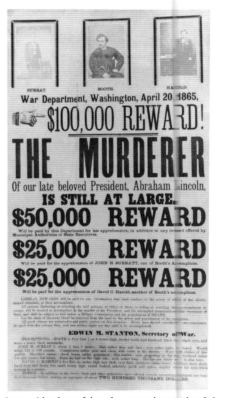

14 Apr.–Abraham Lincoln assassinated by John Wilkes Booth

18 Apr.–General Johnston surrenders to General Sherman near Durham Station, North Carolina

4 May–General Richard Taylor surrenders Confederate forces east of the Mississippi to General Edward R. S. Canby at Citronelle, Alabama

10 May–Jefferson Davis captured near Irwinville, Georgia

26 May–General Edmund Kirby Smith surrenders the last Confederate contingent under arms to General Canby at New Orleans

7 July–Lincoln conspirators hanged

9 Nov.–Confederate raider CSS *Shenandoah* under Commander J. I. Waddell, surrenders at Liverpool, England

Illustrated

Fort Moultrie, in Charleston Harbor—Toward the middle of December, 1860, it became evident from the magnitude of military operations going on, and other indications, coupled with significant threats in the South Carolina Convention, and out of it, that an occupation of Castle Pickney and Fort Sumter was meditated, even if no open manifestation should be made against Fort Moultrie.

The question of the latter, in case Fort Sumter was occupied, was one entirely subordinate, as it was completely commanded by Sumter. Major Robert Anderson, U.S. Army, determined, therefore, to anticipate the South Carolinians in their contemplated maneuver, believing that the contingency had arisen, contemplated in the closing paragraph of his instructions.

Accordingly, on the night of December 26th, at the very time that the South Carolina Commissioners had arrived at Washington to demand the surrender of the forts, he evacuated Fort Moultrie, after spiking the guns and providing for the destruction of the carriages and other material by fire, and with the aid of three small vessels successfully transferred his little command, his flag, and available munitions to Fort Sumter.

The raising of the national flag on Ft. Sumter, which Anderson had brought with him from Fort Moultrie, was one of those imposing scenes which lend a romantic and thrilling inspiration to the exigencies that history is forced to record.

The flag was raised precisely at noon on December 27, 1860. A short time previously, Major Anderson had assembled his little force of soldiers and workmen around the flag-staff. The flag was attached to the cord, and Major Anderson, holding the end, reverently knelt down. Many of the group followed his example, and the chaplain offered an earnest prayer—an appeal for support on earth and mercy in heaven. When his fervent, solemn words were ended, and the men with deep feeling had responded "Amen," Major Anderson drew the cord and the starry flag rose slowly to the top of the staff. The band rolled out the anthem of "Hail Columbia," and the group—officers, soldiers, and laborers—broke into an exultant salute, cheer following cheer, to the national emblem.

United States Arsenal
at Charleston S.C.
seized by the
state authorities
December 28th 1860

22

THE BOMBARDMENT OF FORT SUMTER
April 12, 1861
"At half past four on April 12, 1861, the first gun was fired on Sumter. Gun after gun responded to the signal, until all
the encircling batteries were engaged in the heat of bombardment. For some hours the fort made no reply. At 7 o'clock the first gun was fired in reply.
The bombardment kept up for 36 hours without the loss of a single life on either side. The barracks in Sumter were set on fire, and
the fifty barrels of powder in the magazine were rolled into the sea. On Sunday, April 14, Major Anderson pulled down his flag and evacuated Sumter."
John G. Nicolay, private secretary to President Lincoln

ULYSSES SIMPSON GRANT, U.S.A., 1822–1885

General Grant, Commander of the Union Army in the Civil War, and twice President of the United States, was born at Point Pleasant, Clermont County, Ohio, on the 27th of April, 1822. He was the eldest son of his parents, Jesse R. Grant and Hannah Simpson—people of modest and humble circumstances. General Grant's early years were spent in assisting his father in farm work and obtaining what rudiments of education the village school afforded.

In the spring of 1839 he became a cadet in the U.S. Military Academy at West Point, and it was at this time that his name acquired the middle initial which has caused so much curiosity. Thomas L. Hamer, M.C., who appointed the young cadet to his position, had always heard him called by the name Ulysses, and supposing that this was his first name and that his middle name was probably that of his mother's family, entered him on the official appointment as Ulysses S. Grant, instead of Hiram Ulysses Grant, as he had been christened. Frequent notification was given to the officials concerning this error, but, as no one felt authorized to correct it, he was compelled to carry his new initial through life. Young Grant graduated in 1843, and was immediately commissioned as a brevet second lieutenant, attached to the 4th infantry, on duty at Jefferson barracks, not far from St. Louis. In 1845 he became second lieutenant and accompanied his regiment to Corpus Christi, joining the army there under command of General Zachary Taylor. He rendered excellent service in various battles in Mexico under Generals Taylor, Scott and Worth, for which he

was on several occasions commended highly by his superior officers. For brave action in the battle of Molino del Rey, September 8, 1847, he was breveted first lieutenant; and in the advance against the City of Mexico on September 14 he carried out the daring and novel project of mounting a howitzer in the belfry of an adjacent church, for the purpose of driving the enemy from a defensive work—an idea that resulted so successfully that General Worth sent for him and personally complimented him. A few days after the entrance of the City of Mexico he was promoted to first lieutenant. With the withdrawal of the troops in 1848 he obtained leave of absence, and went to St. Louis. It was here that he married, on the 22d of August, 1848, Miss Julia B. Dent, a sister of one of his West Point class-mates. During the next four years he was ordered to service successively at Sackett's Harbor, N.Y., Detroit, Mich., Panama, California, and Fort Vancouver, Oregon. In 1853 he was appointed captain of a company at Humboldt Bay, Ca. Growing dissatisfied with this service, however, he resigned his commission in July of the year following, and engaged in farming near St. Louis, and later in real estate business in the same city. In 1860 he was compelled through lack of success to give up real estate, and went to Galena, Ill., where he entered his father's hardware and leather store as a clerk. When the news of the firing on Fort Sumter flashed through the country about a year later, Captain Grant took a decided stand for the Union, raising a company of volunteers, whom he drilled thoroughly and

West Point, 1843

Brigadier General, volunteers, August, 1861
Major General, volunteers, February, 1862
Major General, regulars, July, 1863
Lieutenant General, November, 1863
General-in-Chief, November, 1863
General, July, 1866

COMMANDED
District of Southern Missouri, 1861
Departments of the Tennessee, the Cumberland, and the Ohio, 1862
Western Armies, October, 1863
Armies of the United States, November, 1863

accompanied to Springfield, Ill. He was appointed mustering officer by Governor Yates, of Illinois, and later colonel of the 21st Illinois regiment of infantry. This regiment he conducted to the town of Mexico, Mo., where General Pope was stationed, and on July 31, 1861, was appointed under Pope to the command of three regiments of infantry and a section of artillery. In August he became brigadier-general of volunteers, and a few days afterwards was directed to report at St. Louis, where he was placed in command of the District of Southern Missouri, his headquarters being at Cairo. During the remainder of the year he was engaged in an expedition against Colonel Jeff Thompson's Confederate forces and in endeavors to suppress efforts at secession in Kentucky. Early in the following year, 1862, he conceived the plan of capturing Forts Henry and Donelson by the combined efforts of troops and gunboats. General Halleck, to whom he applied, however, slighted his plan, and it was only after urgent application and repeated suggestion that he was enabled to carry it out. On the 1st of February, however, his expedition started, and, with the capture of Fort Henry and later of Fort Donelson, after several days of desperate fighting in harsh weather, the name of General Grant was borne on the clarion note of triumph through every town in the Northern States. This was one of the signal victories of the Civil War, and it was accomplished with an amount of strategic skill that might well command the admiration even of his foes. He was at this time made major-general, a promotion of which he was very shortly afterwards deprived for pushing forward without orders from his superiors in command. On this account he was also compelled to remain at Fort Henry; but on March 13 his services were again required at Corinth. General Grant considerably strengthened the forces there, and immediately after the battle of Corinth turned his attention towards Vicksburg, with the purpose of capturing it. He started on this expedition on November 3, and through all the winter and spring toiled against obstacles greater than he had ever encountered before, and under the most disadvantageous circumstances, with the eventful siege of Vicksburg the prospective point in view. In this campaign he was materially assisted by General Sherman. After a series of minor victories, General Grant was enabled at last on May 18 to close his forces about the outworks of Vicksburg and drive the enemy within. He had a force of 71,000 men to conduct the siege and protect himself from General Johnston's army attacking him in the rear. His lines, therefore, were pushed closer and closer, and General Pemberton, commander of the Confederate troops within the city, at length asked for an armistice. General Grant's reply, however, was, ''Unconditional surrender,'' and on July 4th the city was his. This surrender, with that of Port Hudson later, opened the Mississippi to the Gulf. In recognition of these services General Grant was made major-general in the regular army, and was presented with a gold medal by Congress, together with a formal expression of thanks to him and his army.

In October he was placed in command of the departments and armies of the Tennessee, the Cumberland and the Ohio. After service in this command during the winter he was called to Washington in March, and received from the President his commission as lieutenant-general, this rank having been revived by act of congress during February. He was also placed in command of all the armies, and established his headquarters at Culpepper, Va., with the Army of the Potomac in the later part of the month. General Grant, now fully in command, determined to organize a systematic and combined movement against the Confederate forces. His idea was to form the National forces into several distinct armies, these to act at the same time against the Confederate force opposing them, and to continue vigorous action so as to prevent any detachments on the part of the enemy for relief or raiding purposes. This policy was pursued as steadfastly as possible, with the assistance of Generals Sherman, Sigel, Sheridan and others, in various quarters, General Grant remaining with the Army of the Potomac and directing his forces chiefly against General Lee. Sherman conducted his triumphant march to the sea with the purpose in mind of joining the Army of the Potomac later.

The Floating Battery.

—This novel destructive, anchored off the southern extremity of Sullivan's Island, performed a leading part in the attack on Fort Sumter. It was constructed under a storm of ridicule, which was very effectually silenced by its practical test. The battery was about one hundred feet long, by twenty-five wide, built of sawed pine timber twelve inches square, the bottom flat, the gun side presenting an angular front, the slope of which, upward and downward, was about forty degrees. This front was faced with two thicknesses of railway iron, running vertically, with four thicknesses additional of boiler iron, all bolted firmly to the wooden structure behind, and pierced for four guns of heavy caliber, requiring sixty men to work them properly. Behind the battery, at the time of the attack, was moored a floating hospital, completely protected from horizontal fire by the defenses in front, and only exposed to shell. The magazines were in the hold of the battery, protected by layers of sand bags six feet in thickness, the weight of which served as a counterpoise to that of the guns.

This, it had been first determined, should be accomplished by transporting Sherman's army by sea to Virginia; but this plan was given up, and the determination was formed of marching north by land. Sheridan marched through the Valley of Virginia, defeating Early and scattering the forces under his command; then, turning toward the East, he turned round the north of Richmond and joined the Army of the Potomac. Grant was then ready for his final campaign. President Lincoln visited him at City Point, where he was then stationed, and held a conference with him, in which Sherman and Admiral Porter also participated. Sherman then rejoined his army, the President returned to Washington, and the great campaign began for which General Grant had long been planning, and which ended in Lee's surrender at Appomattox on the 9th of April, 1865.

Immediately after the close of the war General Grant hastened to Washington to stop the further manufacture and purchase of war materials. In the months that followed the enthusiastic greetings to General Grant knew no bounds. Wherever he went he was feted and hailed throughout the Northern States as the hero of the Civil War. Congress also, in July, 1866, created the grade of general, a higher rank than had before existed in the army, and General Grant received his commission for this rank as a reward for his faithful and worthy service. In 1868 he was unanimously nominated by the Republican convention at Chicago as candidate for the presidency and defeated the Democratic candidate, Horatio Seymour, receiving 214 electoral votes to 80 for his opponent. His renomination in 1872 secured for him 286 electoral votes to 66 for Mr. Greeley, after a canvass marked for its exciting and aggressive character, and abounding in personal abuse.

On retiring from his second administration, General Grant determined to visit the countries of the Old World, and sailed for England on the 17th of May, 1877. The distinguished concourse of men that assembled to see him depart formed only the first of a long series of public tributes which greeted him at every point during his travels. From royalty of all nations he received honors rarely bestowed on the most distinguished of their own people, and his trip around the globe was one continued pageant, representing on every hand the most enthusiastic manifestations of welcome. At the Republican convention of 1880 his name was again presented as a candidate for the presidency, and, but for the traditional sentiment against a third presidential term, it may fairly be believed that his nomination would have been secured.

In 1881 General Grant settled in New York City, spending his summers at Long Branch. He had hitherto had neither the leisure nor the inclination for literary work, his only effort in this line having been a vindication of General Fitz-John Porter in the *North American Review*; but in 1884, when he was somewhat straitened in circumstances on account of the great losses incurred by reason of his unfortunate connection with Ferdinand Ward, he was engaged to write a series of articles for the *Century Magazine*, treating of his principal campaigns. This led to his purpose of writing a complete work comprising his personal memoirs—a work upon which he was engaged up to the time of his death, and which has had since an enormous sale. During the summer of 1884 the first symptoms of the disease which finally proved fatal made their appearance. He struggled bravely through the year, hastening the preparation of his work, setting himself in the face of great bodily suffering to complete the volume, the sale of which was to provide for his family. In June, 1885, he was removed to Mount McGregor, near Saratoga, where he lived for five weeks, immediately surrounded by his family and closer friends, and the centre of a greater circle of a nation and world of sympathetic watchers. His work was completed but a few days, when, on July 23, 1885, he passed away, and the sombre shadow of death fell across a name high on the honor roll of our national heroes.

"THE LEXINGTON OF 1861" – BALTIMORE
April 19, 1861

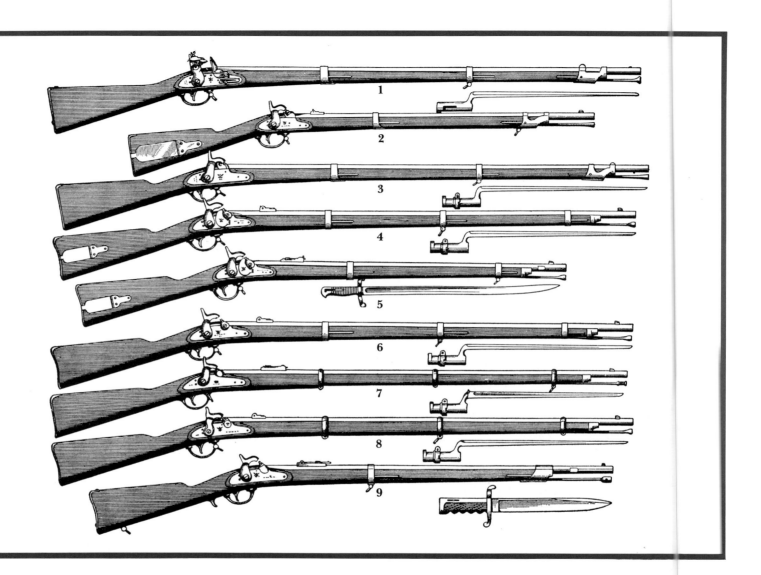

1. U.S. Flintlock Musket
   Model 1822 Caliber .69

2. U.S. Rifle
   Model 1841 Caliber .54

3. U.S. Percussion Musket
   Model 1841 Caliber .69

4. U.S. Maynard Primer Musket
   Model 1855 Caliber .58

5. U.S. Rifle
   Model 1855 Caliber .58

6. U.S. Musket
   Model 1861 Caliber .58

7. English Enfield Musket
   Model 1853 Caliber .577

8. U.S. Springfield Rifled Musket
   Model 1863 Caliber .58

9. U.S. "Whitneyville" Navy Rifle
   Model 1863 Caliber .69

MUZZLE-LOADING RIFLES AND MUSKETS

On Monument Square, Baltimore, Maryland.
—Section of Cook's Boston Light Infantry, with artillery in position, by order of Major General Nathaniel P. Banks, to quell an anticipated riot on account of the arrest of Marshal Kane and the police commissioners.

Major General, volunteers,
May, 1861

COMMANDED
Department of the Gulf, 1863

BATTLES
New Orleans
Winchester
Cedar Mountain
Baton Rouge
Port Hudson
Red River campaign
Sabine Cross Roads
Pleasant Hill

Governor of Massachusetts,
1858–61
Member, U.S. House of
Representatives, 1853–57,
1865–73, 1875–79, 1889–91
Speaker, U.S. House of
Representatives, 1856–57

In the careers of many of the most prominent military leaders who figure in the country's history is found a combination of the soldier and the statesman. Grant developed this quality, as did McClellan and Hancock, and in a more striking degree does the reader find it in the life of General Nathaniel Prentiss Banks. In him is combined an adaptness for managing the affairs of governments as well as those of wars; his introduction, in fact, to public notice was through the prominence he attained in the halls of legislation.

It was in Waltham, Mass., on January 30, 1816, that this famous soldier was born. All the circumstances around his birth were of the most humble kind. His parents were thrifty but poor people, and could give their son but a simple common-school training. But he was an apt scholar, and the country school-room proved confining to the ambitious lad. From its benches he went to a cotton factory and sought employment. His father was the superintendent of the factory, and put his son to learn the trade of a machinist under his di-

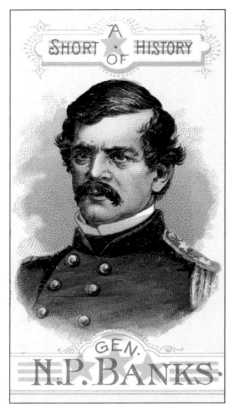

rection. But this was not enough for the lad, and during his leisure hours he began to fit himself for a wider field. Every moment was devoted to diligent study, and his ambition soon led him to public speaking. He secured engagements to speak before meetings and assemblies at a very early age, and never failed to reflect credit upon himself. Then he turned his attention toward journalism, and he soon reached the editorial chair of the village local paper. Even this did not satisfy him, and he turned with longing eyes to the bar. Here he saw fame and

fortune that was not so clearly apparent in the web of journalism. He industriously studied law, was admitted to the bar, and in 1849 stepped on the first rung of the ladder of fame, when, by unanimous vote, he was sent to the Massachusetts legislature. This was the point he had struggled and worked for, and with the enthusiasm and vigor of youth he set out to make a name and place for himself in legislative annals.

An opportunity very soon presented itself. The ancient power of the Whig party was waning in New England, and the Free-soil party was coming to the front, and its influence was beginning to be felt. Mr. Banks advocated a coalition between the Democrats and the new party, and his vigorous part in the discussion showed his admirable qualities as a speaker and statesman. He quickly rose in popularity, and was elected speaker of the State Assembly in 1851, and re-elected in 1852. In the following year he was a delegate to the Massachusetts constitutional convention, and was selected to be its chairman. On the tide of success that attended this political combination he was in 1853 elected to congress as a Coalition Democrat.

During this term of service he withdrew from the ranks of the Democratic party and identified himself with the American or "Know-nothing party," and by an overwhelming vote, as against the Whig and Democratic candidates in his district, he was re-elected to congress. In the preceding congress he had demonstrated his ability, and he was now nominated for speaker of the house of representatives. A contest lasting for more than two months followed, and he was elected by a small majority on the 133d ballot, when the deadlock had been broken by the adoption of the plurality rule. It was a bitter contest, a time of suspense for the rising young statesman, but he bore it as he bore his subsequent part in the battles of his country, bravely and firmly.

The American party went out of existence, and Mr. Banks was elected to the 35th congress as a Republican by a larger majority than before. His abilities having attracted attention throughout the commonwealth, he was next nominated for the gubernatorial chair and elected to the office. Twice again, in 1858 and 1859, he was re-elected governor, serving with distinction and dignity throughout his three terms.

In 1860 he accepted the presidency of the Illinois Central Railroad, but gave up the office when the Civil War began in the following year. Was commissioned a major-general of volunteers and assigned to the command of the 5th corps in the Army of the Potomac. For this duty he was in a degree qualified by experience in the State militia. His first active service was on the Upper Potomac and in the Shenandoah Valley, where a part of his corps acquitted itself well at the battle of Winchester, March 23, 1862.

In April and May he was left to guard the Shenandoah with two divisions. The exigencies of the service caused the withdrawal of one of these (Shields's), and General Banks was left with an army of about 8000 men. Upon this force "Stonewall" Jackson made one of his sudden onslaughts with his whole corps, and the command only escaped capture by rapid and well-ordered marching and stubborn fighting. Through good generalship the bulk of the army crossed the Potomac at Front Royal on May 26, and the Confederate leader failed to realize his reasonable expectation of capturing the entire force.

General Pope was placed in command of the Army of Virginia on June 27, 1862, and he concentrated his forces in the neighborhood of Culpepper Court-house early in August. General Banks's corps was ordered to the front on August 9, and late in the afternoon of that day a severe fight took place,

known as the battle of Cedar Mountain, which lasted well into the night. Banks's force held the position against a largely superior force, received reinforcements during the night, and before the morning of the 11th the Confederates had retreated to the Rapidan.

After participating in General Sigel's campaigns in September, General Banks was placed in command of the defenses of Washington, while preparations were secretly made to dispatch a strong expedition by sea to New Orleans. He was assigned to the command of this expedition, which sailed from New York in November and December, and on reaching New Orleans he succeeded General B. F. Butler in command of the department. Baton Rouge was occupied with a strong force, and during the winter reconnoissances were made toward Port Hudson and other points in the vicinity.

Early in April, 1863, he led the army up the Teche country, encountering no very formidable opposition, as far as the Red River. Then he crossed the Mississippi and invested Port Hudson in connection with the fleet under Admiral Farragut. Several unsuccessful attempts were made to storm the works, involving heavy losses to the assaulting armies. In July the news of the surrender of Vicksburg was received, and on the 9th of that month the garrison of Port Hudson, 6000 strong, capitulated, and the Mississippi River was once more open to the sea.

No military movements of any importance were undertaken in the department until the succeeding spring, when General Banks's army, supported by a powerful fleet, was sent up the Red River with the intention of regaining control of Western Louisiana. At the same time General A. J. Smith, with 10,000 men, descended the Mississippi, reaching the rendezvous first, and was joined by General Banks, who assumed command of the whole force at Alexandria. The army advanced along the south bank of the Red River as far as Sabine Cross Roads, when it suffered a defeat by the Confederates under General Richard Taylor, and was obliged to fall back on Pleasant Hill, having sustained heavy losses in men and material. Here, on

the following day, the Confederates renewed their attack, but were repelled with great loss; and the National army retreated without further molestation to Alexandria, where a new complication arose in consequence of the subsidence of the Red River after the spring freshets. The gunboats were unable to descend the river owing to shoal water, and an obstacle of no small magnitude presented itself. General Banks, however, at once called to his assistance Lieutenant-colonel Joseph Bailey, and through his engineering skill the boats were saved and disaster avoided. The whole force then retreated to the Mississippi.

It was in connection with the failure of this expedition that severe censure fell upon General Banks. The truth, however, was disclosed subsequently that the expedition had been attempted directly contrary to his orders, and in spite of his decided protest. It was deemed feasible, however; but the disaster predicted for it came, and almost with considerable loss. Fortunately, however, this was avoided; but it was plainly shown that no blame could rest upon General Banks, and he was honorably acquitted in the matter.

During his command of the Department of the Gulf he endeavored to reorganize the civil government of Louisiana. He applied all his statesman qualities to the task, but success did not attend him, and he failed to accomplish his desire in a manner satisfactory to the inhabitants.

In May, 1864, he was relieved of his command, and resigned his commission, returning to his home in Massachu-setts. Here the old ardor for public life in the government again seized him, and his constituents sent him to congress, representing his old district. For thirteen successive congresses he was a member, being re-elected each time with increased majorities, and for years he was a member active and often heard in public debates and upon the great questions of the times. The only intervening year of his congressional career was in 1872, when he entered with all his zeal and energy into the campaign for Horace Greeley, who was then the Liberal Democratic candidate for president. He labored without ceasing for the election of Mr. Greeley—made numerous speeches, was very influential—but the result turned against his candidate, as all know.

For a long time he served as chairman on the Committee of Foreign Relations, and became a careful student of our relations with the foreign powers.

Of late General Banks has lived a retired life at Waltham, Mass., his old home, occupying various local offices. In 1886 his daughter Maud entered the dramatic profession, and is at present meeting with success on the boards in legitimate characters. Although having passed the allotted time of three score and ten years, General Banks still retains all his active qualities of mind and brain. He is exceedingly popular among his neighbors, and enjoys the ease and comfort which are his after a life of hard-earned success.

(General Banks died on September 1, 1894.)

Battle of Big Bethel, Virginia.—The first serious reverse which the National forces met in the campaign of 1861 was on the 19th of June, at a point named Bethel Church, about twelve miles from Fortress Monroe, on the road from Hampton to Yorktown, on the James River. Brigadier-General Henry L. Pierce, of Massachusetts, being in command of the Federal troops.

The Confederate troops were commanded by Colonel John B. Magruder. The Confederate force was about 1,800 strong. The Confederate loss was trifling, and they counted another to their succession of victories. The number of Federal troops actually engaged in the affair was about 3,000. The Federal loss was sixteen killed, fifty-three wounded, and five missing.

DON CARLOS BUELL, U.S.A., 1818–1898

West Point, 1841

*Brigadier General, volunteers,
May, 1861
Major General, volunteers,
March, 1862*

*COMMANDED
Departments of the
Cumberland and the Ohio,
November, 1861
District of the Ohio,
June, 1862*

*BATTLES:
Mexican War
Rowland Station
Bowling Green
Gallatin
Shiloh
Perryville
Murfreesboro*

It is an interesting fact, and one which is full of encouragement to American young men, that those of our most illustrious soldiers and commanders who rose the highest in the estimation of the people came from the humblest birth. Not only was their birth amid the simplest surroundings, but their education was scant and their resources for learning limited. The public school of to-day, the village academy of the present, are palaces of instruction to those in which our military leaders received the rudiments of their education. It will be argued by many in connection with this, that the training school of the soldier is the military academy, or West Point, and the argument will be: "These men had the advantages of such places, and here they became the soldiers they subsequently proved." But it must not be forgotten that certain knowledge must first be had prior to an entrance into the military school. These facts present themselves in the life of General Don Carlos Buell.

What is now known as the town of Lowell, Ohio, was the birthplace of General Buell. At the time when the infant who was to develop into so sturdy and gallant a hero first saw the light on the 23d of March, 1818, the place was more of a wilderness than a settlement. It was practically nameless, and wild and uninviting in its aspect. It was scarcely in appearance the birthplace of a famous soldier, but yet such it proved to be.

The early years of the boy Don were spent as they only can be passed in such a place and amid such discouraging surroundings. The country around afforded but scant opportuni-

ties for education, and such as it did boast of were more remarkable for what they failed to teach than for anything else. But the boy had in him the true American spirit of rising above whatever position one finds his lot to be cast in, and with energy and youthful ardor he acquired a self-education. He learned what he could, and what he could not he learned from others. His parents were poor; their income did not allow of their giving him the education they might personally wish to endow upon their son. Every moment that was not spent in work was given over to learning something, however insignificant; and, being a ready scholar, what was once seen, heard or read, was not soon forgotten. The mind of the young lad observed everything with which it came into contact, while the memory was as true as steel to its possessor.

His aspiration for a military life began early, and his eyes were soon turned to the doors of the United States Military Academy. Soon the dream of his youth was realized, and he entered upon his military training. The alertness of the lad became very soon manifest, and he quickly learned the tactics of military science that were to serve him so well in his subsequent career.

In 1841 he left the academy to enter upon active service, and in health and mental equipments few young men were better endowed. He further possessed all the qualities of mind and brain so essential to the successful soldier. He first entered the 3d infantry, and proved so efficient in his initial position that was not long before the title of first lieutenant was accorded him. This he became on June 18, 1846, being then in the 28th year of his age.

He entered the Mexican War at Monterey, and his bravery won for him the brevet of captain. At Contreras and Churubusco he won additional honors, coming out of the battles with the title of major. In these fights his military knowledge received severe tests, and through his daring and bravery he received severe wounds. After he had recovered from the effects of these, his fire and ambition again rose high, and from this point in his career his ascendancy was rapid.

He served as assistant adjutant-general at Washington in 1848 and 1849, and at the headquarters of various departments till 1861. On May 11 of this year he was made a lieutenant-colonel on the staff, and on the 17th—six days later—appointed brigadier-general of volunteers. He was slated for assistance in the organization of the army at Washington, and herein he did much valuable and creditable work. In August he was assigned to a division of the Army of the Potomac.

General Buell was a great believer in discipline in the army, and this fact became at once evident in the men under his charge, until his division became distinguished and was pointed to as an example of rigid and careful discipline.

In November he superceded General Sherman in the Department of the Cumberland, which was reorganized as that of the Ohio. The campaign in Kentucky was opened by an attack upon his pickets at Rowland Station, near Munfordville, on the 17th of December. Bowling Green was the next ground from which he was heard, occupying it on the 14th of February, 1862. On the 23d of that month, with but a small force—which, however, did gallant and heroic work—he took possession of Gallatin, Tenn., and on the 25th he entered Nashville with his troops, supported by a strong fleet of gunboats.

For the services he had thus far rendered his country and flag he was promoted major-general of volunteers on March 21, 1862, and on the same day his district was incorporated with that of the Mississippi, commanded by General Halleck. He arrived with a part of a division on the battle-field of Shiloh near the close of the first day's action, April 6th. On the next day three of his divisions followed, and the Confederates were driven to their intrenchments at Corinth.

On the 12th of June he took command of the District of Ohio. In July and August General Bragg's army advanced into Kentucky, capturing several of General Buell's posts, compelling the abandonment of Lexington and Frankfort, and the removal of the State archives to Louisville, which city was threatened as well as Cincinnati. On the 5th of September General Bragg advanced from Chattanooga, and, entering Kentucky by the eastern route, passed to the rear of Buell's army in Middle Tennessee. This manœuvre was unexpected to General Buell, and compelled him, owing to the endangerment of his communications with Nashville and Louisville, to evacuate Central Tennessee, and retreat rapidly to Louisville along the line of the railroad from Nashville to Louisville.

The advance of General E. Kirby Smith to Frankfort had already caused consternation in Cincinnati, which place, as well as Louisville, was exposed to attack. The march of General Buell's army was a long and tiresome one, and told greatly on the men; and the greatest excitement prevailed when, at midnight of the 24th of September, his army entered the City of Louisville. A fear had been felt all along that Bragg would reach there first with his army. General Buell made his headquarters here for a few days until the 30th, when an order came from Washington instructing him to turn over his command to General Thomas. This order was, however, revoked the same day, and by evening General Buell was again in command.

On October 1st he began a hot and energetic pursuit of the Confederates. He followed them closely, and on the 7th the two divisions of the Confederate army reached Frankfort and formed a junction.

General Bragg had in the meantime taken care to drain the entire country, through which he passed in advance of General Buell, of all food and supplies, sending them southward, before Buell was able to meet him in equal numbers. As fast as the Confederates retreated, the Union troops pressed hard upon their heels, following them so closely that at last General Bragg determined to halt at Perryville and give General Buell a smell of Southern gunpowder. Buell was ready for the fray, and the two armies formed in order of battle on opposite sides of the town. The action was begun, after the opening artillery fire, by a charge of the Confederates early in the afternoon of October 8, and soon became general. The fight was very hot and bitter, and lasted until dark, each side suffering heavy losses. Buell's army, however, had withstood the battle the best, and the next morning found General Bragg withdrawing to Harrodsburg. From here the Confederates retreated slowly to Cumberland Gap, with Buell following them.

In this pursuit General Buell was severely criticised, it being claimed that his following was not swift enough; and that, had he moved his army quicker, and brought the Confederates into action again, it would have been an easy matter for him to have secured a signal victory. His apparent slowness provoked such criticism from Washington that he was ordered to transfer his command to General Rosecrans. He asked that an investigation be made, and accordingly a military commission was appointed. It, however, resulted in nothing of material interest; for, although the commission duly made a report, it was never published. By some General Buell's course has always been freely criticised, while by others it was authoritatively claimed that his men were too much exhausted from a hard day's fighting to give hot pursuit to the retreating forces. As no publication was ever made of the commission's decision, the matter has always remained an open question.

General Buell was mustered out of the volunteer service on May 23, 1864, and on the 1st of June he resigned his commission in the regular army, having been before the military commission from November 24, 1862, until May 10, 1863, and since that time stationed at Indianapolis awaiting orders.

In 1864 he removed to Kentucky, and became president of a large iron manufacturing concern. He went with energy into business, and, with the exception of holding the office of pension agent at Louisville, has not come before the public in anything but in his capacity as a sagacious, honorable and successful man of business. He is at present a resident of Frankfort, Kentucky.

(General Buell died on November 19, 1898.)

The First Ohio State Regiment Surprised by a

Masked Battery.—Four companies of the First Ohio Regiment, commanded by Colonel Alexander McD. McCook, accompanied by Brigadier-General Robert C. Schenck, were ordered to guard the railroad between Alexandria and Leesburg, Virginia. They left their encampment at Alexandria on the 17th of June, 1861, and proceeded cautiously in cars and on trucks, pushed ahead of a locomotive, in the direction of Vienna. McCook and about three hundred of his men had just entered a deep cut, entirely exposed on platform cars, when the cars were swept from front to rear by grape and canister, fired from a masked battery of the Confeder-

ates—supported by a South Carolina regiment commanded by Colonel Maxcy Gregg.

The frightened engineer, instead of drawing the whole train out of the peril, uncoupled the engine and one passenger car and fled with all possible speed toward Alexandria. The troops leaped from the remaining cars, and rallied in a grove, maintaining so bold a front that the Confederates retired to Fairfax Court House, leaving the handful of Ohio troops, whom they might have captured with ease, to make their way leisurely back, carrying their dead and wounded companions on litters and in blankets. The Union loss was five killed, six wounded, and thirteen missing.

AMBROSE EVERETT BURNSIDE, U.S.A., 1824–1881

West Point, 1847

Major General,
R.I. Militia, 1861
Brigadier General, volunteers,
August, 1861
Major General, volunteers,
March, 1862

COMMANDED
Army of the Potomac,
November, 1862–January, 1863
Department of the Ohio, 1863

BATTLES:
Bull Run
Roanoke Island
Frederick City
South Mountain
Antietam
Fredericksburg
Knoxville
Cumberland Gap
Wilderness
Cold Harbor
Petersburg

Governor of Rhode Island,
1866–68
U.S. Senator, 1875–81

Among all the adherents of Charles Edward the Pretender none were more loyal or more faithful than the Scottish family of Burnside. They followed that interesting prince through all the strange vicissitudes of his life until his final defeat at Culloden in 1746, and the destruction of all his hopes to see his claims vindicated. Shortly after that eventful battle, a portion of the Burnside family emigrated to America, settling in South Carolina. General Burnside's grandfather, James, was captain of a company of South Carolina royalists, and when it became evident to him that the Revolution would prove successful he fled to Jamaica, where he remained for some time. He returned to South Carolina, however, and died in that State. He had four sons, who, together with his widow, moved to Indiana after his death, setting their slaves free before their departure. This act was performed from purely conscientious motives, and indicates the deep-seated love of freedom which characterized the family. Their life for a long time thereafter was a hard struggle, particularly in the case of Edgehill, the third son, who settled in the new town of Liberty, where he taught school and entered somewhat into village and county politics. He married Pamelia Brown in 1814, and had nine children, of whom Ambrose was the fourth. The boy was born May 23, 1824, and obtained the best school education that the town could afford; but, as his father felt unable to prepare him for a profession, he apprenticed him to a tailor. Ambrose, after learning his trade, entered into a partnership business in Liberty under the name "Myers &

A SHORT HISTORY OF A.E. BURNSIDE.

Burnside, Merchant Tailors," and secured considerable business success. His first interest in warfare was aroused by hearing a number of veterans of the War of 1812 recalling their experiences, and from that time a passion for the life of a soldier possessed the young tradesman. Of his finally giving up his business and entering the army service the following account is given: "Caleb B. Smith, Congressman from the district, entering the shop to have his coat repaired, found the young tailor with a copy of *Cooper's Tactics* propped up against the 'goose' and kept open by a pair of shears, so that he could study and work at the same time. Some conversation followed, and the congressman was so impressed by the intelligence and appearance of the young man that he sought his appointment as a cadet at the military academy, and, although the first attempt was a failure, fortune at last favored him, and he entered the class of 1847."

At the time of Burnside's graduation the Mexican War was almost over, but immediately on receiving his appointment as second lieutenant of the 3d artillery he was sent with his company to Mexico, and was with the army of the occupation. Burnside was then engaged for several years in Indian warfare on the frontier. In 1852 he married Miss Mary Richmond Bishop, of Providence, R.I., and shortly after resigned his commission in the army, spending the several years following in superintending the manufacturing of a breech-loading rifle which he had invented. His rifle was approved in 1857 by the board of army officers; but his money had run short, and n endeavoring to push the interests of his invention he was compelled to go into bankruptcy. He sold all his personal property, and, by securing a position in Chicago in the Illinois Central Railroad and practicing strict economy, he succeeded before long in discharging all debts honorably.

In the fall of 1860 he went to New Orleans on business, and while in the South became so convinced from the outlook of affairs that war was inevitable that on his return he arranged all his affairs, and was in readiness when, in April, 1861, he was placed in command of the 1st regiment of detached militia of Rhode Island. Leaving Providence, he reached Washington on April 26 and commanded a brigade in the army of General McDowell, which was hastened by popular pressure so prematurely into battle at Bull Run. Burnside took command of his division in that engagement after General Hunter was wounded, and preserved the organization of his command throughout and after that disastrous battle, in which the main body of the National force was completely routed and scattered. In August Burnside was made brigadier-general of volunteers, and in October prepared for operations along the lower Potomac and Chesapeake Bay. His command was composed of regiments recruited on the New England coasts, and was called the "Coast Division." On January 12, 1862, he sailed on 46 transports with a force of 12,000 men against Roanoke Island. A two weeks' storm caused great delay in this expedition, and at times threatened to scatter the fleet completely. On the 25th of January, however, his vessels passed safely through Hatteras Inlet and advanced on Roanoke Island, which was fortified by the Confederates. The island was reached on February 5, a landing was effected, and by February 8 the Confederate garrison was captured, numbering 2500 men. This was a very important success, for it secured the command of the waters of the Albemarle and Pamlico Sounds. It was followed in sharp succession by the capture of Newbern, N.C., on March 14, and Fort Macon and Beaufort, after which General Burnside returned North, where he received high commendation for the successful issue of his campaign.

The next summer Burnside was connected with the Army of the Potomac, commanding his old divisions, reorganized as the 9th corps. General McClellan was relieved of the command of the Army of the Potomac in June, and it was offered to Burnside; but the latter declined it, and General Pope was placed in command. After the second defeat at Manassas and the retreat of the army to Washington, Pope was relieved of the command, and it was again offered to Burnside, who again declined it. This necessitated the recall of General McClellan, whose personal magnetism and remarkable ability in organizing troops soon effected a complete change of affairs, and restored order and confidence among the discouraged and demoralized National force.

On September 3 Burnside left Washington with the 1st and 9th corps to meet Lee's force, which had crossed the Potomac. Burnside encountered the enemy at Frederick City on the 12th, and on the 14th at South Mountain, where he forced Lee to retreat to Antietam Creek. On the 17th the battle of Antietam occurred, and in this engagement Burnside's duty was to capture and hold the stone bridge—a duty which cost an enormous sacrifice of life. After this battle the army remained near Sharpsburg until November. On the 10th McClellan was relieved of the command, and on this occasion Burnside reluctantly accepted it. After reorganizing the army into three great divisions, under Sumner, Franklin and Hooker, Burnside began the famous movement against Fredericksburg, the purpose being to cross the Rappahannock at the city and to crush the two wings of the Confederate army in detail, as they were at that time fully two days' march apart. By November 19 Burnside's army occupied the heights opposite Fredericksburg, but no measures had been taken as yet to effect a crossing of the river. The Confederate army, had, however, been just as rapid in its movements, and now occupied the heights on the south side of the river. Burnside, noting the changed aspect of affairs, since the enemy was now combined, went to Washington and expressed doubt as to the advisability of attempting to cross the river, since Lee's force had not been separated. He

Engagement Near Bealington, Virginia.

—General William H. Morris's force encamped at Bealington, a village at the foot of Laurel Hill, and in close proximity to General Robert S. Garnett's position. Morris had been ordered to engage Garnett in a series of feints which would lead to the belief that the main Federal assault might be expected from that quarter, thus giving McClellan a chance to attack the rear of Garnett's forces. These were estimated at fully 11,000 men, including 3,000 under Colonel John Pegram, at Rich Mountain. So eager were the troops for active work, that skirmishes were incessantly kept up, and one of these, which took place on the 8th of July, 1861, has by many been dignified by even a higher name.

was urged, however, to go on, and returned to conduct the advance. The river was successfully crossed in the face of much opposition, and the enemy was driven back from Fredericksburg. This was on December 13, and the two armies were now ranged opposite each other south of the city, the Confederate lines occupying the naturally strong position along the crest of the hills. Ineffectual attempts were made at all points of the line to dislodge the Confederates, but without success, and Burnside was compelled to recross the river, having lost more than 12,000 men, while the Confederates lost but 5300. As a result of this unfortunate and disastrous engagement much dissatisfaction and insubordination was manifested among the National troops, which increased until Burnside felt compelled to issue an order, subject to the president's approval, dismissing several officers from the service and relieving others from duty. This, however, was not approved, and shortly afterwards General Burnside gave up the command and General Hooker was appointed in his place. Burnside then took charge of the Department of the Ohio, with headquarters at Cincinnati, and was engaged for some time in suppressing the manifestations of Southern sympathizers in that part of the country. He issued a general order on April 13, 1863, "defining certain treasonable offenses, and announcing that they would not be tolerated." The result of this was a series of arrests, of which the best remembered is that of Clement L. Vallandigham, who was accused of making a treasonable speech, and, being convicted, was sentenced to imprisonment during the remainder of the war—a sentence which was afterward commuted to banishment by the president. Shortly after Burnside was nominated for governor by the Democratic party, but was defeated by an overwhelming majority.

During August, 1863, General Burnside, with 18,000 men, crossed the Cumberland Mountains, and, after a march of 250 miles, drove the Confederates from Knoxville and took possession of the Cumberland Gap. He was here, however, met by Longstreet with a much stronger force, and was compelled to retreat to Knoxville, where he fortified and provisioned himself against the expected siege. This action, it is said, was purposely carried out in this manner by Burnside "to draw Longstreet away from Grant's front, and thus facilitate the defeat of General Bragg, which soon followed." After a month the approach of Sherman compelled Longstreet to raise the siege, and Burnside was relieved from the command and was engaged in recruiting and reorganizing the 9th corps. He resumed command with this corps, numbering 20,000 men, in April, 1864, and was connected with the Army of the Potomac under Grant, serving in the battles of the Wilderness and Cold Harbor, and in the action around Petersburg. General Meade accused Burnside of disobedience, founding his charge upon the latter's conduct in these last battles, and a court-martial was ordered to try him. General Grant expressed disapproval of this action, however, and a court of inquiry investigated the case, reporting that they found Burnside "answerable for want of success." Later evidence has gone to prove, however, that Burnside's lack of success was due more to interference with his plans than to incapacity on his own part.

On resigning from the army on April 15, 1865, Burnside entered again into railroad business. He was elected governor of Rhode Island in 1866, 1867 and 1868, and was nominated for a fourth administration, but declined.

During the Franco-Prussian War he was in Europe on business, and, although visiting the headquarters of the Prussians at Versailles simply as a private person, he was pressed into service as an envoy, and served in this capacity for some time, endeavoring to further negotiations for peace between the hostile forces, and securing the confidence and esteem of both nations. On his return to the United States he was elected senator from Rhode Island in 1875, and re-elected in 1880. His career in the senate only confirmed his position in the minds of his countrymen as a brave, patriotic and generous-minded man. He died very suddenly of neuralgia of the heart, at Bristol, R.I., on September 3, 1881, and his funeral services were of an imposing character, worthy of the able and valuable soldier and statesman he had proved himself to be.

BENJAMIN FRANKLIN BUTLER, U.S.A., 1818–1893

General Butler was born in Deerfield, N.H., on November 5, 1818. His father, John Butler, was a portion of his life a soldier, and served as a captain under Jackson at New Orleans. After a preparatory school education Benjamin entered the institution at Waterville, Me., then known as Waterville College—now called Colby University—graduating with credit in 1838. He then pursued the study of law, and was admitted to the bar in 1840, practising first in Lowell, where he soon made considerable reputation for himself, especially as a criminal lawyer. From the first he manifested deep interest in politics and took an active part in political work.

He was at that time a staunch Democrat, and was elected by that party in 1853 as a member of the Massachusetts house of representatives, where he served the interests of his party creditably, and was elected to the State senate in 1859. In the following year he was one of the delegates to the Democratic national convention, then held at Charleston. There was a withdrawal, however, of a portion of that convention taking exception to the policy of the South, and in this movement Butler shared. This portion of the delegates reassembled at Baltimore, and the result of the discussion which took place, and in which Butler took a prominent part, was that they declined to participate any longer in the deliberations of the convention, "On the ground that there had been a withdrawal in part of the majority of the States." Butler also added another reason—"Upon the ground that I would not sit in a convention where the African

slave-trade, which is piracy by the laws of my country, is approvingly advocated." During 1860 he was nominated by the Democratic party for the governorship of Massachusetts, but was defeated.

At the opening of the war, and at the time of the President's call for troops, Butler occupied the rank of brigadier-general of militia, and in response to the summons he accompanied the 8th Massachusetts regiment on the 17th of April to Annapolis, and was there assigned to the command of the District of Annapolis, which included the City of Baltimore. On May 13, 1861, he entered that city with a small force, and on the 16th was made major-general, and placed in command of Fort Monroe, with the Department of Eastern Virginia. While he was in this position it is said that he originated the expression "contrabands," and the incident is thus stated: "Some slaves that had come within his lines were demanded by their masters; but he refused to deliver them up, on the ground that they were contraband of war; hence arose the designation of 'contrabands,' often applied to slaves during the war." During the summer he was engaged in active service, capturing Forts Hatteras and Clark.

An expedition was planned at this time for the Gulf of Mexico and the Mississippi, and to prepare for this General Butler went first to Massachusetts, where he was engaged for some time recruiting, returning in time for the starting of the expedition in the latter part of February, 1862. The military force, consisting of about 15,000 men, sailed from Fort Monroe, reaching the place of rendezvous—Ship Island—on April 17

This expedition was designed first and foremost for reducing the defenses of New Orleans and capturing that place. The fleet, including 21 schooners, was under the general command of Commodore Porter, assisted by Farragut. The duty assigned to Farragut was as follows: "Collect such vessels as can be spared from the blockade and proceed up the Mississippi River and reduce the defenses which guard the approaches to New Orleans, when you will appear off that city and take possession of it under the guns of your squadron." The land force under General Butler was intended to cooperate with the fleet in capturing New Orleans, and to garrison the place after it was taken. The obstructions were most formidable. About thirty miles from the mouth of the river and on either side stood the two forts—Jackson and St. Philip. Above these forts lay a Confederate fleet of 15 vessels, while below the forts two iron chains were stretched across the river, supported by eight hulks anchored. In addition to these, a large number of Confederate sharpshooters kept close watch on the banks. On the night of the 20th of April, however, Captain Bell went silently up the river and unfastened the chains to allow the fleet to pass, and on the night of the 23d the advance began. This was conducted with admirable skill and bravery by Farragut, who moved steadily up the river, silencing the batteries on the forts and almost completely destroying the Confederate fleet. On the 25th the city was compelled to surrender, and General Butler took possession on May 1. His administration of affairs during that time, while conducted with considerable rigor, was in the main just. Both the health and support of the poor of the city received his special attention, and it is said that he compelled many wealthy secessionists to contribute largely to the cause of bettering the condition of the poor. He aroused intense resentment, however, among the inhabitants, as well as the people of the South generally; and what contributed chiefly to the dislike kindled against him was his hanging of William Mumford for taking down the United States flag from the mint building, and his "Order No. 28," to prevent women from insulting soldiers. For these actions he was proclaimed as an outlaw by Jefferson Davis in December, 1862. A more just cause for resentment than the above, however, was to be found in General Butler's seizure of $800,000, deposited in the office of the Dutch consul. His ground for doing this was, as he stated at the time, that Confederate arms and supplies were to be purchased with it, and he purposed to prevent an outlay which would work so seriously against the interests of the North. On the protest of all the foreign consuls, the government looked into the matter, and, considering General Butler's suspicion as unwarranted, required the return of the money.

On December 16, 1862, General Butler was recalled—a proceeding which he himself believed was instigated by Louis Napoleon, the latter's reason being that he felt that General Butler was antagonistic to his Mexican plans.

In the latter part of 1863 Butler was placed in command of the Department of Virginia and North Carolina, his force afterwards being called the Army of the James. He remained in this command hardly a year, and was sent in October, 1864, to the City of New York with a sufficient force to insure peace during the intense excitement of the election.

During the following month he was engaged in an expedition against Fort Fisher, near the mouth of the Cape Fear River. His duty on that occasion was to aid Admiral Porter in capturing the fort, but his own efforts in the engagement were altogether ineffectual. Admiral Porter, who was at that time in command of the North Atlantic squadron, had appeared off Fort Fisher on December 24 with 35 regular cruisers, five ironclads and a reserve of 19 vessels. He had begun to bombard the forts at the mouth of the river, and, as he states, "In one hour and fifteen minutes after the first shot was fired not a shot came from the fort. Two magazines had been blown up by our shells, and the fort set on fire in several places, and such a torrent of missiles was falling into and bursting over it that it was impossible for any human being to stand it. Finding that the batteries were silenced completely, I directed the ships to keep up a moderate fire, in hope of attracting the attention of the transports (containing the military force) and bringing them

Pass Capt Hamilton Wherever He may wish To go April 25 B. F. Butler 1861 Brig Genl

in." General Butler, however, to the surprise and regret of Admiral Porter, decided that the fort was impregnable, and, instead of attempting the assault, took his force back to Hampton Roads, Va. Fortunately, in spite of this, the enterprise was not given up. Admiral Porter held his own steadily, and was reinforced on January 13 by a second military force of 8500 men, under the command of General Alfred H. Terry, and several additional vessels, which formed, as General Grant said, "the most formidable armada ever collected for concentration upon one given point." The works were captured after seven hours of desperate fighting. General Butler's conduct met with considerable disapproval, and his military judgment was somewhat severely censured. He was shortly afterwards removed from his command by General Grant, and, returning to his home in Massachusetts, resumed his political life.

He was elected a member of congress by the Republican party in 1866, and, with the exception of the years 1875–77, he remained a member of the house until 1879. During 1868 he was especially active as a member of the committee conducting the impeachment of President Johnson.

General Butler's politics have varied considerably during the years following the war. He was in 1871 the nominee of the Republican party for governor of Massachusetts, and to that party he owed his seat in congress, although he had in previous years been a pronounced Democrat. He was defeated, however, in his canvass for the governorship. He made another effort in 1878 and 1879 for the position, both as candidate of the Independent Greenback party and of one faction of the Democratic party, but still unsuccessful. Finally, after altering his politics again, he ran as candidate for the Democratic party combined and secured the position.

The chief feature of his administration was his charge of "gross mismanagement against the authorities of the Tewksbury almshouse." The matter was thoroughly sifted by a committee of the legislature, and created a considerable stir at the time. The investigation, however, satisfied the committee that the charge was not well founded, and it was therefore set aside.

In the following year General Butler was nominated for a second term, but was defeated. He was nominated as a candidate for the presidency in 1884 by the Greenback and Anti-monopolist parties, securing 133,825 votes.

(General Butler died on January 11, 1893.)

GENERAL ORDER $\}$ 𝕳𝖊𝖆𝖉𝖖𝖚𝖆𝖗𝖙𝖊𝖗𝖘 𝕯𝖊𝖕𝖆𝖗𝖙𝖒𝖊𝖓𝖙 𝖔𝖋 𝖙𝖍𝖊 𝕲𝖚𝖑𝖋, $\}$

No. 28.   *New Orleans, May 15, 1862.*

As the officers and soldiers of the United States have been subject to repeated insults from the women (calling themselves ladies) of New Orleans, in return for the most scrupulous non-interference and courtesy on our part, it is ordered that hereafter when any female shall, by word, gesture or movement, insult or show contempt for any officer or soldier of the United States, she shall be regarded and held liable to be treated as a woman of the town plying her avocation.

BY COMMAND OF   **MAJOR-GENERAL BUTLER**

GEO. C. STRONG, A. A. GEN., CHIEF OF STAFF

Battle of Rich Mountain, West Virginia.

The battle of Rich Mountain was fought on July 12, 1861, by General William S. Rosecrans, commanding the Federal troops, and General John Pegram the Confederate troops. The movements of General Rosecrans were, however, accidentally discovered through the capture of a courier whom McClellan had sent after Rosecrans, and after a wearisome and in many respects dangerous march in heavy rain, Rosecrans found the enemy prepared to meet him.

The attack commenced at once and was made with such impetuosity that, notwithstanding the fact of Rosecrans's being without cannon, and exposed to the enemy's masked battery, the fight lasted scarcely an hour, and resulted in the total rout of the Confederates, who, in the short time, lost about 400 in killed and wounded, besides their guns and all their ammunition and tents.

THE FIRST BATTLE OF BULL RUN, OR MANASSAS
July 21, 1861
"The Union troops pressed forward with determined courage. The Confederates resisted with
spirit, but under the combined fires of Griffin's and Rickett's batteries, wavered and broke. But the
advantage was not won without serious loss to the Union forces, demoralization of several regiments and loss
of valuable officers. Gen. Hunter, who commanded the advance, was himself wounded with a shell.
John G. Nicolay, private secretary to President Lincoln

DAVID GLASGOW FARRAGUT, U.S.N., 1801–1870

In 1776 George Farragut, the father of the admiral, emigrated to this country. He was born in Minorca in 1755, and traced his lineage through a long line of notable ancestors back to Don Pedro Farragut, who was in the service of James I, King of Aragon. He took an active part in the Revolutionary War, and served the United States as "muster master of the militia of the District of Washington (East Tennessee), employed in actual service for the protection of the frontiers of the United States south of the Ohio, from the 1st of March, 1792, to the 26th of October, 1793." In 1810–11 he was sailing master of an expedition to the Bay of Pascagoula, and afterwards became magistrate at Pascagoula. He had five children—three sons and two daughters. Of the former, David G. Farragut was born at Campbell's Station, near Knoxville, Tenn., on the 5th of July, 1801. From his earliest years he was inured to hardships and dangers by land and sea. His first experience on the sea was extremely distasteful to him; but his father, by constantly taking him out on the water in all sorts of weather, soon overcame his fears, and a strong attachment to the sailor's life replaced his first feeling of distaste. When David was but a little over eight years of age he was adopted by Commodore Porter, who had formed a warm friendship for David's father, and was taken by the commodore to Washington, where he was put to school. During his stay at Washington he aroused the friendly interest of Paul Hamilton, Secretary of the Navy, who assured him that on the completion of his tenth year he should receive a midshipman's warrant.

A SHORT HISTORY OF ADM'L FARRAGUT

The boy then attended school at Chester, Pa., and on the 17th of December, 1810—several months before the promised time—he received the appointment in the navy, and served in the following summer under Commodore Porter, who commanded the *Essex*. David accompanied Porter on his cruise to the West Indies in 1812, and throughout the war of that year displayed a precocity that was remarkable. He was but twelve years of age, but was entrusted with one of the prize vessels captured by Commodore Porter; and it is related of the young prize master, that when the captain of the captured vessel flew into a fury at his diminutive captor's orders, and rushed below to load up his pistols, David, with the coolness of an old seaman, took complete command of the crew, issued his orders promptly, and informed the captain that if he came on deck with his pistols he would be thrown overboard. He took part in the bloody battle between the *Essex* and the *Phoebe* and *Cherub*, where he performed the duties of captain's aide, quarter-gunner, powder boy, and in fact everything that was required of him, as he states in his journal. On his return after the war he again attended school at Chester, Pa. He sailed to the Mediterranean in 1815 under Captain William M. Crane on the *Independence*, again in 1816 on the *Macedonian*, and a third time in 1817, on which occasion he made a very extensive cruise, spending nine months with the U.S. Consul at Tunis, studying languages and mathematics. He made still another cruise in the Mediterranean in 1819, this time as acting lieutenant on the *Shark*, and in the follow-

Rear Admiral, July, 1862
Vice Admiral, December, 1864
Admiral, July, 1866

COMMANDED
West Gulf Blockading Squadron

BATTLES:
Mexican War
New Orleans
Port Hudson
Mobile Bay

Fired One Hundred Guns.—A salute of one hundred guns was fired in front of the State House, Richmond, Virginia, after the battle of Bull Run.

Battle of Bull Run.

The battle of Bull Run, which the Confederates called the battle of Manassas, was the first really important action of the Civil War. The scene lay five miles to the northwest of Manassas Junction, about twenty-nine miles south of Washington, on the banks of the Bull Run.

On the afternoon of July 16, 1861, Union General Irvin McDowell, with about 35,000 men, advanced toward Fairfax Court House, where the Confederates were expected to make a stand.

General Pierre G. T. Beauregard, commanding the Confederate army, had 30,888 men and fifty-five guns. By a singular coincidence, Beauregard had contemplated an attack upon the Federals at the same time, his order for an advance upon the latter at Centerville, though for a later hour, bearing the same date as that of McDowell.

On the 21st of July, both armies met and the bloody battle was fought, which resulted in a defeat for the Federal army, whose loss was 481 killed, 1,011 wounded, and 1,460 missing—total, 3,051, besides twenty-seven guns, nine flags, 4,000 muskets, ammunition, tents, etc. That of the Confederates was 378 killed, 1,489 wounded, and thirty missing—total, 1,887.

ing year sailed home to pass his examination. In May, 1822, he was appointed to the sloop-of-war *John Adams*, carrying the United States representatives to Mexico and Guatemala, and upon his return joined the schooner *Greyhound*, of Commodore Porter's fleet, and assisted in the expedition against the freebooters of the West Indies. He was subsequently made executive officer of the flagship *Seagull* of the same fleet, and remained in that position during a cruise amongst the reefs of the Gulf. In the year 1823 he was married to Miss Susan C. Marchant, and in July of that year was ordered to the command of the *Ferret*, but during his voyage contracted the yellow fever and was taken to Washington, where he was placed in the hospital until his recovery.

He received the commission of lieutenant and was assigned to the *Brandywine* in 1825, on which vessel he again cruised in the Mediterranean, returning home in May, 1826. From then until 1828 he remained at Norfolk, Va., with the exception of the first four months after his return, which were spent attending lectures at Yale College.

During the next ten years he was in command of various vessels, cruising chiefly about the northern coasts of South America and in the Gulf; and at the end of that time he spent two years at home, taking care of his invalid wife, who died in 1840; serving on courts-martial, and learning the trade of carpenter. From 1841–43 he was again cruising in South American waters, and in December of the latter year he married Miss Virginia Loyall, a very superior woman in character and cultivation.

During the Mexican War he obtained command of the *Saratoga*, and sailed to Vera Cruz with the purpose of capturing the castle of San Juan d'Ulloa, but found on his arrival that the castle had just surrendered to the land forces. On his return in 1848 he was appointed to the Norfolk Navy Yard, and in 1850 was engaged at Washington in compiling a book of ordnance regulations for the navy—a work which occupied him about a year and a half, at the end of which he returned to Norfolk.

From 1854 until 1858 he was establishing a navy yard on Mare Island, in the bay of San Francisco; and in July, 1858, he commanded the *Brooklyn*, conveying the U.S. Minister R. M. McLane to Vera Cruz, Mexico. During the latter part of 1860 and the beginning of 1861 Farragut was at Norfolk; but, as the symptoms of war grew more pronounced, he was notified that his free expression of Northern sentiments was distasteful. He therefore moved to Baltimore with his family, and later to Hastings-on-the-Hudson, where he remained nearly a year.

In December, 1861, he was suddenly ordered to Washington to join an expedition against New Orleans, and was placed in command of the steam sloop-of-war *Hartford*. His orders were "to collect such vessels as can be spared from the blockade, and proceed up the Mississippi River and reduce the defenses which guard the approaches to New Orleans, when you will appear off that city and take possession of it under the guns of your squadron. . . ." In the expedition an army of 15,000 men, commanded by General Benjamin F. Butler, constituted the land force. Farragut's fleet consisted of "six sloops-of-war, sixteen gunboats, twenty-one mortar schooners and five other vessels—carrying in all over 200 guns." From the 18th of April the advance began. Farragut was a perfect master of all the details of seamanship, and it was with extreme caution at every step, and with the exercise of the most consummate skill and bravery, that he successfully passed the Confederate obstructions—completely destroying the Confederate fleet, sailing close to the forts (Jackson and St. Philip) on either bank of the river and silencing their guns by sweeping broadsides, until at length, on the 25th of April, the City of New Orleans was at his mercy—he having lost during the expedition 37 men and one vessel. The forts surrendered to Commodore Porter on April 28. It was Farragut's wish immediately afterwards to capture Mobile, but he was retained in the Mississippi for the purpose of effecting an opening throughout the whole length of the river. On July 16 he received the commission of rear-admiral.

In the spring of 1863 he assisted General N. P. Banks in the

Three cheers for the Red, White and Blue.

siege of Port Hudson, blockading the mouth of the Red River and remaining there until the surrender of Port Hudson on July 8. He then sailed to New York in the *Hartford*, and was received at that place with great public enthusiasm. His vessel was found, on examination, to have received 240 shots during her service of the past nineteen months.

In 1864 he was again at the Gulf, awaiting an opportunity for an attack on Mobile. Later he was reinforced by several iron-clads and troops under General Gordon Granger. On August 5 the attack began, and was conducted with even greater care than the advance on New Orleans. It was Farragut's habit to issue the most minute instructions to cover every possible contingency, and in this engagement he surveyed the whole field of action from a position in the port main rigging of the *Hartford*, which led the fleet into the bay. The Confederate fleet was compelled to surrender after a terrible loss of life on both sides. The National fleet lost 335 men, the Confederate fleet losing only a few, many more having been killed in the forts; 280 Confederate prisoners were taken, and a few days later the forts surrendered. At the close of this bloody fight the quartermaster said that the admiral came on deck at the time that the bodies of the killed were laid out, and, he adds, "It was the only time I ever saw the old gentleman cry; but tears came in his eyes like a little child." Mobile could not be captured as New Orleans had been, for the shoals and obstructions in the channel prevented the close approach of a fleet; but the object of his attack was accomplished, viz.: the stoppage of blockade runners with supplies to the Confederacy.

Farragut's health gave way in November, and, returning home, he reached New York on December 12, where another public reception was given him, and he was presented with a purse of $50,000 to purchase a New York home. On July 5, 1865, he was tendered a complimentary dinner by the Union Club of Boston, on which occasion Oliver Wendell Holmes read a poem composed in honor of the admiral.

In July of the following year congress created the grade of admiral and assigned it to Farragut, who assumed command of the *Franklin* and cruised for some time in European waters, during which he visited Minorca, the home of his ancestors. He returned and visited California in 1869. The following summer he spent at the house of Rear-admiral Pennock, in Portsmouth, N.H. One day he stepped aboard a dismantled sloop-of-war in the harbor, and, after a short visit, almost pathetic in its suggestion of former days, he went on shore, remarking sadly: "That is the last time I shall ever tread the deck of a man-of-war." His words proved prophetic indeed; for on August 14, 1870, his spirit gently passed away, leaving the body of our grandest naval officer to receive the well-earned tribute of a nation's tears.

Farragut was a skilled and heroic commander, a thorough and cultured scholar, and a Christian man whose character was notably honest and pure. We append the last lines of the tribute of Dr. Holmes:

> I give the name that fits him best—
> Ay, better than his own—
> The Sea-king of the Sovereign West,
> Who made his mast a throne.

THE BATTLE OF WILSON'S CREEK, OR OAK HILLS
August 10, 1861

Siege of Lexington, Missouri.

The siege and battle of Lexington was fought under Union Colonel James A. Mulligan, whose available force was 2,640 men. The Confederate troops were commanded by General Sterling Price, whose force was 24,000 men. The siege continued from September 17th to the 20th, 1861. At four o'clock on Saturday afternoon, the 21st, the actual surrender of the Federal troops took place. It embraced Colonels Mulligan, Peabody, Marshall, and Grover, Majors Becker and Van Horn, and 118 other commissioned officers, about 2,100 men, six cannon, two mortars, over 3,000 stand of arms, and 750 horses. The Confederates also became possessed of the money (about $900,000), the state records, and the seals hitherto in ex-Governor Claiborne F. Jackson's hands.

The Confederate losses were heavy—between two and three thousand—mainly owing to the judicious explosion by the Federals of six mines during the siege. The Federals lost between three and five hundred, killed and wounded. In the last day's fight Colonel Mulligan was wounded in the leg and in the right arm, Colonel Marshall received a wound in the cheek, and Colonel White was shot through the lungs, dying Saturday morning.

The Battle of Mill Springs, Kentucky,

was the second important engagement of the year 1862. The names of Beach Grove, Fishing Creek, Somerset, and Logan's Cross Roads have been given to this engagement, although it was actually fought at the last mentioned place, about midway between Mill Springs and Somerset. Like the battle of Prestonburg, it proved to be a victory for the Federals.

General Felix K. Zollicoffer, with 5,000 men, left camp to meet the advancing Federals under General George H. Thomas, General Thomas representing in all about 3,000 men. The attack began at six o'clock on the morning of January 19th, the Confederates opening the contest. After a fierce fight for several hours, the Confederates were defeated, with the loss of General Zollicoffer, besides 191 killed, 62 wounded, and 89 prisoners, eight guns, 1,000 stand of arms, 100 wagons, and a large quantity of ammunition. The Federal loss was 39 killed and 208 wounded.

Lieut. General, U.S. Army
Undress

Colonel of Infantry, U.S. Army
Full Dress

Captain of Artillery, U.S. Army
Full Dress

Major of Cavalry, U.S. Army
Full Dress

Sergeant Major, Artillery, U.S. Army
Full Dress

UNIFORMS AND INSIGNIA OF THE UNITED STATES ARMY

Great Coat
For All Mounted Men

Private, Infantry, U.S. Army

Corporal, Cavalry, U.S. Army
Full Dress

Private, Light Artillery, U.S. Army
Full Dress

Brig. General, U.S. Army
Full Dress

UNIFORMS AND INSIGNIA OF THE UNITED STATES ARMY

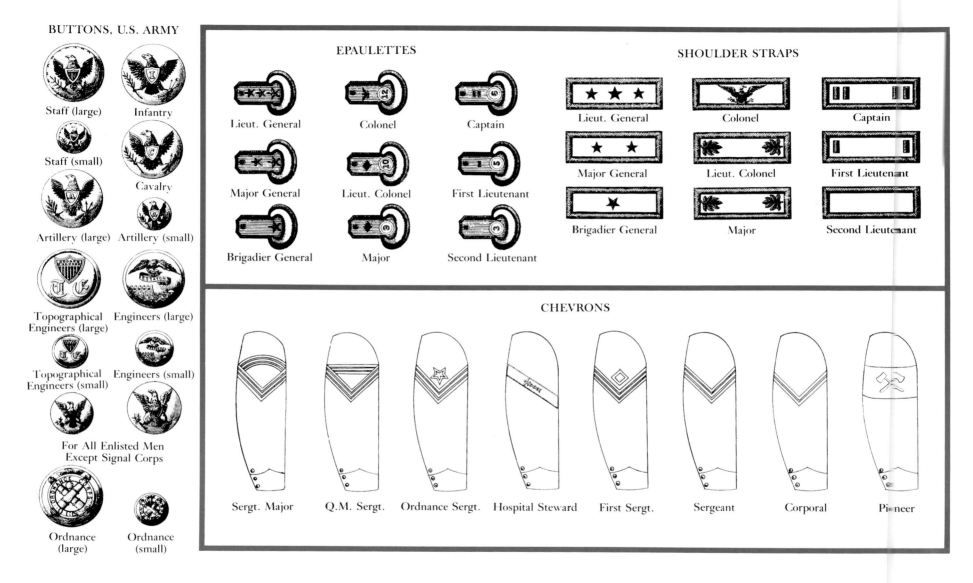

BUTTONS, U.S. ARMY

Staff (large)

Infantry

Staff (small)

Cavalry

Artillery (large)   Artillery (small)

Topographical   Engineers (large)
Engineers (large)

Topographical   Engineers (small)
Engineers (small)

For All Enlisted Men
Except Signal Corps

Ordnance   Ordnance
(large)   (small)

EPAULETTES

Lieut. General   Colonel   Captain

Major General   Lieut. Colonel   First Lieutenant

Brigadier General   Major   Second Lieutenant

SHOULDER STRAPS

Lieut. General   Colonel   Captain

Major General   Lieut. Colonel   First Lieutenant

Brigadier General   Major   Second Lieutenant

CHEVRONS

Sergt. Major   Q.M. Sergt.   Ordnance Sergt.   Hospital Steward   First Sergt.   Sergeant   Corporal   Pioneer

BADGES TO DISTINGUISH RANK, U.S. ARMY

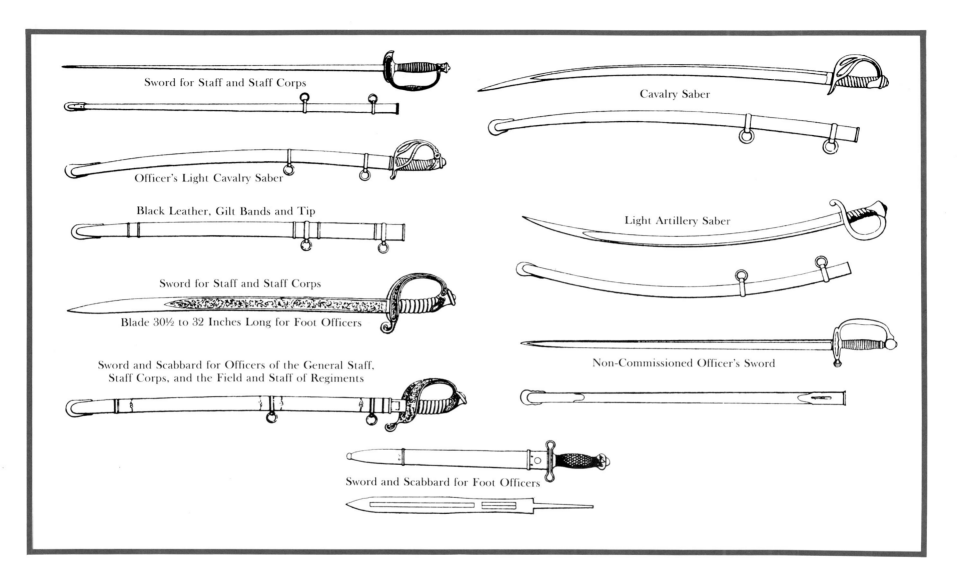

Sword for Staff and Staff Corps

Cavalry Saber

Officer's Light Cavalry Saber

Light Artillery Saber

Black Leather, Gilt Bands and Tip

Sword for Staff and Staff Corps

Blade 30½ to 32 Inches Long for Foot Officers

Non-Commissioned Officer's Sword

Sword and Scabbard for Officers of the General Staff,
Staff Corps, and the Field and Staff of Regiments

Sword and Scabbard for Foot Officers

SWORDS USED IN THE CIVIL WAR

ANDREW HULL FOOTE, U.S.N., 1806–1863

Rear Admiral, June, 1862

COMMANDED
*Naval Operations on
Upper Mississippi, 1861– 62*

BATTLES:
*Fort Henry
Fort Donelson
Island No. 10*

On the roll of brilliant names typical of bravery in naval battles, that of Andrew Hull Foote occupies a conspicuous place. America may truthfully boast of its naval commanders when it can point to a galaxy from which shine forth the glittering deeds of Farragut, Porter, Perry and Foote. Associated with each of these names is a long list of brilliant deeds in naval warfare. In the minds of some the one may be entitled to a higher place than the other, but all alike may be rightfully given a niche in the hearts of patriotic Americans. While Grant, Sherman and Sheridan achieved victories on land, it was the foresight and management of our naval heroes which made their victories more possible and easier. The wars of the seas are ofttimes more fraught with danger than the battles of the shore. Under the feet of the tramping army is at least solid soil, upon which a retreat is possible, if occasion demands; but between fame and death in the case of the naval warrior there are but a few planks, susceptible of being shattered to pieces in the twinkling of an eye if his judgment fails him in discerning the exact location of his enemy; and thus may we rightfully place the name of Admiral Foote high up on the scroll of gallant Americans. All through his eventful career danger was to him an unknown factor. He had but a single thought, and that the preservation of the nation under whose flag his ship sailed. To preserve that flag was his determination at all hazards, and it was the guiding principle of his entire career. When caution was advised, he commanded in a tone of confidence that roused the spirits and failing hero-

ism of his subordinates. With his eye and judgment always keen and on the alert, he had a sublime confidence in himself that knew no failing. He had a masterly judgment of what was best in naval warfare, and while he was always ready to learn, he trusted more to his own foresight. This was not conceit, but a knowledge of years. The man Foote knew only what the boy Foote had learned.

From the fifth or sixth year after his birth at New Haven, Conn., on the 12th of September, 1806, he was an ardent student of ships and the shipping trade. To the boy the water had a peculiar fascination and interest. He longed for it, and was always either in it or by it. To have even the brook trickle over his bare feet, as he sat by its side, was to him a delight and joy. When in the country, he would always seek the lakes, ponds and streams of the neighborhood; by the seashore he was ever paddling on the shore or dancing merrily in its watery embrace. The boy loved the water—its thunder was to him sweet music, and next to the favorite spot in his mother's lap was a cove at the water's brink. And the water loved the boy, for it was always his protector. It seemed to assure him that he was as safe within its embrace as if he were reclining in the sunniest spot on the hills and dales of the Connecticut Valley; and it was a love that was born in the boy himself, without an inheritance. His father was famed in legislative halls, and he had every opportunity given him to follow in the paternal footsteps. But the laws of the land had no interest for him except as they related to its waters and shipping interests. The parents tried to turn the desires and attentions of their boy into different channels, but it proved useless; the boy had set his mind on the navy, and to be in its service was his uppermost wish. Notwithstanding his enthusiasm for the water, he was a close student at school. His young brain doubtless had thought out for him the important fact that education was as essential on the water as on the land, and, stimulated perhaps by this thought, he adhered closely to his studies. But it was not to be for a long time. The love for the water overreached the love for study, and, beginning on his 15th birthday, young Andrew pleaded with his father for an opening in the naval school. The father protested, and counseled his son to go back to his studies and prove their master. "Then," he said, "we shall see." For a year the boy studied hard and industriously, and in less than a year he surprised his father by telling him that he was "master of my studies, and now can't I go on the water?" The father saw it was useless, and, aided by his influence, he secured for his son a midshipmanship in the elder Commodore Porter's squadron. This position he fairly jumped at, and into it he went on December 4, 1822.

In the following year the squadron was sent out to break up the piratical nests which had formed themselves among the West India islands. Young Foote was all enthusiasm when he heard of the proposed voyage, and his youthful ardor asserted itself to the utmost. On the journey no boy on shipboard was more willing or ready to do the slightest bidding of his superiors than he, and it was not long before he commanded the attention and friendship of the officers. Commodore Porter also fixed his eye on the lad, for he perceived the making of a naval commander in the young midshipman. The boy was given hard work as a test, but this he bravely endured and cheerfully performed. Nothing seemed too hard for him to do so long as it advanced him in the respect and opinions of his superiors. There was the true mettle in the lad who worked so faithfully, and none knew this better than the commander of the squadron himself. For five years he worked at different posts and in various positions, but in each he reflected credit upon

himself. True, promotion did not come so quick as he anticipated, but he was willing to work and wait. The following two years brought him hope that his labors were not to go unrewarded, and his boyish fancy began to build castles in the air when he should be commanding squadrons himself. Then it was fancy; little did the boy dream how thoroughly true were to come those fancies.

In 1830 came his first step upward, and in that year he made a strong leap forward direct into the ranks of a lieutenant. In this capacity he again showed his admirable qualities; but there was little to do, and nothing offered itself to show what he could do if put to the test. In 1846 his father died, leaving to his son a name ripe with renown, and symbolic of the true American statesman. The influence of the father was now gone, and the young man stood for himself. But he was fully capable of doing this. In 1849 he was appointed captain of the brig *Perry*, and he felt the importance of his first naval command. Immediately after his appointment he received orders to proceed with his vessel to a cruise to the African coast and suppress the slave trade there, which had grown to large proportions. He set sail at once, and in a few days headed his vessel for the port where he was destined to remain for two years. The task was not an easy or a pleasant one, but his services were very effective, and he kept command of whatever situation he gained.

His next promotion was the command of the sloop-of-war *Portsmouth*, and to this he was transferred in 1856. He was ordered to go at once to China, where he arrived on the eve of the hostilities between the Chinese and the English. He set to work at once and exerted himself to protect American property, and so energetic and determined was he that he soon found himself in conflict, with the guns of the Barrier forts turned full upon him. This he received as an insult to his flag, and he asked for permission to demand an apology. The consent was given, but the apology was refused. He immediately trained his guns and those of his sister ship, the *Levant*, with their full force on the fortifications. His attack was merciless,

and so concerted was it and surprising to those in the forts that he carried them by storm. His guns were far-reaching, and their work meant quick and certain death, and 400 of the enemy's forces fell to the ground, while among his own men the loss was but 40. His quick action and successful attack won attention, and when the Civil War began he was chosen by the government to command the Western flotilla.

This was the turning point in his career, and he determined to show his qualities to their very best. The equipment and organization of the flotilla was almost a herculean task. It called forth his best energies and taxed them to their utmost. He was, however, brilliantly successful, although he always maintained that it was the greatest work he had ever done. He said afterwards that, once through with that task, he felt as if he could accomplish almost anything. The time soon came to give him the opportunity. In the beginning of February, 1862, in connection with the enormous land forces under General Grant, he moved upon Fort Henry on the Tennessee, and on the 6th of that month, after a fierce and hotly contested engagement before the army came up, he carried the fort with his gunboats. In this encounter he showed wonderful skill and a most accurate knowledge of naval warfare. His bravery was conspicuous, and his name flew over the electric wires from one end of the country to the other. The "hero of Fort Henry" was upon everybody's lips, and congratulations and laudations came to him from all sides and from his government. This proved to be the most important achievement in his career, although a few days later he was destined to add more laurels to his already conceded wreath of fame and honor. It was on the 14th, and he helped in the combined assault upon Fort Donelson. For an hour and a half he trained his guns on the fort, and contributed greatly to the demoralization of its garrison. Shells flew in rapid succession from his gunboats, each doing its deadly work. Not a moment did he allow to go unused, and so active was his warfare, and so conspicuous a position did his boats occupy, that he received the full brunt of the enemy's return shots. His fleet after a while became almost

disabled from their hard fighting and the savage assault made upon them from the fort, and he gave orders that his fleet be withdrawn. They had done more than their share in the fight, and Foote was satisfied, not wishing to disable his boats so that they would be unfit for further usage. In this terrific encounter Foote was himself severely wounded; but he soon recovered himself, and went to the assistance of Pope on the Mississippi. After a series of ineffectual attempts, Island No. 10 was surrendered to him on April 7th.

His wounds received at Fort Donelson now became so serious and painful that he was obliged to give up his Western command.

On June 16, 1862, he received a vote of thanks from congress for his brave services, and was made a rear-admiral. On June 22 he was given a deserved position as chief of the Bureau of Equipment and Recruiting.

In 1863 he was again chosen for active service, and was given the honor of succeeding Rear-admiral Dupont in command of the fleet off Charleston. He immediately arranged his matters in Washington and went to New York, to set sail for Charleston to assume his command. But Providence had decreed otherwise; for, arriving in New York, he fell ill, and died in that city on June 26, 1863.

Thus did the gallant commander cease his earthly command in the harness, journeying from one post to another.

He was a man of a high type of Christian character, with the most genial and lovable of traits, but uncompromisingly firm in his principles. Once he fixed a matter as right in his mind nothing could swerve him from it. He was always an ardent advocate of temperance, and believed in it under all circumstances, whether in or out of action. He abolished the spirit ration in the navy, and with this his name will always be associated. Drink was to him a curse, and he did not want to see it inflicted upon his fellows. He was severely honest, upright and true—in fact, a man of the very highest principles, a typical American gentleman, even in the midst of the severest battle. To those under him he was uniformly kind, lenient and gener-

Battle of Roanoke Island, Virginia, February 8,
1862.—Decisive bayonet charge of the Ninth New York Volunteers. Major E. A. Kimball offered to lead the bayonet charge. The Zouaves rushed forward, crying: "Zou, Zou, Zou, Zou," accompanied by Colonel Rush C. Hawkins, and followed by the Tenth Connecticut. The earthworks were soon enfiladed from both sides in such a way as to necessitate the flight of its occupants.

The Federals climbed over the parapets of the three-gun batteries to find that the guns had even been left unspiked, and that all the enemy's dead and wounded had been hurriedly abandoned in a retreat toward Nag's Head, on the other side of Roanoke Sound.

The Federal loss was reported at 235 killed and wounded; that of the Confederates being much greater: over 3,000 in prisoners, besides over 3,000 stand of arms and forty-two heavy guns.

ous. All loved him who knew him—for his manliness as well as for his daring and bravery. He never did anything by halves; like his broadside upon the China forts, all things were done well and thoroughly. What he conceived he undertook, and what was undertaken by him was carried out.

During the four years after 1852, when he remained at home, he devoted himself to literature and placing some of his observations on record; the result was a book entitled, *Africa and the American Flag*—a work rich in its interest and graphic descriptions of men, things and events during his cruise off the African coast. This book was published in 1854, and had a wide sale.

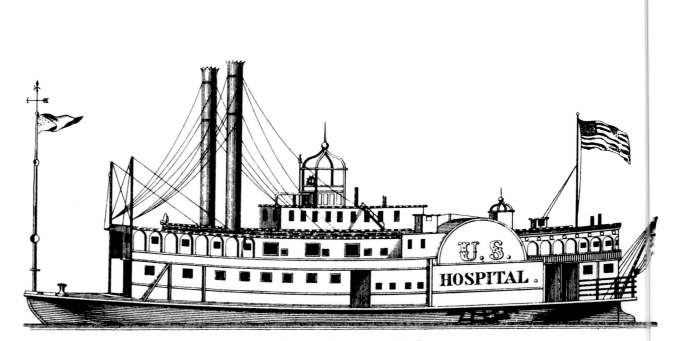

U.S. Army Hospital Steamer D.A. January

JAMES ABRAM GARFIELD, U.S.A., 1831–1881

General Garfield was descended on his father's side from an old Puritan family, and on his mother's side from a Huguenot family that fled from France to America after the revocation of the Edict of Nantes (1685). Abram Garfield, the father, moved West in 1830, and settled in that part of Ohio known as the "Western Reserve," and died there, leaving his wife and four children, of whom James A. Garfield was the youngest. He was born on November 19, 1831, and his early years were spent amidst the struggles and bitter privations of frontier life. His home was simply a log cabin, and his school a similar structure, where he acquired simply the rudiments of the common-school education. But though he acquired little more than the ability to read, he obtained, in his rude and simple home, from the influence and guidance of a pure and high-minded mother, those sterling qualities of mind and character which he displayed throughout his life.

From his third year, when he first went to school, until his fourteenth, he alternated between his studies in the winter and work during the remainder of the year, giving such assistance to his mother as a boy of that age could render. At school he acquired, with his ability to read, a passionate fondness for reading, which remained with him through life; and by the time he was fourteen years of age he was fairly well grounded in grammar, arithmetic and history. His reading had inspired him with a desire for travel and adventure, especially on the sea, and, following this inclination, he went to Cleveland in 1848 with the purpose of shipping as a sailor on one of the lake

schooners. The first glance, however, at this life dissatisfied him so that he gave up the idea, and, not wanting to return home to be laughed at, he worked for some months on the Ohio canal.

The years 1849–50 were spent partly at Geauga Seminary at Chester, Ohio, and partly at work securing the funds necessary to continue his education. Alternating in this manner, he put himself through the seminary, holding an honorable position in his classes and in the respect of his classmates. He was at this period also especially energetic in religious work, and exerted considerable influence on those around him both by the power of his noble example and by his direct efforts in the prayer meetings. At Chester Garfield met Miss Lucretia Rudolph, whom he afterwards married. In 1851 he entered Hiram College, at Hiram, Ohio, and worked his way through this institution by instructing in English and classics during a part of his time.

By the year 1854 he had not only acquired a preparation which would entice him to a place in the junior class of one of our great Eastern colleges, but had laid up a fair sum to meet the expenses of his college life. Having received considerable encouragement from President Mark Hopkins, of Williams College, he determined to enter that institution, and accordingly joined the junior class in the fall of 1854, graduating in 1856 with high honors. He then returned to Hiram as a tutor of Latin and Greek, but in the following year he was made president of the institution, and as such he soon became one of the most influ-

Williams, 1856

Brigadier General, January, 1862
Major General, October, 1863

BATTLES:
Paintville
Middle Creek
Big Sandy
Shiloh
Corinth
Chickamauga

Member,
U.S. House of Representatives,
December, 1863–1880
President of the United States,
1880–1881 (Assassinated July 2)

ential and respected men in the Western Reserve, attracting to Hiram a large number of students simply by the power of his personal magnetism and the love he aroused in his pupils. It was at this period that he began to manifest interest in politics, and his speeches soon brought him prominently into public notice as a sturdy advocate of freedom from slavery. In 1859 he was chosen to be a representative in the senate of Ohio.

At the opening of the Civil War Governor Denison made him a lieutenant-colonel of the 42d regiment of Ohio volunteers, and many of his soldiers were former pupils of his at Hiram. In command of this regiment, which he carefully trained, he was ordered in December, 1861, to report to General Buell at Louisville, Ky., who was favorably impressed by Garfield, and placed him in command of a brigade—his first task being the routing of the Confederate general, Humphrey Marshall, from Eastern Kentucky. This he accomplished under great difficulties. Marshall's force was twice the size of Garfield's; but the latter forced the Confederate army to abandon Paintville and its supplies, and engaged it in a sharp hand-to-hand conflict, holding his own against the superior numbers until reinforced by Generals Graner and Sheldon, when Marshall was compelled to give way, leaving the victory to Garfield at Middle Creek on January 10, 1862. In recognition of the skill displayed during this engagement Garfield was made a brigadier-general by the President.

Garfield displayed an amount of persistence and endurance during the campaign of the Big Sandy that was remarkable. He was engaged in scattering Confederate encampments, and at times his supplies gave out and starvation was close at hand. In order to take Marshall unawares in the Cumberland Gap, Garfield marched his soldiers 100 miles in four days through a severe snow-storm. On rejoining General Buell, he was assigned to the command of the 20th brigade, and took part in the action at Shiloh and in all the operations in front of Corinth; assisting also in the rebuilding of the bridges on the Memphis and Charleston Railroad, and the fortifications of Huntsville.

He contracted a serious illness in July, 1862, and was compelled to return to Hiram on leave of absence, and was confined there two months. On regaining health in September he went to Washington and was engaged in court-martial duty for several months, during which he was assigned to the case of General Fitz-John Porter.

In February, 1863, he again entered into active service, this time with General Rosecrans, commanding the Army of the Cumberland, who made him chief of his staff. In this capacity Garfield exerted considerable influence, and his counsels were of the utmost value and importance during the campaign in Middle Tennessee. During the terrible battle of Chickamauga Garfield volunteered to carry the news of the defeat of the right wing of the army to General Thomas, who commanded the left, and after making a bold and fearless ride through the most exposed portion of the field, brought the information to General Thomas that saved the army. For his gallant conduct during this unfortunate engagement he was promoted to the rank of major-general.

Though his future in the field of action was especially brilliant and promising, he resigned his commission on December 3, 1863, on the request of President Lincoln, and accepted a seat in congress, to which he had been elected some time before. This position he maintained in opposition to a call from General Thomas to assume command of one of the divisions of the Army of the Cumberland. He was only thirty-two years of age when he entered the house; but from the start he commanded the respectful attention of all, not so much by the power of eloquence—for he was not a brilliant orator—but by his strong, shrewd common sense, and for the extensive and accurate information which he was able to impart, especially on military matters. On war subjects he was soon regarded as an authority, and his views were accepted as those of an expert. Shortly after entering congress he was placed on the Committee on Military Affairs, serving in that capacity until 1865, when he was transferred at his own request to the Ways and Means Committee. In 1867, however, he was restored to the congressional Committee on Military Affairs and was elected its chairman.

During the next ten years he was especially active in advocating the resumption of specie payments, and his speech on the national finances, delivered in Boston, was printed and circulated in thousands throughout the country. In the 41st congress he was elected chairman of a new committee—on banking and currency. During the following two congresses he was chairman of the Committee on Appropriations, and in the three congresses after that served on the Committee of Ways and Means. In 1876 Garfield accompanied the Electoral Commission to Louisiana to watch the counting of the votes. During the last three years of his service in the house he was the undisputed leader of the Republican party.

In 1880 the national Republican convention in Chicago was conducted under circumstances of peculiar interest. There was a marked determination on the part of many to re-elect President Grant, but this met with an equally sturdy opposition. The principle of the opposition was worded thus by Mr. Blaine: "Defeat a third term first, and then struggle for the prize of office afterwards. Success in the one case is vital; success in the other is of minor importance." For 33 ballots the Grant party held its own, polling on the 30th ballot 306 votes—the remaining 400 being divided between Blaine, Edmunds and Washburne. On the next ballot, however, Wisconsin announced 36 votes for Garfield, who was one of the leaders of the anti-third-term faction. In the succeeding ballots the deadlock was at last broken, and the votes for Garfield swelled rapidly, and on the 36th ballot he received the nomination. In the following November he defeated Winfield S. Hancock by a large majority.

The first difficulties of his office over, and an especially promising outlook ahead, General Garfield began to feel the cheering and encouraging sense of prosperity assured. It was therefore with relief and pleasure, after the auspicious beginning of his administration, that he prepared to visit the commencement exercises of Williams College on the 2d of July, 1881. At nine o'clock on the morning of that day, as he was passing through the waiting-room of the depot, he was shot twice by Charles J. Guiteau, the second ball entering the back, fracturing a rib and lodging deep in his body. The nation and the world were aroused by the dastardly act, and through the long summer of suffering all nations waited anxiously without his sick-room, and sympathized deeply with his misfortune. Days of national prayer and supplication were set apart, and it seemed at times as if the prayers of thousands must be answered and his recovery assured. Early in September he was removed to Elberon, N.J., by a special train, and under the influence of the sea air again seemed to rally. But on September 15 his blood became poisoned and he lingered but four days more, dying peacefully on the 19th. His body was taken by special train to Washington, where it remained in state in the capitol September 22 and 23, and was then transferred to Cleveland, and interred in the cemetery which overlooks the waters of Lake Erie. It was accompanied throughout its long trip by one constant watch of mourning citizens, by day and night, in town and country.

The nation has never experienced a more sadly impressive ceremony, with the single exception of the only too similar burial of Lincoln. The grand words of Garfield, which rang from the balcony of the custom-house in New York on Lincoln's death, comment fittingly and appropriately upon his own sad end:

"Fellow citizens: Clouds and darkness are around Him; His pavilion is dark waters and thick clouds; justice and judgment are the establishment of His throne; mercy and truth shall go before His face! Fellow citizens, God reigns, and the Government at Washington lives."

ONWARD

QUINCY ADAMS GILLMORE, U.S.A., 1825–1888

West Point, 1849

Brigadier General, volunteers,
April, 1862
Major General, volunteers,
July, 1864

COMMANDED
District of Western Virginia,
September, 1862
Department of the South,
June, 1863

BATTLES:
Hilton Head
Fort Pulaski
Somerset
Morris Island
Fort Sumter
Fort Wagner
Battery Gregg
Swift's Creek
Drewry's Bluff
Bermuda Hundreds
Petersburg

For a profound knowledge of the art of war and the firm grasp of the principles of military science, Quincy Adams Gillmore had but few superiors. General Gillmore was born in Black River, Lorain County, Ohio, on the 28th of February, 1825. He was of mingled Scotch, Irish and German extraction. After the regular four years' course, he was graduated at the head of his class at West Point, July 1, 1849, and was assigned to the corps of engineers as a brevet second lieutenant. He served as assistant engineer in building Forts Monroe and Calhoun at Hampton Roads, Va.

From 1852 to 1855 he was an assistant instructor of practical military engineering at West Point. He was in charge of the fortifications in New York harbor from 1857 to 1859. At the beginning of the Civil War he served for one year as chief engineer of the Port Royal expeditionary corps, and was present at the descent upon Hilton Head, South Carolina, November 7, 1861.

The reduction of Fort Pulaski, defending the water approach to Savannah— a strong fortification, isolated in the centre of a marsh island that was entirely surrounded by deep water— was very essential to the success of this expedition, but was regarded by the ablest engineers of both armies as unapproachable. Different schemes were devised by heads believed to be wise in the science of engineering, but one after another was given up. The engineering knowledge of all was put to the severest test, but nothing could be thought of to successfully accomplish the destruction of the fortress. Finally Captain Gillmore was appealed to, with but little hope that he

would suggest anything which had escaped the others. But the capabilities of the man had been incorrectly judged. It required no great period of time for Gillmore to plan the feat which was destined to make his name remembered in the annals of engineering for years to come. He conceived the establishment of 11 batteries of mortars and rifled guns on an island a mile distant from the fort. The undertaking was a vast one; but after two months of incessant labor, day and night, it was completed. The great bombardment was opened at eight o'clock on the morning of April 10, 1862. Captain Gillmore conducted every detail of the great charge— supervising the elevation, intervals between shots and the minutest details. The bombardment proved one of the most severe in the history of the war, and lasted until two o'clock of the afternoon of the following day, when the fort was surrendered. The fortifications had been so terribly shattered by the terrific rain of shot upon them that they were completely untenable.

Captain Gillmore's triumph was completed—his name became honorably known to hundreds of thousands, and he was at once regarded as the most able of American engineers and batterists. Promotion followed immediately upon his action, and the title of brevet lieutenant-colonel was bestowed upon him. On the day of his promotion he visited Fort Pulaski under the flag of truce and arranged the terms of its capitulation. Returning North, he assisted the Governor of New York in forwarding troops to the front, and in September, 1862, he was placed in command of the District of

West Virginia, and a month later of the 1st division of the Army of Kentucky. He had charge of the Federal forces at the battle of Somerset, Kentucky, in March, 1863, and won the title of brevet colonel for gallantry. In command of the 10th army corps, July 10, 1864, he conducted the operations against the defenses of Charleston, S.C.—comprising the descent on Morris Island, the bombardment of Fort Sumter, and the siege and capture of Fort Wagner and Battery Gregg—and won the title of major-general, United States volunteers. Other operations of the 10th army corps, under General Gillmore's command, were the fight at Swift's Creek, the capture of the right of the enemy's intrenchment at Drury's Bluff, the defense of Bermuda Hundreds, and the reconnoissance of the enemy's lines before Petersburg.

July 11, 1864, he was placed in command of the 19th army corps, defending Washington, and was in pursuit of the enemy under General Early for three days, when a fall from his horse rendered him unfit for service until early in the following September. In February, 1865, he was given command of the Department of the South, with the brevet title of brigadier-general, and subsequently major-general, which commission he resigned December 5, 1865. For the succeeding ten years he was assigned to very many important engineering commissions, such as testing the use of iron in fortifications and of the availability of Gatling guns, and reporting on the feasibility of a ship canal to connect the Mississippi River with the Gulf of Mexico. In these he proved so efficient, and his judgment was found to be so wise and sound, that by executive appointment he was made president of the Mississippi River Commission.

In 1883 a liver and kidney trouble inflicted itself upon General Gillmore, and for five years he was an intense sufferer, although never losing his grip on military and engineering questions of interest. During these years of terrible suffering he never asked a leave of absence from his post of duty in the active service of the government, and in this time his name frequently appeared in connection with responsible public affairs outside his public duties. One of the last positions of trust to which he was called was as a member of the commission for the examination of the aqueduct under construction for increasing the New York water supply, in which he served a year and a half with Generals Newton and Grant.

As an officer of the engineering corps of the army, General Gillmore was given an office in the army building, on Houston Street, New York, and supervised many of the forts and constructing defenses of the Atlantic coast.

At the time of his death, which occurred in the City of Brooklyn on April 7, 1888, he was in charge of the defensive works on Staten Island, N.Y.; at Fortress Monroe and the Hampton Roads, in Virginia; at Forts Sumter and Moultrie, in Charleston harbor; at Fort Pulaski and the Savannah River, and Fort Clinch in the Fernandina River. He had charge of the construction of the jetties in Charleston harbor and in the Cumberland Sound, Florida; the improvements of the Savannah River and harbor, and all the river and harbor work in South Carolina, Georgia and Florida. He was also a member of the board of officers for the construction of various other river and harbor improvements, as notably on the Potomac River.

General Gillmore left various literary monuments of his engineering knowledge and experience. He was the author of *The Siege and Reduction of Fort Pulaski*, *The Engineer and Artillery Operations against the Defenses of Charleston*, practical treatises on roads, streets and pavements, limes, hydraulic cements and mortars, and many other technical works of that nature.

After his graduation at West Point he received the degree of A.M. from Oberlin College and of Ph.D. from Rutgers College. He was a very devout man, his religious principles being of the highest order. For years he was a member of Dr. John Hall's church in New York City, where he attended until his illness became so painful as to make it impossible for him to leave his Brooklyn home and go away from his medical attendants. His brother is Lieutenant Gillmore, of the 8th cavalry, now stationed in Fort Clark, Texas.

General Gillmore will be awarded by the muse of history a

place in the front rank of the great captains whom the War of the Rebellion developed. The quality and character of his mind were early determined by the highest test to which they could be put. He not only passed the intellectual ordeal of the curriculum at the West Point Military Academy, but he passed it with the greatest possible *eclat*, graduating at the head of his class. His genius, as this result demonstrated, was essentially mathematical. In any department of exact science to which he might have devoted himself, he would have been eminent.

Notwithstanding the active labors imposed by his profession, and the various duties that engaged him after the war, he found time to gratify the natural bent of his mind by writing a series of books that are the delight of engineers, both military and civil. There are many men among his soldier contemporaries who have died leaving behind them a record of more showy attainments—men better equipped to provoke the plaudits of the multitude and fix the gaze of the superficial—but for profound knowledge of the art of war and firm grasp of the principles of military sciences, he had few if any superiors. The story of the part he took in the suppression of the rebellion shows that he also possessed the ready judgment, the cool courage and the energetic action essential to the successful commander. He could fight a battle as well as plan it—storm and carry a fortification as well as mathematically conceive and construct one. He was a man, too, who wore his honors meekly, and whose merits were confirmed by the modesty of his nature and demeanor.

In the city of his residence he was one of the most conspicuous figures; his neighbors, one and all, loved and respected him for his qualities, while in the family circle he was a modest husband and father. He bequeathed to all who knew him, and to the country he served so well and earnestly, a memory consecrated by the value of his services, and he will always live in the remembrance which survives the death of a distinguished soldier, a thorough patriot, an honored citizen and a beloved friend.

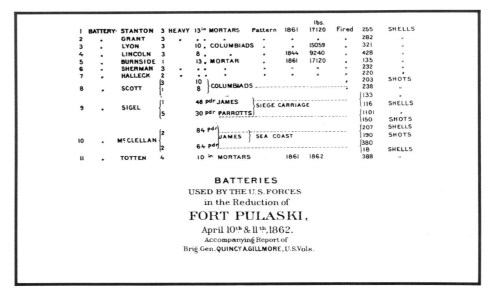

Fort Donelson.—Gallant charge of the Seventeenth, Forty-eighth, and Forty-ninth Illinois Regiments and McAllister's Battery, February 13, 1862. Colonel William R. Morrison, being in command, advanced rapidly up the hill until within forty rods of the battery, when a terrible fire from the entire line of infantry, as well as from the artillery, compelled him for an instant to fall back. He was reinforced by Colonel A. J. Smith's Forty-fifth Illinois Regiment, then supported by Schwartz's and Taylor's Batteries, and made rally after rally, but to no purpose, in face of the superior numbers against him, and after suffering great losses during the full hour he held the ground, fell back to his original position.

THE BATTLE OF FORT DONELSON
February 12 – 16, 1862

"Soon after daybreak on Sunday, 16th, the men of Lauman's brigade heard the notes of a bugle advancing from the fort. It announced an officer who bore to General Grant a letter from General Buckner asking for terms of capitulation, and proposing an armistice until noon. General Grant in his letter replied, *No terms but unconditional surrender can be accepted. I propose to move immediately on your works.* Buckner accordingly surrendered, white flags were displayed along the works, and the national troops marched in, capturing 65 heavy guns and 15,000 prisoners."

M.V. Force, Brigadier General, U.S.A.

HENRY WAGER HALLECK, U.S.A., 1815–1872

General Halleck was born in Westerville, N.Y., on January 16, 1815. He attended the Hudson Academy, and afterwards spent some time at Union College, although he never completed his course there; but entered the Military Academy at West Point, graduating from the latter in 1839. His record at the academy was of the very highest, and at the time of graduation he stood third in a class of 31. Immediately after graduation he was appointed second lieutenant in an engineer corps. His proficiency in the performance of the duties of engineer, as well as his thorough knowledge of all the details which concerned engineering work, soon secured for him considerable reputation. He was sent on a tour of examination of public works in Europe, and while there was promoted to the rank of first lieutenant.

During his first years of engineering service he had prepared a report on the "Coast Defense," which was published by congress and attracted much favorable comment. Among others, the committee of the Lowell Institute, Boston, were struck by the ability shown by Halleck, and requested him to deliver twelve lectures. This he did; and the course was afterwards published in a volume entitled *Elements of Military Art and Science* (New York, 1846)—a work which was widely read, and republished in 1861 with new matter concerning the Crimean and Mexican Wars. This established General Halleck's reputation as a skilled and proficient soldier before any opportunity had been afforded him of showing military tact or bravery on a field of battle.

Immediately on the opening of the Mexican War Halleck was sent as an engineer to the Pacific coast, and sailed under Captain Tompkins's artillery command on the *Lexington*. The vessel was seven months in reaching Monterey, Cal., by way of Cape Horn, and this time was spent by Halleck in preparing a translation of Baron Jomini's *Vie Politique et Militaire de Napoleon*, which was published in four volumes (New York, 1864). Halleck occupied during his stay on the Pacific coast a number of positions, civil and military. He was engaged immediately on his arrival in fortifying Monterey as a port of refuge and a base for expeditions. He accompanied a number of expeditions into California, acted for a time as aide-de-camp to Commodore Shubrick, and was lieutenant-governor of Mazatlan after its capture. He was also secretary of state in the military government which was first established on the coast; and when, after hostilities had somewhat abated, and it became necessary and possible to organize a more permanent and stable form of government, Halleck was a leading and important figure in the convention assembled to frame a constitution, and took an active and prominent part in all the deliberations. For his services, military and civil, he had been promoted to captain; and after the convention was over, and the transactions had ended in the organization of a State government—in which movement he was chiefly instrumental—Halleck acted as aide-de-camp to General Riley, and served also as inspector of light-houses on the Pacific coast, until his resignation from the army in August, 1854.

West Point, 1839

Major General, August, 1861
General-in-Chief,
July, 1862–March, 1864

COMMANDED
Department of Missouri,
November, 1861
Department of the Mississippi,
March, 1862
Military Division of the James,
April, 1865

BATTLES:
Pea Ridge
Island No. 10
Corinth

In 1850 he had been elected director-general of the New Almaden Quicksilver Mine, and on leaving the army he retained this position, also practicing law and preparing a number of books, chiefly of a legal character, including: *A Collection of Mining Laws of Spain and Mexico* (1859); *International Law, or Rules Regulating the Intercourse of States in Peace and War* (1861); also a translation of *De Fooz on the Law of Mines* (1860). A few months after his resignation from the army he was also elected president of the Pacific and Atlantic Railroad. Honors due his ability as a soldier, scholar and author were showered upon him. There was no other officer in the United States service who possessed merits of so widely diverse a character. His military and civil duties were discharged in the most highly commendable manner, and he displayed an amount of intelligence in all his work which few other officers possessed. He had in every case prepared his books in the interest of his profession, and their publication had not only largely benefited his military and legal associates, but had secured for him a wide-spread reputation as a scholar. He received from Union College the degree of A.M. in 1843 and LL.D. in 1863, and in 1848 he was offered the professorship of engineering in the scientific school at Harvard—an offer which he declined.

He continued the practice of law in San Francisco until the opening of the Civil War, and at that time he was one of the most prominent and successful lawyers of the West. He was recommended by General Winfield Scott to the President as being able to fill the highest military position with credit, and accordingly, on his volunteering his services, he was appointed major-general by Mr. Lincoln. He left a prosperous position to accept this commission, and in devoting himself to the country's cause it was at a large sacrifice of personal interests.

On November 18, 1861, he assumed command of the Department of the Missouri, which comprised the States of Iowa, Minnesota, Wisconsin, Illinois, Arkansas and Western Kentucky. The state of affairs at that time has been thus described:

"Around him was a chaos of insubordination, inefficiency and peculation, requiring the prompt, energetic and ceaseless exercise of his iron will, military knowledge and administrative powers. The scattered forces of his command were a medley of almost every nationality. Missouri and Kentucky were practically but a border screen to cover the operations of the seceding South; and even his headquarters at St. Louis, fortified at exorbitant cost and in violation of all true engineering principles, neither protected the city from insurrection within nor from besiegers without." But a few weeks had passed before General Halleck had entirely altered this distressing condition of affairs. After removing all those abusing their power, pruning out and suppressing those who manifested sympathy for the South, he reorganized his command rapidly and with remarkable judgment, repaired the weak points of defense, and then turned his attention to the Confederate forces under General Price, whom he defeated several times successively, and in a few weeks compelled him to retreat to Arkansas, thus clearing all that region of the hostile element.

Then came the general movement of the Northern forces ordered by the President to begin on February 22, 1862, and Halleck early in that month prepared to set in motion the armies under his command on the Mississippi, Tennessee and Cumberland Rivers. Before three months had transpired, General Grant, assisted by Commodore Foote's fleet of gunboats, had captured Forts Henry and Donelson, and gained possession of Nashville; while General Curtis, who was dispatched in pursuit of the Confederate army in Missouri, pushed the enemy into Arkansas, fought successfully the battle of Pea Ridge, and drove the Confederate force before him to the White River. In this manner the first line of the Confederate defense was broken, and they were forced back on their second line, which extended from Memphis to Chattanooga. In order to move with greater unity, the Departments of Kansas and Ohio were placed also under Halleck's command on March 11, 1862, and the whole was called the Department of the Mississippi, and included everything between the Alleghany and

Rocky Mountains. General Buell was ordered to unite with General Grant, and together they moved against Shiloh, securing the great victory at that place on April 6 and 7.

After this battle General Halleck assumed command of all the various armies, and advanced slowly upon Corinth. He acted at this time with an amount of caution which gave rise to considerable criticism. He was accused severely and unfairly for exercising an amount of deliberation which he conscientiously considered at the time most necessary. In gaining the next step, he realized acutely the importance of holding securely the ground already obtained, and of not risking by rash haste the loss of all. On May 30 he was in possession of Corinth; but the enemy had been permitted to evacuate the city and largely destroy its defenses.

Memphis was now to be made the base of operations. General Pope was sent in pursuit of the enemy, General Buell was sent to Chattanooga to restore the railroad connections, and General Sherman was ordered to Memphis. While Halleck was at Corinth, he was ordered to Washington and made general-in-chief of all the armies of the North.

His command thus far had been distinguished for brilliant movements and repeated successes, and had secured for him the highest commendation of the War Department. It was in his new and higher command, however, that he was especially assailed by envious and disappointed schemers. Mistakes he may have made—for so have all commanders—but he was thoroughly undeserving of the criticism to which he was subjected. He acted in all things with a warm feeling of loyalty to the Union and with a view to the best interests of the cause he had at heart. After the glorious campaigns of Vicksburg and Chattanooga, General Grant was appointed lieutenant-general of all the armies, the rank being specially revived for him.

Although General Halleck was requested to remain in discharge of his functions, he said with justice that nothing but the name was left him, and that General Grant, being higher in rank, must necessarily be the commander-in-chief. Halleck continued in service, however, and acted as chief of staff of the army, and between April and July, 1865, commanded the Military Division of the James.

After the war General Halleck was assigned to the Military Division of the Pacific. He remained in this command until March, 1869, when he was transferred to the Division of the South, retaining the latter position until his death, which occurred at Louisville on January 9, 1872. Since his death he has been several times severely criticised, but all his unjust accusers have been ably refuted.

Halleck was a man of surpassing ability, who, by the exercise of superior qualities of mind and character, raised himself to a position which entitled him to the respect of all his countrymen; and it is to be regretted that, in the clashing of petty selfish interests, his reputation should have suffered so severely.

THE BATTLE OF PEA RIDGE, OR ELKHORN TAVERN
March 7–8, 1862

WINFIELD SCOTT HANCOCK, U.S.A.,1824–1886

General Hancock was of Scottish descent, his grandfather being born in Scotland; his father, however, was a native of this country, born in Philadelphia, and by profession a lawyer. His early life was a hard one, for he was thrown altogether upon his own efforts for a living, his guardian having quarreled with him on account of his unwillingness to marry in the Society of Friends, of which he was a member. Mr. Hancock was admitted to the bar in 1828. While still preparing for his profession, and on February 14, 1824, at Montgomery Square, Pa., his son Winfield Scott Hancock was born. General Hancock's early education was received from his father's tutoring, the academy at Norristown (to which place the family moved), and at the public high school. The boy's marked taste for military training led the father to secure his admission to the United States Military Academy at West Point. Young Hancock entered there at 16 years of age, graduating in 1844. He was then breveted second lieutenant and served at Fort Towson, Ind. Ter. At this time the first symptoms of the Mexican War were beginning to manifest themselves, and Hancock's regiment was stationed on the frontiers of Mexico. During his stay there Hancock was commissioned as second lieutenant, and in 1847 he was ordered to the army of General Scott, and an opportunity for active service was afforded him. Of this opportunity he availed himself with considerable credit to himself, taking part in the four principal battles, and, as a reward for brave conduct, he was breveted first lieutenant. During the years 1848–1855 he

A Short History of GEN. HANCOCK

was stationed at St. Louis, serving as regimental quartermaster and adjutant, and in 1855 he was ordered into active service against the Seminoles in Florida, being appointed assistant quartermaster under General W. S. Harney, whose force was stationed at Fort Myers. Hancock accompanied General Harney also to Kansas in 1857–58, and later to Utah to quiet the Mormon troubles that had arisen there. At the opening of the Civil War General Hancock was acting as chief quartermaster of the Southern District of California, and it was at his own request that he was removed to the centre of action. His sentiments in reference to the war were as follows: "My politics are of a practical kind—the integrity of the country, the supremacy of the Federal government, an honorable peace or none at all." President Lincoln appointed Hancock brigadier-general of volunteers, and his first efforts after his appointment were in the direction of organizing the Army of the Potomac. In this work he rendered most valuable and timely service. He was under General McClellan in the Peninsular campaign, playing a very prominent and creditable part in the battles of Williamsburg and Frazier's Farm, and, in the later Maryland campaign, in the battles of South Mountain and Antietam. During this last engagement, on September 17, 1862, Hancock commanded the 1st division of the 2d army corps. A short time afterwards he rendered sharp and trying service while storming Marye's Heights during the battle of Fredericksburg, in which he acted as major-general of volunteers. In May, 1863, he took part in the battle

West Point, 1844

Brigadier General, volunteers, 1861
Major General, volunteers, 1862
Major General, regulars, July, 1866

COMMANDED
Middle Military Division, February, 1865
Army of the Shenandoah
Department of Missouri
Fifth Military District

BATTLES:
Mexican War
Peninsula campaign
Williamsburg
Frayzer's Farm
Maryland campaign
South Mountain
Antietam
Fredericksburg
Chancellorsville
Gettysburg
Wilderness
Spotsylvania
Cold Harbor
Reams Station
Petersburg

of Chancellorsville, and in June of the same year, during the pursuit of General Lee, who was then invading Western Maryland, Hancock received the appointment from the President to command the 2d army corps.

It was at this important juncture of affairs that General Hooker was relieved, at his own request, from the command of the Army of the Potomac, and General Meade was appointed in his place. General Meade was fifteen miles distant when the news of the fighting at Gettysburg reached him. This was on July 1, and General Meade ordered Hancock to take command at Gettysburg. For the success of this eventful battle the greater credit is due to Hancock, and though congress was only too tardy in recognizing his share in the engagement, a resolution was at length passed on April 21, 1866, thanking him for his efficient and faithful services during that campaign. The dispatches between Hancock and Meade at the time are interesting, and serve to show how highly the former's services were estimated by his superior in command. The deciding action of Gettysburg took place on July 3. Hancock was wounded, but remained on the battle-field until he saw how the enemy's lines were broken. His message to General Meade then ran: "The troops under my command have repulsed the enemy's assault, and we have gained a great victory. The enemy is now flying in all directions in my front." The answer from General Meade was: "Say to General Hancock that I regret exceedingly that he is wounded, and I thank him in the name of the country and for myself for the service he has rendered to-day." It is doubtful if General Hancock himself appreciated at that time the full importance of that victory, and the value of the service he had performed; it was at a terrible sacrifice, however, to his corps, almost half their number being lost in those terrible three days. After this battle both General Hancock and his corps obtained a forced rest until March of the following year—the commander recovering from the effects of his wound, and in the meantime recruiting his badly depleted force. This rest was timely and necessary, for it preceded a period of the most severe fighting in which Hancock

was engaged during the war. This was during the campaign of the Wilderness, in which the fiercest action raged between the 5th and 26th of May, and especially in the engagement of Spotsylvania Court-house. This battle occurred on the 12th, and during the whole day Hancock was leading a most exciting and bloody conflict, at times actually hand to hand with the enemy. In spite of the sturdy resistance of the Confederate army, the National forces scored a signal victory, capturing 4000 prisoners, twenty pieces of artillery, a large number of small arms, and thirty or more colors. During this trying period General Hancock was carrying himself bravely in the face of a great disadvantage. His Gettysburg wound, but scarcely healed, caused him much inconvenience and considerable bodily suffering, and on June 17, after the battle of Cold Harbor and the engagement in front of Petersburg, it broke out afresh, compelling him to a second rest. He remained on sick leave only ten days, however, returning to active service at the end of that time. He received appointment on August 12 as brigadier-general in the regular army, in recognition of his able services during the previous months. As the commission reads: "For gallant and distinguished services in the battles of the Wilderness, Spottsylvania and Cold Harbor, and in all the operations of the army in Virginia under Lieutenant-general Grant."

On the 25th of August occurred the most unfortunate incident in Hancock's career. His men were resting at Reams Station, tired, and many of them somewhat disheartened, when a strong force of the enemy set upon them, capturing a large number, while the rest, surprised and overcome, made but a feeble resistance. This was a severe blow to Hancock, and discouraged him greatly. General Morgan speaks of him as standing in the midst of the fight with his hand on a staff officer's shoulder and saying: "Colonel, I do not care to die, but I pray to God I may never leave this field." This was almost the last of Hancock's active service.

He took an energetic part in the expedition against the South Side Railroad in October and November, but on the 26th of the latter month he was ordered to Washington, and during the remainder of the war his duty consisted chiefly in organizing and equipping corps. In February, 1865, he was placed in command of the Middle Military Division, and, relieving General Sheridan at Winchester, Va., from the command of the Army of the Shenandoah, returned to Washington, after the assassination of President Lincoln, to command the forces in defense of the capital.

In July, 1866, Hancock became major-general in the regular army and preceded General Sheridan in the command of the Department of the Missouri, which was engaged in fighting the Indians. On General Sheridan's relieving him there, he was appointed to the Fifth Military District. This extended over Texas and Louisiana, and as commander his headquarters were at New Orleans. This transfer was made in August, 1867, and he remained in command of this district until March, 1868. His opinions, expressed at this time in his "General Order No. 40," concerning the rights of the South and the duties of the military commander in times of peace, were at variance with the policy adopted by congress, and at his own request he was therefore relieved from his Southern command and transferred to the Division of the Atlantic, holding headquarters at New York City. He remained in this position about one year, and in March, 1869, he was placed in command of the Department of Dakota; returning, however, in November, 1872, after the death of General Meade, and resuming again the charge of the Atlantic Division.

General Hancock's name had been brought forward as a possible candidate for the presidency in the Democratic conventions of 1868, 1872 and 1876, and in 1880 he received the nomination—being defeated, however, in the political campaign by James A. Garfield, who secured a popular majority.

Since that time Hancock's life was devoted to the discharge of his official duty. Eminently respected as a soldier and citizen, his courtly bearing, fascinating manners and handsome appearance rendered him an attractive and striking figure on all public occasions. His last public duty of national importance was the sad one of conducting General Ulysses S. Grant's funeral on August 8, 1885.

General Hancock died on Governor's Island on February 9, 1886. A better estimate of him as a soldier and a man than the following by General Grant could not be given: "Hancock stands the most conspicuous figure of all the general officers who did not exercise a separate command. He commanded a corps larger than any other one, and his name was never mentioned as having committed in battle a blunder for which he was responsible. He was a man of very conspicuous personal appearance. Tall, well formed, young and fresh-looking, he presented an appearance that would attract the attention of an army as he passed. His genial disposition made him friends, and his personal courage and his presence with his command in the thickest of the fight won him the confidence of troops serving under him."

We would add to the above the following words of General Sherman to a reporter during the political canvass of 1880: "If you will sit down and write the best thing that can be put into language about General Hancock as an officer and a gentleman, I will sign it without hesitation."

A still higher tribute to General Hancock is to be found in the fact that he passed through the ordeal of a sharp political contest, which subjected him to the evil-minded scrutiny of many, and yet sustained throughout and afterwards his character as a noble, high-minded man, and a soldier who had served his country well.

THE BATTLE OF THE *MONITOR* AND THE *MERRIMACK*
March 9, 1862
"The fight continued with the exchange of broadsides as fast as possible at very short range for
more than three hours, during which Capt. Worden was seriously wounded and the command devolved upon
Lieut. Green. The *Merrimack*, leaking badly, started for Elizabeth River. A few shots
were fired after the retreating vessel as she continued to Norfolk, leaving the *Monitor* in possession of the field."
S.D. Green, Commander, U.S.N.

JOSEPH HOOKER, U.S.A.,1814–1879

"Fighting Joe Hooker"—handsome, brave and dashing, fondly admired by his fellow-officers, and devotedly followed by the soldiers under his command—was one of the most interesting figures of the Civil War.

He was born on November 13, 1814, in Hadley, Mass., and, with an uncontrollable bent towards the life of a soldier, secured an appointment as cadet in the United States Military Academy at West Point, graduating in 1837 in the same class with Generals Bragg and Early. After graduation Hooker served first in Florida as second lieutenant in the 1st artillery, and afterwards on the Maine frontier. He received a promotion to the rank of first lieutenant on November 1, 1838, in which capacity he acted for about two years. In July, 1842, he became adjutant of the Military Academy, remaining there only a short time, and returning to accept the same rank in his own regiment. In 1846 he served in the Mexican War, and between that year and 1848 acquitted himself very creditably under several generals, especially at the siege of Monterey, on which occasion he acted under command of General Zachary Taylor, and as a reward for meritorious conduct was breveted captain. Later, in August, 1847, he received still further promotion, this time as brevet major, for brave action at the National Bridge on the 11th of that month, and after the battle of Chapultepec he received the brevet of lieutenant-colonel.

After the Mexican War he was in the East for about a year, to return in July, 1849, as adjutant-general to the Division of the

A Short History of GEN. JOE HOOKER

Pacific, where he remained until 1851. In the latter year he contracted "California fever," and in 1853 he resigned from the army. From that time until the outbreak of the Civil War he was consecutively a farmer, a superintendent of military roads, and a militia colonel.

In May, 1861, the government, in answer to his offer of services, made him a brigadier-general of volunteers. During 1861 he was engaged in no active service of any importance, being occupied with the defenses of Washington and the Potomac. In the early part of 1862, however, he served throughout the Peninsular campaign, commanding the 2d division of the 3d corps of the Army of the Potomac. Attention was first called to Hooker's remarkable military ability at this time, and his extraordinary coolness and daring then first began to arouse admiration. His services, both at the siege of Yorktown and the battle of Williamsburg, were in the highest degree commendable, and the courage he displayed in the latter engagement earned for him a well-deserved reputation for intrepidity. With his own division he held for a long time the whole Confederate army in check, steadily holding his ground, and only forced to retire after the loss of over 2000 of his men. For his brave conduct at the siege of Yorktown he was made major-general of volunteers. The reputation he had won in these battles was further established by his courageous and efficient service in the battles of Fair Oaks, Frazier's Farm, Glendale and Malvern. With this same division he assisted General Pope in his movement against General Lee's

West Point, 1837

Brigadier General, volunteers, May, 1861
Major General, volunteers, April, 1862
Brigadier General, regulars, September, 1862
Brevet Major General, regulars, March, 1865
Major General, regulars, 1868

COMMANDED
Army of the Potomac, January–June, 1863

Army of Virginia, and it was his conduct in the battles of Manassas and Chantilly that earned for him the title of "Fighting Joe." Hooker was distinctly a military *leader*, and his influence as such was magnetic upon his men. Unlike the great military tacticians, who play their battles like a game of chess, keeping themselves in the background, Hooker was always at the head of his command and in the thickest of the fight. It may be said that where he was there the battle was *always* fiercest. His command to his men was not, "Advance!" but oftener, "Come, boys, follow me!" and the power of his example was great. Almost always at the point of greatest danger, it is remarkable that he should have come through the war alive.

When General McClellan was placed in command of the Army of the Potomac, after Pope was forced back towards Washington, Hooker was promoted to the command of the 1st corps, and rendered distinguished services in the Maryland campaign, especially at the battle of South Mountain, September 14, 1862, and Antietam on September 17. In the latter battle he was wounded in the foot, and had to leave the field— a fact which largely influenced the result of the fight; for so much lay in Hooker's personality that when his presence was removed a great amount of the stimulus that urged his men went with it. His losses in this fight were also very heavy, for he was confronted by a Confederate force which numbered far more than his own. On September 20 he received, as a reward for services in that campaign, and especially in the battle of Antietam, promotion to brigadier-generalship in the regular army. On November 10 he had recovered sufficiently from his wound to join his army, which was preparing for the campaign of the Rappahannock. Burnside had superceded McClellan in command, and Hooker was assigned to the command of the centre division, consisting of about 40,000 men. The unfortunate result of the first part of that campaign is well known. The National army was defeated in the first assault, and it was evident that General Burnside, in expecting to take General Lee off his guard, had counted without his host. Then came the appointment of Hooker to the command of the army, to succeed Burnside. The important letter from President Lincoln containing this appointment ran in part as follows, and is of especial interest as showing Lincoln's clear views of the situation of affairs, and the position in which Hooker was placed

> I have placed you at the head of the Army of the Potomac. Of course, I have done this upon what appear to me sufficient reasons, and yet I think it best for you to know that there are some things in regard to which I am not quite satisfied with you. I believe you to be a brave and skilful general—which, of course, I like. I also believe you do not mix politics with your profession, in which you are right. You have confidence in yourself, which is a valuable if not indispensable quality. You are ambitious, which, within reasonable bounds, does good rather than harm; but I think that during General Burnside's command of the army you have taken counsel of your ambition and thwarted him as much as you could, in which you did a great wrong to the country and to a most meritorious and honorable brother officer. I have heard, in such a way as to believe it, of your recently saying that both the army and the government needed a dictator. Of course, it was not for this, but in spite of it, that I have given you the command. . . . What I now ask of you is military success, and I will risk the dictatorship. The government will support you to the utmost of its ability. . . . And now, beware of rashness! beware of rashness! But, with energy and sleepless vigilance, go forward and give us victory.

The foregoing will suffice to show the one unfortunate characteristic of General Hooker which must be mentioned in any estimate of him. It was a characteristic which worked him some harm in the opinion of his superior officers, and occasionally impeded his chances of promotion. Of the differences between Hooker and Burnside enough reference has been made in the portion of the President's letter quoted above.

Hooker's first work on assuming command was to reorganize the army into corps instead of the great divisions, which he regarded as clumsy. After considerable preparation he spoke most hopefully of the future, declaring that he had "the finest army on the planet." His first engagement, however, at Chancellorsville was attended with unfortunate results. Hooker was stunned by the force of a cannonball, which struck

McClellan between Big Bethel and Yorktown,

Virginia. —On the 2nd of April, 1862, Union General George B. McClellan had 58,000 men and, with much of his artillery, was in front of Yorktown. The Confederate force was 50,000 men. But very little fighting was engaged in from the 2nd of April to the 3rd of May. By the 3rd of May, McClellan had completed and armed all his works, and had an effective force of 112,000 men, with which he contemplated advancing three days later. His works consisted of fifteen redoubts, mounting 111 guns and mortars.

While constructing them he had but once departed from his original resolution not to open upon the Confederates until all were finished. That was when he had fired upon vessels discharging at the Yorktown Wharf, and had driven them across the Gloucester Point, with shot and shell from his 100 and 200 pounders. Late in the afternoon of the 3rd, the Confederates began shelling General Samuel P. Heintzelman's camp, and kept up firing at intervals until after midnight. At daylight a great conflagration was visible in Yorktown, and the report having been made that the latter place was being evacuated, Heintzelman ascended in his balloon and found that many of the Confederate guns had in reality been abandoned. The Confederates had, in fact, evacuated Yorktown.

The Federals entered Yorktown on the 4th of May, and took possession of it, as well as of the fifty-three guns remaining there uninjured, and at once organized a vigorous pursuit.

the pillar of the Chancellor House, against which he was leaning, and his army was left with insufficient command at a time when every moment was precious. It was expected that Lee would fight again in Maryland, and the National forces were arranged with that in view; but they were disappointed in this, and it became evident soon that Lee was invading Pennsylvania by way of Chambersburg. The Army of the Potomac therefore hastened northward in pursuit, looking for a suitable place for action. At this juncture Hooker, who felt that his force needed considerable reinforcement for so important an engagement as the one now impending, asked that French's force at Harper's Ferry, consisting of 11,000 men, should be added to his command. On this request being refused, Hooker sent in his resignation, and June 27, 1863, the President appointed General Meade to succeed him—the latter, with the assistance of Hancock, leading the troops to Gettysburg and fighting that eventful battle. On parting from his troops, Hooker spoke frankly and feelingly of the matter as follows: "Impressed with the belief that my usefulness as the commander of the Army of the Potomac is impaired, I part from it, yet not without the deepest emotion."

The next few weeks Hooker spent in utter retirement, but on September 24 he was again called into action as commander of the 11th and 12th army corps (afterwards consolidated into the 20th corps), and served in Tennessee under Rosecrans and Grant. On November 24 Hooker led his corps gallantly through the engagement at Lookout Mountain, which has been called "the battle above the clouds," and assisted afterwards in the defeat of Bragg at Missionary Ridge.

Under Sherman Hooker took part in the invasion of Georgia, doing excellent work, for which he naturally expected, on the death of General McPherson, to succeed in the command of the Army of the Tennessee; but in this he was disappointed, owing, it is said, to General Sherman's suggestion that the President should appoint General Howard. For what he regarded as unfair treatment General Hooker again resigned command, and remained for about two months inactive. For his brave conduct in this last campaign, however, he was breveted major-general in the regular army on March 13, 1865.

The war over, General Hooker served in 1865 in command of the Department of the East, and in 1866 in command of the Department of the Lakes, with headquarters at Detroit. A stroke of paralysis unfitted him for all duty, and on October 15, 1868, he was placed on the retired list, retaining his rank as major-general. His home was in New York and Garden City until his death, on October 31, 1879, and in the latter place he was buried.

Somewhat too impetuous, hasty and strong-headed, General Hooker in action was one of the most efficient servants the country had in the Civil War, and some of those same strongly marked characteristics which interfered with his official promotion served him and his men in the highest stead in the heat of battle. His few faults were counter-balanced by rare military talents, and though at times his own worst enemy, it may be said, the more to his credit, that he attained great eminence in spite of himself. Had he acted somewhat more judiciously at times, he would undoubtedly have obtained military honors that were denied him; but even greater faults than his could not have concealed the bold, brilliant and skilful soldier that he was.

THE BATTLE OF SHILOH, OR PITTSBURG LANDING
August 6–7, 1862
"The firing grew closer, and it became manifest that a considerable force of the enemy were upon
us. The whole division fell back to the tents and again rallied, although no line of battle was
formed, yet from every tree a deadly fire was poured upon the enemy which held them in check for
an hour; when being reinforced we were forced to fall back with loss of four pieces of artillery."
Colonel Francis Quinn, 12th Michigan Infantry

The Final Stand at Shiloh, or Pittsburg Landing, Tennessee.

—At about three o'clock on Sunday morning April 6, 1862, the Confederate army moved forward very quietly in three lines of battle, General William J. Hardee's being in the lead, across the Corinth road, while General Leonidas Polk's forces were deployed on his left toward Owl Creek, and General Braxton Bragg's division stood on his right opposite Bridge Road, with General John C. Breckenridge's reserves extending behind Bragg's right wing toward Lick Creek.

At about five o'clock all was in readiness for the attack. Almost simultaneously the Confederate forces struck the Federal line, the attack proving a complete surprise. The Confederate onslaught was so fiercely made that, by seven o'clock, almost the whole army was engaged, and the battle raged with varying results, but generally favorable to the Confederates, until 5 p.m. The Federal loss on this day was 4,000 killed, wounded, and prisoners.

Among the killed of the Confederates, on Sunday, was General Albert Sidney Johnston, who ranked among the most able commanders in the Confederacy, and whose loss was more keenly felt than any other misfortune of the battle. He received his death wound while leading his troops in an assault against the Federal lines.

General Ulysses S. Grant, having been reinforced during Sunday night by General Don Carlos Buell, advanced against General P. G. T. Beauregard in the morning, and after most stubborn fighting, lasting until about 4 p.m., regained not only the lost ground of the previous day, but drove the Confederates in disastrous defeat from the entire field.

The reported losses in the two days' battle were 1,673 killed, 7,495 wounded, and 3,022 missing, a total of 12,190 on the side of the Federals; and 1,728 killed, 8,012 wounded, and 959 missing, a total of 10,699 on the side of the Confederates. Among the Confederate officers lost were George W. Johnson, the Provisional Governor of Kentucky, killed; General Gladden, who died from wounds; General Cheatham, who had three horses shot under him, and was also wounded; and Generals Bowen, Clark, and Hindeman, who were wounded on the first day. On the Federal side, General William T. Sherman was twice wounded on the first and second days, and had three horses shot under him during Monday's battle; Colonel Stewart was wounded severely early the same morning, but kept the field till weakness compelled him to waive to Colonel T. Kirby Smith; Colonel Hicks and Lieutenant Colonels Kyle, E. F. W. Ellis, and Walcutt were mortally wounded.

Capture of Union Gen. John A. McClernand's

Headquarters.—Sunday, April 6, 1862. The Confederate attack was so fiercely made, that by seven o'clock the whole of Sherman's line and McClernand's left were engaged. An overwhelming force had, meanwhile, been opposed to General Benjamin M. Prentiss's First Brigade, which had become entirely separated from the rest and had to fight its way unaided. With his few regiments, Prentiss maintained his ground for several hours, fighting steadily all the while until, his rear being gained by the Confederates, the force was compelled to surrender. At noon the Confederates held possession of the camps which McClernand, Prentiss, Sherman, and Stewart had occupied in the morning, and, in addition to the capture already mentioned, had taken many prisoners, nearly half of both McAllister's and Schwartz's Artillery, besides several of Dresser's cannon, some caissons, and a large number of horses.

The Confederate effective force at Pittsburg Landing was about 40,335, and that of the Federals about 45,000.

Recapture of artillery by the First Ohio Regiment, under

General Lovell H. Rousseau, at Pittsburg Landing, on Monday, April 7, 1862.

The giving way of the Confederate right allowed Rousseau to push along more freely until he met the troops that had been withdrawn from Nelson's front and were being massed in McClernand's camp of the previous day. There an obstinate contest took place, but the camp was finally yielded to Rousseau's troops who, in addition, captured one of the batteries which the Confederates had taken on Sunday, and from whose fire Rousseau had suffered greatly.

Gen. Lew Wallace at Shiloh.—On the extreme Federal right, Wallace had begun the attack before sunrise on the 7th of April, by shelling with Turber's and Thompson's batteries the Confederate positions situated in a deep wooded ravine opposite. He soon silenced one of the enemy's guns, and followed up the first attack by an advance upon the Confederates' left, commanded by General Braxton Bragg, whose position on the hill he shortly afterward occupied.

OLIVER OTIS HOWARD, U.S.A., 1830–1909

General Howard was one of the youngest officers of our late war, and among the younger officers his name occupies a most honorable position; and, owing to his peculiarly fervent piety, which has earned for him the title of the "Christian Soldier," he has commanded the sincerest respect and admiration of all with whom he has been associated.

He was born in Leeds, Me., on November 8, 1830; was prepared by a good school training for Bowdoin College, which he entered in 1846. In 1850, after graduation with credit, he entered the Military Academy at West Point, completing his course there in 1854. The usual rank obtained by the West Point graduate at first was brevet second lieutenant; or, if some special circumstances favored him, he became second or even first lieutenant. Howard immediately upon graduation was appointed first lieutenant and instructor in mathematics—a position which he retained until the opening of the Civil War, when he resigned to take charge of the 3d Maine regiment of volunteers. With this command he went to Washington, and was assigned to the Army of the Potomac, under the command of General McDowell. During the late spring weeks of 1861 the organizing and training of this army was pushed with all possible speed.

Since the first news of the firing on Fort Sumter had flashed through the Northern States, there had been a steadily growing impatience for some definite and decided action. On a few weeks' notice the Army of the Potomac was organized, drilled, and pushed forward to battle; and the result, considering the

condition of the army, was what might have been expected. Before leaving Washington, the entire force consisted of about 30,000 men, and of these all but about 700 were the rawest recruits. The preliminary preparations at Washington were brought to a close by popular outcry for immediate action; and General McDowell was ordered to advance against the Confederate army at Manassas Junction, under General Beauregard. McDowell had under him, besides Howard, a number of able officers, including Hooker and Burnside, and his plan was well arranged. His purpose was "to turn the enemy's left flank while threatening the front, which was well posted behind Bull Run on an elevation that commanded the entire plateau."

On the 18th of July a small preliminary engagement took place at Blackburn's Ford, after which the National troops were forced to fall back. After a rest of two days the battle of Bull Run was opened by a fierce onslaught by the National troops, in which they drove the enemy back with considerable loss. The Confederates reformed in a line on the crest of the hill, and the fight then centred at that point. The position of advantage was lost and won three times, but at three o'clock in the afternoon it was held by the National army. Victory seemed almost within their grasp, when the sudden arrival of a Confederate force, which McDowell had supposed to be held in check by General Patterson in the Shenandoah Valley, turned the whole fate of the battle; and the National forces, weary and worn with prolonged fighting, and disheartened by the sight of so large a

West Point, 1854

Brigadier General, volunteers, September, 1861
Major General, volunteers, November, 1862
Brigadier General, regulars, December, 1864
Brevet Major General, regulars, March, 1865
Major General, regulars, 1894

COMMANDED
Army of the Tennessee, July, 1864

reinforcement of fresh troops, turned and retreated in disorder to Washington. The disastrous results of this battle have been charged severely to the discredit of the National commanders, particularly McDowell; but this is altogether unmerited; for it was an unexpected turn of affairs that won the day, and one which the best commander could scarcely forecast. The victory hung for some time in the balance, and the condition of the Confederate army before the arrival of reinforcements argued well for a Northern victory. After the battle, the Confederate forces were in an extremely disorderly state, and to this fact is largely due their failure to follow up the great advantage they had gained.

Among all the officers who shared in that unfortunate battle no one rendered better service than Howard; and it is to his credit in a large proportion, and to the excellent work performed by his brigade, that the advantages gained by the Northern troops during that day are due. It is a fact for special mention that, among the few that received acknowledgments of service in the battle of Bull Run, Howard stood prominently forward, receiving on September 3, 1861, the appointment as brigadier-general.

McDowell was relieved of the command, and McClellan was called to Washington, and on July 27 was placed in command of the Army of the Potomac, which, as might be expected, was in a most chaotic state. McClellan declares that on reaching Washington "he found no army to command—a mere collection of regiments cowering on the banks of the Potomac—some perfectly raw, others dispirited by recent defeat, some going home. There were no defensive works on the Southern approaches to the capital. Washington was crowded with straggling officers and men absent from their stations without authority." To restore this force to some sort of order was McClellan's first task, and he was engaged upon it during the fall and winter. This delay was increased by McClellan's illness in December, so that the Peninsular campaign was not opened until March, 1862.

Howard commanded under McClellan in this campaign with conspicuous bravery. He shared in the siege of Yorktown, and in the pursuit of the enemy up the Peninsula. Later, in the battle of Fair Oaks, which was contested so hotly by Sedgwick's division, Howard was severely wounded, losing his right arm. This wound, which threatened to prove fatal, compelled Howard to go on sick leave for some time. As soon, however, as it was possible for him to go about, he was ready and eager to resume service. He was at first engaged in recruiting work, and afterward participated in the battle of Antietam, in September, for which he received the warm commendation and sympathy of his fellow officers. Shortly after this battle he took charge of Sedgwick's division of the 2d corps, and in November he became major-general of volunteers.

McClellan had been removed from the command on November 7 and Burnside appointed in his place. The National army was at this time near Sharpsburg, and Burnside, having reorganized the army under three divisions, commanded by Sumner, Franklin and Hooker, purposed to cross the Rappahannock at Fredericksburg and crush the two Confederate wings separately, the latter being at that time about two days' march apart. Awkward and almost inexcusable delays, however, afforded the Confederate army an opportunity to combine, and by the time that Burnside had his army on the heights opposite Fredericksburg, and was ready to cross the river, Lee's army had occupied and fortified the other side of the river. The crossing of the river was effected in opposition to sharp resistance, and then followed the disastrous and ineffectual efforts to dislodge the Confederate lines from the crest of the hills in the rear of Fredericksburg. It was an engagement which resulted in the utter discomfiture of the National army, and they were compelled to recross the river, after having lost about 12,000 men. Howard was in command of the 11th corps, under General Hooker, and occupied the centre during the fight. Hooker's division was the last to attack the heights, and was repelled, as his predecessors had been, with great loss. Burnside was relieved of the command of the Army of the Potomac after this campaign and Hooker was appointed.

Another reorganization of the army now took place—Hooker restoring the old corps system and doing away with the cumbrous grand divisions. Howard served under Hooker through the Chancellorsville campaign, and followed the army of Lee in its march north into Pennsylvania, sharing in the battle of Gettysburg, after which Lee was driven back across the Potomac. In September the 11th and 12th corps were consolidated into one, and constituted the 20th corps, which, under the command of Hooker, was sent south to the relief of Chattanooga. In the battle at Lookout Mountain and Missionary Ridge in November, and later in the expedition for the relief of Knoxville, where Burnside was besieged by Longstreet, Howard was ever actively engaged, and his thorough and able service was raising him daily in the estimation of his superiors in command.

From December, 1863, until the following July Howard was at Chattanooga, and at the end of that time he was assigned to the Army of the Tennessee. Hooker being retained by General Sherman in command of the 20th corps.

Sherman's army at the opening of the Georgia campaign numbered about 99,000 men, while Johnston's army, which opposed him, was about 65,000 men. The Army of the Tennessee, which numbered at this time about 25,000 men, was under the command of General McPherson. The campaign opened early in May, Johnston at that time occupying a strongly fortified position at Dalton. Sherman's plan was to threaten Johnston in front with the armies of Thomas and Schofield, while McPherson's army was to go around through Snake Creek Gap, and, by throwing himself across the railroad near Resaca in Johnston's rear, was to force the latter to evacuate Dalton. McPherson passed around through the gap, found Resaca too strongly fortified to justify, in his judgment, an assault, and retired into the gap, threatening the railroad. As a result, Sherman brought his whole army to the left of McPherson, and Johnston retreated to Resaca. On the 15th an attack was made; Johnston was defeated and compelled to fall back to Cassville. During the months of May, June and July there were incessant skirmishing engagements between the two armies, culminating in battles at New Hope Church, Dallas, Kenesaw Mountain and around Atlanta, the last-named battle occurring between July 19 and 22.

After the death of General McPherson on July 22, General Hooker expected to succeed him, but in this he was disappointed; for, at the suggestion of General Sherman, Howard was appointed to the command of the Army of the Tennessee, and shared in the pursuit of the Confederate army in Alabama, under General Hood, from October until December, 1864.

Howard commanded the right wing of Sherman's army in the march to the sea, and on December 21, 1864, he received in recognition of his services the commission of brigadier-general in the regular army. He remained with Sherman, in command of the Army of the Tennessee, throughout all the various operations from January to April, 1865, and shared in all the small engagements which terminated with the surrender of General Johnston at Durham, N.C., April 26, 1865.

Howard had already received numerous commendations for his valuable service during the Atlanta campaign, and in March, 1865, he received a more substantial recognition from the government in the form of promotion to the rank of brevet major-general. This was given him especially for gallantry at Ezra Church, and concerning his service in that engagement, and the confidence which Sherman had in him, General Howard tells the following: "Our skirmishers cleared the field and the battle of Ezra Church was won, and with this result I was content. One officer, who was a little panic-stricken, ran with the first stragglers to Sherman, and cried substantially, as I remember: 'You've made a mistake in McPherson's successor. Everything is going to pieces!' Sherman said: 'Is General Howard there!'—'Yes, I suppose he is.'—'Well, I'll wait before taking action till I hear from him!' So Sherman sustained and trusted me and I was content."

Immediately after the war Howard was appointed commissioner of the Freedmen's Bureau at Washington—a position which he retained until 1874, when he became commander of

OUR CAUSE IS JUST.

Surrender of Confederates.—Surrender of Confederate forces under Generals McCall and Gantt to General Charles J. Paine, at Tiptonville, Tennessee, on April 8, 1862. The Confederates abandoned their works at Island No. 10, fleeing toward Tiptonville, where they surrendered 7,273 men, including Generals McCall, Walker, and Gantt, besides 123 cannon and mortars, nearly 10,000 stand of arms, a floating battery, many horses and mules, and a large quantity of ammunition and stores.

THE SPLENDID NAVAL TRIUMPH ON THE MISSISSIPPI
"Farragut's fleet of 16 ships passed up the river in silence until the head of the fleet was opposite the forts, when one incessant roar of heavy cannon commenced from both sides of the Mississippi and from the gunboats. The Union vessels returned the fire as they came in range. A lurid glare was thrown over the scene by the bombshells and by the fire rafts sent down against the fleet. In an hour and ten minutes the affair was virtually over, and Farragut was steaming on up to New Orleans, to open the way for the Union troops."
David D. Porter, Rear Admiral, U.S.N.

the Department of the Columbia. In 1877 and 1878 he led expeditions first against the Nez Perces Indians, and then against the Bannocks and the Piutes.

During the years 1881–82 he was superintendent of the United States Military Academy, and in 1886 he was made major-general and assigned to the Department of the Pacific, with headquarters at San Francisco. This position he retained until the close of 1887, when he superceded General Schofield in the command of the Department of the Atlantic, the latter being appointed commander of the United States Army.

General Howard has done considerable literary work, and his scholarly attainments have received recognition in the form of the degree of A.M. conferred on him by Bowdoin College, and LL.D. from Shurtleff College and Gettysburg Seminary. In 1884 he was made a chevalier of the Legion of Honor by the French government.

(General Howard died on October 26, 1909.)

8-Inch Smooth-bore Mortar Cannon

Fort Pulaski, on Cockspur Island, Georgia, was built by the United States Government in 1829–31, for the defense of the Tybee Roads and the Savannah River approach to the city of Savannah. In January, 1861, it was seized and occupied by the military authorities of the State of Georgia, and held by them until transferred to the Confederate Government, by whom it was strongly armed and garrisoned. The lighthouse, known by all coast-wise sailors as Tybee Light, 108 feet in height, and to be seen at a distance of twelve miles, was extinguished, together with all the other lighthouses in the hands of the Confederates, and, shortly before the Federal troops took possession of the island, was set on fire. The capture of Fort Pulaski had been determined upon shortly after the taking of Port Royal, and Tybee Island was occupied on the 24th of November, 1861, for the purpose of erecting batteries, and to enable the making of reconnoissances with gunboats and land forces. On April 12th, Colonel Charles H. Olmstead surrendered the Fort with 360 prisoners, 47 guns, and a large supply of stores and ammunition.

JOHN ALEXANDER LOGAN, U.S.A., 1826–1886

General Logan's father came to this country from Ireland when a young man, settling successively in Maryland, Kentucky, Missouri and Illinois. He was a sturdy Democrat, and served several terms as the representative of that party in the legislature. General Logan was born in Jackson County, Ill., on February 9, 1826, and was educated first at a common school and with a private tutor, and afterwards at Shiloh College. In the Mexican War he first volunteered as a private, but soon became lieutenant in the 1st Illinois infantry. His service throughout the war was entirely creditable, and he acted for some time as quartermaster of his regiment. At the close of the war he returned from Mexico and began the study of law, entering somewhat into politics also.

In 1849 he was chosen clerk of Jackson County. He graduated from Louisville University in 1851 and was admitted to the bar. As a lawyer and political speaker he soon became popular, and was elected to the legislature in 1852, and again in 1856. In this same year he was also a presidential elector on the Buchanan and Breckinridge ticket. He was elected to congress by the Democratic party in 1858, and was re-elected in 1860. He was a firm advocate of Stephen A. Douglas; but on first hearing news of trouble in the South, he said that, in case Abraham Lincoln were elected, he would "shoulder his musket to see him inaugurated;" and in support of this statement he actually did take the field; for in July, 1861, while the extra session which President Lincoln had called was still in session, Logan left the house, overtook the

army of the North as they were leaving Washington, and took part in the battle of Bull Run. On his return in August, he resigned his seat in congress and organized the 31st Illinois infantry, of which he was made colonel. He led his regiment gallantly at Belmont in November, and later in the assaults on Forts Henry and Donelson, and in the last-named engagement he received a serious wound which disabled him for some time.

On March 5, 1862, he was made brigadier-general of volunteers, and shared actively in the important movement against Corinth. He was afterward placed in command at Jackson, Tenn., with orders to guard the railroad communications.

General Logan's reputation as a statesman had already secured for him an extensive and faithful constituency at home. His forcible style of oratory, pleasing address and fine voice had won him many admirers, while his good judgment and thorough information on political matters had inspired all who knew him with confidence. Logan was a natural orator in the best sense of the word; strong, earnest and convincing in debate, he possessed an indomitable will, which overcame all opposition, and a remarkable faculty of clear presentation, which rendered him a most formidable opponent in the courtroom and the senate hall, and commanded the enthusiastic admiration of friends and foes alike.

As concerns his behavior at the opening of the Civil War, it must be said in justice to him that General Logan was a noble example of sacrifice of self-interest for the sake of the country.

Some of our greatest generals at the opening of the war were in humble condition of life, faring badly in business, and, speaking generally, only too ready for something to turn up to engage their services. Others, including such names as Garfield, Rosecrans and Logan, were in prosperous condition and with a most encouraging outlook in life. To step out of their professions meant a great sacrifice of personal interests. Logan had, from his graduation from the law school, steadily built himself up in his profession, with increasing success, until, by the year 1862, he had attracted to himself a host of warm admirers—the lawyer's and politician's surest guarantee of future success. During the summer of 1862 his friends requested him, therefore, to become a candidate for re-election to congress. His reply was characteristic and manly: "I have entered the field to die, if need be, for this government, and never expect to return to peaceful pursuits until the object of this war of preservation has become a fact established," and with this declination they were forced to rest content.

In the Northern Mississippi campaign Logan was in command of the 3d division of the 17th army corps, and performed excellent service in the battles of Port Gibson, Raymond, Jackson and Champion's Hill. He received the promotion to major-general of volunteers, dating from November 26, 1862. He commanded the centre under McPherson during the siege of Vicksburg, and was among the first to enter the city when captured. He was appointed its military governor.

In November, 1863, he succeeded General Sherman in the command of the 15th army corps, and in the following May served under Sherman, who was at that time preparing for his advance into Georgia, and in the various engagements of that famous march rendered brilliant and distinguished services. Sherman had received his final orders to move against Atlanta on April 10, and he moved at once to Chattanooga, making that his headquarters on the 28th. Starting from that point, the National force came up with the Confederate army under General Johnston at Dalton, May 14, and succeeded in driving him back to Resaca. Here he was assaulted, and compelled to re-

treat to Cassville and behind the Etowah on the 17th. After the several severe battles at New Hope Church and near Dallas, Johnston was forced to retreat still further to a strong position on Kenesaw Mountain, also covering Marietta with his flanks. Sherman attempted several attacks on the fortified Confederate lines during the latter part of June, but without success; and at last, on July 3, he moved a portion of his force towards the Chattahoochee, compelling Johnston to retire to the northwest bank of that river, and as Sherman crossed the river the Confederate army fell back on Atlanta.

By July 17 the direct attack on Atlanta began, General Hood having succeeded Johnston in command of the Confederate army. In the three battles at Peach Tree, the east side of the city, and Ezra Church, on July 20, 26 and 28, the National forces were victorious. Sherman then, drawing off five corps, marched to Jonesboro—twenty-six miles south of Atlanta—defeated the enemy there, and took possession of the railroad, thus stopping all means of supply, and forcing the City of Atlanta to capitulate on September 1.

General Logan shared actively in all these engagements. He led the advance in the battle of Resaca, repulsed the enemy at Dallas, and at Kenesaw Mountain drove them from their line of works. In the operations around Atlanta, when Sherman was extending his left flank to envelop the city, General Hood was endeavoring to frustrate the movement, and a series of sharp encounters resulted. On the 22d of July General Hood concentrated his whole force upon the National left, which was commanded by General McPherson, and made a terrific and almost overwhelming onslaught. The movement was almost entirely unexpected, and McPherson was at the time in General Sherman's headquarters in consultation. Immediately mounting his horse, McPherson hastened to the field, to dispose his troops in the best form to receive the attack and repulse it. In the confusion of the battle, he endeavored to cross from one column to another and rode into the enemy's lines, where he was killed. This left the National forces in an almost demoralized condition, and but for the brave and prompt ac-

tion of General Logan, who succeeded McPherson, all might have been lost. Speaking concerning the battle of Atlanta, General Sherman said in his report: "General Logan commanded the Army of the Tennessee through this desperate battle with the same success and ability that has characterized him in the command of a corps or division." The greatest credit is due General Logan for his able command during this campaign; in fact, in the battle of Atlanta it may be said that it was mainly due to his skill and determination that a serious disaster to Sherman's army was averted. With the downfall of Atlanta Logan severed his connection with his command—returning to Washington and taking an active part in the presidential campaign. He rejoined his troops, however, at Savannah, and remained with the army until the surrender of General Joseph E. Johnston.

At the close of the war he was appointed commander of the Army of the Tennessee, but resigned his commission, and was shortly after appointed minister to Mexico. This office, however, he also declined. In 1866 he was elected a representative from Illinois to congress by the Republican party, and was one of the managers in the impeachment trial of President Johnson. He was re-elected to the next congress, and served as chairman of the Committee on Military Affairs. In this office he secured the passage of an act for the reduction of the army. In the next congress he was again re-elected; but before entering on this office he was chosen senator by the Illinois legislature, his term beginning March 4, 1871.

On December 2, 1872, he succeeded Vice-president Wilson as chairman of the Senate Committee on Military Affairs. His term of office expired in 1877, and for two years he resumed his pursuit of the law profession, practicing in Chicago. In 1879, however, he was again elected to congress, where his brilliancy and oratorical powers secured him always a high position of honor. Among some of his more famous speeches may be mentioned the following: "On Reconstruction" (1867), "Impeachment of President Johnson" (1868), "Removing the Capitol" (1870), "Vindication of President Grant against the Attack of Charles Sumner" (1872), "Ku-klux in Louisiana" (1875), "The Power of the Government to Enforce the United States Laws" (1879). He delivered, moreover, on June 6, 1880, a very able speech on the Fitz-John Porter case in which he took the ground that General Porter was justly condemned, and should not be readmitted to the army.

At the Republican convention of 1884 General Logan was nominated vice-president, with Mr. Blaine as candidate for president; but the ticket was defeated by a small majority, after a very closely contested campaign.

The last years of General Logan's life were spent quietly, a part of his time engaged in literary work, which has borne fruit in two volumes, entitled, *The Great Conspiracy* (1886), and *The Volunteer Soldier of America* (1887).

He died in Washington, D.C., on December 26, 1886. His wife, who survived him, was the daughter of John M. Cunningham, Sheriff and County Clerk of Williamson County, Il., and appointed register of the land office at Shawneetown, Ill., by President Pierce. She married General Logan on November 27, 1855, and was identified with her husband's career, acting as his best adviser on all questions.

Mr. Blaine has ably summed up the character of General Logan as follows:

"General Logan was a man of immense force in a legislative body. His will was unbending; his courage, both moral and physical, was of the highest order. I never knew a more fearless man. He did not quail before public opinion, when he had once made up his mind, any more than he did before the guns of the enemy when he headed a charge of his enthusiastic troops. In debate he was aggressive and effective. . . . I have had occasion to say before, and I now repeat, that, while there have been more illustrious military leaders in legislative halls, there has, I think, been no man in this country who has combined the two careers in so eminent a degree as General Logan."

Concerning his personal appearance we would quote the following: "His personal appearance was striking. He was of medium height, with a robust physical development, a broad and deep chest, massive body, and small hands and feet. He had fine and regular features, a swarthy complexion, long, jet-black hair, a heavy moustache, and dark eyes."

For the personal sacrifice which Logan made freely at the opening of the war, he received afterwards full recompense. More honors, in fact, were tendered him than he cared to accept; for he was ever a man of independent, self-reliant spirit, scorning to accept what he could not justly earn. He resigned his commission, when the war was over, on the ground that he did not wish to draw pay without rendering active service. And besides, another field of honor awaited him—to vindicate, in discharge of civil and political duties, the stern integrity of character and noble manliness which had already secured for him the love and admiration of his fellow-soldiers on the field of battle.

NATHANIEL LYON, U.S.A., 1818–1861

West Point, 1841

Brigadier General, May, 1861

COMMANDED
Department of the West,
May, 1861

BATTLES:
Mexican War
Jefferson City
Booneville
Dug Spring
Springfield
Wilson's Creek (Killed)

General Lyon was born at Ashford, Conn., July 14, 1818, and after a common-school education entered the Military Academy at West Point, graduating in 1841, and serving first with the 2d infantry in the Seminole War in Florida.

In 1847 he served in the Mexican War under Generals Scott and Worth. General Scott had in that year been assigned to the command of the army in Mexico, and, drawing a portion of the troops under General Taylor, operating at the Rio Grande, he prepared in March to lay siege to Vera Cruz. Scott assembled his force at Lobos Island, numbering 12,000 men, and on the 9th the siege began. The city yielded on the 26th, and the garrison of about 5000 men in the castle of San Juan d'Ulloa formally surrendered on the 29th. Lyon rendered able service in this engagement, and was promoted to the rank of first lieutenant, leading his company with credit through the several battles which followed. On the advance the American army met the Mexican force under Santa Anna, occupying the mountain pass of Cerro Gordo, surprised them at sunrise, and completely routed them. The Mexican army numbered 12,000, while Scott's force was at this time only 8500, but notwithstanding the victory was complete. Three thousand Mexicans were taken prisoners, five generals were captured, besides killing and wounding more than 1000, and taking a large number of arms—this with the total loss on the American side of scarcely 500. In the march against Mexico Lyon carried himself with considerable honor, and for his brave services in the battles at Contreras and

A Short History of Gen'l N. Lyon.

Churubusco he was breveted captain. On September 8 Molino del Rey was attacked by General Worth and taken; on the 13th Chapultepec was assailed and captured, and on the 14th the American army entered the city, taking possession of the national palace. In the assault on the city Lyon was wounded.

After the close of the war he served under General Persifer F. Smith, who commanded the departments of California and Texas. Lyon led several successful expeditions against the Indians, and was commended highly by his superior officer. In 1851 he was promoted to the rank of captain, and returned East with his regiment in 1853.

He was sent to Fort Riley in 1854, and it was here that he first manifested strong abolition principles. He was amongst men of hostile disposition, however and in 1856, when the troops were ordered to enforce the laws against the abolitionists, he felt seriously inclined to resign his commission, believing that he was acting "as a tool in the hands of evil rulers for the accomplishment of evil ends"; and he would probably have acted upon this belief had he not been removed shortly after and ordered to Dakota. He returned in 1859, and served under General W. S. Harney.

Early in February, 1861, he was sent to St. Louis and for some time after was engaged in a contest with Major P. V. Hagner concerning the command of the arsenal. Hagner was major of ordnance, and had held that position for ten years. On April 25, 1861, he was assigned to the duty of ordering, irspecting and purchasing arms and ordnance stores. Lyon had reasons for believing that Hagner sympathized with the cause of the South, and on this ground appealed to General Harney, and afterwards to President Buchanan, asking for the removal of Hagner from command. His efforts in this direction, however, were of no avail, and shortly after he and F. P. Blair, Jr., were busily engaged in organizing the home guards as an opposition body to Hagner. Blair went to Washington and endeavored to persuade the president to transfer the command of the arsenal to Lyon, representing the dangerous situation of affairs, but was unsuccessful in accomplishing his purpose. This was a short time before the inauguration of President Lincoln, and there did not at that time seem to be provocation enough for the removal of Hagner. But when on inauguration day there was a decided movement of hostility on the part of the secessionist minute-men of St. Louis, the government began to realize the situation, and appointed Lyon commander of the troops on March 13. General Harney was, however, most reluctant in altering affairs, and still left Hagner in charge of the arms and war materials which Lyon needed for his home guards. It was only after Governor C. F. Jackson showed his sympathy with the secession movement by promoting the interests of the minute-men, and placing the city police force under the command of Basil W. Duke, the leader of the secessionist minute-men, and after the city election transferred the municipal government into the hands of the secessionists, that General Harney placed Lyon in complete control of the arsenal. When the president issued his call for troops, Governor Jackson prepared to place batteries on the hills overlooking the arsenal, and in other ways manifested a spirit of hostility to the North. Lyon was therefore reinforced by three regiments to assist his garrison. Lyon also had obtained, through Blair in Washington, authority to issue 5000 stand of arms for volunteer service. General Harney vigorously opposed the arming of volunteers, and also Lyon's attempts to guard the city by placing armed forces at various points. For this chiefly Harney was removed from the command of the department on April 21,

and immediately after his departure Lyon assumed charge, and was the recognized commander of the department. He had under him four regiments, and, after taking the arms and materials necessary for equipping his own force, he dispatched all the rest of the arms and ordnance stores to the Illinois State authorities. This virtually defeated the purpose of the governor, who ordered the militia into camp in the city, having in mind the capture of the arsenal. Lyon, whose force had now been increased by volunteers (chiefly German) to five regiments, surrounded the camp of the militia-men on May 10, and made prisoners of war of the entire corps. General Harney shortly afterwards resumed command again, and although he expressed approval of the capture of the militia-men, was opposed to Lyon's efforts to interfere with the organization of forces by the governor, although the latter's operations were plainly hostile to the North. On May 21 General Harney entered into an agreement with the Confederate General Sterling Price, commanding the Missouri militia, to make no military movement so long as peace was maintained by the State.

On May 17 Lyon had received the commission of brigadier-general, and on the 31st was appointed commander of the Department of the West in the place of General Harney. Shortly after this the governor and General Price endeavored, in an interview with General Lyon, to obtain his consent to a continuance of the agreement made with General Harney; but Lyon opposed it vigorously, and maintained "the right of the United States Government to enlist men in Missouri, and to move its troops within or across the State." This resulted in hostile operations, and Lyon, anticipating a Confederate advance from Arkansas, sent one force to meet it, while with another he captured Jefferson City, pursued the enemy to Booneville, and defeated the force under Colonel John S. Marmaduke on June 17.

The utmost credit is due General Lyon for his unabated efforts in the early portion of his St. Louis command, when he had opposition to overcome on the part of friends and foes alike; and he is entitled to special commendation for his prompt-

ness of action on assuming the command of the department. He had in no single case awaited developments. Realizing the necessity of immediate action, he had anticipated each time the purpose of the enemy and frustrated it, so that he was now master of the whole State of Missouri, with the exception of a small section in the southwestern corner. It was his purpose to pursue Price, and on July 3 he started from Booneville; but, hearing that Sigel's force had been defeated at Carthage, and that the Missourians had combined with the Confederate force under General McCulloch, Lyon stopped at Springfield, hoping to receive reinforcement. The Confederate force advanced on Springfield, and General Lyon saw small hope of successfully meeting them. His force he knew was scarcely more than one-fourth the number of the enemy. However, he met them in a small skirmishing engagement at Dug Spring, and was compelled to fall back again to Springfield. He determined on the 9th of August to meet the enemy in battle on Wilson's Creek; for he saw that, in spite of their superior numbers, it was the only thing left him to do, as retreat was even more dangerous. He therefore attempted to take the Confederate camp by surprise early in the morning, attacking them in the rear, while General Franz Sigel assailed the right wing. The latter conducted his share of the battle with great success at first, and drove the enemy a considerable distance back, but made a fatal mistake later in supposing one of the Confederate regiments to be Iowa troops. In the confusion which resulted Sigel was defeated.

Lyon could now see little hope, and his last heroic charge is thus described: "Lyon, perceiving new troops coming to the support of Price, brought all his men to the front for a final effort. His horse was killed, and he was wounded in the head and leg; but, mounting another horse, he dashed to the front to rally his wavering line, and was shot through the breast, expiring almost instantly."

The battle already lost, the death of their leader only added to the dismay of the National troops, and Major Samuel D. Sturgis shortly afterward commanded a retreat, having lost 1317 men, while the Confederates lost 1230.

General Lyon supplies a striking example of whole-souled devotion to the cause of the North. Throughout his life he had been ever the most active in upholding the Union. He died in one last brave effort in her behalf, and after his death it was found that he had bequeathed $30,000—almost his entire property—to the government to aid in the cause of freedom

Engagement between the U.S. Gunboat *Varuna* & the Confederate Ram *Breckinridge* & Gunboat *Governor Moore*.

—Shortly after one o'clock on the morning of the 24th of April, 1862, everybody was called to action, and about an hour later two small red lights were shown as a signal for advance. At about half-past three the entire fleet was well under way. Fort Jackson and Fort St. Philip were passed by without experiencing much damage. As the *Cayuga* got beyond Fort St. Philip, she was attacked by the Confederate flotilla, under command of Captain Mitchel, of the *Louisiana*. The *Varuna* was about moving ahead when she was fiercely assailed by the *Governor Moore*, which, under the command of Beverley Kennon, suc-ceeded in ramming her simultaneously with the delivery of a raking fire that killed four and wounded nine of the *Varuna*'s crew. Captain Boggs, of the *Varuna*, managed, however, to get some 3-inch shells and rifle shots abaft the *Moore*'s armor, compelling her to drop out in a disabled condition. He was then attacked by another vessel having a concealed iron prow, which was driven twice into the *Varuna*, the second time crushing in her side to such an extent that she sank some fifteen minutes later. Before the *Varuna* settled, however, the Confederate vessel had become entangled and was so drawn around as to expose her unarmored side, into which, later, Captain Boggs was enabled to fire some of his 8-inch shells. After this, the Confederate vessel went ashore.

Surrender of New Orleans, April 25, 1862. —In the midst of the rain, Captain Theodorus Bailey, bearing a flag of truce, put off in a boat, accompanied by Lieutenant George H. Perkins, with a demand for the surrender of the city, as well as for the immediate substitution of the Federal for the Confederate ensigns. They stepped ashore and made their way to the City Hall through a motley crowd, which kept cheering for the South and for Jefferson Davis, and uttering groans and hisses for President Lincoln and the Yankee fleet.

GEORGE BRINTON McCLELLAN, U.S.A., 1826–1885

General McClellan was born in Philadelphia on December 3, 1826. He was educated at first by tutors, and during the years 1840–42 studied at the University of Pennsylvania, where he shared the first honors of his class. At the age of fifteen years and six months he entered the United States Military Academy at West Point, and graduated on July 1, 1846. His record at the academy was of the highest, both in scholarship and performance of military duty. Upon graduation he was appointed brevet second lieutenant in the engineer corps, and in this capacity served during the Mexican War, being present at Malan, Camargo, Tampico and Vera Cruz, and taking an active part in the battle of Cerro Gordo. On April 24, 1847, he was made second lieutenant, and distinguished himself by brave conduct in the battles of Contreras and Churubusco, and in the assault against Chapultepec. For gallant and meritorious conduct in the first two engagements he was breveted first lieutenant, and for his share in the last he was made captain.

At the close of the war he became instructor in practical engineering at West Point, and remained there until 1852, when he joined Captain Marcy's expedition up the Red River, exploring that region. During the next two years he was engaged in engineering work in Oregon and Washington Territories, and later on the Northern Pacific Railroad.

In the spring of 1855 he was sent on a military commission to Europe to report on the operations in the Crimean War. His report, representing with admirable fulness and clearness the

details concerning the organization and equipment of European armies, was published in 1861 under the title, *The Armies of Europe*. Shortly after his return McClellan resigned his commission, and during the years 1857–61 was engaged in railroad work; and at the opening of the Civil War he was President of the St. Louis, Missouri and Cincinnati Railroad.

He was made major-general of Ohio volunteers, commanding the Department of the Ohio, on April 23, 1861, and at the end of a month had crossed into Virginia and occupied Parkersburg. General Garnett commanded the Confederate army opposing McClellan, and in the eight days' campaign which followed the latter drove the enemy from their position by the Great Kanawha, scattering them and taking 1000 prisoners—in short, completely annihilating the enemy of Western Virginia. At the convention held at Wheeling on June 11, 1861, in which 40 counties were represented, this part of the State adhered to the Union, and, splitting from the rest of Virginia, entered the Union as a separate State, by act of congress, December 31, 1862.

General McClellan was made major-general in the regular army, and after the battle of Bull Run was called to Washington and appointed to the command of the Department of Washington and Northeastern Virginia. On August 20 he was placed in command of the Army of the Potomac, while in November he became the commander of all the armies of the United States.

No other general during our late war passed through such a

West Point, 1846

Major General, volunteers, April, 1861
Major General, regulars, May, 1861
General-in-Chief, November, 1861–March, 1862

COMMANDED
Department of the Ohio, April, 1861
Department of Washington and Northeastern Virginia, July, 1861
Army of the Potomac, July, 1861–July, 1862; September, 1862–November, 1862

rapid series of promotions, and this fact must be borne in mind in estimating McClellan's ability. He was placed in the highest position of command without being retained long enough in any of the lower positions to acquire the full and complete knowledge of the power and resources of his forces necessary to one who fills the highest rank. His successors had all served long in subordinate positions before entering on the performance of the duties of commander. By the time that General Grant was called to the command of the armies, he had acquired, by long and hard service in lower commands, a thorough knowledge of all the branches of the army; and he came, moreover, into command of forces well organized and trained. This training they owed to McClellan. When he entered into command, he found, as he states, "no army to command—a mere collection of regiments cowering on the banks of the Potomac: some perfectly raw, others dispirited by recent defeat, some going home." Of the other armies he could, of course, know nothing, except by report from their commanders. It was not to be wondered at that his progress in bringing the Army of the Potomac into order was slow, and yet for this slowness he was subjected to suspicion. The progress was still further delayed by McClellan's illness in December, 1861; and it was not until March, 1862, that his army was in motion and he entered on the Peninsular campaign. Immediately on his leaving Washington, however, he was accused of having left the capital unprotected, and detachments were made from his force to render the city secure, and he was in other ways interfered with; while a short time afterwards he was suddenly relieved of the general command of the armies, retaining simply his rank as Commander of the Army of the Potomac.

In his progress against Yorktown and Williamsburg, and later against Richmond, McClellan was again accused of slowness; and his caution, owing to his lack of knowledge of the real strength of the force opposing him, and his systematic habits as an engineer, together with his careful deliberation, give this accusation considerable justice; for he was unnecessarily slow during the early part of the campaign. After the engagement near Richmond the position of the National army was very precarious. Its supplies had been largely cut off by Confederate raids, and it became evident that the only plan was to fall back and reorganize and plan anew. Then followed the seven days' battles, from June 25 to July 1, during which the National force continued to fall back, warding off the repeated attacks of the enemy in a series of engagements which severely tested the mettle of the excellent but exhausted troops. On the 28th of June, during this great retreat, McClellan asserted that if the government had lent him its full support, he could, with 10,000 additional troops to reinforce him, have captured Richmond. In his dispatch to Secretary Stanton at this time he states: "If I save this army now, I tell you plainly that I owe no thanks to you or to any other person in Washington. You have done your best to sacrifice this army."

On the 7th of July President Lincoln visited the army, which was found to number over 80,000 men. McClellan requested reinforcements and another trial, but without success, and on the 11th General Halleck was appointed commander-in-chief, and McClellan was relieved of his command, and ordered to send all available soldiers to General Pope, who was commanding the new Army of Virginia, formed by consolidating the forces under Generals Fremont, Banks and McDowell. But on the 30th of August, 1862, occurred the second battle of Bull Run—more disastrous than the first—and early in September General Pope resigned his command. In this predicament the services of McClellan were again needed, and so urgently that he departed to assume the command without the official word from the Secretary of War. On his arrival he was received with enthusiasm by the dispirited soldiers, who were devoted to "Little Mac," as they styled him.

McClellan's personal magnetism was remarkable, and his influence over his men similar to that which Napoleon exercised. In the battle of Antietam, which followed shortly after, McClellan virtually accomplished a signal victory in holding his ground and forcing the Confederate line back. This is usually regarded as a drawn battle; but, all circumstances considered—especially the failure of Burnside's troops to accomplish their share of the work—the result of the engagement redounds considerably to McClellan's credit. He had taken "13 guns, 39 colors, about 15,000 stand of arms, and more than 6000 prisoners, while he had not lost a gun or color." For what he accomplished, however, he received from Washington only expressions of dissatisfaction at his delay in Warrenton, where he had paused to recruit. He was awaiting reinforcements and supplies, which he believed to be absolutely necessary for his forces, and only received from Washington repeated and urgent orders to move, while all manner of insinuations were hurled at him. On November 7 he at length received a message from the President relieving him of the command, while Burnside was appointed as his successor. The latter, however, expressed his indisposition to accept the position.

McClellan was then for a short time at Trenton, and afterwards at New York, awaiting orders. He took no further part in the war, but his popularity followed him everywhere. During 1863 he visited Boston, where he was treated with the utmost honor and received the most enthusiastic welcome. In 1864 a monument was erected at West Point to the memory of the officers and soldiers of the regular army, and McClellan was invited to deliver the memorial oration at the unveiling.

During his inactive months he prepared his work entitled, *Report on the Organization and Campaigns of the Army of the*

THE PLATFORMS
AS INTERPRETED BY THE SOLDIERS.

Mc'Clellan Platform.	Union Platform.

"Cessation of Hostilities."	"For a vigorous prosecution of the War."

Potomac. In the same year (1864) he was appointed by the Democratic convention at Chicago as their candidate for the presidency, but it was of course to be expected that his chances would be at such a time very small; in fact, the election of any new candidate at such a critical juncture of our National history would have been attended with too great a risk. McClellan's defeat was therefore a bad one, he receiving but 21 electoral votes against 212.

On September 8, 1864, he resigned his commission in the army and spent the following four years in Europe. In 1868 he returned to the United States, and during that year and the year following received the offers of the presidency of the University of California and Union College, both of which he declined. He became engineer-in-chief of the Department of Docks in New York City in 1870, retaining the position for about two years. During the following few years he received a number of offers from various quarters, chiefly from engineering corporations. He spent the years, however, very quietly, traveling and writing.

In 1877 he was elected Governor of New Jersey, and served one administration, at the close of which he was renominated for the position, but declined. In 1881 he became, by appointment of congress, a member of the Board of Managers of the National Home for Disabled Soldiers.

During the latter years of his life he contributed a number of articles to various magazines, while amongst his more pretentious works will be found the following: *A Manual of Bayonet Exercise* (1852), *Government Reports of Pacific Railway Surveys* (1854), *Report on the Organization and Campaigns of the Army of the Potomac* (1864), *McClellan's Own Story* (1886).

While apparently in sound health, he was suddenly attacked by heart disease, and died at his country residence at Orange, N.J., on October 29, 1885.

General McClellan was a man of modest and retiring disposition, and genuine worth. His character was eminently pure and lovable, and his control over his men and the adoration he inspired in them surpassed that of any general in the war.

McCLELLAN ARMY SADDLE

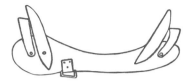

Side view

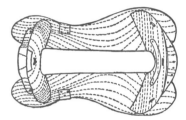

Top view

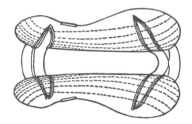

Bottom view

THE BATTLE OF WILLIAMSBURG
May 5, 1862

IRVIN McDOWELL, U.S.A., 1818–1885

General McDowell was born in Columbus, Ohio, on October 15, 1818, and received his first educational training at the College of Troyes, in France. On returning to this country he entered the United States Military Academy at West Point, graduating in 1838. He was then appointed second lieutenant in the 1st artillery, and served first on the Northern frontier, where there was a threatened collision with Great Britain, growing out of the disputed boundary line between Maine and New Brunswick. The dispute, however, was settled without war, chiefly through the efforts of General Scott, and the whole affair was satisfactorily closed by the Ashburton-Webster Treaty in 1842. On his return in 1841 McDowell was made assistant instructor of infantry tactics and adjutant at West Point, retaining that position until 1845, when he became aide-de-camp to General John E. Wool. In that capacity he served in the battle of Buena Vista, and for gallant conduct on that occasion was promoted to brevet captain, receiving the same rank in the adjutant-general's department on May 13, 1847. General Scott had been assigned to the general command of the army in Mexico, and in March previous had assembled his army, numbering 12,000 men, at Lobos Island, with the purpose of laying siege to Vera Cruz. The siege began on the 22d, and on the 26th, after 7000 missiles had been fired, the city and castle of San Juan d'Ulloa capitulated, and the garrison of the latter, comprising 5000 men, grounded their arms before the city on the 29th.

Then followed the march to Jalapa, on which the Mexican

army, 12,000 strong, under Santa Anna, was surprised in the mountain pass of Cerro Gordo and completely routed. Jalapa was captured on the 19th of April, Perote on the 22d and Puebla on May 15. This left the advance on the City of Mexico almost entirely cleared of obstructions, and had Scott's army been able to march directly against the capital, victory would have been an easy matter and much bloodshed spared. But the American army was in a sadly depleted condition after its recent hard service, and thoroughly exhausted from continued fighting against heavy odds, so that a delay for some time was absolutely necessary until reinforcements should arrive and the tired men should be in condition to resume the march. This delay, however, enabled Santa Anna to gather together the scattered remnants of his force, create a new army and fortify the capital. On August 7 the American army was again in motion, and Scott, instead of following a direct line to the City of Mexico, made a detour to San Augustin on the south, attacking and carrying successively Contreras and Churubusco. An armistice followed, lasting until September 7, to enable the peace commissioner an opportunity to arrange matters. The operations were resumed by General Worth storming Molino del Rey. This was successfully and gallantly conducted in the face of enormous odds; and, after storming and carrying Chapultepec on the 13th, Scott's army entered the City of Mexico.

McDowell served with most commendable skill and bravery during the war, and was with the army of the occupation,

West Point, 1838

Brigadier General, May, 1861
Major General, volunteers,
    March, 1862
Brevet Major General, regulars,
    September, 1866
Major General, regulars,
    November, 1872

COMMANDED
Department of Washington and
    Northeastern Virginia, 1861
Army of the Potomac,
    May, 1861
Army of the Rappahannock, 1862

which remained several months in the city. On their first entrance, the troops had met with considerable opposition from the inhabitants, and had been fired upon from the houses, but order was soon restored and the city was reduced to a state of submission. A civil organization, under the protection of the troops, was organized; a contribution of $150,000 was levied on the city, and taxes were imposed to meet the expenses of the army. A treaty between Mexico and the United States was at length negotiated, and McDowell was for a time occupied in mustering out and discharging troops. This over, he returned to Washington, where he became assistant adjutant-general in the War Department. He filled this office afterwards in New York and other places until 1857. In 1856 he was promoted to the rank of major.

After an absence of a year in Europe he returned to Washington in 1859, where he remained in the discharge of the duties of the adjutant-general's department, and acted as aide-de-camp on the staff of General Scott. He served Scott chiefly as inspector of troops, and was engaged in this work at the opening of the Civil War. General Scott, whose reputation and experience would naturally have entitled him to the command of the Northern troops, was too advanced in age to accept such a position, and an excellent opportunity for rapid promotion was afforded to likely members of his staff. McDowell was looked upon with considerable favor, and his efficient performance of duty had met with high commendation.

During the early part of the year 1861 he was busily engaged in mustering and drilling volunteers, and on May 14 he was made brigadier-general and was placed in command of the Department of Northeastern Virginia and of the defenses of Washington south of the Potomac. The recruiting, organizing and drilling work had gone on actively during the spring weeks, the people of the North manifesting a growing impatience for some definite action. McDowell took command of the Army of the Potomac on May 29, 1861, and between that time and July 16 preparations for an advance were urged with all possible speed. McDowell's army numbered about 30,000 men, of which all were raw recruits with the exception of about 800 regulars. With this force he was ordered to march against the Confederate army at Manassas Junction, commanded by General Beauregard. McDowell had planned his campaign carefully and well, and the disastrous results of it were due chiefly to an unforeseen circumstance. The principal feature of his plan was "to turn the enemy's left flank while threatening the front, which was well posted behind Bull Run, on an elevation that commanded the entire plateau." The first fighting took place at Blackburn's Ford on the 18th, and the National troops were forced to fall back to Centreville. This engagement occurred entirely without the authority of McDowell, although he has since been severely censured for it and the results which followed. The National army remained at Centreville two days, and on the 21st made an attack on the Confederate left, throwing that portion of the line into such confusion that both General Beauregard and General Johnson were forced to take part in the fight in order to rally the troops. The Confederate line was then re-formed on the crest of the hill, and the brunt of the battle was there. The ground was fought and re-fought, the hill was three times won and lost, but at about three o'clock in the afternoon the National force held the position. It was then that the unforeseen and fatal incident of the battle occurred. Victory seemed assured to the Northern army, when suddenly a large reinforcement to the Confederate army arrived in the form of a force under General E. Kirby Smith, which McDowell had all along supposed to be held in check by General Robert Patterson in the Shenandoah Valley. This completely turned the battle, and the exhausted and discouraged Northern troops broke into confusion and retreated to Washington, demoralized and in the utmost disorder, leaving the Confederate army an open opportunity to march directly to the capital. This unfortunate engagement was a severe blow to the North and to General McDowell. General Sherman has characterized it as "one of the best planned battles, and one of the worst fought." The Northern army, in spite of a decided defeat, suffered scarcely less than the Confederate force. General Johnston says: "The Confederate army was more disorganized by victory than that of the United States by defeat"—a fact which goes largely to account for the failure of the Confederate army to push their advantage. Public opinion made General McDowell solely responsible for this defeat, and this charge stood in the way of all advancement for him during the war. He was removed from the general command and General McClellan was appointed in his place.

McDowell was then placed in command of the 1st army corps of the Army of the Potomac—a corps which was afterwards detached and called the Army of the Rappahannock. In March, 1862, he was appointed major-general of volunteers, and during the summer, when the four commands in Virginia were concentrated into the Army of Virginia under General Pope, McDowell was assigned to the 3d corps. With this army McDowell shared in the campaign of Northern Virginia, taking a prominent part in the battles of Cedar Mountain, Rappahannock Station and the second battle of Manassas. This campaign ended in August, and during the last part of it McDowell's corps was in a most distressing condition, "either making forced marches, many times through the night and many times without food, or was engaged in battle. Though worn out with fasting, marching and fighting, his men were neither demoralized nor disorganized, but preserved their discipline to the last."

On September 6, 1862, General McDowell was retired from active field service, and no further command was given him during the Civil War. This slight was deeply felt by him, and he made an appeal for a court of inquiry, but without success, and the matter was dismissed. He acted as president of the court of investigation of cotton frauds during 1863, and afterward as president of the board for retiring disabled officers. In 1864 he went to San Francisco to assume command of the Department of the Pacific, and in the following year commanded the Department of California, remaining in the latter charge until 1868. On September 1, 1866, he had been commissioned brevet major-general in the regular army. From 1868–1872 he was in command of the Department of the East, and on November 25 of the latter year he was promoted to major-general. He then succeeded General Meade in the command of the Division of the South, remaining there until 1876, when he was again placed in command of the Division of the Pacific.

He retired from the army on October 15, 1882, and spent the remaining years of his life in San Francisco, during which he was one of the park commissioners of that city. His death occurred on May 4, 1885.

General McDowell was handled very severely for his action in the battle of Bull Run, both by the press and the public. He was not, however, entitled to the treatment he received, and it was with considerable justice that he asked for a court of inquiry. The refusal of this on the part of the government, while it may have been partially justified by the pressure of most important and momentous events, absorbing attention, was none the less unfair; and the response to General McDowell's request was worded in a manner that did his conscientious service but poor justice. His appeal was dismissed with the following curt sentence: "The interests of the public service do not require any further investigation into the conduct of Major-general McDowell."

In estimating McDowell's services one must consider fairly a number of circumstances which go a great way to mitigate his personal responsibility for the disastrous results of the battle of Bull Run. He had been placed in charge of a horde of raw recruits, who never had experienced a battle. He was then hastened by the impatient voice of the people to an action which, considering the condition of the Northern forces, was a little premature. But this would have counted for nothing had he received the support upon which he justly relied. General Robert Patterson crossed the Potomac at Williamsport on June 15, and was instructed to watch and hold back the Confederate troops at Winchester, Va. He failed, however, to do this. His reason for this failure, according to his own statement, is that he had been directed to await orders from General Scott, which

the latter failed to send. However this may be, the blame was surely not McDowell's. He had virtually carried the day at Bull Run, and held the upper hand, when the reinforcement of fresh troops told him only too well that General Patterson had failed to co-operate with him. In view of these facts, it scarcely seems fair that he should have been treated as an inefficient and blundering officer. The battle was thoroughly well arranged. It was not a great blunder, but a great misfortune, and its evil results cannot be laid solely to McDowell's discredit. He was an excellent disciplinarian and organizer, a brave and able officer, and, though most unfortunate, careful and conscientious in the performance of duty.

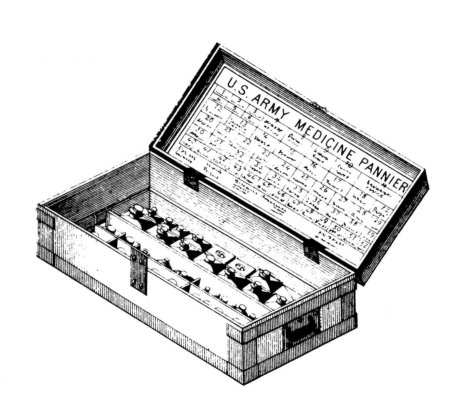

THE BATTLE OF FAIR OAKS, VIRGINIA
May 31, 1862

The Pennsylvania Bucktails, at Harrisonburg,

Virginia, June 6, 1862. The Confederates were fiercely engaged, and, although reinforced by General Alexander P. Stewart's brigade, were, after a sharp fight of several hours, compelled to fall back into a neighboring pine forest, with the loss of a portion of their camp equipage. Toward evening, General Bayard ordered Colonel Kane, with a detachment of the Pennsylvania Bucktail Rifles, numbering about 125 men, to explore the forest, and, if possible, dislodge the enemy. They entered a dense pine thicket on the left, but had not proceeded far when they found themselves almost completely surrounded by Confederates, which afterward proved to be detachments from four regiments of cavalry, with a strong support of artillery. The Bucktails flinched only temporarily in face of the almost overwhelming force suddenly opposed to them. Fire was opened upon the Confederates, who promptly returned it, wounding Colonel Kane, and rapidly thinning out the force of Federals opposing them. Such as remained of the Bucktails succeeded, however, in fighting their way out in the darkness, after a loss of 6 killed and 46 wounded and missing, the latter including Colonel Kane, who had been made a prisoner.

Battle of Cross Keys, June 6, 1862.—Before General "Stonewall" Jackson's forces could cross the north fork of the Shenandoah, General John C. Frémont was close upon them, and on Sunday, the 7th of June, he attacked the brigades under Generals Stewart, Elzey, and Trimble, which formed the rear of Jackson's army, and which were admirably posted upon a ridge commanding the road close by the Cross Keys Church. These were opposed by the Federals under Generals Stahl, Schenck, and Milroy, who moved steadily up the slope, under a heavy fire of shot and shell, gradually pressing back the Confederates until late in the afternoon, when, in view of their heavy loss of nearly 700 in killed and wounded, the Federals were ordered to retire.

GEORGE GORDON MEADE, U.S.A.,1815–1872

West Point, 1835

Brigadier General, volunteers,
August, 1861
Major General, volunteers,
November, 1862
Brigadier General, regulars,
July, 1863
Major General, regulars,
August, 1864

COMMANDED
Army of the Potomac,
June, 1863
Military Division of
the Atlantic, 1865

BATTLES:
Mexican War
Peninsula campaign
Mechanicsville
Gaines's Mills
Frayser's Farm
White Oak Swamp
Second Bull Run
South Mountain
Antietam
Fredericksburg
Chancellorsville
Gettysburg

The name of Meade has been intimately associated with various public and national movements during the past hundred years. George Meade, the grandfather of General Meade, was a signer of the non-importation resolutions of 1765, and was notably patriotic during the Revolution, subscribing large sums of money to aid the government in defraying the war expenses, and in other ways manifesting his sturdy allegiance to the cause of the United States. He was associated also with many prominent public actions in the City of Philadelphia, of which he was a resident.

His son, Richard Worsam, was a merchant and ship-owner, trading between America and Spain. During the Peninsular War he exported thousands of barrels of flour, placing Spain in a state of indebtedness to him from which, in her extremely low financial state, she was unable to free herself. In his endeavors to collect the amount due him he was summarily disposed of for a time by imprisonment in the prison of Santa Catalina at Cadiz. There he remained for two years, when he was released through the action of the United States minister. In 1819 the treaty of Florida was made between America and Spain, and, according to the terms of that treaty, our government was to receive Florida, and in return to assume the responsibility of discharging all debts on the part of Spain to American citizens. Mr. Meade therefore returned to this country armed with a certificate for $491,153.62—the amount due him—signed by the King of Spain. Then came a long, fruitless course of solicitation. Bills were passed through the senate,

and the ablest lawyers—including Webster, Clay and Choate—were engaged, but all to no end; and to this day, in spite of the correctness of the documentary proofs, the famous Meade claim has profited nothing to the family.

This was General Meade's father; and it was on December 31, 1815, while he was living in Cadiz, Spain, that General George Gordon Meade was born. The family returned to America when George was about three years of age, and it was at Philadelphia, and afterwards at Salmon P. Chase's school in Washington, and Mt. Hope institution, near Baltimore, that he received his first education. He then entered the United States Military Academy, graduating in 1835, and serving first with the 3d artillery in Florida, in the war against the Seminoles. Neither the climate nor his surroundings, however, were congenial to him there, and before a year had passed he was so reduced in health that the necessity for a change became evident. He was therefore sent with a party to Arkansas, and from there was ordered to ordnance duty at Watertown Arsenal, Mass. From this duty he resigned October 26, 1836, and entered into civil engineering work on the railroad at Pensacola, Fla.

During the years 1838 and 1839 he was engaged by the War Department on the government survey of the Sabine River and the Delta of the Mississippi; and in the year following he was employed on survey work, first on the boundary line between United States and Texas, and afterwards in the north on the boundary between United States and British America

Up until the opening of the Mexican War General Meade's employment was almost continuously in government survey at one place and another. In December, 1840, he was married to Margaretta, daughter of John Sergeant. He remained on the northeastern boundary, connected with the corps of topographical engineers, until the end of the year 1843, and during the following two years was engaged in the survey of Delaware Bay. His rank in the above corps was that of second lieutenant.

During the Mexican War he was connected with the staff of General Zachary Taylor, and shared in the battles of Palo Alto and Resaca de la Palma. His first service of note, however, was in the battle of Monterey, in which he was serving under General Worth. In this engagement he led the advance on Independence Hill, and took part later in the march to Tampico. In appreciation of his brave conduct at this time he was breveted first lieutenant. He took part in the siege of Vera Cruz, and in this battle served as a member of the staff of General Robert Patterson.

This ended for a time his active field service; for, from the year of his return from Mexico (1847) until the opening of the Civil War, he was again engaged in survey work.

During 1847–49 he was employed in the construction of light-houses on the Delaware Bay, and later in surveying the Florida reefs. On returning to Delaware in 1850 he was made first lieutenant of the topographical engineer corps. In 1851 he was sent again to the Florida reefs, where he was engaged for five years in light-house construction, and in 1856 was made captain of the corps conducting the geodetic survey of the Northern lakes.

At the beginning of the Civil War General Meade was placed in command of the 2d brigade of Pennsylvania reserves in the Army of the Potomac. He was made brigadier-general of volunteers, and in June, 1862, was promoted in the topographical engineer corps to the rank of major. His future services were, however, devoted to his brigade, and during 1862 he took part in the battles of Mechanicsville, Gaines's Mills, and Glendale. In the last-named battle he was badly wounded, and compelled to leave the army for a time. He had been removed to Philadelphia; but his wound recovering more rapidly than was at first expected, it was not long before he was able to rejoin his army and enter again into active service.

The enemy was at this time advancing toward Washington, and it was therefore at a most critical juncture of the war that General Meade resumed command of his brigade, opposing the advance of the Confederate army and sharing in the second battle of Bull Run. When the enemy later on invaded Maryland, General J. F. Reynolds being absent, General Meade was in command of the whole division of Pennsylvania reserves. He rendered distinguished services in the battles of South Mountain and Antietam; and in the latter engagement, in which General Hooker was wounded, General Meade was assigned on the battle-field to the command of Hooker's corps, and was complimented for his skill and bravery.

To the reputation already secured in these battles General Meade added materially, in November, 1862, in the battle of Fredericksburg. The enemy was commanded by "Stonewall" Jackson, and during the battle the only marked advantage that was gained by the National forces was won by General Meade's division, which drove everything before it, and penetrated the enemy's lines as far as their reserves. Two horses were shot under General Meade during the action. Had the whole National force accomplished as much in proportion, the results of that battle would have been different; but General Meade, after having made a most gallant attack, and having won a great advantage, was compelled to fall back through lack of sufficient support.

Shortly after this engagement General Meade was made major-general and commanded the 5th corps, taking part in the battle of Chancellorsville, where, after having successfully overcome considerable resistance, he was unfortunately recalled and ordered to his former position. The lack of good management in this battle was owing largely to the fact that General Hooker was stunned by a cannon ball, thus leaving the army at a most important point without sufficient command. It

became evident soon after that the Confederate army intended marching further north. While affairs were so disposed General Hooker requested further reinforcement, and, on this being refused by the President, suddenly sent in his resignation—General Meade being placed in command of the army.

This was the most trying time of Meade's experience. He was unfamiliar with the army at large and its resources, and a most important action was pending. Not a moment was to be lost, and yet he was not in possession of all the knowledge essential to a commander. It was in June, 1863, and while Lee's army was moving north, that the National forces were lying near Frederick, Md. General Meade's purpose was to follow the Confederate army in a parallel line, to prevent a descent on Baltimore, and, on finding a fitting place, to engage Lee in battle. In this manner the two armies approached Gettysburg, and on July 1 the first action of that eventful battle took place. General Reynolds led the advance National forces on that day, but was driven back by the Confederate army, Reynolds himself being killed. General Meade sent General W. S. Hancock ahead with additional forces. The result of that terrible third day of the battle, the 3d of July, and the importance of that result to the interests of the Northern cause, is well known and appreciated. As long as the Civil War is remembered, so long will the gallant and hard-earned victory at Gettysburg be recorded, with the warmest praises of the able military leadership of General Meade, and the efficient and skilful assistance of General Hancock. In view of his valuable and illustrious services, General Meade was promoted to the rank of brigadier-general in the regular army, his commission dating from July 3, 1863.

Under previous commanders the Army of the Potomac had suffered a number of reverses, and either through inefficiency or petty differences between officers in command had lost important points in the war. But under General Meade's command the army experienced no marked repulses, and he retained his position under Grant after the latter's appointment to the rank of commander-in-chief of the Northern armies. On August 18, 1864, General Meade was promoted to major-general, and led his army in the grand review in Washington at the close of the war.

During the years 1866–1872 he commanded successively the Department of the East, the Military District of Georgia and Alabama, the Department of the South (comprising Georgia, Alabama, South Carolina, Florida), and the Military Division of the Atlantic.

He died in Philadelphia on November 6, 1872, of an attack of pneumonia, which was aggravated by the results of he wound he had received at the battle of Glendale.

It has been charged against General Meade that he planned a retreat on the second day of the battle of Gettysburg. This grave charge, however, cannot be substantiated, and was solemnly denied by him before the Congressional Committee on the conduct of the war in the following words:

"I deny ever having intended or thought, for one instant, to withdraw that army, unless the military contingencies which the future should develop during the course of the day might render it a matter of necessity that the army should be withdrawn."

A complete statement of this question will be found in a pamphlet entitled "Did General Meade desire to Retreat at the Battle of Gettysburg!" (Philadelphia, 1883), and no one can read this reinstatement of General Meade without being convinced that the charge was an unjust one.

Battle of White Oak Swamp, June 30, 1862.—

Not long after the termination of the battle of Savage's Station, the Federals continued on their retreat, and by eight o'clock on the morning of the 30th they had crossed White Oak Swamp and Creek. General "Stonewall" Jackson, who reached Savage's Station early on the 30th, there found a large amount of property which the Federals had had no time to destroy, as well as fully 2,500 Federal sick and wounded, which they had likewise been unable to remove. He had orders to pursue the Federals, which he did, in company with the forces of Generals James Longstreet and A. P. Hill. After crossing White Oak Creek, the Federals had quickly formed a new line of battle in readiness for the attack.

Longstreet and Hill now pushed on, and the conflict became a severe one along the entire front. One point, then another, was vainly tried in the determined effort to break the Federal line. At length General Cadmus M. Wilcox's Alabama brigade rushed across an open field and, after a desperate hand-to-hand fight, captured Cooper's and Randall's batteries, which had been doing terrible execution. A charge was then ordered for the recapture of the guns, which were finally recaptured, but not without severe losses on both sides. The Federal loss was about 1,800 killed and wounded, that of the Confederates was somewhat over 2,000.

"At 6 P.M. General Lee came to the front and ordered an advance all along the line. Brigade after brigade charged up the hill with impetuous courage, breasting the storm of grape, shell and canister which devastated their ranks. Night came on, and yet the fight continued. The lurid flashes from the artillery, the hoarse shriek of the shells from the gunboats, made it a scene of terrific grandeur. At 9 o'clock the sound of battle ceased, and cheer after cheer went up from the victors on the hill."

—*Alex S. Webb,*
Commanding General,
2d Division, 2d Corps

Battle of Malvern Hill.—At nine o'clock on the morning of July 1, 1862, the Confederates had formed a line of battle in General Darius N. Couch's immediate front. After some desultory firing, General Robert E. Lee concluded that the Federal position could be carried only by assault. He therefore ordered a simultaneous attack to take place along the whole line as soon as the concentrated fire from his artillery had succeeded in silencing most, if not all of the Federal batteries. When this was done, part of General Benjamin Huger's division was to advance with a shout, which was to be the signal for a general movement "to drive the invaders into the James." The artillery was in position and began its fire at about three o'clock, and at a little after six the divisions of Couch and Porter were assailed by D. H. Hill's forces, who had misinterpreted a loud shout for the intended signal. The Federals were bitterly assailed, and the Confederates held their ground well, but not having any support they were soon driven back in confusion to their original position. The dash displayed by the assailants was heroic, but it availed little in face of the artillery and infantry fire, that was studiously reserved until the Confederates were within a short distance of the crest, and then poured destructively into them. A bayonet charge would then generally follow, and the Confederates would fall back to renew the attack elsewhere, until finally all were repulsed with terrible slaughter. The Federal loss was 15,249, Confederate loss 19,370.

DAVID DIXON PORTER, U.S.N.,1813–1891

The United States Government is indebted to the Porter family for many years of faithful service. Five generations of Porters served in the navy, and from the early colonial days until the present some member of that family has filled a prominent position of command. Alexander Porter commanded a merchant ship, and rendered service in behalf of the colonies; his sons, David and Samuel, served in the Continental Navy, commanding vessels commissioned by George Washington. Both of David's sons, John and David by name, rendered similar service, especially David, whose bravery in the War of 1812 secured for him the rank of commodore, and the reputation of being one of the most active and intrepid officers of the United States Navy. The end of his career, however, was unfortunate. In his pursuit and investigation of some pirates at Porto Rico, he took measures which were regarded by the government as beyond his powers, and he was therefore suspended for six months. He resigned his commission and joined the cause of Mexico, serving as commander-in-chief of the Mexican Navy—a position which he gave up a few years later, on account of treacherous treatment received, and returned to the United States. He had four sons, three of whom served in the navy, and one—Theodoric Henry—in the army.

His second son, David Dixon—the subject of the present sketch—was born on June 18, 1813, in Chester, Pa. He obtained his education at Columbia College, Washington. He was with his father in his expedition to the West Indies for the

A SHORT HISTORY of ADML PORTER

suppression of pirates, and served later as midshipman in the Mexican Navy. David D. entered the United States Navy in 1829 as midshipman, and, after cruising in the Mediterranean, was engaged in the coast survey, where he remained until February, 1841. He was then promoted to lieutenant, and during the following years, until 1845, he was continually cruising in the Mediterranean, and later off the coast of South America. He then returned to Washington and was engaged at the Naval Observatory there.

He served throughout the Mexican War, first as lieutenant and then as commander of the *Spitfire*, and in this capacity had charge of the naval rendezvous at New Orleans, and took part in every engagement on the coast during the war.

From that time until the opening of the Civil War he had charge of the California mail steamers *Panama* and *Georgia*, running between New York and the Isthmus of Panama. This latter, however, was not government naval service, but a position secured by himself, after obtaining a furlough, in consequence of the largely increased transportation between the East and California after the discovery of gold in the Pacific States.

Shortly after the opening of the Civil War Porter's services were required by the government, and he was placed in command of the *Powhatan*, a steam frigate. He was then ordered to Pensacola, to aid the Gulf blockading squadron and the reinforcement of Fort Pickens. He received, in April, 1861, the appointment as commander, and a few months later was

Rear Admiral, October, 1862
Vice Admiral, July, 1866
Admiral, 1870

COMMANDED
North Atlantic Squadron, 1866

BATTLES:
Mexican War
New Orleans
Grand Gulf
Arkansas Post
Vicksburg
Red River campaign
Cape Fear River
Fort Fisher

placed in charge of a fleet of 21 schooners, carrying mortars, and five steamers. In April, 1862, Porter's fleet, in conjunction with the fleet of Farragut, bombarded Fort Jackson and Fort St. Philip. The enemy's fleet of 15 vessels was destroyed, and the forts surrendered on April 28, 20,000 bombs having been exploded in the Confederate works during the action.

Porter's fleet was not of as much assistance in the campaign against Vicksburg as it was at first thought it would be, but this was owing not to any fault on the part of the commander or fleet, but to natural obstacles. All the assistance that his fleet could render under the circumstances, however, Porter gave, and conducted his share of that famous action skilfully and efficiently. His own words concerning it are interesting: "The navy has necessarily performed a less conspicuous part in the capture of Vicksburg than the army; still it has been employed in a manner highly creditable to all concerned. The gunboats have been constantly below Vicksburg in shelling the works, and with success, co-operating heartily with the left wing of the army. The mortar boats have been at work for forty-two days without intermission, throwing shells into all parts of the city. . . . I stationed the smaller class of gunboats to keep the banks of the Mississippi clear of guerrillas, who were assembling in force and with a large number of cannon to block up the river and cut off the transports bringing down supplies, reinforcements and ammunition for the army. Though the rebels on several occasions built batteries, and with a large force attempted to sink or capture the transports, they never succeeded, but were defeated by the gunboats with severe loss on all occasions."

The *Indianola* had been captured by the Confederates, and while they were attempting to repair the vessel Porter fitted up an old scow in a manner to resemble his "turtle" gunboats and set it adrift. The result was a terrific cannonading on the part of the Confederates, and they had wasted shot for an hour and had destroyed the *Indianola* before they discovered the trick.

In July, 1862, Porter took his flotilla to Fort Monroe, and, resigning charge of it there, he was appointed rear-admiral in the Mississippi squadron in September. He considerably improved the condition of this squadron, constructing a temporary navy yard at Mound City, and adding several new vessels.

In January, 1863, he assisted General Sherman's army in the capture of the Arkansas Post. During the next few months the National forces on land and water were closing slowly around Vicksburg. Porter captured the Confederate forts at Grand Gulf, and thus secured means of communication with General Grant, who, with the assistance of the fleet, on May 18 placed himself in the rear of Vicksburg. The city was at length compelled to surrender, after a prolonged and obstinate resistance, on July 4. For his valuable services at Vicksburg Porter was presented with the commission of rear-admiral and received the thanks of congress. After the surrender of Vicksburg and during the remainder of the year Admiral Porter was occupied in keeping the Mississippi River open.

During the spring of 1864 he was engaged with General Banks in the Red River expedition, which, however, was altogether unsuccessful. In the fall of the same year he was assigned to the command of the North Atlantic Squadron, comprising the coast from the Cape Fear River to the Port of Wilmington, N.C.

In December and January Admiral Porter conducted the most notable and distinguished engagement during his career. On the 24th of December he began a bombardment of the forts at the mouth of the Cape Fear River. The outlook was extremely unpromising, and General Benjamin F. Butler, who was in command of the military force, looking the ground over carefully, came to the conclusion that Fort Fisher was inpregnable, and that all attempts at storming it were useless. Admiral Porter speaks of this assault as follows: "In one hour and fifteen minutes after the first shot was fired not a shot came from the fort. Two magazines had been blown up by our shells and the fort set on fire in several places, and such a torrent of missiles was falling into and bursting over it that it was impossible for any human being to stand it. Finding that the batteries were silenced completely, I directed the ships to keep up a

Long Shall it Wave.

moderate fire, in hope of attracting the attention of the transports and bringing them in." Admiral Porter was persistent in his purpose to force the fort to surrender, and on the return of General Butler to Hampton Roads, Va., requested that the enterprise be pushed vigorously, as he felt confident that victory could be secured. In response to this, General Terry arrived on January 13 with a second military force, comprising almost 9000 men; and after some further reinforcement later, and a desperate and bloody fight of seven hours, the works were captured on January 15, and Admiral Porter had proved the truth of his previous convictions. For his gallant behavior in this engagement congress tendered him a vote of thanks.

This was the culminating act of Porter's service during the war, and from that time till the close no further opportunity was afforded him of exhibiting his skill. In fact, it may be said that the Civil War throughout gave a naval commander but few opportunities; but whenever a fleet could be handled with advantage to the land forces, or to conduct an independent assault, Admiral Porter managed his command with masterly skill.

On July 25, 1866, he received promotion to vice-admiral, and until 1869 filled the position of Superintendent of the United States Naval Academy. In 1869 he was engaged in the Navy Department at Washington, and in the following year was appointed admiral of the navy, a position which he has held ever since.

Admiral Porter is reputed not only as a naval commander of eminence, but also as a scholar. He has written several books, including a *Life of Commodore David Porter,* a novel entitled *Allan Dare and Robert le Diable*, *Incidents and Anecdotes of the Civil War*, *Harry Marline*, and a *History of the Navy in the War of the Rebellion*.

Admiral Porter is a first cousin of General Fitz-John Porter, who was court-martialed on the charge of disobeying orders at the second battle of Bull Run, and whose name has been prominently before the public ever since the war in connection with petitions for remittance of sentence and bills for relief. In May, 1882, the sentence of the court-martial disqualifying him from further service under the United States Government was remitted, and in August, 1886, he was restored to the army as colonel.

(Admiral Porter died on February 13, 1891.)

President Abraham Lincoln, with General George B. McClellan, reviewing the troops at Harrison's Landing on the James River, Virginia, July 8, 1862.

WILLIAM STARKE ROSECRANS, U.S.A.,1819–1898

General Rosecrans was born on September 6, 1819, in Kingston, Ohio. In his early school education, and afterward at West Point, he showed himself superior in scholarship, and thorough and conscientious in the performance of duty. He graduated from the United States Military Academy in 1842, holding the fifth position in his class, and was immediately appointed brevet second lieutenant in the engineer corps. During the following year he was occupied at Hampton Roads, Va., as assistant engineer in the construction of fortifications, and on the completion of his work there returned to West Point as assistant professor. He remained at the academy as an instructor until 1847, teaching first natural and experimental philosophy and then engineering. From 1847 until 1854 he was engaged in superintending engineering work at Fort Adams, R.I.; then on surveys on the Taunton River and New Bedford harbor, and repairing the Providence and Newport harbors; and lastly he was connected with the Washington navy yard. He had by this time been promoted to the rank of first lieutenant, and on April 1, 1854, resigned his commission and entered the profession of architect and civil engineer at Chicago. During the next year he became interested in coal industries and connected himself with the Cannel Coal Company. In 1856 he was President of the Coal River Navigation Company, and in the year following organized the Preston Coal Oil Company, devoted to the manufacture of kerosene. He was in this business at the opening of the Civil War, and volunteered as aide to General McClellan,

who was at that time in charge of the Department of the Ohio. Rosecrans was at first engaged in organizing and equipping troops. He then served as chief engineer of Ohio, and on the 10th of June, 1861, was made colonel of the 23d Ohio volunteers. Shortly after he received the commission of brigadier-general in the regular army, and was placed in command of a brigade under General McClellan in Western Virginia, fighting his first battle at Rich Mountain on July 11, 1861, and scoring a victory. Shortly after General McClellan was appointed to the chief command of the armies, and was transferred to the Army of the Potomac, Rosecrans succeeding him in the West on June 25. His command consisted of the Department of the Ohio, comprising Western Virginia, Ohio, Michigan and Indiana. His command was thorough, efficient and satisfactory. He defeated General J. B. Floyd at Carnifex Ferry, September 10, 1861, and prevented Lee's attempts to make progress in Western Virginia. He guarded his ground successfully at every point; and in appreciation of his able and efficient services he received the thanks of legislatures of Ohio and West Virginia. In May he was appointed to the command of General Eleazar A. Paine's and General David Stanley's divisions in the Army of the Mississippi, which was at that time under the command of General Pope. In this capacity Rosecrans took part in the siege of Corinth during the period between April 22 and May 30. At the end of June General Pope was summoned to Washington and assigned to the command of the Army of Virginia, consisting of Fremont's,

Banks's and McDowell's corps, and this left Rosecrans as his successor in the command of the Army of the Mississippi. On September 19 Rosecrans defeated General Sterling Price at the battle of Iuka, and immediately after this action returned to Corinth in anticipation of an attack and fortified that place. On the 3d and 4th of October, 1862, the Confederate army, under the command of Generals Price and Earl Van Dorn, attacked Corinth; but met the most disastrous defeat from General Rosecrans, who forced them into precipitate retreat, and pursued them 40 miles before he was recalled.

Following after his able service in this command came a still more difficult and trying duty. He was summoned on October 25 to Cincinnati, where he received orders to supercede General Don Carlos Buell in the command of the Department of the Cumberland. This was left largely to him to make, for it comprised all the territory south of the Cumberland that he might be able to wrest from the enemy. Rosecrans more than confirmed the trust that had been placed in him; for during the year following, while he remained in the Cumberland command, he carried on a campaign which was one of the most notable of the war for brilliant action and hard fighting. The first battle, which occurred on December 30, 1862, was fought at Stones River, against a Confederate force under General Braxton Bragg, and is summed up as follows: "The Confederates attacked the right wing of the National army and drove it back, while the left wing engaged the Confederate right. Meanwhile Rosecrans was obliged to reinforce his right, and personally directed the re-formation of the wing, thereby saving it from rout, although not without very hard fighting, in which both sides lost heavily. Two days later the battle was renewed by a furious assault on the National lines; but after a sharp contest the enemy was driven back with heavy loss. Unwilling to engage in a general action, the Confederate army retreated to the line of Duck River, and the Army of the Cumberland occupied Murfreesboro." The loss on both sides during this engagement was very heavy, the ranks of the National army being lessened by 9511 men, and the Confederate army

losing 9236. Bragg's forces were intrenched at Shelbyville and Tullahoma; but Rosecrans toward the latter part of June succeeded, by a brilliant flank movement, in forcing the Confederate forces from their intrenchments and driving them from Middle Tennessee. This was accomplished by July 7, and from that time until August 14 Rosecrans was busily engaged in repairing bridges and railways, and obtaining supplies, preparatory to advancing against Bragg at Chattanooga. During the latter part of August Rosecrans was crossing the Cumberland Mountains and the Tennessee River, and, attacking Bragg, forced him to withdraw from Chattanooga and to retire behind the Chickamauga, where he was reinforced by Longstreet's corps. On the 19th occurred that most eventful and bloody battle of Chickamauga. The National right, under General McCook, was driven from the field; but General Thomas held the centre firmly, and General Crittenden commanded the left. Bragg manœuvred to turn the left wing and prevent Rosecrans from gaining possession of the road to Chattanooga, but Rosecrans defeated this attempt and succeeded in placing General Thomas's corps and the divisions of Generals R. W. Johnson and J. M. Palmer firmly on the road. During the night Longstreet came up and was placed in command of the Confederate left. On the next day, when the fight was renewed with special vigor on the National right and centre, General Wood's division was drawn from the centre, through some misconception of an order, and a gap was left in the midst of the National army. General Longstreet quickly availed himself of this advantage and plunged into the gap, thus splitting the National forces and throwing the right wing out of the fight. For a time the battle seemed irrevocably lost; but General Thomas, whose orders had been to hold his position at all hazards, remained firm; Sheridan rallied many soldiers from the retreating centre to his ranks and then joined Thomas; and, in spite of the fierce and repeated attacks of the enemy, the entire force fell slowly back in good order within the defenses of Chattanooga, where the army was concentrated.

This battle, while conceded as a victory to the Confederate

army, was not altogether a defeat for the National forces; for the latter had gained and remained afterward in possession of Chattanooga, which was the objective point of the campaign. The army, however, was in a very much reduced condition. The loss on the National side was 16,179 men, and on the Confederate side 17,804; but the latter had much the more advantageous position. They commanded the approaches by land and water, and but for the timely assistance of General Grant's forces might have starved the National army at Chattanooga into submission.

On October 23 General Thomas was placed in command, and General Rosecrans in January, 1864, was assigned to the command of the Department of the Missouri, holding headquarters at St. Louis. During September General Sterling Price made a raid into Missouri and had many engagements with Rosecrans's army, which resulted in the latter driving Price from the State and into Southwestern Arkansas. This was the last active service of General Rosecrans, as he was placed on waiting orders at Cincinnati on December 10, 1864, and so remained through the last months of the conflict—the centre of interest and activity during that time being entirely in Virginia. For his services, especially at the battle of Stones River, Rosecrans was breveted major-general, and shortly after, on March 28, 1867, resigned his commission. During the same year he declined the Democratic nomination for governor of California. On July 27, 1868, he received the appointment of Minister to Mexico—an office which he held one year, returning to the United States to receive the Democratic nomination for governor of Ohio. This nomination, however, he also declined, and resumed some time later his profession of engi-

neer. His short stay in Mexico had aroused in him a deep interest for that country, and he was engaged during 1872–73, at the instigation of President Juarez, in endeavoring to bring about the construction of a system of narrow-guage railway in Mexico. In 1871 he was President of the San Jose Mining Company, and in 1878 of the Safety Powder Company in San Francisco. While he was Minister at Mexico he had urged the republic to grant a charter for an inter-oceanic railway from the Gulf of Mexico to the Pacific. This charter was intrusted to him, with the request that he would use his influence in securing the support of American capitalists and the co-operation of skilled American builders in carrying out the project. He bent all his efforts to the end of interesting congress in cultivating close commercial relations with Mexico and assisting the progress of that country. He went to Mexico at the instance of American railway builders and President Juarez, and succeeded in obtaining from the legislatures of 17 of the Mexican States unanimous resolutions urging their National Congress to enact the legislation advocated, the governors of six other States sending official recommendations to the same effect

General Rosecrans was extremely popular throughout the West. In addition to the nominations for governor already mentioned, he was in 1876 nominated for congress by the Democratic party in Nevada. This he declined, although in 1881 he was nominated for congress by the same party in California and was elected, serving until March 4, 1885. In June following he was appointed Register of the United States Treasury, and has remained in that position ever since.

(General Rosecrans died on March 11, 1898.)

Pontoon Bridge.—Volunteers for the Federal army crossing from Cincinnati, Ohio, to Covington, Kentucky, on a bridge of coal boats, hastily constructed, that they might defend Kentucky from the invasion of Confederate General Edmund Kirby Smith, in August, 1862.

WINFIELD SCOTT, U.S.A., 1786–1866

William and Mary

Brigadier General, March, 1814
Brevet Major General, 1814
General-in-Chief, 1841
Lieutenant General, 1852

BATTLES:
War of 1812
Blackhawk War
Seminole War
Mexican War

General Scott was one of the most—if not *the* most—impressive figures in the military history of our country. Bold, spirited and fearless, he combined the greatest qualities of a soldier with a presence at once so majestic and commanding that to see him once was to remember him with respect forever.

He was born near Petersburg, Va., on June 13, 1786, and after a good school preparation entered William and Mary College. After graduation he studied law and was admitted to the bar in 1806. He first entered the army in 1808 as captain of light artillery. His first year of service, however, was unfortunate. He was stationed at Baton Rouge, La., under the command of General Wilkinson, and on one occasion expressed his opinion of the conduct of his superior officer with an amount of spirit that brought him before a court-martial. No defense being possible, Scott was suspended for one year. This period the young officer devoted to the study of military tactics. He was appointed lieutenant-colonel in 1812, and was ordered to the Canada frontier. The only feature of interest at that time was the following:

"Arriving at Lewiston while the affair of Queenstown Heights was in progress, he crossed the river, and the field was won under his direction; but it was afterwards lost, and he and his command were taken prisoners, from the refusal of the troops at Lewiston to cross to their assistance." He was retained for several months, but in the January following was exchanged, and was then connected with General Dearborn's

A SHORT HISTORY OF

GENERAL WINFIELD SCOTT

army, acting as adjutant-general. He served in the attack on Fort George on May 27, 1813, and was severely wounded by the explosion of a powder magazine during the engagement. During the operation against Montreal, which took place in the fall, Scott was once more connected with his former commander, General Wilkinson, accompanying him in his descent of the St. Lawrence—an expedition which was at length given up. Scott was made brigadier-general in March, 1814, and was occupied for some time at Buffalo establishing a camp of military instruction.

During the month of July were fought the engagements which first established the military reputation of General Scott. The first of these occurred on the 3d of July, when the brigades under Scott and Ripley, and Hindman's artillery, after crossing the Niagara River, captured Fort Erie and made prisoners of many of the garrison.

Two days later the battle of Chippewa was fought, in which the enemy was defeated, while on the 25th of July the famous engagement at Lundy's Lane took place. In this last battle General Scott distinguished himself signally. He was twice severely wounded and had two horses killed under him. For a time it was feared that his recovery was doubtful, but he rallied after a slow and painful convalescence, carrying with him through life, however, the effect of his misfortune in the form of a partially disabled arm. In recognition of these services he received a gold medal, with the thanks of congress, and was offered the position of secretary of war in the cabinet. This latter honor, however, he declined, and, after superintending the reduction of the army at the close of the war, he visited Europe in a military and diplomatic capacity.

On his return to the United States in 1816, he lived for several years quietly, devoting a portion of his time to the compilation and elaboration of a manual of fire-arms and military tactics. In 1817 he married Miss Mayo, a young lady of Richmond, Va. In the year 1833 considerable trouble was caused by the hostilities against the Sac and Fox Indians, and General Scott set out from Fort Dearborn, Ill., in command of a detachment to quell the disturbance. He was too late, however; for before his arrival the chief, Black Hawk, had been captured, and with that incident the war was virtually ended. During the same year he was present at Charleston harbor, commanding the Federal forces, and to his tact and decision is largely ascribed the prevention of serious civil trouble. Three years after, in the Seminole War in Florida, General Scott was actively engaged, and later in similar warfare in the Creek country.

In 1838–39 General Scott was engaged in a service of a far different nature from that to which his life was devoted. This consisted, first, in effecting the peaceful removal of the Cherokee Indians from Georgia to their present reservation beyond the Mississippi; and in the following year the prevention of a threatened collision with Great Britain, consequent upon the dispute over the boundary line between Maine and New Brunswick. This was settled largely through the pacific efforts of General Scott, and was confirmed in the Webster-Ashburton treaty (1842).

Scott became commander-in-chief of the United States Army in 1841, after the death of General Macomb, but up until the Mexican War was afforded no opportunity to exercise his authority actively. In 1847, however, he was appointed to the chief command of the army in Mexico, and, after drawing a part of General Taylor's troops from the Rio Grande, he gathered his force at Lobos Island—numbering 12,000 men—and laid seige to Vera Cruz. His operations were begun on March 22, and lasted but four days—the city and castle of San Juan d'Ulloa capitulating on the 26th, and the garrison of 5000 men grounding their arms outside the city on the 29th. The next step was towards Jalapa, and the advance was begun on the 8th of April. On the 17th Scott met the Mexican army under Santa Anna at the mountain pass of Cerro Gordo, and, surprising the Mexicans at sunrise, Scott's army, which numbered nearly 4000 men less than their opponents, defeated them at every point. This was a most overwhelming and decisive victory, Scott capturing five generals, 3000 men, 4500 stand of arms and 43 cannon, and killing and wounding more than 1000, with a loss of less than 500. This effectually cleared all obstruction, and his advance on Jalapa met no further opposition, the city surrendering on the 19th. The capture of Perote followed shortly after on the 22d, and Puebla on the 15th of May. Had Scott commanded a sufficient force to have admitted of his advancing upon Mexico without delay, the way would have been almost entirely clear, and the victory an assured and easily obtained result. Through a considerable depletion of his force, which was at no time large, General Scott was compelled to remain at Puebla, waiting for reinforcements, until August 7. His new troops, moreover, in opposition to his expressed desire, had not been properly disciplined and instructed in the United States before they were sent to the army in Mexico. The time spent in drilling new men, therefore, contributed also to the delay. This seriously affected the interests of the American army, for it afforded Santa Anna the opportunity to create a new army and to fortify the City of Mexico. General Scott began his advance on August 7, and approached the capital in an indirect way, making a detour to San Augustin on the south. Then followed the battles at Contreras and Churubusco, in both of which Scott scored a decided victory. This left Mexico open to capture, and Scott would have made his attack at that time, but that an armistice was agreed upon to allow the peace commissioner, Nicholas P. Trist, an opportunity to arrange terms. On the 7th of September operations were once more begun on the southwest of the city by General Worth. This gallant and brave officer attacked Molino del Rey

with a force not exceeding 3500 men, in opposition to a Mexican army of about 14,000 men. General Worth captured more than 800 prisoners and conducted the attack most successfully, though at the loss of about one-fourth of his force and 58 officers. This was one of the most notable engagements of the war, and reflected the utmost credit on the brave and intrepid leader.

On the 13th of September Chapultepec was captured, and on the next morning General Scott entered the city and occupied the national palace. Though at first there was considerable disturbance within the city, and the troops were fired upon from the houses, all trouble was soon stopped, and the inhabitants were reduced to a state of complete submission. A contribution of $150,000 was levied, also a tax for the support of the army, and a civil organization was created under the protection of the troops. On the 2d of February, 1848, the treaty of Guadalupe Hidalgo was signed, and a short time afterward the city was evacuated by the United States troops. General Scott returned to receive approval of the committee on the conduct of the war, and the praise due to his distinguished services.

In 1852 he was candidate of the Whig party for the presidency, but was defeated by his opponent, General Pierce. In 1859 he acted as commissioner in the dispute concerning the boundary line between the United States and British Columbia, and successfully arranged the difficulty. On October 31, 1861, he retired from service, on account of age and infirmity, retaining his rank and pay. After a short visit to Europe, he returned to spend the remainder of his days at West Point, remarking, as he arrived there, "I have come here to die." He lived but a few weeks after, and on the morning of the 29th of May, 1866, he passed away so quietly that the exact moment of his death was not known. A touching incident of his parting moments was his injunction to his servant in the last words he ever uttered: "James, take good care of the horse"; and the magnificent animal that had carried him to victory over many a bloody field followed the impressive funeral that accompanied his master to the grave a few days later, forming in that sad pageant the most affecting figure of all. General Scott was buried at West Point, and there gathered to do him honor many of the most illustrious men of the land.

Captain Knapp's Battery. —Captain Knapp's Battery engaging the Confederates at the Battle of Cedar Mountain, August 9, 1862. The Confederate loss in this battle was about 1,300 men, and the Federals loss 1,800 killed, wounded, and missing.

THE SECOND BATTLE OF BULL RUN, OR MANASSAS
August 29 – 30, 1862
"The infantry was now massing not 500 yards away to charge and capture our guns. Our ammunition
being exhausted, there was but one way to save them, and that was to run them off the field. More than half
our horses having been killed, we divided the remaining animals among the guns, limbered up and fled.
The charging infantry gained the crest of the hill in time to give us one volley, but with no serious damage."
John B. Imboden, Captain, Staunton Artillery

JOHN SEDGWICK, U.S.A., 1813–1864

Among the names of those brave men who fell in the country's cause none occupy a more honorable position than John Sedgwick. From his earliest years he was decided in his taste for a military career, and till the day of his sad death he was ever prompt and efficient in his performance of a soldier's duty. He was born in Cornwall, Conn., on September 13, 1813, and after an ordinary school education entered the Military Academy at West Point in 1833, graduating four years later, a classmate of Generals Hooker, Bragg and Jubal A. Early. The Seminole War in Florida was at this time in progress, and Sedgwick's first service was in that region, and his first battle was that of Fort Clinch, May 20, 1838. In this war he served side by side with many a young officer that afterwards secured undying fame in the civil conflict. The Seminole and Mexican Wars were the schools in which all our great generals of the War of the Secession were trained, and to the practical experience gained in those minor conflicts they owe largely their later military success. Sedgwick was not a prominent sharer in the Seminole War, but played the part assigned him most creditably. During 1838 he was engaged in conducting bands of Cherokees from Florida to their new home beyond the Mississippi. On April 19, 1839, he was promoted to the rank of first lieutenant of artillery.

Nothing of importance occurred to alter the condition of Sedgwick until the Mexican War; but from the opening of that conflict his services were of the highest value, and promotion rapid.

A SHORT HISTORY

GEN'L
John Sedgwick.

General Macomb died in 1841, leaving General Scott commander of the United States Army, and it was under his direction entirely that the Mexican War was conducted. There were associated, however, with Scott many who are entitled to most honorable and grateful recognition for able and brilliant actions. The name of General Worth can only be mentioned in terms of the highest tribute, while even in the lower commands were officers whose services during that war obtained immediate and thankful recognition, and whose names have since become as familiar as a household word. Grant, Sheridan, Hancock, Lyon, Sedgwick, and a host of others were banded in the force which advanced under Generals Scott and Worth against the Mexican capital. With excellent officers, Scott was considerably handicapped at times by the undrilled and undisciplined troops with which he was compelled to act; and in opposition to his expressed desire, the United States Government continued to send him, at a time when time was most precious, the rawest troops, thoroughly unfit for service until days had been wasted in organizing and drilling them.

Scott took command of the army in Mexico in 1847. Drawing away a portion of the troops under General Taylor on the Rio Grande, Scott assembled a force of about 12,000 men in good condition and well disciplined. This was at Lobos Island on March 9, and on the 22d he began the siege of Vera Cruz. His mortar battery and siege-guns made short work of the city, which surrendered on the 26th, together with the fort of San

West Point, 1837

Brigadier General, volunteers, August, 1861
Major General, volunteers, December, 1862

Juan d'Ulloa. The garrison, comprising 5000 men, formally surrendered their arms on the 29th. After this victory the American army set out for Jalapa, and met a Mexican force of 12,000 men, under General Santa Anna, occupying the strong mountain pass of Cerro Gordo in a defile formed by the Rio del Plan. The American army had been reduced to about 8500; but, by surprising the Mexicans at sunrise, a complete and overwhelming victory was secured, and Santa Anna's army was scattered throughout the mountains. Scott captured five generals, 3000 men, 4500 stand of arms and 43 cannon, at a loss of about 500 men. The prisoners were paroled and their stores destroyed, while the Americans continued their march against Jalapa, capturing it on the 19th of April, Perote on the 22d, and Puebla on May 15. At this latter place it was that Scott was compelled to delay, awaiting reinforcements to his depleted force, only to find on their arrival that they were, as previously stated, untrained and undisciplined troops. To organize these and bring them to some degree of order necessitated still further delay, which afforded Santa Anna an opportunity to create a new army and fortify the City of Mexico. It was not until August 7 that the army of Scott resumed the advance, and, approaching the capital, made a detour to the south, attacking and capturing Contreras and Churubusco. In both of these engagements Sedgwick displayed great bravery and skill, as also in the storming of Chapultepec on September 13; and in recognition of his gallant services he was promoted to brevet captain and then major. On the 14th the city was carried, Sedgwick leading his command most commendably in the attack on the San Cosmo gate, and entering with the army in its almost entirely unopposed march through the city and occupation of the national palace. Sedgwick was with the army of occupation for some time, returning to the United States to engage in frontier service for a number of years.

In January, 1849, he was made captain—a position which he retained for a long time, as the service was at that time slow, and chances of promotion small. It was a period when Grant, Sherman, Rosecrans, Burnside, and a number of other officers

of the army resigned their commissions, on account of the small prospect of promotion and little opportunity for activity, and followed various walks of business and political life.

On the 15th of March, 1855, Sedgwick was promoted to major of the 1st cavalry, and continued serving in Kansas and on the Western frontier until the opening of the Civil War, at which time he was lieutenant-colonel of the 2d cavalry. With the beginning of the Civil War, however, the opportunities for activity and promotion became numerous enough, and the many graduates of West Point, hastily leaving their private pursuits, once more gathered on the field of battle to do service to the cause they upheld. Sedgwick was appointed colonel of the 4th cavalry on April 25, 1861, and in the following August received the commission of brigadier-general of volunteers and was connected with the Army of the Potomac.

General McClellan had recently been placed in command of the armies of the United States, and the hopes of the people of the North ran high. During the fall months, however, and the beginning of the year 1862 little of importance was done. The army, when McClellan first assumed command, was in a badly disorganized condition, and a long delay was necessary to bring order out of the chaotic troops. This delay was increased, moreover, by McClellan's illness in December; so that it was not until March, 1862, that the army was in motion. The prolonged delay, and the conflicting opinions as to the best plan of conducting the campaign, had already begun to arouse suspicion in the minds of some as to the ability of General McClellan to carry the operations through with success. The plan at length decided upon for the Peninsular campaign was to proceed by York River, with the co-operation of the navy. The campaign following contained a series of unfortunate actions. McClellan's enemies, as soon as his back was turned, began their work against him, and he was deprived of the reinforcements to which he looked at various points; while, after his departure from Washington, he was relieved from the position of commander-in-chief, and retained only the command of the Army of the Potomac. On McClellan's side, too great delibeation, and unwarrantable delay in the operations around York-town and in the subsequent pursuit of the enemy up the Peninsula, naturally increased the suspicion which had taken root at Washington, and subjected him with some justice to the charge of incapacity.

At the siege of Yorktown Sedgwick's division constituted a portion of the left wing, and both in that engagement and in the following movements he rendered most efficient services, especially in the battle of Fair Oaks, where McClellan's army was divided by the Chickahominy and the left wing was heavily attacked. The Confederate army in this battle attempted to pass between the left wing and the river, and to seize Bottom's Bridge. Sumner was ordered to cross the bridge, and it was Sedgwick's division that rushed across, planted a battery of 24 Napoleon guns so as to flank the advance of the enemy, and hurled them back upon Fair Oaks Station.

Later, in the bloody and sharply contested battle of Antietam, Sedgwick conducted himself with an amount of skill and bravery which secured for him the warmest praise of his fellow-officers. He was at the most exposed portion of the battle, and with a recklessness and daring that seemed at times to insure his death he led his command throughout that terrible fight, although twice wounded and urged to retire from the field.

He was made major-general of volunteers on December 3, and in the beginning of the next year took command of the 6th corps, serving under General Burnside in the Chancellorsville campaign. The Confederate army was at the beginning of this campaign divided into two wings and separated by about two days' march. The plan of Burnside was to cross the Rappahannock at Fredericksburg and defeat the two wings of the enemy in detail. For this purpose, therefore, Burnside assembled his force on the heights opposite Fredericksburg; but, instead of pursuing his plan speedily, a sufficient delay was incurred to allow the Confederate forces to combine and arrange themselves on the other side of the river. After still further delay, while Burnside visited Washington for a consultation, the National force crossed the river in the face of considerable op-

position and drove the enemy to the rear of Fredericksburg, where they ranged themselves on the hills. In the attack which then followed nothing could be gained, although Sedgwick's assault on Marye's Hill was attended with more success than the other sallies during that disastrous battle. The National army was at length compelled to recross the river, having lost about 12,000 men and gained nothing.

During the summer of 1863 Sedgwick bore a prominent part in the movements of the Army of the Potomac, commanding the left wing in the advance into Maryland, and sharing in the battle of Gettysburg, beginning with the second day, "after one of the most extraordinary forced marches on record, his steady courage inspiring confidence among his troops."

In the fall of that year his most noted service was at the crossing of the Rapidan River on November 7, when he succeeded in capturing a whole confederate division, with guns and colors.

During the following spring he commanded his corps in the campaign of the Wilderness, where his division for the most part had to bear the brunt of the battle. General Grant was at this time personally superintending the movements of the Army of the Potomac, of which army Sedgwick was one of the oldest and ablest officers. The chief command had been offered him previous to the appointment of General Meade, but he declined it, preferring to remain to the end with his own division, which soon became the best disciplined and most useful in the army.

General Sedgwick's death was a most unfortunate loss to the army, and it occurred under circumstances more harrowing than if he had been struck down in the heat of battle and fallen with a host of his comrades. On May 9, 1864, he was superintending the arrangement of artillery in the intrenchments near Spottsylvania Court-house, when he suddenly fell forward dead, struck in the head by the bullet of a sharpshooter. In his death the army lost an able officer of marked military skill, and one who had endeared to him all with whom he came in contact by his simple, generous and honest manliness of character.

PHILIP HENRY SHERIDAN, U.S.A.,1831–1888

General Sheridan was born in Albany, N.Y., March 6, 1831, and received his early education at the public schools of that city. He entered West Point Academy as a cadet in July, 1848, and was a class-mate of Generals James B. McPherson, John M. Schofield and John B. Hood. During his life at West Point a quarrel arose between himself and a cadet file-closer, in consequence of which young Sheridan was suspended from the acad-emy. He was allowed to return at the end of a year, however, and graduated July 1, 1853. On the same day he was appointed brevet second lieutenant in the 3d infantry, serving in Kentucky, Texas and Oregon. In November, 1854, he became second lieu-tenant in the 4th infantry, and in 1861 was promoted to first lieutenant. In May of the same year he was appointed captain of the 13th infantry, and in December he was chief quartermaster and commissary of the army in Southwestern Missouri. Between April and September, 1862, he served as quar-termaster under General Halleck during the Mississippi campaign.

At the time of the advance upon Corinth he was selected for active field-service, made colonel of 2d Michigan cavalry, and at the beginning of July was ordered to make a raid on Boone-ville. He availed himself so well of this first opportunity for display of military skill, and performed such efficient service during that month, that he was rewarded by the appointment as brigadier-general of volunteers, and in October of the same year commanded the 11th division of the Army of the Ohio, and participated in the battle of Perryville; and the success of

A Short History of G͞e͞n Phil. Sheridan

the National forces in this engagement may be largely credited to the gallant action of Sheridan. After carrying relief to Nashville in the month following, he was placed in command of a division of the Army of the Cumberland. His share in the battle of Stone River, December 31 and January 1, was prominent and in the highest degree commendable. He was act-ing under General Rosecrans—General Bragg, commanding the Confederate army, opposing. Sheridan was compelled to stand the brunt of the fight, and at one time the fate of the day rested on him. It was only by the most courageous resistance, the most daring and brilliant action, that he was enabled with his own division to hold the entire opposing force in check while Rosecrans should have opportunity to form new lines; and General Bragg was at length forced to fall back, leaving Sheri-dan with but a handful of men. "Here are all that was left," said Sheridan to Rose-crans after that engagement.

In recognition of his valiant behavior he was made major-general of volunteers, and during March, 1863, pursued Van Dorn to Columbia and Franklin, taking many prisoners. During the summer of that year he participated in the capture of Winchester, crossed the Cumberland Mountains and Tennessee River, and assisted in the terrible battle of Chickamauga in September. The battle of Missionary Ridge was the occasion of some of Sheridan's most dashing and brilliant service during the war. This occurred in November, and in this engagement Sheridan's distinguished action first recommended him to the favorable opinion of General Grant, under whose direction that battle was conducted. From that day forth Grant marked Sheridan as pre-eminently a man to be selected for important service, where skill and daring should be required.

On April 4, 1864, Grant placed Sheridan in command of the cavalry corps of the Army of the Potomac, and in this capacity he participated with Grant in the battle of the Wilderness in May. As a cavalry leader Sheridan was now at his best and thoroughly at home. The next few weeks saw a series of brilliant, dashing raids, success following success, until, by the end of June, scarcely a company of the Confederate forces in Virginia had escaped suffering at one time or another from his fierce onslaughts. Having under his command similar men to himself, in Merritt, Custer and others, he cut his way by quick, daring charges, from place to place, harassing and threatening the enemy at every point. In August Sheridan was appointed commander of the Army of the Shenandoah—consisting of the 6th corps, two divisions of the 8th, and two cavalry divisions—while a few days after his command was extended to the Middle Military Division. The duty that now lay before him was to rout the enemy from the Valley of Virginia and destroy their supplies. This was a portion of General Grant's plan. The latter was stationed with the Army of the Potomac at City Point, opposing Lee. Sheridan's force had been augmented by the 18th corps under Emory, while the opposing Confederate army was commanded by Early. In spite of the great confidence which Grant placed in Sheridan, he was willing to give the final order only with great caution. Going from City Point to Harper's Ferry, Grant met Sheridan, and instructed him to remain quiet until Lee had drawn away some of the Confederate force in the valley. Immediately after this was done, the final order was given and Sheridan was instantly on the advance. General Grant's report reads as follows: "He was off promptly on time, and I may add that I have never since deemed it necessary to visit General Sheridan before giving him orders." Starting on September 19, Sheridan met General Early crossing the Opequan, and routed him completely, pur-

suing him through Winchester past Fisher's Hill, thirty miles south, and through Harrisonburg and Staunton, finally scattering his forces throughout the passes of the Blue Ridge. He then ordered a detachment under Torbert to devastate Staunton and the adjoining country, so that Early's troops might be unable to find means of living should they return there and endeavor to reorganize. In this rout Sheridan took 5000 prisoners and five guns. His forces were now resting near Cedar Creek, and Sheridan himself, appointed brigadier-general in the regular army for his successes, had gone to Washington.

The Confederate army in the meantime received a considerable reinforcement from Longstreet, and, acting with the utmost celerity and secrecy, crossed the Shenandoah, and on October 18 approached within a short distance of the camp of the National forces. Early in the morning of the next day they suddenly attacked the camp, utterly surprised Sheridan's army and forced it to make a precipitate retreat. Sheridan had by this time reached Winchester, twenty miles distant, and, hearing the sound of a battle, leaped on horseback and covered the twenty miles with breathless speed, meeting his retreating troops at about ten o'clock. With his arrival the men took heart again, and almost instantly the tide of the battle changed. "Face the other way, boys," he shouted; "we are going back." And back they went, carrying overwhelming victory with them. The Confederate troops, partially disorganized, were devoting themselves chiefly to plundering the camp, and were least of all things expecting such a spirited return of the force which they had so recently routed. The part of the Confederate army still in line was thrown back and overwhelmed, while the whole force was scattered and pursued as far as Mt. Jackson. Then, acting under Grant's orders, Sheridan completely devastated the valley, thus destroying all possible resources of the enemy in that region. Sheridan's ride was one of the most brilliant and successful exploits of the Civil War, and has been deservedly immortalized in painting and sculpture, as well as by the well-known poem by R. Buchanan Read.

Sheridan was made major-general in the regular army, and

The Federal artillery
taking position
at the Battle of
South Mountain.

Harper's Ferry.

Harper's Ferry.—Early on the morning of the 14th day of September, 1862, the Confederates had almost completely invested Harper's Ferry, then in the charge of Colonel D. H. Miles, who had a total force of nearly 12,000 men, including the troops which General Julius White brought with him there after abandoning Martinsburg. Miles still held batteries on Bolivar Heights in the rear; but the Confederates commanded both the Maryland and Loudon heights across the Potomac and Shenandoah rivers, and from these an artillery fire was opened in the afternoon.

Instead of holding out to the last extremity and endeavoring to re-occupy Maryland Heights, as General McClellan had directed, Miles sent away his cavalry in the evening and made no effort to regain the Heights, which Colonel T. H. Ford, after repelling a heavy Confederate attack, had been compelled to abandon during the night of the 13th.

At dawn on the 15th the investment was complete, for General Jackson had brought up his force in the rear of Harper's Ferry and opened upon the Bolivar Heights batteries simultaneously with the firing from Loudon and Maryland heights. The position was, of course, untenable, and a white flag was soon displayed by Colonel Miles, who, however, was mortally wounded before it could be distinguished.

The surrender devolved upon General White, who had waived the command in Miles's favor, and to the Confederates Harper's Ferry was transferred, with 11,583 prisoners, 13,000 stand of arms, 200 wagons, 73 cannon, some ammunition, a large quantity of stores, and camp equipage.

the President's order reads: "For personal gallantry, military skill, and just confidence in the courage and patriotism of his troops, displayed by Philip H. Sheridan on the 19th of October at Cedar Run—where, under the blessing of Providence, his routed army was reorganized, a great national disaster averted, and a brilliant victory achieved over the rebels for the third time in pitched battle within thirty days—Philip H. Sheridan is appointed major-general in the United States Army, to rank as such from the 8th day of November, 1864." In honor of Sheridan's victories Grant ordered that a salute of a hundred guns should be fired by each of his armies, and he further stated of Sheridan: "I have always thought him one of the ablest of generals."

Sheridan's greatest raid was in March, 1865, with 10,000 cavalry, which extended from Winchester to Petersburg. During this raid he met Early at Waynesboro, routed and pursued him to Charlottesville. Afterwards, joining the Army of the Potomac, he served with consummate skill and bravery at the engagement of Five Forks, which was one of the most decisive of the war, and had much to do with compelling Lee to evacuate Petersburg and Richmond. Grant, speaking of Sheridan's action, said: "Here he displayed great generalship."

The remaining few days of the war Sheridan was engaged in harassing the army of Northern Virginia, carrying his raids as far down as South Boston, N.C., and as late as the 24th of April—several days after Lee's surrender and the formal close of the war.

During the years immediately following the war Sheridan served as commander in various departments throughout the country. From July, 1866, to March, 1867, he commanded the Department of the Gulf. From September of the latter year until March, 1868, he assumed charge of the Department of the Missouri, with headquarters at Fort Leavenworth, Kansas, during which he was engaged in a campaign against the Indians. He then was placed in command of the Military Division of the Mississippi, holding headquarters at Chicago.

Congress had revived the rank of lieutenant-general and general-in-chief for Grant, and upon his election to the presidency in 1869, Sherman, who had followed him as lieutenant-general, became general-in-chief, and Sheridan was promoted to the lieutenant-generalship.

Sheridan visited Europe in 1870, and was present with the German staff during a portion of the Franco-Prussian War. He was married in 1879 to Miss Rucker, a daughter of General D. H. Rucker, of the United States Army. In 1883 General Sherman retired, leaving Sheridan his successor as general-in-chief of the United States Army.

The last years of General Sheridan have been very quiet. In May, 1888, he contracted the illness which proved fatal to him a few weeks later.

Like all the eminent generals of our late war, he has left behind him in his personal memoirs the record of his distinguished services to his country. His courage was indomitable, and from the very jaws of defeat he frequently sprang to victory. Faithful and trustworthy in the performance of duty assigned him, he was far more than this. His unflinching bravery in moments of utmost danger, his brilliant and daring leadership, and his rare military skill—which at times seemed almost inspiration—entitle him to the highest place in the admiration and esteem of his fellow-countrymen.

THE BATTLE OF ANTIETAM
September 17, 1862

"At length the thunder of cannon on the left announced Burnside's advance. The long dark columns, with arms and banners glittering in the sun, was one of the most brilliant and exciting incidents of the day. At this crisis McClellan, followed by his staff, rode forward to a bluff nearer the scene of action. As he passed through the long columns hurrying to the front, he received such a magnificent reception from his men as was worth living for. The cheers and shouts of 'Little Mac' were heard over the roar of the battle. The cheers went with him and after him, till the sound, receding with the distance, died away."

Francis Winthrop Palfrey, Brevet Brigadier General, U.S.A.

Opening of the Battle of Antietam. Hooker's division fording the creek to attack the confederates.

Burnside Carrying Antietam Bridge.—General

Ambrose E. Burnside had been ordered at eight o'clock, September 17, 1862, to carry the lower stone bridge, take possession of the Sharpsburg Heights, and then advance along their crest upon the town. He made several attempts, but failed in the presence of a raking fire that the Confederate infantry and sharpshooters directed upon him. Failing to hear of any progress, McClellan twice sent to him, but this not producing any result he commanded Burnside to carry the bridge at the point of the bayonet. This was finally done at one o'clock in the afternoon, when the Fifty-first Pennsylvania and the Fifty-first New York drove the Confederates from the bridge to the heights.

Hawkins' Zouaves.—Colonel E. A. Kimball, commanding, of Burnside's Division charging on the Confederate battery on the hill, at Antietam, September 17, 1862, routing the Confederates.

THE BATTLE OF CORINTH
October 3–4, 1862
"In the attack upon Gen. Rosecrans' batteries fronting Corinth, two divisions of Moore's brigade entered Battery Robinett and there engaged in a desperate hand to hand encounter. The heroic Col. Roger, 2d Texas, was killed, bravely fighting in the very midst of the works. The survivors were then driven out by the Union forces, after a desperate and stubborn resistance, during which the guns from Gen. Rosecrans' Battery Robinett created fearful havoc among the retreating Confederates."

Frances Vinton Greene, Lieutenant, Engineers, U.S.A.

WILLIAM TECUMSEH SHERMAN, U.S.A.,1820–1891

In 1634 three Shermans came from England to this country. Of these three two were brothers, and the third a cousin, and to one of these brothers, Rev. John Sherman by name, General W. T. Sherman traces his lineage. The family first settled in Connecticut, whence a later branch moved to Lancaster, Ohio; and in that place, on the 8th of February, 1820, General Sherman was born. His father, a lawyer, and for five years judge of the Supreme Court, was the head of a large family, William Tecumseh being the sixth of eleven children. After his father's death William was adopted by Thomas Ewing, and attended school in Lancaster until 1836, when he became a cadet at West Point, a classmate of George H. Thomas, and graduated standing sixth in a class of 42. In 1840, the year of his graduation, he was commissioned as second lieutenant in the 3d artillery, and his first service was in Florida, where a small remnant of the Indian War still remained. In 1841 he was placed in command at Picolata as first lieutenant. He served later at Fort Morgan, Ala., and Fort Moultrie, Charleston harbor; but neither of these places were calculated at that time to satisfy a taste for war, the latter being more of a fashionable summer resort for the inhabitants of Charleston than a site for active military service. Sherman was more than the ordinary practical military man, with a taste for adventures. Both at West Point and in his first days of service he displayed those superior qualities of the scholar and soldier combined which earned for him his later position of honor. His ideals were ever high, and he was al-

ways seriously impressed with the glory and honor of service to his country. In 1843 he began the study of law, and this not with the purpose of practising at the bar, but simply to make of himself a more skilful and intelligent soldier. In the Mexican War he acted as adjutant to Generals S. W. Kearny, P. F. Smith and Colonel Mason, and for his service in California he was breveted captain. In 1850 he returned to Washington, and on May 1 married Miss Ellen Boyle Ewing, a daughter of his old friend, at that time Secretary of the Interior. Sherman shortly after his marriage was appointed captain in the commissary department and was sent to St. Louis and New Orleans. As all his old West Point mates were pursuing quiet paths of life, and there seemed to be little chance of promotion in such peaceful times, Sherman resigned his commission in September, 1853, and accepted an appointment as manager of a branch bank of Lucas, Turner & Co., of San Francisco. The following few years his life and pursuits were varied. The banking firm closed up its affairs in 1857, and in 1858–59 Sherman practiced law in Leavenworth, Kansas, and in the year following superintended the State Military Academy at Alexandria, La. On the secession of that State, however, he went to St. Louis, where he was for a brief period the president of the Fifth Street Railroad.

On the opening of the Civil War, Sherman entered with heart and soul into the cause of the Northern States. On the 13th of May, 1861, he was commissioned colonel of the 13th regiment of infantry, to be commanded by General Scott, then

West Point, 1840

Brigadier General, volunteers,
August, 1861
Major General, volunteers,
May, 1862
Brigadier General, regulars,
July, 1863
Major General, regulars,
August, 1864
Lieutenant General,
July, 1866
General-in-Chief, 1869

COMMANDED
Army of the Tennessee
Military Division of
the Mississippi

at Washington. Sherman was placed in command of a brigade in Tyler's division of the army, marching to Bull Run. This brigade consisted of the 13th, 69th and 79th New York, and the 2d Wisconsin regiments, which in the terrible engagement that followed suffered serious losses. In August Sherman was made brigadier-general of volunteers, and was sent from the Army of the Potomac to serve under General Anderson in Kentucky. In November General Buell relieved him of this command, and Sherman was ordered to report to General Halleck, who placed him in command of Benton Barracks.

It was in February, 1862, that General Grant moved on Forts Henry and Donelson, and after their capture Sherman was placed in command of the 5th division of the Army of the Tennessee. In the battle of Shiloh Sherman's service was especially notable. This occurred on the 6th and 7th of April; and as Sherman's position was in the very centre of the fight, an excellent opportunity was afforded him of showing his superior mettle. Of his behavior during that engagement General Grant wrote in his report: "I feel it a duty to a gallant and able officer, Brigadier-general W. T. Sherman, to make mention. He was not only with his command during the entire two days of the action, but displayed great judgment and skill in the management of his men. To his individual efforts I am indebted for the success of that battle." General Halleck also said: "Sherman saved the fortunes of the day on the 6th, and contributed largely to the glorious victory of the 7th." General Halleck became general-in-chief, with Grant appointed to the command of the Department of the Tennessee, and with this change Sherman was made major-general of volunteers, and was ordered by General Grant to Memphis, with directions to place the city in a state of defense. The next move of the National forces was against Vicksburg, which was covered by a Confederate army commanded by General Pemberton, and in the advance Sherman proceeded with his forces from Memphis to Wyatt, turning Pemberton's left, who retreated to Grenada. The plan then proposed and attempted was that Sherman should return to Memphis with one brigade, reorganize a suffi-

cient force, and move down the river in gunboats against Vicksburg, conducted by Admiral Porter, while Grant retained Pemberton in check at Grenada. Natural causes, however, rendered this plan impracticable, and shortly after General McClernand, arriving with orders from the President to assume command of the expedition, the Army of Tennessee was divided into the 13th, 15th, 16th and 17th corps, and Sherman was placed in command of the 15th. In the engagement which followed shortly after, and which ended with the capture of Vicksburg on July 4, 1863, General Sherman's service was most active, and as a reward for his able and brilliant share in that notable fight he was appointed brigadier-general in the regular army. At this time Rosecrans was expelling the enemy from Central Tennessee, and after forcing them from Chattanooga, and fighting the terrible battle at Chickamauga, he was compelled to rest in Chattanooga awaiting relief for his depleted force. Sherman was ordered with his corps to proceed by way of Memphis toward Chattanooga, but received on his way orders from Grant to march with all speed to Bridgeport, on the Tennessee. In the sharp action which took place shortly afterwards at Mission Ridge, Sherman's corps was the centre of the enemy's attack. Without treating that engagement in detail, it may be said that Sherman's best service there was in drawing the enemy to his flank, enabling Thomas to make a successful attack upon the ridge. On the 25th of November the enemy were driven before Sherman on the roads north of the Chickamauga. On December 3, under Grant's orders, he proceeded to Burnside's relief to Knoxville, and after rendering sufficient assistance returned to Chattanooga. During the early part of 1864 Sherman was engaged at Jackson and Meridian, breaking up Confederate combinations and destroying communications. In March Grant assumed command of the armies, and Sherman was placed in command of the Mississippi division, comprising the Departments of the Ohio, Tennessee, Cumberland and Arkansas, with headquarters at Nashville. For his recent service in the Chattanooga campaign General Sherman received the formal thanks of Congress. It was on the

10th of April that he received final orders to move against Atlanta, and the great triumphal march began which has ever since been associated in words of highest eulogy with the name of Sherman. His advance towards Atlanta was steady and sure. Pressing the opposing force under General Johnston constantly backward, he began the direct attack on Atlanta July 17. In the several battles at Peach Tree Creek, Ezra Church, and again on the east side of the city, the National forces were notably successful. Sherman sent General Thomas to Nashville to resist the advance of General Hood—an expedition that resulted in the disastrous defeat of the latter. Sherman, with the remainder of his forces, moved on against Savannah, finding nothing now to oppose his advance. Savannah was promptly taken, and General Sherman wrote to President Lincoln: "I beg to present you, as a Christmas gift, the City of Savannah, with 150 heavy guns, plenty of ammunition, and 25,000 bales of cotton."

The march of Sherman has received many a tribute of praise, but the value of the achievement cannot be too highly estimated by the adherents to the Northern cause. In August he was appointed major-general in the regular army and in January following he again received the thanks of Congress.

Sherman, leaving Savannah in February, marched north, meeting some opposition, but reaching Goldsboro on March 24, where he met Schofield. Leaving his troops there, he joined the conference of General Grant, Admiral Porter and President Lincoln at City Point. This interview over, and the policy adopted which brought the war to a close soon after, he returned to Goldsboro, ready to cut off Lee's retreat or to reinforce Grant in front of Richmond for a final attack, if necessary.

On April 9 Lee surrendered to Grant at Appomattox, and Johnston, receiving the news at Greensboro, sent a message to Sherman on the 14th asking on what terms he would receive a surrender. The terms arranged in the interview and correspondence which followed were considered by the government as entirely too lenient, and they were therefore disapproved of,

and the matter was re-negotiated. This slight to General Sherman was undeserved, for an examination of the matter will reveal the fact that he acted throughout the part of a courteous, considerate and humane commander. The great tide of feeling in Washington, aroused by the assassination of President Lincoln, may have given partial cause for the curt manner in which the government treated the matter. General Sherman's behavior throughout was above reproach. On the President requesting to see him, he stated in the interview that the offense to him lay in the tone and style of the publication, the insinuations it contained and the false inferences it gave rise to, and not the disapproval on the part of the government of his terms of agreement with Johnston.

In the grand review at the close of the war, and in fact on all fitting public occasions since, General Sherman received the genuine and enthusiastic tributes which he has well earned.

His life since the war has been very quiet. From June, 1865, to March, 1869, he had headquarters at St. Louis, commanding the Military Division of the Mississippi, comprising the Departments of the Ohio, Missouri and Arkansas. In July, 1866, he became lieutenant-general, and on the election of General Grant to the presidency in 1869 Sherman succeeded him as general and took up his headquarters at Washington.

On February 8, 1884, he was placed, at his own request, on the retired list, with full pay, leaving General Sheridan his successor as general-in-chief.

To his military honors he has added the degree of LL.D., conferred upon him by Dartmouth, Yale, Harvard and Princeton, in recognition of his superior worth as a scholar as well as soldier. The sterling qualities which General Sherman displayed on the battle-field commanded the admiration of friends and foes alike, while the genuine, noble and sympathetic heart which beats within his breast has made friends of foes, and won for him the love and respect of a nation.

(General Sherman died on February 14, 1891.)

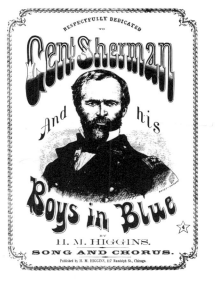

THE BATTLE OF FREDERICKSBURG
December 13, 1862

"On the ridge northwest of Fredericksburg, Lee's army was strongly posted in an impregnable position behind stone walls reinforced with earth banked up on the face of it. The distance the Union troops had to march in attack was 1,700 yards, exposed to a murderous fire of musketry and artillery, without being able to return a single effective shot. 'Six times,' says Lee, 'did the enemy press on with great determination to within 100 yards of the foot of the hill, but here encountering the deadly infantry fire, his columns were broken and fled in confusion to the town.' The bloody day came to an end and the Army of the Potomac was no nearer Richmond than when the sun arose."

Francis Winthrop Palfrey, Brevet Brigadier General, U.S.A.

FRANZ SIGEL, U.S.A.,1824–1902

There is no more truly representative body of Americans than the commanders in our late war. Almost all of them were of humble birth, and exemplified in their own hard struggles against adversity the life and spirit of the sturdy and progressive nation of which they so proudly claimed citizenship. They were distinctly Americans in birth, life and character, and it is no matter for wonder, therefore, that the internal dissension and civil strife which threatened to throw the government into chaos should have aroused in the minds of these brave men the intensest and most fervid feelings of patriotism. It is not to be wondered at that these citizens, born and reared under the rough but kindly care of the land of liberty, should have readily responded to the first summons of war, sacrificing personal interests and life even for the cause they had learned to love so well. But among the names on the honor list which the Civil War has left us there is one which is a marked exception to the rest—the name of Franz Sigel. His honorable service in behalf of the United States was the voluntary offering of a foreigner, and that he served so well is worthy the most thankful acknowledgment.

Sigel was born at Sinsheim, Baden, on November 18, 1824, and was educated first at the gymnasium of Bruchsal, after which he entered the military school at Carlsruhe, graduating from there in 1843. He was stationed first at Mannheim as lieutenant. He was ever of a bold and independent disposition, and with a tendency to revolutionary ideas. During his stay at Mannheim he published a number of writings which contained

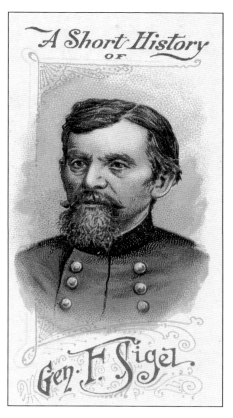

very free expressions of disapprobation of the condition of the standing army, and as a result a number of quarrels with his fellow-officers ensued. From one of these satisfaction was required, and in the duel, which was the only method by which such affairs were then settled, Sigel's antagonist was killed, and Sigel himself was compelled to resign. This was near the end of the year 1847. The following year the Baden revolution began, and Sigel found it impossible to remain quiet. In February, therefore, he raised a body of about 4000 volunteers, who rallied readily to his call, and, having organized them, marched against Freiburg. He was unfortunate, however; for, while encountering the royal troops twice, he was badly beaten both times. This was nothing more, however, than was to be expected; for Sigel's force consisted of men hastily trained, and many of them fighting together for the first time, while he was opposed to an army of well-disciplined soldiers of experience.

After these unfortunate engagements Sigel, left almost alone, escaped across the border into Switzerland. In May, 1849, however, an insurrection at Baden recalled him to that place, and his service during that year is briefly summed up as follows: "He was made commandant of the Lake and Upper Rhine District, then placed in charge of the Army of the Neckar, met the royal forces at Heppenheim on May 30, became minister of war, and finally succeeded to the chief command of the troops. He fought in several battles under General Louis Mieroslawski, whom he succeeded; conducted the army of 15,000 men in retreat

Brigadier General, volunteers, August, 1861
Major General, volunteers, March, 1862

COMMANDED
Department of West Virginia
Army of West Virginia

through three hostile army corps, and crossed the Rhine with the remnant into Switzerland on July 11." Considerable search was made for him during the following months, and early in 1851 he was arrested by the Federal authorities at Lugano, who handed him over to the French Government. They purposed disposing of this man of revolutionary disposition by shipping him to a country in which a few years later a full opportunity was given for the exercise of those qualities that had already rendered him so conspicuous in Europe. With the purpose of sending him to the United States, he was taken by the French police to Havre; but the plan was altered, and Sigel went to England instead, living in London and Brighton until May, 1852, when he sailed for the United States, and made his new home in New York.

He was engaged for several years in teaching, translating German works, and editing *Die Revue*, a military magazine. During this time he married a daughter of Rudolf Dulon, in whose school he was a teacher. In 1858 he left New York, having received a call to the professorship of mathematics in the German Institute in St. Louis. Sigel's active and restless disposition was not satisfied with the quiet and prosaic life of a teacher, and he was constantly occupied in urging progressive ideas on educational and political subjects. He edited a military journal, and through its columns, as well as those of the other city journals, he defended the cause of the Northern States. His patriotic activity recommended him to the attention of the public, and he was elected director of the St. Louis public schools.

In 1860 Claiborne F. Jackson, a decided sympathizer with the Southern States, was elected governor of Missouri, and endeavored to draw the State into secession. The city of St. Louis was at that time in a very precarious condition, and there were in the city government many bitterly conflicting elements. Governor Jackson was active in behalf of the South; Major P. V. Hagner, who commanded the arsenal and all its supplies, was also a Southern sympathizer; and General W. S. Harney, who commanded the Department of the West, with headquarters at St. Louis, was covertly interested in the secessionist cause. At this time General Lyon, a man of indomitable will and courage, was placed in command under General Harney, and with his arrival a warm and bitterly contested conflict arose within the city. Lyon was loyal and true to the Northern cause, and his bold, uncompromising nature could not tolerate the hostile parties in power and the luke-warmness of those avowedly Northern in their sympathies. Lyon suspected Major Hagner from the first, and, realizing the great danger of permitting the arsenal and ordnance supplies to remain under the control of one who might at any time play into the hands of the South, he made an appeal first to General Harney, requesting that Major Hagner should be removed. His appeal, however, was without success; and he then turned to President Buchanan, from whom he got as little satisfaction. Thrown upon his own resources, Lyon, together with Francis P. Blair, Jr., Franz Sigel and other Unionists, determined to take an independent and decided stand. In order, therefore, to have in readiness a sufficient force for emergencies, Lyon, Sigel and their associates, organized the home-guards, comprising volunteers from the city and neighborhood. These were chiefly of German extraction, and drawn by the lead of Sigel. A short time before the inauguration of President Lincoln, Francis P. Blair, Jr., went to Washington to solicit the attention and assistance of the government, indicating the dangerous condition of affairs in Missouri, and requesting especially that the arsenal should be placed in the command of General Lyon and his associates. The necessity of this, however, did not seem to impress the authorities, and it was only on the occasion of an attempted outbreak of the secessionists of St. Louis on inauguration day that the government realized the danger and took any steps to relieve it. Lyon was placed in command of the troops, but General Harney still retained Hagner in charge of the arms, etc., with which Lyon and Sigel wished to arm their volunteers. This movement, however, produced as decided an opposition, and Governor Jackson organized a secessionist militia force, and in other ways expressed his determination o thwart the efforts of Lyon. General Harney at length placed Lyon in command of the arsenal, and a complete change was effected. Jackson was forced to leave St. Louis, while the secessionist militia went into camp near the city. They were here surprised and captured in a body by Lyon's force, and the city was restored to a more orderly condition.

Sigel had been an active and energetic assistant in the work of organizing troops, and commanded a regiment in the occupation of the arsenal and in the capture of the secessionist camp. General Harney had made an agreement with General Sterling Price, the Confederate commander in Missouri, to make no military movement as long as peace was maintained by the State authorities, and an endeavor was made by General Price and Governor Jackson to secure a renewal of this agreement from General Lyon; but the latter insisted on the right of the United States Government to move their troops as they chose in the State. A Confederate advance from Arkansas being anticipated, Sigel was sent in June, 1861, to Rolla; marching from there to Neosho, and driving Sterling Price and his force into Arkansas. Lyon in the meantime had advanced on Jefferson City, capturing that place, and proceeded to Booneville, where he defeated Colonel J. S. Marmaduke's Confederate force. Sigel, after driving Price back, turned north to meet Claiborne Jackson at Carthage. The Confederate force was so much greater than Sigel's that he was compelled, after a hard struggle, to retreat to Springfield and Mount Vernon. Lyon was about leaving Booneville in pursuit of Price when he learned that Sigel had been repulsed at Carthage, and, altering his plan, he halted at Springfield, awaiting the anticipated advance of the Confederate army, which he knew far outnumbered his own. Lyon and Sigel went forward early in August to meet the advancing enemy, but after a skirmish at Dug Springs were compelled to fall back upon Springfield. On August 9 Lyon endeavored to surprise the enemy in their camp at Wilson's Creek, and in this fight Sigel's force had driven the enemy back, and was gaining a decided advantage, when, through an unfortunate mistake in supposing one of the regi-

ments of the enemy to be Iowa troops, he was taken off his guard and badly defeated. Lyon, rallying his column for one final charge, was killed, and Sigel conducted the retreat of his army toward Rolla. Sigel was made brigadier-general, and served during the fall campaign, commanding two divisions under General John C. Fremont, and later gained the battle of Pea Ridge, commanding the right wing of the troops under General Samuel R. Curtis.

In the spring of 1862 Sigel was made major-general, and was ordered east to take command of the troops at Harper's Ferry, and shared in the movement against General Thomas J. Jackson, which took place shortly after. Near the end of June the Army of Virginia was organized and placed under the command of General Pope. This consisted of three corps, under Banks, McDowell and Sigel—the latter having in charge the 1st corps, formerly commanded by Fremont. Sigel served in all the engagements of the unfortunate and disastrous campaign which ended in the second battle of Bull Run. In this engagement Sigel's corps was the only one which gained any advantage, holding the enemy successfully in check throughout the first day. Likewise in the retreat to Centreville, and, it may be said, in all that campaign Sigel's corps was conducted with skill and bravery proportionate to the unfortunate circumstances in which he was placed. Shortly after he was compelled to go on leave of absence, and was superseded in command by General Howard.

He took command of the reserve army of Pennsylvania in June, 1863, and while in that charge organized a force of 10,000 men to assist in meeting Lee, whose invasion was continually expected, and who a few weeks later encountered the combined Northern forces at Gettysburg, where he was defeated and driven back to Virginia. Early in 1864 Sigel was assigned to the command of the Department and Army of West Virginia, and organized an expedition in the Kanawha Valley, which was placed under the charge of General George Crook; and conducted another against Lynchburg and Staunton, being defeated at New Market by General John C. Breckinridge.

Contraband, or Jeff on Cotton.
Our Union Flag has caught a prize,
Which will, no doubt, create surprise—
And they will safely tow them into land,
Cotton, Jeff and Contraband.

In June, 1864, Sigel was assigned to the command of the troops at Harper's Ferry. His health, however, which had been for some time past very poor, compelled him to consider a resignation. He met General Early at Maryland Heights and repelled his attack successfully, and with that engagement Sigel's service in the field ended. He was relieved from command, and retired to Bethlehem, Pa.

Resigning his commission in May, 1865, he entered into journalistic work as editor of the Baltimore *Wecker*. He removed to New York City in September, 1867, and two years later was the Republican candidate for Secretary of State of New York. In 1871 he filled the offices first of Collector of Internal Revenue and then of Register of the City of New York. During the following years he pursued journalistic work as editor of a weekly paper, and lectured at times on political and social subjects, altering his politics in 1876 and espousing the cause of the Democratic party. He was appointed pension agent in New York City in 1886.

(General Sigel died on August 21, 1902.)

REVIEW OF THE ARMY.

THE BATTLE OF STONES RIVER
December 31, 1862 and January 2, 1863

Hand-to-Hand Combat.

—On the 17th day of March, 1863, Union General William W. Averell had crossed the Rappahannock at Kelly's Ford, to raid the country in the direction of Culpepper Court House. The Federals had proceeded about a mile from the ford, when they encountered General Fitzhugh Lee's brigade of cavalry. They were in line of battle, and first made an effort to turn the Federal right, but the Sixth U.S. subjected them to such a scathing fire as to promptly cause their retirement from the road. An attempt was then made upon Averell's left, but without any great success, for Duffi's brigade boldly attacked the Confederate troops and by its superiority in number was enabled to drive back the assailants with great loss. Charges and counter-charges followed rapidly until darkness set in, when General Averell withdrew across the river, having lost in all about seventy men, while the loss sustained by his antagonist was nearly twice as great in killed and wounded alone.

GENERALS AND ADMIRALS OF THE CONFEDERACY

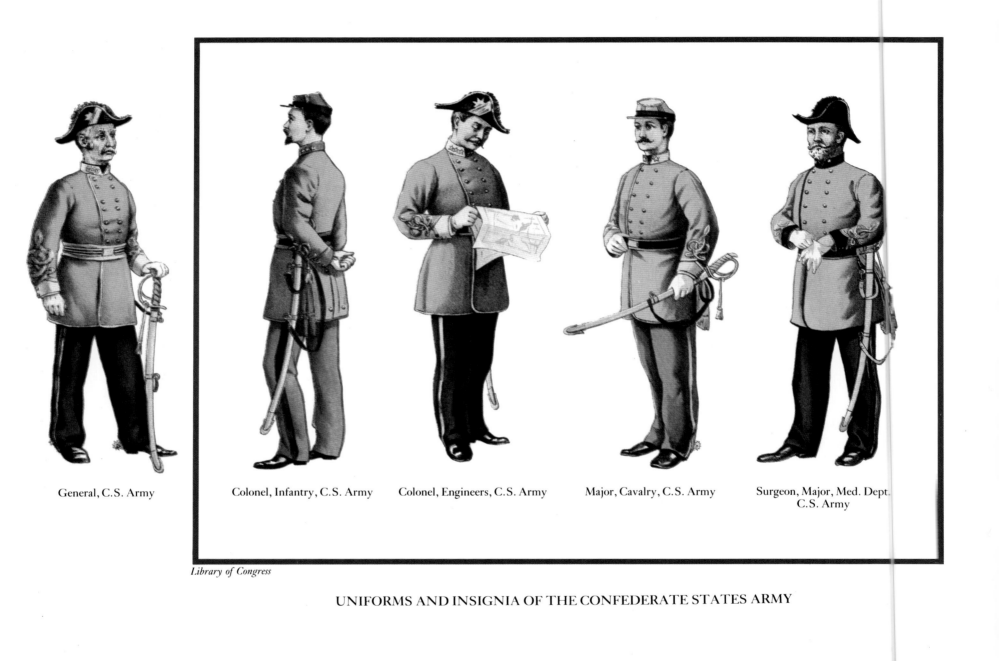

General, C.S. Army

Colonel, Infantry, C.S. Army

Colonel, Engineers, C.S. Army

Major, Cavalry, C.S. Army

Surgeon, Major, Med. Dept. C.S. Army

UNIFORMS AND INSIGNIA OF THE CONFEDERATE STATES ARMY

Sergeant, Cavalry, C.S. Army   Corporal, Artillery, C.S. Army   Infantry, C.S. Army
Overcoat   Private, Infantry, C.S. Army   Cavalry, C.S. Army
Overcoat

UNIFORMS AND INSIGNIA OF THE CONFEDERATE STATES ARMY

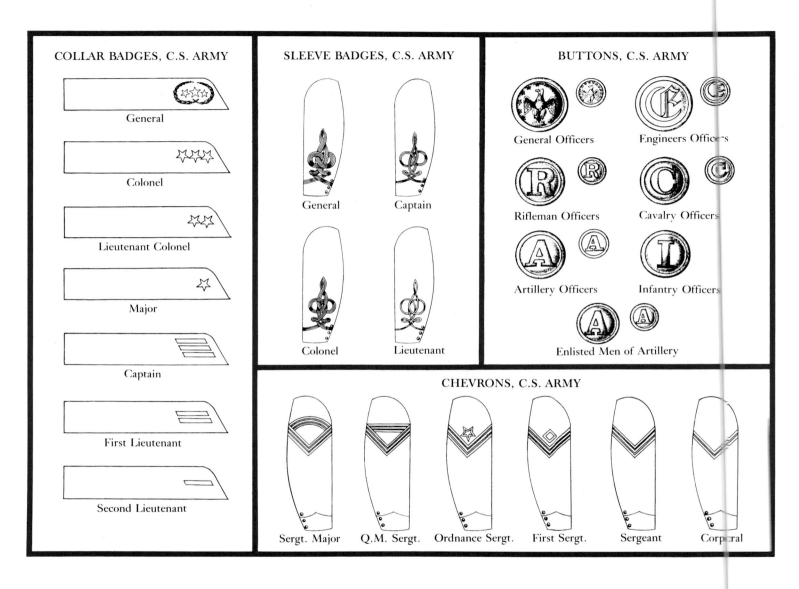

COLLAR BADGES, C.S. ARMY

General

Colonel

Lieutenant Colonel

Major

Captain

First Lieutenant

Second Lieutenant

SLEEVE BADGES, C.S. ARMY

General

Captain

Colonel

Lieutenant

BUTTONS, C.S. ARMY

General Officers

Engineers Officers

Rifleman Officers

Cavalry Officers

Artillery Officers

Infantry Officers

Enlisted Men of Artillery

CHEVRONS, C.S. ARMY

Sergt. Major   Q.M. Sergt.   Ordnance Sergt.   First Sergt.   Sergeant   Corporal

BADGES TO DISTINGUISH RANK, C.S. ARMY

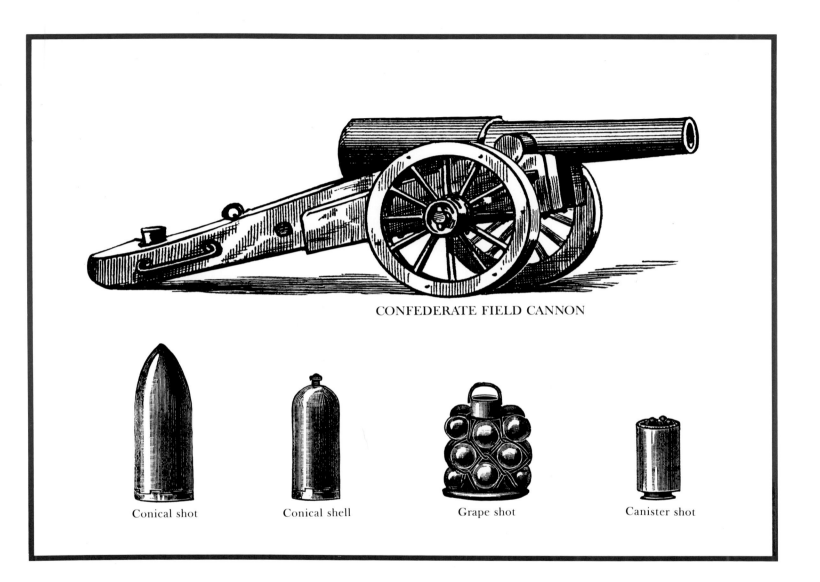

CONFEDERATE FIELD CANNON

Conical shot   Conical shell   Grape shot   Canister shot

ROBERT EDWARD LEE, C.S.A.,1807–1870

Lord Wolseley, who visited General Lee's headquarters in 1862, subsequently wrote that "Lee is stamped on my memory as a being apart and superior to all others in every way." The man who elicited this somewhat extravagant eulogium was descended from fine stock. The Lees of Virginia, to whom the eminent Confederate soldier owed his origin, were an illustrious family of the State that has been designated the "Mother of Presidents." He was the son of the Revolutionary General Henry Lee, known as "Light-horse Harry," and was graduated from West Point in 1829, ranking second in a class of forty-six, and was commissioned as second lieutenant in the engineers. At the beginning of the Mexican War he was assigned to duty as chief engineer of the army under General Wool, with the rank of captain. His abilities as an engineer and his conduct as a soldier won the special recognition of General Scott, who attributed the fall of Vera Cruz to his skill, and repeatedly singled him out for commendation. He was thrice breveted during the war, his last brevet to the rank of colonel being for services at the storming of Chapultepec.

In 1852 he was assigned to the command of the Military Academy at West Point, where he remained about three years. He wrought great improvements in the academy, notably enlarging its course of study, and elevating it to a rank equal to that of the best military schools of Europe.

On April 20, 1861—three days after the Virginia convention adopted an ordinance of secession—Lieutenant-colonel Lee

resigned his commission in the United States Army, in obedience to his conscientious conviction that he was bound by the act of his State.

At that time, in a letter to his sister, the wife of an officer in the National army, he gave the only authenticated expression of his opinions and sentiments on the subject of secession:—

"We are now," he wrote, "in a state of war which will yield to nothing. The whole South is in a state of revolution, into which Virginia, after a long struggle, has been drawn; and though I recognize no necessity for this state of things, and would have forborne and pleaded to the end for redress of grievances, real or supposed, yet in my own person I had to meet the question whether I should take part against my native State. With all my devotion to the Union, and the feeling of loyalty and duty of an American citizen, I have not been able to make up my mind to raise my hand against my relatives, my children, my home. I have therefore resigned my commission in the army, and, save in defense of my native State—with the sincere hope that my poor services may never be needed—I hope I may never be called upon to draw my sword."

Repairing to Richmond, he was made commander-in-chief of the Virginia State forces, and in May, 1861, when the Confederate government was removed from Montgomery to Richmond, he received his commission as full general. During the early months of the war he rendered inconspicuous services in the western part of Virginia. In the autumn he was dispatched to the coast of South Carolina, where he planned and in part constructed the defensive lines which successfully resisted all efforts directed against them till the very close of the war. General Lee was ordered to Richmond on March 13, 1862, assigned to duty "under the direction of the President," and "charged with the conduct of military operations in the armies of the Confederacy."

The campaign of the preceding year in Virginia had embraced but one battle of importance; it was that known as Bull Run, or Manassas, and the Confederate success there had not been followed by any demonstration more active than an advance to Centreville and Fairfax Court-house, with advanced posts on Mason's and Munson's Hills. Meantime McClellan had been more or less successfully wrestling with the problem of converting raw levies into disciplined troops, and reorganizing the National army. When, after many delays, he was finally prepared to advance, the Confederates retired to the south side of the Rappahannock; whereupon McClellan transferred his base of operations to Fort Monroe, and advanced upon Richmond by way of the Peninsula. To counteract this move, General Joseph E. Johnston removed his army to Williamsburg, leaving Jackson's division in the valley, and Ewell's on the line of the Rappahannock. In May Johnston fell back to make his stand in defense of Richmond, immediately in front of the town. McClellan advanced to a line near the city with his army of more than 100,000 men, and, under the mistaken impression that Johnston's force outnumbered his own, waited for McDowell, who was advancing with 40,000 men from the neighborhood of Fredericksburg, to join him. To checkmate the advance of this reinforcement, General Lee ordered Ewell to join Jackson, and directed the latter to attack Banks in the Shenandoah Valley, drive him across the Potomac, and thus seem to threaten Washington. The strategy was entirely successful. Washington was alarmed and McDowell was recalled. McClellan now established himself on the Chickahominy, with a part of his army thrown across the stream. A flood came in the end of May, and, believing that the swollen river effec-

tually isolated this force, General Johnston attacked it on May 31. Thus eventuated the battle of Seven Pines, or Fair Oaks, in which Johnston was seriously wounded. McClellan now fortified his lines, and General Lee confronted him with a great army, and with the full confidence of the Confederate government. Lee's preparations were promptly and energetically executed. His capacity as a strategist and commander was first demonstrated in that sanguinary and brilliant series of conflicts and manœuvres known as "the Seven Days' Battle," by which he successfully frustrated McClellan's plans against Richmond. "General Lee's plan," say Messrs. Nicolay and Hay in their *Life of Abraham Lincoln*, "was to herd and drive down the Peninsula a magnificent army, superior in numbers to his own, and not inferior in any other respect—if we except the respective commanders-in-chief. . . . The measure of success he met with will always be in the general judgment a justification of his plan."

Having thus raised the siege of Richmond, Lee's ambition was to transfer the scene of operations to a distance from the Confederate capital, and thus relieve the depression occasioned in the South by the general retreat of its armies in the West. McClellan lay at Harrison's Landing, below Richmond, with an army that was still strong, and "while the Confederate capital was no longer in immediate danger, the withdrawal of the army defending it would invite attack and capture, unless McClellan's withdrawal at the same time could be compelled." For effecting this, General Lee calculated on the excessive anxiety felt at the North for the safety of Washington. If he could so dispose of his forces as to place Washington in actual or apparent danger, he felt assured that McClellan's army would be speedily recalled. The series of movements and manœuvres that followed culminated on the morning of August 29, on the same field that the first battle of Manassas or Bull Run was fought in 1861. Pope's army, reinforced by McClellan's, was in position, and battle was joined in the afternoon. After many determined but unsuccesful assaults upon Lee's lines, the National army was driven across Bull Run to Centreville.

The way now seemed clear to the Southern commander. The *esprit de corps* of his army was at the highest pitch. He felt that he could act on the aggressive and transfer the scene of operations to the enemy's territory. "The plan involved the practical abandonment of his communications; but the region into which he proposed to march was rich in food and forage, and, with the aid of his active cavalry under Stuart, he trusted to his ability to sustain his army upon the Northern territory." The advance movement was at once inaugurated. On September 5 the army, 45,000 strong, crossed the Potomac and took up a position near Frederick, Md., from which it might move at will against Washington or Baltimore, or invade Pennsylvania. Simultaneously "Stonewall" Jackson had been dispatched to Harper's Ferry, which, with 11,000 men and all its extensive stores, fell into his hands. Both Lee and McClellan reached Sharpsburg, and on the 17th of September battle was joined.

"The conflict of Sharpsburg, or Antietam," says a writer on the war, "is called a drawn battle. It was such if the immediate result is considered. There might be no actual advantage in the fight, but McClellan had partly gained his point, and Lee's invasion of Northern territory was brought to an end. On the other hand, if we include the capture of the garrison at Harper's Ferry, Lee had inflicted greater loss upon the enemy than he had suffered."

The order assigning General Burnside to succeed McClellan in command was received at General Lee's headquarters, at Culpepper Court-house, about twenty-four hours after it reached Warrenton.

Burnside's plan of campaign was to threaten Richmond by an advance over a short line, while at the same time he kept Washington covered. He made his base upon the Potomac, and planned to cross the Rappahannock at Fredericksburg. Lee moved promptly to meet this new advance, and occupied a line of hills in the rear of the town. In the engagement that followed the National commander lost nearly 13,000 men, while the Southern loss was but a trifle beyond 5000. Without effect-

ing anything, the Northern army recrossed the river on December 15, and operations were suspended for the winter.

After the retreat General Lee went to Richmond "to suggest other operations," according to Longstreet, "but was assured that the war was virtually over, and that we need not harass our troops by marches and other hardships. Gold had advanced in New York to 200, and we were assured by those at the Confederate capital that in thirty or forty days we would be recognized and peace proclaimed. General Lee did not share in this belief."

"Fighting Joe Hooker," who succeeded Burnside in command of the Army of the Potomac, planned a campaign for the purpose of driving Lee out of his intrenched position at Fredericksburg. His plan was well conceived, and we are assured that "no operation of the war so severely tested the skill of the Confederate commander, or so illustrated his character, as did the campaign that followed." About the end of April, 1863, Sedgwick with 30,000 men crossed below Fredericksburg, while Hooker with the main body crossed the fords above. Leaving about 9000 men in Fredericksburg, Lee marched on May 1 to meet Hooker's advance, which he encountered, attacked, and drove back at Chancellorsville. Dividing his force, he sent Jackson with one division of the army to strike Hooker in the rear. In the fighting that followed, Jackson received a mortal wound from the fire of his own men; but in the end the Northern army was "driven with great loss from the field." Meantime Sedgwick had carried the position at Fredericksburg, and had in turn been driven across the river by Lee. These contests raised the confidence of General Lee's army to the highest pitch, and he again resolved to carry the scene of active operations to Northern soil.

The campaign of 1864 began with the advance of the Northern army under General Grant, who crossed the Rapidan on May 4 with 120,000 men. Lee's opposing force was about 60,000, and he attacked his adversary with his usual promptitude and courage. Lee's plan of striking the flank of Grant's army as it passed through the Wilderness has been pronounced

9ᵗ Apr '65 —

Genl
I have rec'd your note of this date. Though not entertaining the opinion you express of the hopelessness of further resistance on the part of the Army of N. Va. — I reciprocate your desire to avoid useless effusion of blood, & therefore before Considering your proposition ask the terms you will offer on Condition of its Surrender —

Very respy your Obdt
R E Lee
Genl

Lt Genl U. S. Grant —
Commd Armies of the U States

above criticism; yet Grant's persistent hammering and superior force told the inevitable tale. "It's no use killing these fellows; half a dozen take the place of every one we kill," is said to have been a common remark in Lee's army at this time.

Pages might be filled with the touching scenes of the great commander's surrender. "General," cried one of his men, "take back the word 'surrender'; it is unworthy of you and of us. I have a wife and children in Georgia; I have made up my mind to die, but not to surrender." Lee placed his arm around the brave fellow's neck, and, with tears streaming down his face, said: "We have done all brave men can do. If I permitted another man to be slain, I would be a murderer."

General Lee laid down his sword in a manly, magnanimous manner, without moroseness or sullen vexation. His mind was pure, his character upright. In a remarkable degree he exhibited that inflexible devotion to duty which is exemplified in a perfect readiness to sink the consideration of self. As the biographers of Abraham Lincoln most truly and eloquently say: "Lee's handsome presence and cordial manner endeared him to his associates, and made friends of strangers at first sight."

Three days after his death his remains were buried beneath the chapel of the University at Lexington. In accordance with his request, no funeral oration was pronounced.

THE BATTLE OF CHANCELLORSVILLE
May 2 – 4, 1863
"At dawn of day, Jackson, with his own corps of 26,000 men, made a masterly detour through the woods
and fell upon the right flank of Howard's line in overwhelming numbers. The whole of Howard's corps fled in the greatest disorder.
This was Stonewall Jackson's last battle. As he was coming in from the front in the gathering twilight, his own men fired,
thinking it was Union cavalry advancing, and Jackson, with nearly all his escort, were killed or wounded."
Abner Doubleday, Brevet Major General, U.S.A

PIERRE GUSTAVE TOUTANT DE BEAUREGARD, C.S.A., 1818–1893

There is a page in the book of fame,
On it is written a single name
In letters of gold, on spotless white,
Encircled with stars of quenchless light;
Never a blot that page hath marred,
And the star-wreathed name is BEAUREGARD.

General Beauregard entered life in the Parish of St. Martin in Louisiana in 1816. His great-grandfather sprung from a noble family in France, which emigrated to this country during the reign of Louis XV, and settled in Louisiana. The name of the family was Toutant *de* Beauregard, until James, the father of Pierre Gustave, discarded the titular portion of it, for the reason, some allege, that it was repugnant to the old gentleman's republican tastes.

James Toutant, the father, married Helene Reggio, whose earliest American ancestor came to this country about the time of the Beauregards. The family of Reggio is also of noble origin, being an Italian branch of the house of Este. The fruit of the marriage was three sons, of whom Pierre Gustave was the second, and three daughters.

General Beauregard entered West Point as a cadet in 1834, and graduated June 30, 1838, taking second honors in a class of 45. On June 16, 1839, he was promoted to a first lieutenantcy in the engineer corps, and in that capacity entered the Mexican War, obtaining two brevets in it, and serving generally with great distinction. Two incidents of his Mexican career are worth recording as illustrating the peculiarly practical and methodical character of the man: Lieutenant Beau-

regard was sent out before Vera Cruz by his colonel with a party of sappers to dig and prepare a trench, according to a profile and plan made by his superior officer. No sooner had Beauregard examined the ground than he discovered great objections to the plan. To assure himself, he climbed a tree, and with the aid of a field-glass he made a reconnoissance, and saw plainly that the trench as planned would be enfiladed by the enemy's guns. Here was a delicate and difficult position for a subaltern officer. He decided promptly. He returned to headquarters without sticking a spade in the ground. The colonel met him and expressed surprise that he had so soon accomplished his mission. Beauregard replied that he hadn't even touched it. The colonel, with the astonishment military men feel on hearing that their orders have not been obeyed, acridly inquired the reason. The lieutenant explained; the colonel was incredulous. "The ground has been examined," he said; "the reconnoissance was perfect."—"The reconnoissance may have been perfect," replied the subaltern, "but it was not made from up a tree." Like a sensible man, the colonel concluded to make another examination, and the plan was changed in accordance with the young lieutenant's views. The work done from those trenches is a matter of history. The second incident occurred before the City of Mexico. A night or two before the attack a council of war was held. There were asembled all the eminent warriors, from Lieutenant-general Scott, Worth, Twiggs, etc., down to the youngest lieutenant. The debate went on for hours. General Scott was alone in his

West Point, 1838

Brigadier General, 1861
General, August, 1861

COMMANDED
Army of the West

BATTLES:
Mexican War
Fort Sumter
Bull Run
Mill Springs
Shiloh
Corinth
Fort Wagner
Drewry's Bluff
Charleston
Richmond

opinion. Every officer present, except one, had spoken, and all concurred in their views; the silent member was Lieutenant Beauregard. At last General Pierce crossed over to him and said: "You have not expressed an opinion."—"I have not been called on," said Beauregard. "You shall be, however," said Pierce, and, resuming his seat, announced that Lieutenant Beauregard had not given his opinion. Being thus called out, he remarked that if the plan, which had received the assent of all but the commanding general, were carried into effect, it would prove disastrous. He then gave at length the objections to the scheme of the majority, and, taking up General Scott's plan, urged the reasons in its favor with equal earnestness. The council reversed its decision, and the City of Mexico was entered according to the plan urged by the young lieutenant.

On August 20, 1847, he was breveted captain for gallant and meritorious conduct. At the Belen Gate he was wounded, and after his return home was presented with an elegant sword. Subsequently he was placed by the government in charge of the construction of the mint and custom house at New Orleans, as well as the fortifications on and near the mouth of the Mississippi.

At the beginning of 1861 he was appointed Superintendent of West Point Military Academy, but was relieved by President Buchanan within 48 hours, as a rebuke, it is alleged, to the secession speech of Senator Slidell, who was a brother-in-law of Beauregard. Shortly after he resigned his commission in the service of the United States, and was appointed by Governor Moore, of Louisiana, colonel of engineers in the Provincial Army of the South. From this position he was called by President Davis to the defense of Charleston, with the rank of brigadier-general.

General Beauregard was singularly impassioned in the cause which he served. He was the author of some rather weak letters in the early part of the war, deriding the power of the North. He continually asserted that the South would easily whip the North, even if the former "had for arms only pitchforks and flint-lock muskets." Of the army which General

GENERAL BOAR-A-GUARD
ON DUTY

Scott was marshalling on the borders of Virginia he wrote, that the enemies of the South were "little more than an armed rabble, gathered together hastily on a false pretense and for an unholy purpose, with an octogenarian at its head."

Beauregard's personal appearance always attracted attention. He was a small, thin man, with features wearing a dead expression, and hair prematurely whitened. "His manners were distinguished and severe, but not cold; they forbade intimacy; they had the abruptness without the vivacity of the Frenchman; but they expressed no conceit and were not repulsive. He had ardor, a ceaseless activity, and an indomitable power of will."

On April 11, 1861, General Beauregard demanded the evacuation of Fort Sumter. Major Anderson, in his reply, regretted that his sense of honor and his obligation to his government prevented his compliance. Next day the first gun was fired, and on the 13th the fort surrendered. "As an honorable testimony to the gallantry and fortitude with which Major Anderson and his command had defended their posts," General Beauregard not only agreed that they might take passage at their convenience for New York, but allowed him on leaving the fort to salute his flag with 50 guns.

At the beginning of June Beauregard was in consultation with President Davis and General Lee at Richmond. With the *eclat* of the first victory of the war, and the attractions of a foreign name and manners, he at once became the ladies' favorite among the early Southern generals. "He was constantly receiving attentions from them in letters, in flags, and in hundreds of pretty missives."

General Beauregard took a leading part in the first battle of Bull Run, increasing his popularity insomuch that he began to be talked of in some quarters as the next Confederate president; upon which he wrote a flimsy theatrical letter to the newspapers, dated "Within hearing of the enemy's guns," and declaring: "I am not either a candidate, nor do I desire to be a candidate, for any civil office in the gift of the people or executive."

Shortly after the Confederate disaster at Fishing Creek, General Beauregard was sent from the Potomac to General Johnston's lines in Kentucky. When General A. S. Johnston fell mortally wounded at Shiloh, Beauregard assumed chief command of the army. He did not follow up the Confederate victory gained on that sanguinary field. Of the abrupt termination of the conflict, and the condition of the Federals at the time, a Confederate officer writes: "From some cause I could never ascertain a halt was sounded, and when the remnants of the enemy's divisions had stacked arms on the river's edge, preparatory to their surrender, no one stirred to finish the business by a *coup de main*. It was evidently 'drown or surrender' with them, and they had prepared for the latter, until, seeing our inactivity, their gunboats opened furiously, and, save a short cannonade, all subsided into quietness along our lines." In his official report Beauregard gave this explanation: "Darkness was close at hand; officers and men were exhausted by a combat of over twelve hours, without food, and jaded by the march of the preceding day through mud and water."

The Federal army being reinforced, General Beauregard retired to Corinth, in pursuance of his original design to make that the strategic point of his campaign. When the immense forces under Generals Grant and Buell advanced upon him, he made a masterly retreat. "By holding Corinth, he had gained time, and held the enemy in check without a battle; and by retreating when he did, he out-generaled Halleck, rendered him powerless to move, and saved the Mississippi from the inroads of a large army." At this period General Beauregard had sought to recuperate his health by a short respite from duty. He turned over his command to General Bragg during his intended three weeks' absence. No sooner had President Davis heard of this step than he telegraphed General Bragg to assume permanent command, "taking this opportunity to inflict upon General Beauregard a mark of his displeasure, and in fact to encourage the curious report in Richmond that he had become insane, and was no longer fitted for a command."

General Beauregard's next appearance of importance was in the defense of Charleston against an imposing naval demonstration by the Federals during the summer of 1863. General Gillmore assumed command of the National land forces on June 12, and commenced a base of operations on Folly Island. The assault on Fort Wagner took place on the morning of June 11, and was a surprise to Beauregard. It was repulsed by the Confederate commander with a loss of 300 killed and wounded, including 16 officers. It now remained for General Beauregard to repair the error he had committed. Well did he do this secondary duty. Admitting the impraticability of defending Morris Island after the Federal position on it was fully established and covered by the iron-clads, Beauregard appreciated the opportunity of holding the island long enough to replace Sumter by interior positions. He saw clearly enough that every day of defense of Wagner was vital to that of Charleston; and for two months this policy was successful.

Under General Gillmore a second unsuccessful attempt was made on Fort Wagner. After this, during the remainder of July and the early part of August, the Federals were employed in erecting siege-works and mounting heavy siege-guns. Beauregard and the Mayor of Charleston issued an appeal to the land proprietors to send in their Negroes to work on the fortifications. "Though an act of the legislature had been passed involving a penalty on refusal, many of the planters preferred paying it rather than allow their Negroes to be so employed."

On August 21 General Gillmore addressed to General Beauregard a demand for the evacuation of Morris Island and Fort Sumter, and threatening, if not complied with "in less than four hours, a fire would be opened on the City of Charleston from batteries within easy reach of the city." Beauregard made a bitterly sarcastic reply and the siege went on, and when September came the Confederate flag still floated over Sumter.

In April, 1864, the services and command of General Beauregard had been called into requisition from Charleston to strengthen the defenses around Richmond. On April 21 he passed through Wilmington with a large body of troops, and assumed command of the district on the south and east of

Richmond. On May 16 he attacked General Benjamin F. Butler in his advanced position in front of Drury's Bluff. The action was sharp and decisive. Butler was forced back into his intrenchments between the forks of the James and Appomattox Rivers, and Beauregard, intrenching strongly in his front, "bottled" Butler effectually up.

In anticipation of Sherman's triumphal march, Beauregard directed the evacuation of Charleston, and under General Hardee it was completed February 17, 1865. Wilmington was next occupied, Bragg having remained there idle for a month, despite the earnest protest of Beauregard, who in vain had represented to President Davis that, with the fall of Fort Fisher, Wilmington became useless, and that the command there should be used at the earliest possible moment in the field against Sherman.

Beauregard subsequently joined forces with General Joe Johnston in the futile attempt to oppose General Sherman. He surrendered with his commanding general to the Federal commander in April, 1865.

After the war he became President of the New Orleans, Jackson and Mississippi Railroad Company, adjutant-general of the State, and manager of the Louisiana State Lottery. He is, moreover, the author of a work entitled, *The Principles and Maxims of the Art of War.*

(General Beauregard died on February 20, 1893.)

BRAXTON BRAGG, C.S.A., 1817–1876

One of General Bragg's warmest Southern admirers has said of him, that he "was famous for his profuse censure of his officers, and his ascription of every failure in his campaigns to the fault of some subordinate officer." At the same time he found no encomium too high, no honor too great, for the private soldier. Writing after the battle of Murfreesboro, he said: "However much of credit and glory may be given, and probably justly given, to the leaders in the struggle, history will yet award the main honor where it is due, to the private soldier, who, without hope of reward, and with no other incentive than a conscientiousness of rectitude, has encountered all the hardships and has suffered all the privations."

General Braxton Bragg was born in Warren County, North Carolina, March 22, 1817, and graduated at the United States Military Academy in 1837, standing fifth in a class of fifty. Among his classmates were Generals Besham, Townsend, Sedgwick and Hooker, on the Federal side; and Early and Pemberton on the Confederate side. He was appointed lieutenant of artillery, and served mainly in Florida till 1843, during the war with the Seminoles.

In May, 1846, he was made captain by brevet for gallant conduct in the defense of Fort Brown, Texas, and in June was promoted captain of artillery. He was present at the battle of Monterey, and was breveted major for gallant conduct there; and in 1847 he was breveted lietenant-colonel for gallant and meritorious conduct at Buena Vista. From 1848 up to 1855 he was engaged in frontier service at Jefferson Barracks, Mo. In

March, 1855, he was appointed major of cavalry, but declined, and received leave of absence. In January, 1856, he resigned his commission and retired to his plantation at Thibodeaux, La., and for two years officiated as commissioner of the board of public works of the State.

When the Civil War broke out he was appointed brigadier-general, and placed in command of Pensacola, Fla. In February, 1862, he was made major-general, and ordered to join the Army of the Mississippi. At the battle of Shiloh, when General Sidney Johnston was killed, and the Confederate forces exhibited a great lack of discipline, General Bragg held a few thousand of the better disciplined troops firmly in hand and restored some approximation to order.

Subsequently General Bragg commanded the whole Confederate Army of the West, in place of General Beauregard, and early in August, 1862, made preparations for the Kentucky campaign, which was to be conducted amid intricate and formidable combinations of the Federal forces. After considerable successful manœuvring, he sent the following somewhat fulsome dispatch to Richmond, which greatly excited the hopes of the government there: "My advance will be in Glasgow to-day, and I shall be with them to-morrow; my whole force will be there on the 14th. We shall then be between Buell and Kirby Smith, for which I have been struggling. The troops are in good tone and condition, somewhat footsore and tired, but cheerful. With arms we can not only *clear* Tennessee and Kentucky, but, I confidently trust, *hold*

West Point, 1837

Brigadier General, 1861
General, April, 1862

COMMANDED
Army of Tennessee
Army of the West
Military Adviser to
*   President Davis, 1864*

169

them both.'' On the 17th September the Federal garrison at Munfordville surrendered to his advanced divisions, and 4267 prisoners, ten pieces of artillery, 5000 small arms, and a proportionate quantity of ammunition, horses, etc., fell into his hands. His whole army was now on the road between Nashville and Louisville—the road by which Buell would be forced to march. Yet Bragg did not take advantage of the situation, and ''his remarkable failure to deliver battle at Munfordville was the subject of much censure and criticism, which never obtained any reply from him but a weak and insufficient explanation in his official report.''

After considerable marching and manœuvring, Bragg, deceived as to the real strength of his adversary, found himself forced to give battle at Perryville, October 8, 1862, at serious disadvantage. The action began a little past noon, and was fought with gallantry and persistent determination on the Confederate side. Finding, however, that the Federals had concentrated their three corps against him, and aware that his loss had been already quite serious, General Bragg fell back on Harrodsburg. This move was a sore disappointment to the Confederate authorities, whose hopes had been unduly excited by the commander's sensational dispatches. Instead of his performance keeping pace with his promise, four weeks after passing Cumberland Gap Bragg's army was found ''with serried ranks in front of the enemy at Nashville, with the bulk of his army in camp at Murfreesboro.'' Here in December, 1862, he confronted Rosecrans, and prepared for an important battle, likely to decide the fate of Tennessee. Bragg's cavalry was absent, being employed in harassing Grant's rear in West Tennessee, and the absence of this arm of his service encouraged Rosecrans to attack. By seven o'clock in the morning of December 31st the troops of both armies were preparing for battle. As the result showed, the battle of Stones River was a desperate but undecided contest; yet the advantage remained with the Confederates. They had driven the Federal right almost upon its left, captured nearly one-third of its artillery, compelled a change of front under fire, and occupied that part of the field

from which the National army had been driven in the morning. The next day—January 1, 1863—General Bragg telegraphed to Richmond: ''God has granted us a happy new year.''

Each army kept its position on the field, and each general anticipated an attack from his opponent, yet neither appeared willing to begin a new battle. Meanwhile ''Bragg was deceived into the belief that the enemy was receiving reinforcements, and, in view of the exhausted condition of his army, determined to withdraw from the unequal contest.'' In the night of January 3, 1863, the retreat was effected, the Confederate army retiring to Tullahoma.

From March till June, 1863, Bragg's forces remained in comparative inactivity—his line stretching from Shelbyville to the right—while the Nationals, ''holding a line from Franklin to Woodbury, again and again,'' according to a Confederate writer, ''afforded opportunities of attack on detached masses, which the dull secession commander never used.''

Meantime drafts had been made upon Bragg's forces for the defense of Richmond, and with his army so reduced, he insisted upon regarding it as one merely of observation. Rosecrans was in his front, and Burnside was in a position to threaten his rear. An injudicious disposition of the Confederate commander's forces incited Rosecrans to advance upon Hoover's Gap. Bragg commenced a retreat, which was eventually continued to Chattanooga. To save the State of Georgia, he found it necessary to abandon Chattanooga, and on September 7, 1863, he began the retreat that precipitated several minor engagements, and culminated in the great battle of Chickamauga.

At dawn of the 20th September General Bragg was in the saddle, surrounded by his staff, listening for the sound of Polk's guns. The sun rose and was mounting in the sky, and still there was no note of attack from the right wing. Bragg chafed with impatience, and dispatched Major Lee to ascertain the cause of Polk's delay. ''Major Lee found Polk seated at a comfortable breakfast, surrounded by brilliantly dressed officers, and delivered his message with military bluntness and brevity. General Polk replied that he had ordered Hill to open the action, that he was waiting for him, and added: 'Do tell General Bragg that my heart is overflowing with anxiety for the attack—overflowing with anxiety, sir.' Major Lee returned to the commanding general and reported the reply literally. Bragg uttered a terrible exclamation, in which Polk, Hill, and all his generals were included. 'Major Lee,' he cried, 'ride along the line and order *every captain* to take his men instantly into action.'" In fifteen minutes the battle was joined; but three hours of valuable time had been lost, and Rosecrans had strengthened his position. It was ten o'clock in the morning when the battle opened. When it closed the Federal army was totally routed from right, left and centre, and was in full retreat to Chattanooga. Polk's wing captured 28 pieces of artillery and Longstreet's 21, making 49 pieces of cannon. General Bragg reckoned the Confederate loss as "two-fifths of his army."

At this juncture starvation or retreat seemed to stare the Federal army in the face. Its supplies had to be dragged sixty miles over abominable roads, and even if it ventured to retreat it would have to abandon its artillery and most of its *materiel*. At this critical period General Thomas relieved Rosecrans, and a few days afterwards General Grant was on the scene, and relief was at hand. But, although the Federal army had now no fears of starvation or retreat, Grant hesitated about assuming the offensive against the strong positions in his front. What was his surprise then to learn that Longstreet, with 11,000 infantry, had been detached from Bragg's front, and that this veteran commander had gone to Knoxville to attack Burnside. The announcement of this enterprise determined the Federal general to attack. The battle of Missionary Ridge was the consequence of this decision. There were 80,000 troops in the Federal lines. The Confederate army numbered not half so many, yet had a position that should have decided the day. "It was late in the afternoon," says a Confederate writer, "when Grant ordered a general advance of his lines to the crest of the Ridge. As the Federal columns moved up at a rapid rate, in face of the batteries, the Confederate centre gave way, and in a few moments what had been a regular and vigorous battle became a panic and a rout. The day was shamefully lost. General Bragg attempted to rally the broken troops. He advanced into the fire and exclaimed, 'Here is your commander,' and was answered with derisive shouts of a prevalent slang phrase in the army, 'Here's your mule.'"

"An army notoriously lacking confidence in their commander," writes a military critic, "made weak and suspicious by the detachment from it of Longstreet's veteran divisions, and utterly demoralized by one of Bragg's freaks of organization before the battle, in shuffling over all the commands, broke into disorderly retreat from a line which might easily have been held against twice their numbers, and gave to the Confederacy what President Davis unwillingly pronounced 'the mortification of the first defeat that had resulted from misconduct by the troops.'"

The consequence of this disaster was that General Bragg left in the hands of the Federals all his strong positions, and retired with his whole army to Dalton, where he was displaced in command by General Joseph E. Johnston.

General Braxton Bragg did not again appear on the military stage till January, 1865, when he was sent by President Davis to take part in the second defense of Wilmington. A Virginia newspaper irreverently announced the event as follows: "General Bragg has been appointed to command at Wilmington; good-by, Wilmington!" The name of this Confederate commander inspired no further confidence and, although Fort Fisher held out against a naval bombardment, and its garrison was largely increased when Bragg took command, it was generally felt that some disaster would ensue. These fears were to be realized. It was evidently the first and most important concern to prevent a landing of the Federal troops. Bragg's forces were disposed with that view. On January 13, 1865, several troops under Terry were landed five or six miles above Fort Fisher. The Federal landing-place was well chosen. Bragg at first gave the order to charge the enemy, but after a reconnois-

Confederate Button

sance determined to withdraw, after reinforcing the fort, held by General Whiting, with a garrison increased to about 2500 men. As everybody knows, General Whiting and his garrison surrendered themselves on January 15 as prisoners of war. Wilmington was thereupon occupied without resistance; and "the command of General Bragg, which had remained there idle for more than a month, despite the earnest protest of General Beauregard, was at last moved into the scene of hostilities in the Carolinas."

Early in March two columns of Federal troops—one from Wilmington, the other from Newbern—moved to supply Sherman by Cape Fear River. The column from Newbern was attacked on the 8th March near Kingston by General Bragg, with his own troops and Hill's division of the Army of the Tennessee, and completely routed, 1500 prisoners being taken. On March 9 General Bragg found the enemy several miles in the rear, strongly intrenched, and after a faint attack drew off.

General Bragg's military career may be said to end here. He took no prominent part in any subsequent action, and in other respects seemed to have outlived his fame and usefulness. He made no noticeable appearance after the war, and died at Galveston, Texas, September 27, 1876.

That Feed Won't Do

JOHN CABELL BRECKINRIDGE, C.S.A., 1821–1875

This distinguished Kentuckian was born at Lexington, January 21, 1821. He was the grandson of John Breckinridge, United States Senator and Attorney-general, and was educated at Centre College, Danville, subsequently studying law at Transylvania Institute. After a short residence at Burlington, Iowa, he settled at Lexington and practiced his profession with conspicuous success. At the inception of the Mexican War in 1847 he was elected major in a regiment of Kentucky volunteers. On his return he was elected to the Kentucky house of representatives.

In 1851 General Breckinridge was elected to congress, and was re-elected in 1853, and declined the Spanish mission offered him by President Pierce. In the presidential election of 1856 he was chosen Vice-President of the United States, with Buchanan as President, and was the youngest man that ever held that office. In 1860 he was candidate for president as the representative of the slave-holding interest nominated by the Southern delegates of the Democratic convention. In the electoral college he received 72 votes to 180 for Lincoln, 39 for Bell, and 12 for Douglas. In the same year he was elected United States Senator as the successor of John J. Crittenden, and took his seat in March, 1861.

At the beginning of the Civil War he defended the Southern Confederacy in the senate. About that time the Kentucky legislature had passed a resolution to the effect that the State should remain neutral in the contest pending, and would not permit the troops of either party to pass over or occupy her soil for

belligerent purposes.

An election for members of her legislature ensued in August. After the returns were made "it became evident that the Federal government intended to occupy Kentucky, and to use her roads and mountains for marching invading columns upon the Confederate States. . . . It was not long before Federal agents were making daily arrests of persons suspected of entertaining designs hostile to the Government at Washington." Among many other notable persons, John C. Breckinridge hastened within the Confederate lines. Soon after he proceeded to Richmond and was appointed a brigadier-general.

On assuming his new functions, General Breckinridge published a manifesto to the People of Kentucky. The following are extracts from that address:

"The Federal Government—the creature—has set itself above the creator. The atrocious doctrine is announced by the president, and acted upon, that the States derive their power from the Federal Government and may be suppressed on any pretense of military necessity. . . . The fortresses of the country are filled with victims, seized without warrant of law, and ignorant of the cause of their imprisonment. . . . A subservient congress ratifies the usurpations of the president, and proceeds to complete the destruction of the constitution. . . . The great mass of the Northern people seem anxious to sunder every safeguard of freedom; they eagerly offer to the government what no European monarch would dare to demand. The president and his generals are unable to pick up the liberties of

Centre College, 1839

Brigadier General, 1861
Major General

the people as rapidly as they are thrown at their feet. General Anderson, the military dictator of Kentucky, announces in one of his proclamations that he will arrest no one who does not act, write or speak in opposition to Mr. Lincoln's government. It would have completed the idea if he had added: or *think* in opposition to it."

At the battle of Shiloh, April 6, 1862, General Breckinridge commanded the reserve of General Albert Sidney Johnston's army.

When, in the summer of 1862, General Earl Van Dorn was assigned to the defense of Vicksburg, Breckinridge's division occupied the city; and when it was resolved by the Confederate commander to attempt the capture of Baton Rouge, and so open the navigation of the Mississippi, General Breckinridge was ordered to move to that point with a force of 5000 men, picked from the troops at Vicksburg, with the force of General Ruggles added to his command. By epidemic disease Breckinridge's forces were reduced to less than 3000 effective men within the period of ten days after he reached Camp Moore. "Advised by telegram every hour of the progress of the ram *Arkansas* towards Baton Rouge, and counting on her co-operation, he, on the morning of the 5th of August, determined to attack the enemy with his whole effective force, then reduced to about 2500 men." The attack was gallantly made, and the Federal forces, driven from their position, were forced to seek protection under the cover of their gunboats. Breckinridge had listened in vain for the guns of the ram *Arkansas*. She never reached the scene of the contest. "After arriving within a short distance of Baton Rouge, in ample time for joint action, she had suddenly become unmanageable from a failure in her machinery." She was therefore abandoned, her guns shotted and the Confederate flag run up to her prow. The torch was applied, her guns were discharged as the flames reached them, and when her last shot was fired the career of the *Arkansas* was ended.

"Unable, without the co-operation of this vessel, to penetrate the cover of the enemy's gunboats, General Breckinridge withdrew his troops at ten o'clock in the morning." He had fought a brilliant action, but was unable to follow up he victory.

At the battle of Murfreesboro, December 26, 1862, General Breckinridge commanded the right wing of the army under Bragg. After the resolutely fought but indecisive battle, Breckinridge was transferred to the right of Stones River, to resume the command of that position now held by two of his brigades. On January 1, 1863, Bragg telegraphed to Richmond: "God has granted us a happy new year." Next day more fighting ensued. Breckinridge with his division, together with the cavalry forces of Wharton and Pegram and ten Napoleon guns, was instructed to carry the hill occupied by the Federals, intrench his artillery, and hold the position.

The attack was made at 4 p.m. Van Cleve's division gave way, retired in confusion across the river, and was followed by the Confederates. "The enemy, however, had disposed his batteries on the hill on the west side of the river, and Negley's division was ordered up to meet the onset. The firing was terrific. In about half an hour the Confederates lost 2000 men." Breckinridge's command was driven back in much disorder, but the pursuit of the Federals was checked by Anderson's brigade of Mississippians.

At the battle of Chickamauga Breckinridge and his division, which had come up from Mississippi, fought in the corps of General D. H. Hill. Breckinridge took a prominent part in the two days' terrible fighting that followed. On the 19th Helm's brigade of Breckinridge's division crossed over and attacked Negley's infantry and drove it off. "Riding over the ground with Breckinridge," says General D. H. Hill, "I counted 11 dead horses at the Federal battery, and a number of dead infantry men who had not been removed. The clouds of dust rolling down the valley revealed the precipitate retirement of the foe."

Breckinridge's division moved at 9:30 a.m. on the battle of the 20th. Forrest dismounted Armstrong's division of cavalry to keep ahead with Breckinridge. The latter's two right brigades met but little opposition, but the left of Helm's brigade encountered the left of the Federal breastworks and was badly cut up. The heroic Helm was killed and his command repulsed. "General Breckinridge suggested," writes General D. H. Hill, "and I cordially approved the suggestion, that he should wheel his two brigades to the left and get in the rear of the breastworks." These brigades had reached the Chattanooga road, and their skirmishers had pressed past the Federal field hospital; "while," says Breckinridge in his report, "Adams had advanced still further, being actually in rear of his intrenchments. A good supporting line to my division at this moment would probably have produced decisive results."

On November 25, 1863, the Federals prepared for a grand assault. Sherman's force had come up and occupied the northern extremity of Missionary Ridge. Hooker had scaled the rugged height of Lookout Mountain, and the Federal forces maintained an unbroken line from the north end of this eminence to the north end of Missionary Ridge. The Confederate army held the crest of the ridge from McFarlan's Gap to the mouth of the Chickamauga, the position being from four to six hundred feet in elevation. The Confederate right wing was held by Hardee; Breckinridge commanded on the left his old division, Stewart's, and part of Buckner's and Hindman's. The enemy's first assault was made on the right wing, which was repulsed with great slaughter. A second attack was made on Breckinridge's corps, which was also repulsed. Late in the afternoon General Grant ordered a general advance, and the greater part of the Confederate army became completely demoralized and fled from the field. Grant claimed as the fruits of his victory 7000 prisoners and 47 pieces of artillery.

Early in April, 1864, Grant conceived a plan for taking Richmond without capturing the government machinery, and without overthrowing Lee's army. General Sigel, in furtherance of this plan, was ordered to organize all his available forces into two expeditions, to move from Beverly to Charleston against the East Tennessee and Virginia Railroad. Subsequently Sigel gave up the Beverly expedition and formed two columns—one on the Kanawha and another on the Shenandoah; General Butler commanded one column, Sigel himself the other. Butler manœuvred so as to place himself in a position which Grant pithily described as being "in a bottle strongly corked;" General Sigel moved up the Shenandoah Valley, and on May 15 was encountered near Newmarket by General Breckinridge, who drove the Federal forces across the Shenandoah, "captured six pieces of artillery and nearly 1000 stand of small arms, and inflicted upon him a heavy loss. Sigel abandoned his hospitals and destroyed the larger portion of his train."

The singular fortune of war had again made the Peninsula the blood-steeped battle-ground. Lee had been joined at Hanover Junction by Pickett's division of Longstreet's corps, a brigade of Early's division of Ewell's corps, and two small brigades, with a battalion of artillery under Breckinridge. "The force under General Breckinridge, which Grant estimated at 15,000, did not exceed 2000 muskets." When he fell back to the lines immediately about Richmond, General Lee was further reinforced; but at the same time Breckinridge and his division were sent back into the Shenandoah Valley, where he was defeated by Sheridan in September, 1864. He was again defeated by General Gillam in East Tennessee, November 12, 1864.

On December 15, 1864, his command fought under General Hood against the Federal commander General Thomas at Nashville. At 4 p.m. it was thought that the day was to be decided for the Confederates; but, alas! "Finney's Florida brigade in Bates's division, which was on the left Confederate centre, gave way before the skirmish line of the enemy. Instantly Bates's division took panic and broke in disorder." A wild panic ensued, and "everything that could impede flight was thrown away as the fugitives passed down the Granny White and Franklin pikes, or fled wildly from the battle-field." Fifty pieces of artillery and nearly all the Confederate ordnance wagons were left to the Federals. Hood, Breckinridge and others escaped across the Tennessee with the remnant of the brilliant force they had conducted across that river a few

THE BATTLE OF MISSIONARY RIDGE

"As our troops advanced, the Confederates opened fire with shot and shell. Dashing over the open plain, capturing the works at the foot of the hill, the troops continued on up to the crest of the ridge, and captured the guns at the point of the bayonet. When General Grant saw the troops charging up the hill to capture it, he turned sharply to General Thomas and asked—'By whose orders are those troops going up the hill?' Thomas, taking in the situation, replied—'Probably their own orders.' General Grant remarked 'that it was all right if it turned out all right; if not, somebody would have to suffer.' As it turned out 'all right,' Grant complimented the troops."
Henry M. Cist,
Brevet Brigadier General, U.S.A.

175

THE BATTLE OF CHAMPION'S HILL
May 16, 1863

weeks before. This was the last action in which General Breckinridge was engaged. Soon after he became Secretary of War in Jefferson Davis's cabinet, and remained in that position till the surrender of General Joe Johnston to General William T. Sherman in April, 1865.

A small slip of paper, sent up by General Breckinridge from the War Department to President Davis as he was seated in his pew in St. Paul's Church, contained the most momentous item of news of the whole war. Lee had telegraphed to the War Department, advising that the Richmond authorities have everything in readiness to evacuate the capitol at 8 p.m. that Sunday. Soon after the streets were filled with bustling throngs, making their way to the railroad depots. Wagons were being hastily laden at the War Department with boxes, trunks, etc., and driven to the Danville depot. In the afternoon a special train carried from Richmond President Davis, Breckinridge and some other members of the Confederate Cabinet.

After it was decided to abandon the now hopeless contest, General Breckinridge left the fallen president and party at Washington, Ga., and made his escape to Cuba, and from thence sailed to Europe. After spending some time abroad, he returned in 1868, determined to take no further part in politics, but to devote himself to his profession.

General Breckinridge died in Lexington, Ky., May 17, 1875.

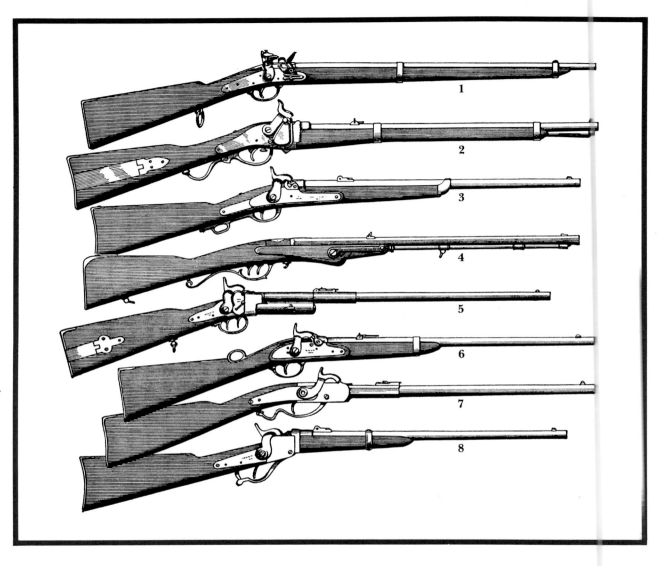

1. Jenks Flintlock Carbine
   Model 1839 Caliber .69

2. Symmes Breech-loading Carbine
   Model 1858 Caliber .54

3. Gibbs Breech-loading Carbine
   Model 1856 Caliber .52

4. Schroeder Breech-loading Carbine
   Model 1856 Caliber .53

5. Greene Breech-loading Carbine
   Model 1854 Caliber .53

6. Joslyn Breech-loading Carbine
   Model 1855 Caliber .54

7. Cosmopolitan Breech-loading
   Carbine
   Model 1861 Caliber .50

8. Starr Breech-loading Carbine
   Model 1858 Caliber .54

BREECH-LOADING SINGLE-SHOT CARBINES

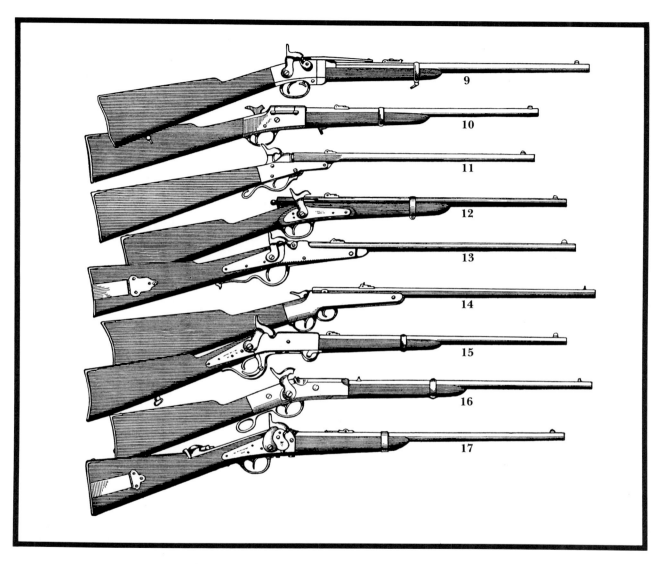

9. Smith Breech-loading Carbine
   Model 1861 Caliber .52

10. Warner Breech-loading Carbine
    Model 1864 Caliber .50

11. Maynard Breech-loading
    Percussion Carbine
    Model 1859 Caliber .50

12. Palmer Breech-loading
    Bolt-action Carbine
    Model 1863 Caliber .50

13. Gallagher Breech-loading
    Percussion Carbine
    Model 1860 Caliber .54

14. Wesson Breech-loading
    Carbine
    Model 1859 Caliber .44

15. Burnside Breech-loading
    Percussion Carbine
    Model 1856 Caliber .54

16. Perry Navy Breech-loading
    Carbine
    Model 1855 Caliber .54

17. Merrill, Latrobe, and Thomas
    Breech-loading Carbine
    Model 1856 Caliber .54

BREECH-LOADING SINGLE-SHOT CARBINES

JUBAL ANDERSON EARLY, C.S.A.,1816–1894

General Lee was in the habit of calling Jubal Early his "bad old man." The designation was apropos to the picture of a commander who garnished his speech with oaths, dressed in the careless fashion of a stage-driver, and who was famous for his hard direct blows in battle.

Early was born in Franklin County, Virginia, November 3, 1816. He graduated from the United States Military Academy in 1837, was appointed lieutenant of artillery, and assigned to duty at Fort Monroe, Va. He served in the Florida War in 1837–38, and in the latter year resigned his commission in the army for the purpose of beginning the practice of law in Virginia. He served in the legislature of his native State during 1841–42, and was commonwealth attorney in 1842–47, and again in 1848–52. During the Mexican War he was major in a regiment of Virginia volunteers, serving from January, 1847, until August, 1848; and was acting governor of Monterey in May and June, 1847. After the Mexican campaign he returned to the practice of civil law.

At the beginning of the Civil War he entered the Confederate service as a colonel. A graphic pen has described him at this period as a man of vigorous and athletic appearance. His stature approached, if it did not reach, six feet, and he seemed to be capable of undergoing great fatigue. His hair was black and curling, and just touched with gray; his eyes dark and sparkling; his smile ready and expressive, but somewhat sarcastic, as was the bent of his character. His dress was plain gray, without decoration. His face, set upon a short neck,

A Short History of GEN. J. A. EARLY.

joined to stooping shoulders, attracted attention from every one. In the dark eye you could read the resolute character of the man, as in his satirical smile you saw the evidence of that broad, trenchant humor for which he was famous. The keen glance drove home the sarcastic speech, and almost every one who ventured upon word combats with Lieutenant-general Early sustained a "palpable hit." The soldiers of his army had a hundred jests and witticisms about him. They called him "Old Jube," and sometimes "Old Jubilee." They delighted to relate how, after the defeat of Fisher's Hill, when the troops were in full retreat, their commander had checked his horse, raised his arms aloft, and exclaimed, "My God! won't any of my men make a rally round Old Jubal!" To which a philosophic foot-soldier, calmly seeking the rear, replied: "Nary rally, gen'ral." He is said to have exclaimed when he heard of Lee's retreat: "Now let Gabriel blow his horn; it is time to die."

Everything about "Old Jube" was characteristic and marked. Speaking slowly, and with a species of drawl in his voice, all that he said was pointed, direct, and full of sarcastic force. These "hits" he evidently enjoyed, and he delivered them with the coolness of a swordsman making a mortal lunge. All the army had laughed at one of them. While marching at the head of his column, in his dusty, dingy, gray uniform, and with his faded hat over his eyes, he had seen, leaning over a fence and looking at the column as it passed, a former associate in the Virginia Convention who had violently advocated secession. This gentleman was clad in citizen's clothes—black coat and irreproachable shirt bosom—and greeted Early as he passed. The reply of the general was given with the habitual smile and sarcastic drawl: "How are you!" he said. "I think you said the Whigs wouldn't fight." The blow was rude and made the whole army laugh. Of this peculiar humor a better instance still is given. After Fisher's Hill, when his whole army was in complete retreat, and the Federal forces were pressing him close, he was riding with General Breckinridge. It might have been supposed that their conversation would relate to the disastrous events of the day, but General Early did not seem to trouble himself about that subject. In full retreat, as they were, and followed by an enraged enemy, his companion was astounded to hear from Early the cool and nonchalant question: "Well, Breckinridge, what do you think of the decision of the Supreme Court in the Dred Scott case, in its bearings upon the rights of the South in the territories?" As has been aptly said, "the man who could amuse himself with political discussions between Fisher's Hill and Woodstock on September 22, 1864, must have been of hard stuff or peculiar humor. There were many persons in and out of the army who doubted the soundness of his judgment, but there were none who ever called in question the tough fibre of his courage."

General Early commanded a brigade at the battle of Bull Run, and at the battle of Williamsburg, May 5, 1862, he was supposed to be mortally wounded. Under "Stonewall" Jackson he took an active part at the engagement of Cedar Run in August of the same year, and again at the second battle of Bull Run. He was promoted brigadier-general in May, 1863, and commanded the division that held the lines at Fredericksburg while Lee was fighting the battle of Chancellorsville. Again at Gettysburg General Early was in the thick of the fray, his division being selected to storm the ridge. He succeeded in capturing the first line of breastworks, but was driven back by the weight of numbers.

On November 6, 1863, the Federals came in force upon Lee's army at Rappahannock Station, and General Rodes, who had fallen back before superior numbers, was reinforced. To meet the demonstration at the bridge, near where Ewell's force was stationed, Early's division was put in motion. The night was very dark, and a high wind effectually prevented the movements of the Federals being heard. Early was afraid of using his artillery, because some of his men were commingled with the enemy. Hence the unlucky commander witnessed the loss of the greater portion of two of his brigades without, as he declared, the possibility of an effort to extricate them. Some of his men effected their escape by swimming the river, and others by making their way to the bridge; but not less than 2000 prisoners were left in the Federal camp.

In the operations west of the Blue Ridge in June, 1864, it became necessary for General Lee to detach a considerable portion of his force to meet and overthrow the Federal commander Hunter, who was moving up the Shenandoah Valley. General Early was selected for this purpose. He had latterly commanded Ewell's corps, and with the greater portion of this he moved rapidly to Lynchburg. On July 3, 1864, he approached Martinsburg, accompanied by a cavalry force under Ransom. The Federal forces retreated and took up a position at Monocacy Bridge. The National troops held the east bank of the river, and were drawn up along the railroad. General Early, having crossed the river, sent forward a brigade to develop the Federal strength. In the engagement that followed "the enemy broke in shameful confusion. His losses were more than 1000 killed and wounded, and 700 prisoners." Flushed with success, Early moved on Washington, reaching Rockville on the evening of July 10. He was now within sight of the capitol, and the fire of his skirmishers was heard at the White House and in the departmental buildings. The toiling march, however, had depleted his army. The 500 miles of incessant advance at 20 miles a day left him only 8000 infantry, about 40 field-pieces and 2000 cavalry, with which to assault the works around Washington. On the 12th July a severe skirmish occurred in front of Fort Stevens, but "General Early declined to follow it up, and, by a decisive blow, attempt the capture of Washing-

ton. Reflecting that he was in the heart of the enemy's country, and not knowing what force defended the capital, he abandoned his design upon it, and in the night of the 12th commenced his retreat. Respecting this, some Northern writers have declared that if Early had made a vigorous attack when he first came up, and not lost a day in a fruitless reconnoissance, it would have resulted in the capture of the city, so feebly was it defended.

General Early, having broken up his camp before Washington, retreated, and stood at bay on the Opequon to protect the Shenandoah Valley. He carried off with him 5000 horses, 2500 beef cattle, and accomplished the primary object of the march. At the end of July a portion of his cavalry advanced into Pennsylvania as far as Chambersburg, which they burnt.

On September 19, 1864, he was defeated by Sheridan, and lost 2500 prisoners and five pieces of artillery. Early then retired to Fisher's Hill, near Strasburg. This position has been described as one of the strongest in the whole Virginia valley. But a Confederate officer, who has reviewed the campaign, says: "When Early took up a position on the great range of hills above Strasburg and waited to be attacked, he committed an error under the circumstances which the general himself at this day would probably acknowledge. . . . General Jackson is said to have expressed this opinion, and it is certain that he never made a stand there. General Early did so, and was flanked on the left." Be this as it may, the Confederate forces were easily defeated by Sheridan's army, and Early retired in great disorder, leaving 11 pieces of artillery. General Early had lost half his army, and his career seemed to be close at an end. However, his army was reinforced, and in October he returned to the valley. On the 18th he was again in Cedar Creek with a force of "less than 10,000 men, and about 40 pieces of artillery." His force was inadequate for open attack, and his only chance was to make a surprise. The Federals were posted on a low line of hills. "Early's dispositions for attack were to make a feint with light artillery and cavalry against the enemy's right, while the bulk of his forces marched towards the left."

The movement commenced a little past midnight. At dawn he flanking column was across the ford. The Federal pickets had not yet taken alarm. Early had brought his column unperceived to the rear of the left flank of the National army. The surprise was complete. The Confederates, in the action that followed, "captured 18 pieces of artillery, 1500 prisoners, small arms without number, wagons, camps, everything on the ground."

Sheridan had not been present. The incident of his famous "ride" comes in here. The Federal counter-charge was made at three in the afternoon. The Confederates were not prepared. "They had been demoralized by pillage, and when urged forward they moved without enthusiasm." At the first contact with Sheridan's army Gordon's division broke; Kershaw's and Ramseur's followed in retreat, and the field became covered with flying men. . . . Many ordnance and medical stores, and 23 pieces of artillery, besides those taken in the morning by Early, were captured. About 1500 prisoners were taken. . . . The day was completely turned against the Confederates, and night closed with the enemy's infantry occupying their old camps, and his cavalry pursuing the wreck of Early's army."

After the grave disaster of Cedar Creek, General Early published an address to his troops which was far from being complimentary. He said: "I had hoped to have congratulated you on the splendid victory won by you on the morning of the 19th at Belle Grove, on Cedar Creek, when you surprised and routed two corps of Sheridan's army, and drove back several miles the remaining corps. . . . But I have the mortification of announcing to you that by your subsequent misconduct all the benefits of that victory were lost, and a serious disaster incurred. Had you remained steadfast to your duty and your colors, the victory would have been one of the most brilliant and decisive of the war. . . . But many of you, including some commissioned officers, yielding to a disgraceful propensity for plunder, deserted your colors to appropriate to yourselves the abandoned property of the enemy."

General Early had received an overwhelming defeat, from which his army never recovered. The battle of Cedar Creek practically closed the campaign in the valley, and most of Early's infantry were returned to General Lee's lines.

A short time after he was relieved by General Lee from the command in the valley. With characteristic generosity the commander-in-chief said: "Your reverses in the valley, of which the public and the army judge chiefly by the results, have, I fear, impaired your influence, both with the people and the soldiers, and would add greatly to the difficulties which will, under any circumstances, attend our military operations in Southwestern Virginia. While my own confidence in your ability, zeal and devotion to the cause is unimpaired, I have nevertheless felt that I could not oppose what seems to be the current of opinion, without injustice to your reputation and injury to the service."

After the war General Early spent some time in Europe, and on his return resumed the practice of law in Richmond. He subsequently took up his residence in New Orleans (alternately with Lynchburg), where, with General Beauregard, he became a manager of the Louisiana State Lottery. He is president of the Southern Historical Society, and has published a pamphlet entitled, "A Memoir of the Last Years in the War for Independence of the Confederate States."

(General Early died on March 2, 1894.)

The "Rucker" Ambulance-wagon

RICHARD STODDERT EWELL, C.S.A., 1817–1872

General Ewell was a native of Georgetown, District of Columbia, and was born February 8, 1817. He graduated from West Point in 1840, served in Mexico, and was engaged at Contreras and Churubusco. He was promoted to captain in 1849.

When the Civil War began he resigned his commission and entered the Confederate army. He was promoted to major-general, and fought at Blackburn's Ford July 18, 1861. Three days later his command was at Bull Run, where he was directed to make "a demonstration of his front, in order to retain and engross the Federal reserves and forces on their flank at and around Centreville." The following year he distinguished himself in Jackson's campaign in the valley of Virginia. Ewell's division reinforced Stonewall Jackson. The two men were warm friends, and the most harmonious relations existed between them.

On June 7, 1862, the main body of Jackson's command had reached the vicinity of Port Republic. General Ewell was some four miles distant, General Fremont had

arrived with his forces in the vicinity of Harrisonburg, and General Shields was moving up the east side of the south fork of the Shenandoah. Fremont had seven brigades of infantry, besides numerous cavalry. Ewell had three small brigades and no cavalry; his force was 5000 men. After ten o'clock the foe felt along his front, posted his artillery, and with two brigades made an attack on Trimble's brigade on the right. General Trimble repulsed this force, and advancing, drove the Federals more than a mile. At a late hour of the afternoon General

Ewell advanced both his wings, drove in the Union skirmishers, and when night closed was in possession of all the ground previously held by the enemy. This victory, known as Cross Keys, had been purchased by a small Confederate loss—42 killed and 287 wounded.

General Ewell participated in the battle of Cedar Run, in which the Confederates claimed a victory. On August 27 a considerable force of the enemy under Brigadier-general Taylor approached from the direction of Alexandria and pushed forward boldly towards Bull Run. After a sharp engagement, the Federal forces were routed and driven back, General Taylor himself being mortally wounded. In the afternoon the enemy advanced upon General Ewell at Bristol. They were attacked by three regiments and the batteries of Ewell's division, and "two columns of not less than a brigade each were broken and repulsed." Their places were soon supplied by fresh troops, and it was apparent the Federal commander had now become aware of the situation of affairs and had turned upon the Confederates with his full force. General Ewell, upon perceiving the strength of the enemy, withdrew his command, and subsequent manœuvrings led up to the second battle of Bull Run, in the operations preceding which General Ewell lost a leg. When General Jackson was fatally wounded at Chancellorsville, Ewell, at his request, was promoted to lieutenant-general.

In the late spring of 1863 General Lee on the plains near Culpepper effected preparations for a grand campaign. By the

1st of June all was in readiness and the advance was ordered. General Ewell's corps, in the lead, pushed rapidly forward, and marched across the Blue Ridge Mountains, by way of Front Royal, into the Shenandoah Valley upon Winchester. Here he surprised General Milroy and defeated him. Three thousand prisoners, 30 pieces of artillery, over 100 wagons and a great quantity of stores were captured in and near Winchester.

The failure of General Ewell, at the head of Jackson's veterans, to seize "Cemetery Hill" and adjacent positions, has frequently been assigned as the cause of the loss of Gettysburg by the Confederates. Respecting this theory General E. M. Law writes: "It is very doubtful whether General Ewell could have occupied those heights had he made the attempt; for General Pleasonton has asserted very positively that on the night of July 1 'we (the Federals) had more troops in position than Lee'; and General Lee qualified his instructions to General Ewell to seize the heights by the words, 'if practicable.' Under the circumstances, the fact that General Ewell did not seize them is very strong presumptive evidence that it was not practicable."

In the two days' desperate fighting that followed the corps of General Ewell did brilliant work, and subsequently in the engagements that followed in the Wilderness. The Confederate army on the Rapidan, at the beginning of the last-named campaign, consisted of two divisions of Longstreet's corps, Ewell's corps, A. P. Hill's corps, three divisions of cavalry, and the artillery. "General Lee's whole effective infantry did not exceed 40,000 muskets. With this force he was called upon to cope with the 180,000 men of the Federal army. Meantime the Confederate commander-in-chief adopted precautionary measures to meet the enemy. He kept open his communications with Richmond, while by way of Fredericksburg he destroyed the bridges and rails, in order to prevent Grant's advance in that direction. The works occupied by Lee's army on the Rapidan extended on the right three miles below Raccoon's Ford. General Ewell's corps lay behind those defenses, and with A. P. Hill's stretched out on each side of Orange Court-house along a line of 20 miles. As soon as Lee ascertained that Grant had certainly cut loose from his base at Culpepper Court-house, and was moving rapidly past his right, "he put his own army in motion, sending Ewell's corps down the turnpike and A. P. Hill's down the plank road; and ordering Longstreet, who had arrived at Gordonsville, to move his corps down on the right of Ewell's line of march, so as to strike the head of the enemy's column." The advance of Ewell's corps arrived within three miles of Wilderness Run in the evening and encamped, Rodes lay in his rear, and Early was next at Locust Grove, all ready to strike at Grant's advance next morning. About six o'clock on the morning of May 6 the skirmishing between the advance posts of the two armies began. The 5th Federal corps assailed the Confederate line at the intersection of the road. "The decisive moment of the battle was not at hand. Stewart moved from his position to close the gap left in it by the brigade of Jones, whose broken troops had fled and Jones himself killed. As the Federal masses poured through, his men rushed forward with a cheer, and, driving them back by the impetus of their charge, captured their guns. At the same time Ewell ordered two brigades of Rodes's division to form on the right and charge." The work of carnage went desperately on. Hundreds of Confederates lay weltering in their gore; but when the work of the day ended, the Southern army was still in possession of their improved position and advanced lines.

In the fighting next day Longstreet was severely wounded. So far the Federals had been held back on the Confederate right, and were firmly held in check. On the left General Ewell, battling desperately, held his own, and joined his line of battle with that which had been restored on the right wing. The movement was a decided success.

"In these two days of terrible battle in the Wilderness," says a Confederate historian, "our wounded, by the official reports of the surgeons, were estimated at 6000, and our killed at less than 1000. The wounds were comparatively slight, owing to

the protection afforded by the trees and the absence of artillery, which could not be used in consequence of the dense forest. The Federal loss was out of all proportion to what it had inflicted: 269 officers and 3019 men killed, 1017 officers and 18,261 men wounded, and 177 officers and 6667 men missing—making an aggregate of 27,310.''

General Ewell next came into conspicuous notice in the series of events accompanying the evacuation of Richmond. When that evacuation became on that Sunday night, April 2, 1865, a foregone conclusion, ''it was proposed to maintain order in the city by two regiments of militia; to destroy every drop of liquor in the warehouses and stores, and establish a patrol through the night. But the militia ran through the fingers of their officers, the patrols could not be found after a certain hour, and in a short time the whole city was plunged into mad confusion and indescribable horrors.'' The Federal force, on the north side of the James River, consisted of three divisions under the command of General Weitzel, while General Ewell covered this approach to the capital with a force about 4000 strong. General Ewell silently withdrew his forces from Weitzel's front, their rear guard traversing the city before daybreak. Later in the day the Federal general found that Richmond was at his mercy. For the people of the doomed city it had been a hideous night. Disorder, pillage, revelry ran riot, while the gutters ran with a liquor freshet whose fumes filled the air. But a new horror was to commemorate the distressing scene. To General Ewell had been left the duty of blowing up the iron-clad vessels in the James River and destroying the bridges across that river. ''The *Richmond, Virginia*, and an iron ram were blown to the winds; the shipping at the wharves was fired; and the three bridges that spanned the river were wrapped in flames as soon as the last troops had traversed them. The work of destruction might well have ended here; but General Ewell, obeying the letter of his instructions, had issued orders to fire the four principal tobacco warehouses of the city—one of them, the Shockoe warehouse, situated near the centre of the city, side by side with the Gallego flour mills,

just in a position and circumstances from which a conflagration might extend to the whole business portion of Richmond. ' In vain Mayor Mayo and a committee of citizens had remonstrated against this reckless military order. General Ewell seemed to think that he had no alternative, and the warehouses were fired. A wildly widening conflagration followed. When morning broke on the scene of devastation, the fire was devouring whole blocks of buildings. It leaped from street to street, and raged with unchecked fury. Weitzel and his troops meantime had arrived on the scene and planted their guidons on the capitol. Late in the evening the fire had burned itself out, and it had destroyed the most important part of Richmond

Jefferson Davis had gone on to Danville, and from thence issued the last of his many sanguine proclamations. It gave new color to the evacuation of Richmond; but ''the hopeful and ingenious minds which constructed the new theory of Confederate defense therein enunciated had failed to take in a most important element in the consideration. That element was the moral effect of the fall of the Confederacy's capital.'' In the retreat and surrender of General Lee's army, which quickly followed the evacuation of Richmond, Ewell and Elzey, with the Richmond garrison and other troops, took the road nearest the James River. During the day following the evacuation of Petersburg the Confederates made good progress; but after the junction of Gordon's corps with Mahone and Ewell, ''with thirty miles of wagons, containing the special plunder of the Richmond departments,'' they went at a rate so slow that it was apparent that an enterprising enemy would have little trouble in overtaking them.

On the 6th, the Federals having changed the order of pursuit, Sheridan with his cavalry struck the Confederate line of retreat near Sailor's Creek. Ewell's corps of 4200 men was called upon to support Pickett, who, with his division of 800 men, were being sorely pressed by Sheridan. The Federal force advanced with spirit, and, without being able to assist Pickett, Ewell with his small force was compelled to hold his ground against overwhelming numbers. ''The enemy's forces,'' wrote an eye-witness, "confident and exulting over the prospect of success, were hurled upon the brave men of Ewell's corps. It, however, with an exhibition of valor never surpassed, continued to stand at bay. At last the unequal contest was ended; General Ewell was captured, and then the greater portion of his command surrendered."

After the war General Ewell retired to private life. General Grant says in his "Memoirs": "Here (at Farmville) I met Dr. Smith, a Virginian and an officer of the regular army, who told me that in a conversation with General Ewell, a relative of his (who had just been made prisoner), Ewell had said that when we had got across the James River he knew their cause was lost, and it was the duty of their authorities to make the best terms they could while they still had a right to claim concessions. . . . He said further, that for every man that was killed after this in the war somebody is responsible, and it would be but very better than murder. He was not sure Lee would consent to surrender his army without being able to consult with the President, but he hoped he would."

General Ewell died in Springfield, Tenn., January 25, 1872.

Officer Parker, of the U.S. Gunboat *Essex*, hoisting the Federal ensign on the State Capitol, Baton Rouge, Louisiana, on its occupancy by General Cuvier Grover's troops.

Unloading military stores for the Federal troops from the transport *North Star*, over the Mississippi steamer *Iberville*, on the levee, Baton Rouge.

THE SIEGE OF VICKSBURG
May 18 – July 4, 1863
"Our place of meeting was on the hillside, a few hundred yards from the enemy's lines, near a stunted oak tree. Pemberton and I had served together in Mexico, and greeted each other as old acquaintances. He soon asked what terms I proposed giving his army. My answer was the same as proposed in my letter to you, unconditional surrender."

Ulysses S. Grant, General, U.S.A.

NATHAN BEDFORD FORREST, C.S.A., 1821–1877

While to the soldier the value of an education is almost incalculable, bravery and a record of gallant deeds are not always fostered by the training of the mind. To rise from poverty and obscurity to the heights of fame and fortune is creditable under whatever circumstances, but it becomes a double credit to the man who can make the ascent without the advantages which education brings. Two-fold glory should therefore attach itself to the name of Nathan Bedford Forrest, for few of the many gallant men whose names grace the roll of honor of the Confederacy rose from such obscure birth to fortune, and subsequently to renown.

The South did not possess its present unequaled educational institutions when, in Bedford County, Tennessee, on July 13, 1821, the subject of this sketch was born. His entrance into this world was hardly conspicuous, except for the pleasure which it gave to the proud parents. But even they realized only too well how impossible it was for them to raise their children as perhaps they might have wished. The neighborhood boasted of no privileges for training the mind; it was as barren of school-houses as it was of dwellings. Nathan was therefore brought up amid surroundings not calculated to attract the boy of the 19th century. It was perhaps the lack of all advantages which governed the course of the parents when, after a few years after the birth of Nathan, they decided to pack up their belongings and remove to Mississippi. Here the improvement was not found to be material in any sense of the word, but civilization seemed at least to be more complete,

and the Forrest home was once more reared. Misfortune, however, followed the journeyings of the family; for it was but a brief time after the removal that the head of the little flock fell a victim to a serious illness and died. It was a heavy blow to the household, and its guidance now rested almost solely upon the shoulders of the boy Nathan. Young as he was, the lad seemed to feel the responsibility, and resolutions and ambitions doubtless crowded themselves upon the youthful mind. He must now steer the domestic ship: the only question was, How? But ready hands do not seek long for something to do, and even in the unproductive fields wherein young Forrest's boyhood had been cast the lad found opportunities. True, they were not brilliantly attractive, but they at least held out the prospect of some financial returns. But it was a hard struggle—the struggle for bread against the most adverse circumstances—and up to the time of his 21st year young Forrest made but little headway. But now young manhood had come to him, and with it its never-failing ambitions and energies. His first step was to remove the family to a spot where his labors would be more productive, and in 1842 the homestead was again broken up and reared on new soil in the town of Hernando, Mississippi. Hernando was a thriving little village, with some prospects for an energetic young man, equipped with full physical powers and a willingness to begin at almost anything. After a year he saw signs of establishment, and he went into the planting trade. In this he proved successful, and light broke for the first time in the dark clouds of

Brigadier General,
  July, 1862
Major General,
  December, 1863
Lieutenant General,
  February, 1865

COMMANDED
Confederate Cavalry,
  Nashville campaign, 1862

NATHAN B. FORREST

BATTLES:
Fort Donelson
Nashville
Huntsville
Shiloh
Iuka
Murfreesboro
Parker's Cross Roads
Chickamauga
Oklona
Fort Pillow
Brice's Cross Roads
Tupelo
Memphis
Gainesville
Selma

his life. He began in a small way, but soon doubled his capital, and in a little while it increased still more. In five years he was as far as he hoped to be in ten. After ten years of life in Hernando, and having succeeded as well as the resources of a small town would allow, he removed to Tennessee and settled in Memphis, becoming a real estate broker and dealer in slaves. Having saved some capital, he was enabled to start on a comfortably good scale. Success came slow at first, but it came, and finally in generous measure. Fortune was now repaying the man for the hardships of his boyhood, and when the Civil War broke out he was the possessor of a handsome fortune.

He was a loyal believer in the doctrines of the Confederacy, and when war was proclaimed he did not hesitate to offer his services. Early in 1861 found him enlisted in the Tennessee mounted rifles, with a determination to fight his way upward into the realms of fame. He had always been a close friend of Governor Harris, and when the State's executive saw Forrest enlisted he sent him a request that he raise and equip a regiment of cavalry. This he did, and for his adaptness in the work he was made lieutenant-colonel. In October he moved with his men to Fort Donelson, where he remained until the approach of General Grant. He participated actively in the defense of the fort, but his foresight quickly told him that the Union forces were too great, and before the flag of truce was sent he arranged a successful escape of all his men and himself. He then started out upon an extended raiding excursion, visiting Nashville, Huntsville and Iuka.

His next participation in any fighting was at the battle of Shiloh. In the following June another promotion came to him, and he was assigned to a more important command—that of the cavalry at Chattanooga. His first active work with this new command was in the attack on Murfreesboro on July 13, 1862. In this he showed a daring, pluck and bravery that attracted the attention of his superiors. By several dexterous movements of his men, he showed a wonderful capability in the art of war tactics, and he greatly annoyed the Union forces by

his tricky and stealthy methods. On July 21 he was made brigadier-general, and the promotion inspired within him new hopes and determinations.

All this while he was constantly forwarding dispatches and documents to headquarters which were simply marvelous examples of inaccurate spelling and the most reckless grammar. In the case of some decipherment was almost impossible, yet their contents were always ascertained, even though some time was required in special cases.

The following September found him in command at Murfreesboro, and in the following December he was engaged at Parker's Cross Roads. During the next few months following these participations, Forrest's career was marked with but few important episodes. In the little skirmishes to which he was called he always showed bravery and quickness of dispatch. His next battle of moment was on the 19th and 20th of September, 1863, when he participated in the battle at Chickamauga, reflecting much credit upon himself and his men.

In November he was transferred to Northern Mississippi to await orders. For a month he rested, when there came to him at a most unexpected moment the promotion to major-general, with an assignment to the command of Forrest's Cavalry Department. When the idea of storming Fort Pillow was conceived, in April, 1864, General Forrest was placed in command of the attacking Confederate forces. In this encounter a curious incident in Forrest's life occurred. After a heavy storming of the fort by Forrest's forces, the signal for negotiations of surrender was shown by the fortifications, and the firing ceased. While the negotiations, however, were in progress, Forrest conceived the project of moving his forces to a point of attack which it would be impossible to attain in any other way. This he thought would be an advantage in case the negotiations for the surrender of the fort proved unsuccessful. When the move was discovered by Major Bradford, commander of the fort, he positively refused to surrender, although fully realizing that Forrest's position was a dangerous one to the fortifications. General Forrest afterwards explained that he had a right

Gallant Charge of the Sixth U.S. Cavalry, under General Alfred Pleasonton, upon the Confederate Cavalry commanded by General J. E. B. Stuart, at Brandy Station, Virginia, June 9, 1863.

to move his forces wherever he chose, and gain whatever advantage he could, so long as the flag of the fort had not been hauled down as a token of surrender. Upon the commander's refusal to surrender, the assault of the Confederate forces was renewed, with the result of a signal victory, wherein General Forrest had taken no small part. The garrison, consisting mainly of colored troops, were given no quarter by Forrest's men, who had fought with all the ardor and daring bravery of their commander.

General Forrest's next move was seemingly to become as annoying as was possible to the Union forces, and during the operations of Generals Hood and Thomas in Tennessee he proved a source of the most irritating annoyance.

In February, 1865, he was promoted to the rank of lieutenant-general. But he was destined to be at last conquered, and on April 2, 1865, he was badly routed by General James H. Wilson, meeting with heavy losses on the part of his men, and barely escaping with his own life. His great courage, however, never failed him even in this moment, when defeat seemed so certain. Surrender stared him in the face, but he refused to meet it. "I will rather run," was his remark, and he retreated to Gainesville; but here surrender was inevitable, and on May 9, after holding out to the last, he delivered over his sword to the Union forces.

Much amusement is still occasioned by the originals of General Forrest's remarkable war documents, which are yet in existence. Their orthography and phraseology are both wonderful. For example, in his dispatch announcing the fall of Fort Pillow, he wrote: "We busted the fort at ninerclock and skated the nigers. The men is still a cillanem in the woods." Accounting for some prisoners, he wrote in another report: "Them as was cotch with spuns and brestpins and sich was cilled, and the rest of the lot was payrold and tolled to git."

At the close of the war he entered into commercial life and was elected to fill the presidency of the Selma, Marion and Memphis Railroad. He had always been interested in railroading, and he became an intelligent student of the railroad system of America and the world. But confinement proved too much for the soldier of the battle-field, and, rather than lose his health, he resigned his position in 1874.

He retired to private life, and enjoyed the peace and quiet which his struggles had earned for him. But his retirement lasted but for a short period, and on October 29, 1877, he died, respected by the community in which he lived, and loved by all who knew him intimately. General Forrest never entered politics save in one instance, when, on July 4, 1868, he was sent as a delegate from Tennessee to the Democratic National Convention at its session in New York City.

THE BATTLE OF GETTYSBURG
July 1 – 3, 1863
"At 1 P.M. a signal gun was fired, and 115 guns opened on Hancock's command. The object of this terrific cannonade was to prepare the way for Pickett's charge. Gen. Hunt, chief of Union artillery, immediately posted 80 guns on Round Top to answer the fire. At 3 P.M. Gen. Hunt ordered 'cease firing,' to retain ammunition for close quarters. Pickett at once gave the order for his famous charge, in column a mile and a half long, and numbering 17,000 men. They were opened on by grape and canister at close quarters. Two-thirds of Pickett's command were killed, wounded or captured, and every officer except one fell."

Abner Doubleday, Brevet Major General, U.S.A.

Siege of Vicksburg.

Siege of Vicksburg.—As soon as General Ulysses S. Grant deemed his line of entrenchments strong enough to guard against all possibility of a sortie, he assigned to General William T. Sherman the duty of watching the movements of General Joseph E. Johnston, who was reported to have collected a large army at Jackson, for the purpose of attacking the Federals' rear and raising the siege of Vicksburg. Grant had made preparations subsequently for another and more extended assault, to take place on the 6th of July, but at about half-past seven o'clock, on the morning of the 3rd, a flag of truce was seen approaching the position held by General Stephen G. Burbridge. This was accompanied by General John C. Brown and Colonel Montgomery, of Pemberton's staff, who were the bearers of a letter to General Grant, asking terms for the capitulation of Vicksburg. At General Brown's request, Grant appointed three o'clock as the hour for meeting General John C. Pemberton, and at the designated time the latter appeared, in company with General Brown and Colonel Montgomery. General Grant stood at the meeting place, under an oak, close by a fruit orchard, about halfway between the fronts of the two contending forces, attended by his staff and Generals McPherson, Logan, Ord, and A. S. Smith. The two commanders shook hands, and after a few moments held a private conference, whereat Grant promised to send his proposition in writing the same day, which proposition was accepted by General Pemberton, who surrendered the city of Vicksburg, public stores, etc. at 8 a.m., July 4, 1863.

The surrender of Vicksburg included 27,000 officers and men as prisoners; 128 pieces of artillery; 80 siege guns; arms and ammunition for fully 60,000 men.

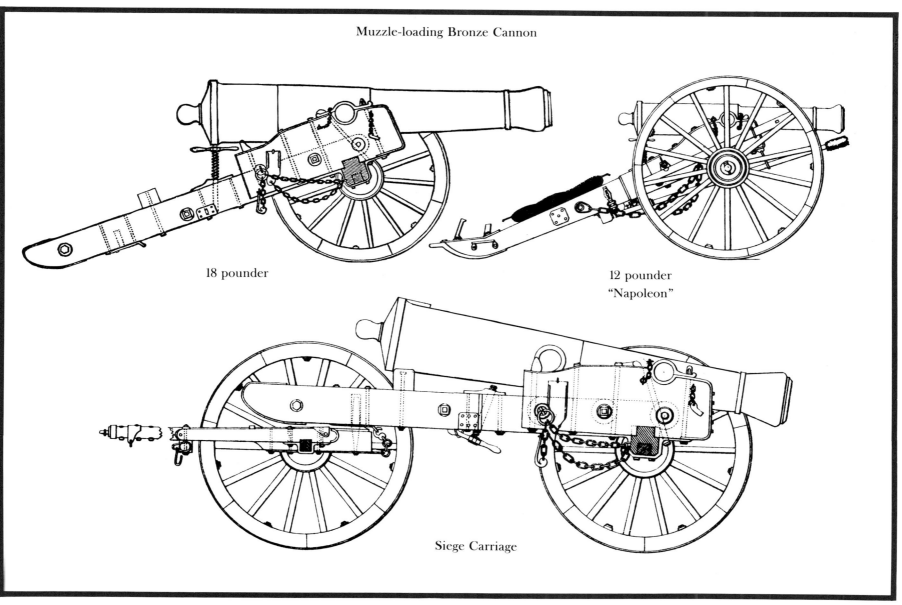

Muzzle-loading Bronze Cannon

18 pounder

12 pounder
"Napoleon"

Siege Carriage

FIELD ARTILLERY

THE STORMING OF FORT WAGNER
July 18, 1863

JOHN BROWN GORDON, C.S.A.,1832–1904

The present Governor of Georgia was born in Upson County, Georgia, on February 6, 1832. He was educated at the university of his State, studied law and was admitted to the bar. He practised his profession for only a short time, and when the War of Secession began he entered the Confederate army as a captain of infantry, and rose successively to the rank of lieutenant-general. We obtain glimpses of his dash and *elan* all through the war. During the thirty days' struggle from the Wilderness to Cold Harbor there were few more active combatants than he.

Fighting in Ewell's corps on May 6, 1864, Gordon's brigade "crushed through the enemy's first lines, and captured as they went forward a whole regiment—men, offices and colors. Driving on furiously, he struck back the Federal front in confusion upon its supports, and, scattering both like leaves in a storm, forced them off the field in utter rout." Towards twilight of the same day Brigadier-general Gordon attacked the Federal left, captured General Seymour and a large portion of his brigade, and excited a panic which put Grant's whole army on the verge of rout. "Brigade after brigade," writes an on-looker, "fled from the Federal works, and attempting, one after another, to wheel around into line in order to check the advance, was borne back under the rapidity of Gordon's movement. The woods in front were alive with masses of men struggling to escape with life. Gordon swept all before him for a distance of two miles; but the forest through which he advanced was so dense with undergrowth that by nightfall he had

become separated from his supports. He paused before he had completed a movement that came near completely routing the entire Federal right. The enterprise, notwithstanding its incompleteness, was crowned with brilliant success. The Confederate loss in that service numbered in killed and wounded but 27, while on the enemy's side Generals Shaler and Seymour, with the greater part of their commands, were taken prisoners, and the entire 6th corps of the Army of the Potomac had been broken up with panic."

After the Confederate artillery had been withdrawn on the night of May 11, General Johnston discovered that the enemy was concentrating on his front. The men in the trenches were kept alert all night, and when at dawn on the morning of the 12th a dense column of Federals emerged from the pines and rushed to the attack, they came on, to use General Johnston's words, "in great disorder, with a narrow front, but extending back as far as I could see." In the onward rush General Johnston himself, 20 pieces of artillery and 2800 men—almost his entire division—were captured. General Gordon's division was in reserve, and, under orders to support any part of the line about the salient, hastened to throw it in front of the advancing Federal column. As the division was about to charge, General Lee rode up and joined General Gordon, evidently intending to go forward with him. Gordon remonstrated, and the men, seeing his intention, cried out: "General Lee to the rear!" which was taken up all along the line. The two moving lines met in rear of the captured woods,

University of Georgia

Brigadier General, 1862
Major General, 1864
Lieutenant General, 1865

and after a fierce struggle the Federals were forced back to the base of the salient. But Gordon's division did not cover their whole front. On the left, where Rodes's division had connected with Johnston's, the attack was still pressed with great determination. Three brigades from Hill's corps were ordered up. Perrin's, which was the first to arrive, rushed forward through a fearful fire and recovered a part of the line on Gordon's left. All day long and far into the night the battle raged with unceasing fury in the space covered by the salient and the adjacent works. Every attempt to advance on either side was met and repelled from the other. The hostile battleflags waved over different portions of the same works, while the men fought like fiends for their possession. It was, as one of the "Rebs" remarked, "War to the knife, and the knife to the hilt."

While the battle was raging at the salient, a portion of General Gordon's division was busily engaged in constructing a new and shorter line of intrenchments in rear of the old one, to which Ewell's corps retired before daylight on the 13th. The five days of comparative rest that followed the terrible battle of Spotsylvania were never more welcome to the wearied Confederate soldiers, who had been marching and fighting since the 4th of May almost without intermission. "Their comfort," writes a Confederate general, "was materially enhanced by the supply of coffee, sugar and other luxuries to which they had long been strangers, obtained from the haversacks of the enemy who had been killed in their front."

"In the last days of March, 1865," writes a Confederate chronicler, "General Lee made his last offensive demonstration, which ended in failure, and plainly and painfully revealed the condition of his troops. He determined to try Grant's lines south of the Appomattox. The attack was immediately directed by General Gordon on the enemy's works at Hare's Hill. The project of assault was bold and its promises were large, while one success might lead to another." If Gordon's troops once got possession of a part of the Federal line, in the flush of success, with such a daring commander, they might be carried to the capture of the neighboring works. After that Lee might even venture on the great enterprise of getting possession of Grant's military road, and cutting his entire right from its base at City Point and from the army north of the James.

The assault of March 25 was made two miles south of the Appomattox and just to the left of the Crater. Massing two divisions, General Gordon in the early light of the morning dashed on the Federal works. "The enemy was surprised," writes a Confederate historian; "the sharpshooters of Grimes's division, composing the advance, succeeded in driving the Federal troops from their works, and the Confederates occupied their breastworks for a distance of a quarter of a mile, with comparatively slight loss, and with the loss to the enemy of one principal fort (Steadman) and some 500 prisoners. Had this advantage been utilized, there is no telling the result; but the troops could not be induced to leave the breastworks they had taken from the enemy, and to advance beyond them and seize the crest in rear of the line they had occupied. They hugged the works in disorder until the enemy recovered from its surprise; and soon the artillery in the forts to the right and left began their murderous fire on them. When fresh troops were brought up by the enemy, their advance was almost unresisted, and an easy recapture of the fort was obtained, the Confederates retiring under a severe fire into their own works. Nearly 2000 men took shelter under the breastworks they had captured, and surrendered when the enemy advanced, and the result was a Confederate loss much greater than that of the foe. This affair demonstrated to all that the day of offensive movements on the part of the Confederates was gone."

A Federal eye-witness of this affray depicts the trap in which General Gordon found himself when his daring onslaught had so disastrously miscarried: "It was now no longer a question of forging ahead for Gordon, the dashing leader of the sortie, but of getting back out of the net into which he had plunged in the darkness. A cordon of fortified batteries commanded all the ground whereon his ranks were spread, and our artillery reserves stationed between the main batteries created an unbroken chain of cannon, barring him from the railway. Supporting these guns was a solid line of infantry just gathered hastily from the left, and covering every line of advance. The way of retreat was back over the ridge before Steadman. This was swept by two withering fires, for Fort Haskell commanded the southern slope of the ridge and McGilvery the northern. With either slope uncovered, the retreat would be comparatively easy and safe for Gordon, and the Haskell battery was the one at once able to effect the severest injury to his retreating ranks. . . . The whole mind sickens at the memory of it, for Gordon and his men were not fighting, but struggling between death and home."

General Gordon, during an interview had with him in 1878 by the writer of the magazine article from which the foregoing is extracted, stated that "his purpose in making this assault had been 'to roll up the Union line' from left to right, beginning with Fort Haskell, and as soon as he saw that Haskell could not be silenced he determined to withdraw. He did not do this immediately, because he required Lee's sanction. The Union counter-assault, as it had been called, did not expel him nor hasten his movement, but simply destroyed and captured such of his command as had not retreated. Henry W. Grady, an intimate friend and companion of the general, who was present at the interview, subsequently stated that General Gordon always gave this version of the fight, and desired it to stand so in history."

Had this battle happened at a period earlier than the wind-up of the war, it would have found a more prominent place in history. Fort Haskell was the size of an ocean steamer's deck, and one may well imagine that scores of cannon and hundreds of rifles playing upon such a space for the greater part of three hours would make it a hot spot.

On the night of April 1, 1865, General Grant celebrated the victory of Five Forks, and performed the prelude of what was yet to come by a fierce and continuous bombardment along his lines in front of Petersburg. As dawn broke next morning, he prepared for the final attack, which was made in double column at various points on the Confederate line. The most deter-mined effort was made on Gordon's lines, and here the enemy succeeded in taking a portion of the breastworks near the Appomattox. But they could not use the advantage which they had struggled so hard to obtain, because Gordon's men held an inner cordon of works, and the position which the Federals had taken exposed them to a raking fire of artillery. In other parts of the field, however, important advantages were gained by the Union troops. Finally Fort Gregg was taken, and with it the Confederate army was cut in two.

On leaving Petersburg, Gordon's troops took the river road. His division formed the rear guard of Lee's retreating army, and on reaching Sailor's Creek, and whilst deploying his troops into line of battle, the Confederate commander-in-chief discovered that "Gordon had taken another road, following after the wagon train, and that the Federal forces in his rear occupied high ground and were opening upon his troops a rapid and deadly fire of artillery."

The retreat of what remained of the Confederate army was continued, Gordon's troops at the High Bridge going into bivouac on the opposite side of the river from Longstreet's command. At early dawn the Federals made an attack on Gordon at the bridge, and on Longstreet on the hills near Farmville. Firing the bridge, and leaving one brigade to check the enemy, the remainder of Gordon's corps took the railroad track to Farmville, leaving the brigade skirmishing sharply. On the high hills on the upper side of the Appomattox, just beyond Farmville, it appeared as if the Confederates intended to give battle. The artillery was placed in position and lines of infantry were formed; but it was only done to cover the movement of the wagons as the army took up its line of retreat.

During all day of the 7th the Confederate army marched without molestation in the rear. Occasionally the enemy's cavalry would dash down on the wagon train, kill a few horses, frighten the drivers and quartermasters, and then scamper away. Lee's army dwindled down to 8000 armed men, and he was in a position from which it was impossible to extricate his command without a battle, which it was no longer capable of

Confederate Bullet Mold
Augusta Arsenal, Georgia

fighting. General Gordon was thrown out with about 2000 men in front; the wreck of Longstreet's command covered the rear. Such was the condition and disposition of General Lee's army when Gordon attempted the last desperate task of cutting himself through Sheridan's lines. The Confederate cavalry was drawn up in mass in the village of Appomattox Court-house. The fields, gardens and streets were strewn with troops bivouacking in the line of battle. In the early light of morning Gordon's troops marched through and to the west of the village. Dispositions were made for attack, and about 10 a.m. Gordon's line was ordered forward. Success seemed to follow his initiatory movement, but before long Gordon sent word to General Lee that the enemy was driving him back. Just as his divisions had formed anew to resist a flank movement of Sheridan, a flag of truce appeared, and the action suddenly ceased.

General Gordon was the Democratic candidate for Governor of Georgia in 1868; but, though his election was claimed by his party, his opponent, Rufus B. Bullock, secured the office. He was a member of the National Democratic Conventions of 1868 and 1872; and in January, 1873, was elected to the United States Senate. He was re-elected in 1879, but resigned his seat in 1880. In 1886 he was elected Governor of Georgia.

(General Gordon died on January 9, 1904.)

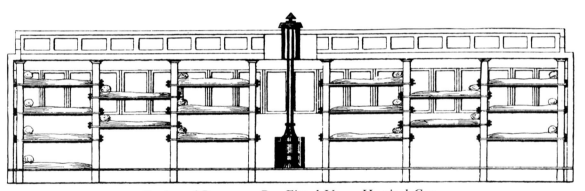

Section of Passenger Car Fitted Up as Hospital Car

WADE HAMPTON, C.S.A.,1818–1902

This distinguished soldier of the Confederacy was a son of the second Wade Hampton, and was born in Columbia, S.C., in 1818. His daring was proverbial and his powers of endurance remarkable. His tone of character was heroic and his impulses chivalrous. He graduated at the University of South Carolina, and afterward studied law. Under his father's training he became a good horseman and a famous hunter. He served in the legislature of South Carolina in early life, but his political views were those of a national rather than a secession Democrat, and were not popular in his State. His speech against the reopening of the slave trade was pronounced by Horace Greeley in the *New York Tribune* "a masterpiece of logic, directed by the noblest sentiments of the Christian and patriot."

His earlier life was devoted to his plantation interests in South Carolina and Mississippi.

When the Civil War began, Hampton first enlisted as a private, but soon raised a command of infantry, cavalry and artillery, which was known as "Hampton's Legion." It won distinction wherever it appeared in the war. At Bull Run 600 of his infantry held for some time the Warrenton road against Keyes's corps, and were sustaining General Bee when Jackson came to their aid. A colonel of artillery, writing of the first Bull Run battle, says: "To reach my horse, after General Jackson had given me permission to rejoin my battery, I had to pass the infantry of Hampton's Legion, who were lying down in supporting distance of our artillery, then in full play. (Colonel

Wade Hampton's 'Legion' at that time, as I remember, consisted of a regiment of infantry, a battalion of cavalry and a four-gun battery of horse artillery.) Whilst untying my horse a shell exploded in the midst of Hampton's infantry, killing several and stampeding fifteen or twenty nearest the spot. I tried to rally them, but one huge fellow, musket in hand, with bayonet fixed, had started on a run. I threw myself in his front with drawn sword, and threatened to cut him down; whereupon he made a lunge at me. I threw up my left arm to ward off the blow, but the bayonet-point ran under the wrist-band of my red flannel shirt, and raked the skin of my arm from wrist to shoulder."

In the Peninsular campaign the fire-eaters of the Legion were again distinguished, and at Seven Pines lost half their number, while Hampton himself was severely wounded in the foot. Soon after he was made brigadier-general of cavalry, and with his Legion assigned to "Jeb" Stuart's command. He was frequently selected for detached service by General Stuart, in which he was uncommonly successful. Hampton was constantly on the most advanced line, or skirmishers, cheering them on—the most conspicuous mark to the enemy. He used to laugh when warned against such exposure of himself, and said he was not afraid of any ball aimed at him.

In the Maryland and Peninsular campaigns of 1862–63 Hampton was actively engaged; and he distinguished himself at Gettysburg, receiving three wounds. It is said that 21 out of 23 field-officers and more than half the men in Hampton's

South Carolina College, 1836

Brigadier General, June, 1862
Major General, August, 1863
Lieutenant General, August, 1864

COMMANDED
Confederate Cavalry, 1864

command were killed or wounded in this battle.

Hampton was made major-general August 3, 1863, and in 1864, after several days' fighting, he gave Sheridan a check at Trevillian's Station which broke up a plan of campaign that included a junction with Hunter and the capture of Lynchburg. In 23 days he captured over 3000 prisoners and much material of war, with a loss of 719 men. General Hampton was made commander of Lee's cavalry in August, 1864, with the rank of lieutenant-general. In September of the same year he struck the rear of the Federal army at City Point, bringing away 400 prisoners and 2486 beeves. Soon after in another action he captured 500 prisoners. In one of these attacks he lost his son in battle.

Subsequently Hampton was detached to take command of General Joe Johnston's cavalry, and did what he could to arrest the advance of Sherman's army northward from Savannah in the spring of 1865. It had been hoped to the last by the people of Columbia, S.C., that the town would be vigorously defended and made a point of decisive contest in Sherman's devastating pathway. General Hardee failed to grasp the situation, believing that Charleston was the objective point of the Federal commander's attack. In this dubiety of perception and purpose there was no adequate force to check the onward march of the Union army. The only Confederate troops which contested Sherman's advance upon Columbia consisted of General Hampton's mounted command, and, though they made a stubborn resistance, their opposition could not, of course, be more than that of severe skirmishing. Yet to the last it was hoped that Columbia might be saved. "It was asserted that the corps of Cheatham and Stewart were making forced marches, with a view to a junction with the troops under Beauregard; and such was the spirit of the Confederate troops, and *one* of the generals at least, that almost at the moment when Sherman's advance was entering the town Hampton's cavalry was in order of battle, and only awaiting the order to charge it." But the horrors of a street fight in a defenseless city, filled with women and children, were prudently avoided, and the Confederate troops were drawn off from the scene at the very hour when the Federals were entering it. The gallant and chivalrous Hampton was eager to do battle to the last. When it was proposed to display a white flag from the tower of the city hall he threatened to tear it down. "He reluctantly left the city, and so slowly that a portion of his command passed on the road to Winsboro' in sight of the advance column of the enemy, giving it the idea of a flank movement of cavalry."

Columbia was surrendered to the Federals on the morning of February 17, 1865, by the mayor, Mr. Goodwyn, who asked for the citizens "the treatment accorded by the usages of civilized warfare." Sherman promised this. "As the night approached," says a Southern historian, "perceiving that the mayor was exhausted by his labors of the day, Sherman counseled him to retire to rest, saying: 'Not a finger's breadth of your city shall be harmed, Mr. Mayor. You may lie down to sleep, satisfied that your town shall be as safe in my hands as if wholly in your own.' He added: 'It will become my duty to destroy some of the public or government buildings; but I will reserve this performance to another day. It shall be done tomorrow, provided the day be calm.' With this assurance the mayor retired." A few minutes later fire broke out in twenty distinct quarters.

"An attempt has been made," says the historian quoted above, "to relieve General Sherman of the terrible censure of having deliberately fired and destroyed Columbia, and to ascribe the calamity to accident or to carelessness, resulting from an alleged order of General Hampton to burn the cotton in the city. . . . To the imputation against General Hampton, that chivalrous officer, whose word friend or foe never had reason to dispute, has replied in a public letter: 'I deny emphatically that any cotton in Columbia was fired by my order. I deny that the citizens "set fire to thousands of bales in the streets." I deny that any cotton was set on fire when the Federal troops entered the city. . . . I pledge myself to prove that I gave a positive order by direction of General Beauregard that no cotton should be fired; that not one bale was on fire when

General Sherman's troops took possession of the city; that he promised protection to the city; and that, in spite of his solemn promise, he burned the city to the ground, deliberately, systematically and atrociously.' The facts are that Columbia was fired in twenty different places at one time; that several hours before the commencement of the fire a Federal officer had given warning at the Ursuline Convent that Columbia was doomed.''

Sherman himself in his memoirs tells the fate of Columbia in these brief and suggestive words: ''The army, having totally ruined Columbia, moved on towards Winnsboro'.''

Just at this juncture the Confederate forces were much dispersed. Hardee was moving towards Fayetteville in North Carolina; Beauregard was directing Stevenson's march to Charlotte; Cheatham, with his division from the Army of the Tennessee, had come from Augusta, and was moving towards the same point as Stevenson; while on the west side of the Congaree and Broad Rivers the cavalry under General Hampton kept in close observation of the Federal advance. With these forces General Joe Johnston formed the army with which he fought the battle of Bentonville. Writing of this battle, General Wade Hampton says: ''General Johnston realized that unless the advance of the enemy could be checked, it would only be a question of time before Sherman would effect a junction with Grant, when their united armies would overwhelm the depleted and exhausted army of Northern Virginia.''

It is hard nowadays to realize the condition of the Confederate soldiers at this period in the spring of 1865. There was death at the cannon's mouth in front of the hungry, foot-sore, shivering rebel, and starvation in his rear. Even so early as February, 1863, the money value of a day's rations for 100 soldiers, which in the first year of the war had been about $9, was at market prices $123. In the corresponding month of the following year a day's rations had no estimated market value. ''The necessaries of the life of to-day were the luxuries of that storm and stress time. With 'seed-tick' coffee and ordinary brown sugar costing fabulous sums, and almost impossible to

be obtained, it is small wonder that the unsatisfied appetite of the rebel sharpshooter, at his post far to the front, often impelled him, though at the risk of detection and death, to call a parley with the Yankee across the line—his nearest neighbor—and persuade him to a barter of the unwonted delicacies for a twist of Virginia homespun tobacco.''

With soldiers in this condition, the Confederate general, according to Wade Hampton, had two alternatives presented to him: ''One was to transport his infantry by rail rapidly to Virginia, where the reinforcements he could thus bring to General Lee might enable these two great soldiers to strike a decisive blow on Grant's left flank. The other was to throw his small force on the army confronting him, with the hope of crippling that army, if he could not defeat it. As we could hope for no reinforcements from Virginia, or indeed from any quarter, my judgment was that the first-named plan held out the best promise of success, and, if my memory serves me right, I think General Johnston mentions in his 'Narrative' that he suggested it.'' However the case may have been, that plan was not adopted, and General Johnston resorted to the other.

About twelve o'clock on the night of March 17, 1865, General Hampton received a dispatch from the commanding general, asking if he could give him information respecting the positions of the several corps of the Federal army. Johnston furthermore asked for Hampton's opinion of the practicability of attacking these corps, and when and where the attack could be made to most advantage. General Hampton replied at once, telling him that ''the 14th corps is in my immediate front; the 20th corps is on the same road five or six miles in the rear; while the other two corps are on a road some miles to the south, which runs parallel to the road my command now occupies. I suggested,'' General Hampton continues, ''that the point on which I was camped was an admirable one for the attack contemplated, and that I would delay the advance of the enemy as much as possible, so as to enable our troops to concentrate there. In a few hours a reply came from General Johnston, saying that he would move at once to the position

Confederate Belt Plate

indicated, and directing me to hold it if possible. In obedience to these orders, I moved out on the morning of the 18th to meet the enemy, with whom we skirmished until the afternoon, when I was pressed back by force of numbers."

As an illustration of the quick perception of private soldiers, during the battle of Bentonville, General Hampton tells this: "After getting the guns in position, I rode off. Turning to some of his companions, a soldier said to his fellows with a laugh: 'Old Hampton is playing a bluff game, and if he don't mind Sherman will call him.'" The battle of Bentonville was a Confederate failure.

After the war General Hampton engaged in cotton planting. He accepted from the first all the legitimate consequences of defeat—an entire submission to the law, and the civil and po-

litical equality of the Negroes—but he has steadily defended the motives and conduct of his people and their leaders In 1866, speaking of the Negroes, he said: "As a slave, he was faithful to us; as a free man, let us treat him as a friend. Deal with him frankly, justly, kindly."

In 1878 he met with an accident by which he lost a leg, but while his life was despaired of he was elected to the United States Senate, where he is still serving.

General Hampton married early in life Margaret Preston, youngest daughter of General Francis Preston. His second wife was the daughter of Senator George McDuffie, of South Carolina.

(General Hampton died on April 11, 1902.)

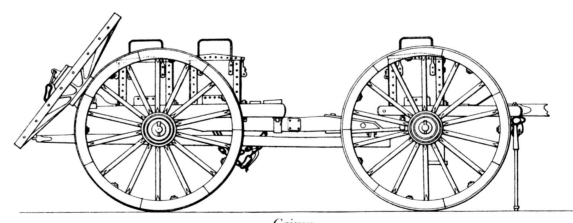

Caisson

WILLIAM JOSEPH HARDEE, C.S.A.,1815–1873

This conspicuously brave and dashing soldier was a Georgian, and was born at Savannah in that State about the year 1817. He graduated from the West Point Military Academy in 1838, and after serving in the Florida War in the 2d dragoons, he was promoted to be first lieutenant on December 3, 1839. He was so promising and zealous a soldier that he was sent by the Secretary of War to the celebrated military school of St. Maur in France. While there he was attached to the cavalry department of the French army. On his return to his native country, he was stationed for a time on the Western frontier, and appointed captain of dragoons September 18, 1844. He accompanied General Taylor across the Rio Grande in 1846, and his company was the first to engage the enemy at Curricitos, where he was overwhelmed by superior force and made prisoner. He was exchanged in time to take part in the siege of Monterey, after which he was promoted major for gallantry. At the end of the war he was breveted lieutenant-colonel, and a little later was appointed major in the 2d cavalry, of which Albert Sidney Johnston was colonel and Robert E. Lee lieutenant-colonel.

About this time he received instructions from the War Department to prepare a system of tactics for the use of infantry. He completed that work in 1856. According to competent military authorities, Hardee's *Tactics* is a work "eclectic rather than original, and drawn mainly from French sources." When his work was in the press, Hardee was ordered to West Point as commandant of cadets, with the local rank of lieutenant-

colonel. He remained at West Point—with the exception of one year, during which he was absent in Europe—till the end of January, 1861. He then joined the Confederate army, with the rank of colonel, and was assigned to duty at Fort Morgan, Mobile.

In June, 1861, he was made brigadier-general, and sent to Arkansas under General Polk. He had been made a major-general before the battle of Shiloh, where he led the first line, composed of the 3d army corps, augmented by Gladden's brigade and Bragg's corps. He took a brilliant share in the battle of Perryville, October 8, 1862. His was the plan of battle and his was rightly the glory of the success.

After this he was transferred to Kentucky, and commanded the Confederate troops at the battle of Murfreesboro, January 1, 1863, under General Bragg. "At the break of day," says a Southern chronicler, "on the cold and cloudy morning, General Hardee gave the order to advance, and commenced the battle by a rapid and impetuous charge on McCook's position. The enemy was taken entirely by surprise; general and staff officers were not mounted, artillery horses not hitched, and infantry not formed." One of McCook's divisions, after a short but fruitless contest, to use General Rosecrans's words, was "crumbled to pieces." The Federals formed a new line of battle, and for two hours the conflict raged with horrible slaughter, and neither side receded till 5 p.m. Then the worn and decimated armies suspended operations for the night. It had been a drawn battle, but both sides claimed a victory. For

West Point, 1838

Brigadier General, June, 1861
Major General, March, 1862
Lieutenant General, January, 1863

BATTLES:
Mexican War
Shiloh
Perryville
Murfreesboro
Missionary Ridge
Atlanta campaign
Bentonville

205

his conduct during this campaign Hardee was made lieutenant-general and ranked after Longstreet.

At the battle of Missionary Ridge he commanded the Confederate right wing, and received the Federal first assault, repulsing it with great slaughter. "The attack was made by Sherman, and his bleeding columns staggered on the hill. A second attack was ordered at noon and repulsed." By and by the Confederate centre gave way, and in a few minutes a vigorous, well-fought battle became a rout and a stampede.

Subsequently, under General Joseph E. Johnston, General Hardee took a prominent part in the military operations which opposed Sherman's advance to Atlanta. When Lieutenant-generals Polk and Hood urged the commanding general to abandon his position at Kingston, and when he yielded because, as he said, "I became apprehensive that, as the commanders of two-thirds of the army thought the position untenable, the opinion would be adopted by their troops, which would make it so," Hardee was strongly opposed. "Lieutenant-general Hardee, whose ground was the least strong," writes Johnston, "was full of confidence."

In the successive stages of Sherman's victorious march he had gained the peninsula formed by the Salkahatchie and Edisto Rivers, and had now the choice of going to Augusta or Charleston. He declined both places. On February 16, 1865, his advance was drawn up on the banks of the Saluda in front of Columbia. It had been hoped to the last by the people of Columbia, says a Confederate authority, that the town would be vigorously defended, and made a point of decisive contest in Sherman's pathway. "But the old wretched excuse of want of concentration of the Confederate forces was to apply here. General Hardee was not the man to grasp the business of a large army, and he had never had his forces well in hand. The remnants of Hood's army, the corps of Cheatham and Stewart, had been brought to Augusta, to find that Sherman had given the cold shoulder to it and moved down the railroad. On the lower part of the road Hardee could not be persuaded that Charleston was not the chief object of Sherman's desires, and

so lay behind his fortifications at Branchville to protect it In this uncertainty of purpose there was no force afield sufficient to check Sherman's course."

Columbia was surrendered to the Federal forces on the morning of February 17, 1865, and subsequently sacked and burned. Sherman's onward march was decisive of the fate of Charleston. The loss of this place was a severe trial to President Davis, who had a peculiar affection for the city. Even when Beauregard directed its evacuation, so as to provide a force with which to fall upon Sherman, the President of the Confederacy wrote such a letter to General Hardee, commanding there, as led him to suspend the evacuation, and obliged Beauregard to resume command, and to imperatively direct the measure to be completed. Hardee completed the evacuation of Charleston February 17. He destroyed the cotton warehouses, arsenals, two iron-clads, and some vessels in the shipyard. But he was compelled to leave all the heavy ordnance, including 200 pieces of artillery, which could only be spiked and temporarily disabled. "A terrible incident of the evacuation was an accidental explosion of powder in the large building at the depot of the Northwestern Railroad, destroying hundreds of lives. The building was blown into the air, a whirling mass of ruins. From the depot the fire spread rapidly, and, communicating with the adjoining buildings, threatened destruction to that part of the city. Four squares—embracing the area bounded by Chapel, Alexander, Charlotte, and Washington streets—were consumed before the conflagration was subdued."

"Charleston," says a Confederate writer, "came into the enemy's possession after General Hardee's evacuation a scarred and mutilated city. It had made a heroic defense for nearly four years. For blocks not a building could be found that was exempt from the marks of shot and shell. What were once fine houses presented great gaping holes in the sides and roof, or were blackened by fire. At almost every step were to be found evidences of destruction and ruin wrought by the enemy. After a display of heroism and sacrifice unexcelled in the war, this most famous city of the South fell, not by assault or dramatic catastrophe, but in consequence of the stratagem of a march many miles away from it."

The evacuation of Charleston having been successfully accomplished, Hardee and Beauregard retired to Charlotte, whither Cheatham was making his way from Augusta to join them. It was easy for Bragg and Hoke in North Carolina also to effect a junction with these forces, swelling them, it would be supposed, to a formidable army. But this army, which appeared so imposing in the enumeration of its parts, was no match for Sherman. When the Federal campaign in South Carolina began, General Hardee had 18,000 men. He reached Cheraw with 11,000, Averysboro with about 6000. Eleven hundred State troops left him between those places by order of Governor Magrath, of South Carolina; but the balance of his great loss was due almost entirely to desertions. These figures, from an official source, show, without the aid of commentary, how low had fallen the military spirit of the Confederacy.

The traditional rebel soldier in the persimmon tree, who told his captain that he was eating the green persimmons in order to fit his mouth to the size of his rations, epitomized in his epigrammatic speech the economic conditions of the Confederate soldiers under Hardee at this period. After the war ended a monthly magazine, dedicated to perpetuating the records of the war from a Southern standpoint, and soon perishing in the vain endeavor, published a woodcut, which, with its concomitant inscription, expressed with great pith and point the extremities to which soldiers and homefolk were alike reduced. It represented two lank, lean, lantern-jawed Confederates in a blackberry patch; one of them, on his knees, the more readily to reach the palatable fruit, is looking at his comrade with a grim smile and saying: "They can't starve us, nohow, as long as blackberries last." The other responds with an even larger and more catholic faith: "Naw, sir! And not as long as thar's huckleberries, nuther. And when they're gone, come 'simmons!"

One reads with curious interest the suggestive item of news in the Virginia newspapers of January, 1865, that "Thompson Taylor, Esq., who had charge of the cooking of the New Year's dinner for the soldiers of General Lee's army, sold the surplus grease from the meats cooked to one of the railroad companies for seven dollars per pound." But in the hardest times following the evacuation of Charleston, when provisions were the scarcest, the latch to the larder of every Southern housekeeper hung out to each soldier of Hardee's army, no matter how ragged or humble. For him the best viands about the place were always prepared; and his was the high prerogative of receiving the last cup of real coffee, sweetened with the solitary remnant of sugar.

It was from such demoralized forces, such *disjecta membra*, that General Joe Johnston, who was assigned to the command of this department February 23, 1865, had to form the army with which he fought the battle of Bentonville. When General Johnston reached Bentonville, Hardee's troops had not been able to form a junction. Meantime Wade Hampton had been reconnoitring the ground, and the general commanding had issued his directions. The movements were carried out successfully, except that General Hardee had not reached his position in the centre when the Federals struck Bragg's corps. This absence of Hardee left a gap between Bragg and Stewart. About the time that Hardee's column came up a heavy attack was made on Hoke's division, and Hardee was directed to send a portion of his force to help Hoke. This movement has been regarded as a mistake, and General Johnston in his report admits as much. He says: "The enemy attacked Hoke's division vigorously . . . he therefore applied for strong reinforcements. Lieutenant-general Hardee, the head of whose column was then near, was directed most injudiciously to send his leading division to the assistance of the troops assailed."

The fighting that evening was close and bloody. General Johnston says: "The Confederates passed over 300 yards of the space between the two lines in quick time and in excellent order, and the remaining distance in double-quick, without pausing to fire until their near approach had driven the enemy

DIXIE !

THE BATTLE OF CHICKAMAUGA
September 19–20, 1863

"Thomas was the only general officer on the field. Hearing of the perilous position of Granger on the right, he gathered
his troops together from all parts of the field to reinforce him. Posting his troops on the lines designated, he, so to speak, placed his back against
a rock, and refused to be driven from the field. Here he stayed, repulsing every attack, and when the sun went down he was
still there. Well was he called the *Rock of Chickamauga*. All things considered, this battle was the hardest fought and bloodiest in the rebellion."

Henry M. Cist, Brevet Brigadier General, U.S.A.

from the shelter of their intrenchments in full retreat to their second line. After firing a few rounds, the Confederates again pressed forward, and when they were near the second intrenchment, now manned by both lines of Federal troops, Lieutenant-general Hardee, after commanding the double-quick, led the charge, and with his knightly gallantry dashed over the enemy's breastworks on horseback in front of his men. . . . Four pieces of artillery were taken; but, as we had only spare harnessed horses enough to draw off three, one was left on the field."

General Wade Hampton writes concerning Hardee's famous charge at Bentonville: "General Hardee, who assumed command when he reached the field, led this charge with his usual conspicuous gallantry; and as he returned from it successful,

his face bright with the light of battle, he turned to me and exclaimed: 'That was nip and tuck, and for a time I thought tuck had it.'" A sad incident marred General Hardee's triumph. His only son, a gallant lad of sixteen, who had joined the 8th Texas cavalry two hours before, fell in the charge led by his father.

General Hardee finally surrendered at Durham Station, North Carolina, April 26, 1865, and at the close of hostilities retired to his plantation in Alabama. He died at Hydesville, Va., November, 1873. Of him it might be justly said that

The prize he sought and won
Was the crown for duty done.

Confederate Perry Breech-Loading Percussion Carbine Caliber .52

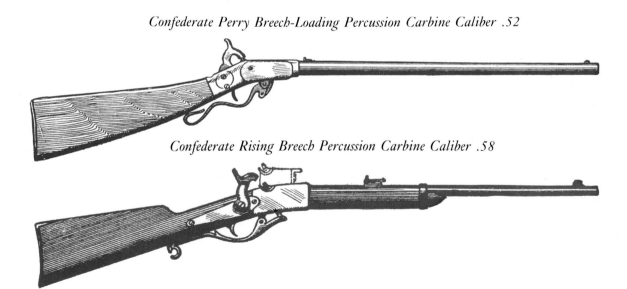

Confederate Rising Breech Percussion Carbine Caliber .58

THE BATTLE OF CHATTANOOGA
November 23, 1863

AMBROSE POWELL HILL, C.S.A., 1825–1865

It is the law of nature that services to a lost cause should be soon forgotten. However able and brilliant the service may be, and however plausible the cause may be, the soldier who has devotedly laid down his life in behalf of an unsuccessful cause has fought himself into oblivion, while the lowest private on the winning side is borne to immortality on the wings of victory. To the winners all is glory; weaknesses and errors are indulgently overlooked—some blunders are even misconstrued to their credit; while to the most valiant of the conquered small consideration is extended, and their best services avail their reputation but little. The severe handling of the record of General Lee after the close of the late Civil War instances this but too well. General Lee's services can scarcely be over-estimated. Had he been associated with the winning side in that contest, he would have stood with irreproachable honors by the side of Generals Grant and Sherman. He was the foremost soldier of the South—brave, skilful, and thoroughly versed in the science of war—while actuated by the purest and most loyal spirit of devotion to the Confederate cause; and yet, in spite of four hard years of danger and hardship, of sturdy opposition against steadily increasing odds, in spite of a remarkable display of able and efficient soldiership, he was compelled to share the fate of the hero of a lost cause, and to suffer the suspicion of the unjust. Truly

> The painful warrior, famoused for fight
> After a thousand victories, once foiled
> Is from the book of honor razed quite,
> And all forget the cause for which he toiled.

In the graveyards of the South lie many soldiers whose names should be breathed only with the accents of love and admiration; and yet they lie for the most part buried in body and in name. Could the graves give up their records, we would hear a roll call of honor which would not come short of that of their more fortunate countrymen in the North. Amongst the first on that roll would stand the name of one about whom only too little has been spoken—Ambrose Powell Hill.

General Hill was born in Culpepper County, Va., on November 9, 1825, and near the town of Petersburg, which became identified with such momentous engagements during the Civil War. During his early boyhood General Hill had often played carelessly close to the very spot upon which he fought his last battle. The boy's father, Major Thomas Hill, was a merchant, and quite a prominent and zealous politician. General Hill from the earliest boyhood showed a marked taste for active out-door life. He was fond of sports and manly exercises of all kinds, and with the advance into youth he developed a distinct leaning towards the military profession. After his school education was completed, therefore, he entered the Military Academy at West Point, and the pleasure that he derived from the smallest details of a soldier's life soon convinced him that he had not mistaken his calling.

He graduated from West Point in 1847, and almost immediately was made second lieutenant in the 1st artillery. He was ready, therefore, to enter at once into the war in Mexico, which

at that date was approaching its close. On the 9th of March previous General Scott had assembled his army at Lobos Island, and, moving against Vera Cruz, had taken the city on the 26th, together with the castle of San Juan d'Ulloa and its garrison of 5000 men. This brilliant feat had been promptly followed by a series of victories of the most decisive nature. On the 17th of April General Scott came up with Santa Anna and his army of more than 12,000 men, encamped in the strong mountain pass of Cerro Gordo. Surprising them at sunrise, General Scott had almost annihilated them, took many prisoners, and scattered the rest throughout the mountains. Jalapa was then captured, and afterwards Perote and Puebla. At the latter place Scott was compelled to wait until he received reinforcements from the government. It was not until August 7 that he was able to resume his advance, and in the meantime Santa Anna had gathered together a new army and hastened to the defense of the City of Mexico. This delay, of course, rendered a large amount of additional fighting necessary; for, had Scott been able to march direct to Mexico after his overwhelming victories at Cerro Gordo, Perote, and Puebla, he would have found the capital but weakly protected. Hill joined the army about this time, and assisted in the following engagements, which resulted in the capture of Mexico. Scott made a detour, and captured Contreras and Churubusco; and after a short armistice, during which a negotiation for peace was conducted by Commissioner Nicholas P. Trist, the attack against the city began with General Worth's brave assault and capture of Molino del Rey on the southwest. This was on September 8. On the 13th Chapultepec was stormed and carried, and on the morning of the 14th the American army entered the city and took possession of the palace.

After the close of the Mexican War Hill returned to the United States and was engaged during 1840–50 in Florida in the war against the Seminoles. On September 4, 1851, he was promoted to first lieutenant of the 1st artillery and afterward to a captaincy. In November, 1855, he was made an assistant on the coast survey, and was stationed in Washington until shortly before the opening of the Civil War.

Hill had from his earliest years been a warm sympathizer with the South, and the experience at West Point and in the field had only served to confirm him in his loyalty to the Confederacy. The association, during the Mexican and Seminole Wars and at Washington, with strong friends of the North had only intensified his Southern sentiments. It became evident to him, therefore, early in 1861 that he should soon be compelled to leave Washington for the South. He remained at his post as long as possible; but as the spring advanced national feeling ran higher, and accordingly Hill resigned on March 1, and formally adopted the cause of the Confederate States. On the secession of Virginia he was appointed colonel of the 13th regiment of Virginia volunteers and was ordered to Harper's Ferry, where General Joseph Johnston was in command. General Robert Patterson, commanding a National force, was at that time advancing from the north of the Potomac, and General Johnston withdrew his army from Harper's Ferry and took up his position at Winchester. This force of Johnston's was called the Army of the Shenandoah, and had all to do with the fate of the battle of Bull Run. When General Beauregard was attacked by the National army under General McDowell on July 3, 1861, Johnston, covering his movement with Stuart's cavalry, left Patterson behind him and rapidly moved to Beauregard's relief. This most unfortunate mistake of Patterson's turned the fate of that terrible day. General McDowell has been especially blamed for the terrible defeat, but the fault was not his. The battle had been well planned, and would have resulted quite differently had McDowell's trust in Patterson been realized. The former fully counted on the latter's checking the advance of the Army of the Shenandoah, and such was the special mission of Patterson. The excuse offered by him for his failure in executing this mission was that he was held back awaiting necessary orders from General Scott at Washington, which never reached him. However that may be, the army of Beauregard, which alone would have scarcely been equal to the well-arranged attack of McDowell, when reinforced by the Army of the Shenandoah, succeeded in utterly routing the National army. Hill shared actively in this fight, and his service was distinguished by cool courage and military skill. He was promoted to brigadier-general, a rank which he retained until the battle of Williamsburg in May, 1862, on which occasion he fought with such spirit that he was made major-general.

In the notable council of war which was held at Richmond on June 25, 1862, Hill was present, and his voice commanded a respectful hearing as coming from one who, even in the short experience of one year, had proven himself a soldier of more than common ability. His sentiments received approbation, and his opinions weighed as well with those of Generals Lee, Jackson, Longstreet and other eminent Confederate leaders who participated in that meeting.

In the seven days' battles about Richmond, Hill began the long and memorable series of engagements with the National army under McClellan by driving the latter from Meadow Bridge, thus clearing a way for Longstreet and D. H. Hill to advance. Throughout all the following engagements during the slow retreat of McClellan, Hill occupied the centre of Lee's army, and conducted the forces under him with the utmost bravery and skill, securing thereby a reputation for himself which few of his fellow-officers equaled. Hill's force bore the brunt of the fight during the whole of the campaign, and took the lead in all the offensive movements. The success of these may justly be attributed to his distinguished services in handling the troops. He was also most active in the succeeding campaign against General Pope, and at the second battle of Bull Run, July 29, and 30, 1862.

When the National troops had been compelled to surrender at Harper's Ferry on September 17, A. P. Hill remained at that place for a time, caring for the prisoners and stores; and, after making a forced march, arrived at Antietam in time to enable General Lee to hold his ground. The battle of Antietam is called a drawn battle, and it was such if only the immediate result is taken into consideration. Neither army overcame the other, or gained a decisive advantage. If we include the capture of the garrison by Hill's forces at Harper's Ferry, Lee had inflicted greater loss upon the enemy than he had himself suffered; but, on the other hand, McClellan had the upper hand in the fight at Antietam, and Lee's invasion of the Northern territory was brought to an end. This was most important, and the battle was therefore in effect a victory for the National army.

At the battle of Fredericksburg, on December 13, 1862, Hill's division formed the right of Jackson's corps, and during all that hotly contested fight Hill managed his force with notable success, and personally distinguished himself by brave conduct.

At Chancellorsville, on May 5 and 6, he occupied the centre, and took a prominent part in the brilliant flank movement that crushed Hooker's right. This engagement very nearly cost brave Hill his life. He was borne from the battle severely wounded, and was for some time in a very critical condition. For his notable gallantry during this battle he was made lieutenant-general on May 20, and was placed in command of one of the three grand corps into which the army was divided.

Recovering from his wound, he participated in the battle of Gettysburg, and during the terrible and bloody three days' fight was associated most prominently with all the movements of the Confederate forces. With the brilliant charge of Pickett and its disastrous result, the Confederate army was compelled to resign the field and retreat to Virginia, while the fate of the Southern cause was virtually settled. Gettysburg, although, like Antietam, not an occasion of decisive victory for either side, yet gave the National forces a most important advantage in the repulse of Lee. The latter was not routed, but he had failed to overthrow his adversary, and his project of invading the enemy's country was therefore at an end. "With an invading army, as with an insurrection, an indecisive action is equivalent to a defeat."

Hill's next engagement, at Bristow Station, October, 1863, was most unfortunate, as he was repelled with considerable loss. In the following June his corps and Longstreet's repelled the attack on the Weldon Railroad.

A short time after, Hill was taken sick and compelled to

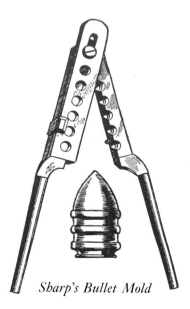

Sharp's Bullet Mold

THE BATTLE OF LOOKOUT MOUNTAIN
November 24, 1863

THE BATTLE OF MISSIONARY RIDGE
November 24 – 25, 1863

leave the army. It would have been better for him had he not recovered so rapidly, for he arose from his sick-bed to go to his death. He could not, however, tolerate the thought of lying idle on an invalid's couch while the fate of his army hung in the balance. He returned to the seat of action before his leave of absence had expired, and on Sunday morning, April 2, 1865, while engaging in the struggle for the possession of the works before Petersburg, he endeavored to cross over to Heth's division, in opposition to General Lee's wishes, and was shot from his horse by sharpshooters. General Lee ordered a charge, and the body of the brave man was recovered. It was buried first in Chesterfield County, but was removed later to Hollywood Cemetery, Richmond, Va. And so, in the last month of the war, died one of the most courageous, honorable and brilliant soldiers of the South, who fought nobly in behalf of the cause which his heart and conscience urged him to support.

The "Wheeling" or "Rosecrans" Ambulance-wagon

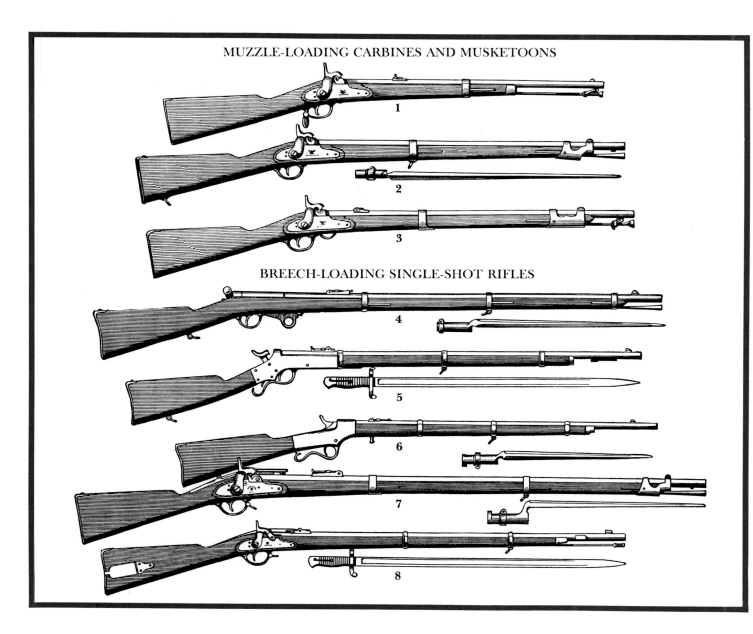

MUZZLE-LOADING CARBINES AND MUSKETOONS

BREECH-LOADING SINGLE-SHOT RIFLES

1. U.S. Springfield
   Muzzle-loading Carbine
   Model 1842 Caliber .54

2. U.S. Springfield
   Artillery Musketoon
   Model 1842 Caliber .54

3. U.S. Springfield
   Cavalry Musketoon
   Model 1842 Caliber .54

4. Greene Rifle
   Model 1857 Caliber .535

5. Sharp and Hankins Rifle
   Model 1861 Caliber .54

6. Ballard Rifle
   Model 1861 Caliber .44

7. Merrill Alteration of
   Model 1842 Musket Caliber .69

8. Merrill Patent Rifle
   Model 1858 Caliber .54

JOHN BELL HOOD, C.S.A., 1831–1879

President Davis looked upon General Hood as "a fighting general"; yet, when Sherman heard that Hood was to be his future antagonist, "he jumped to his feet, made a significant motion around his forefinger, and exclaimed: 'I know that fellow!'" Hood was a Kentuckian, born at Owenville, Bath County, June 1, 1831, and graduated at the United States Military Academy in 1853. After serving two years in California, he was transferred in 1855 to the 2d cavalry, of which Albert Sidney Johnston was colonel and Robert E. Lee lieutenant-colonel. In the fight at Devil's Run with the Comanche and Lipian Indians, in July, 1857, he was severely wounded in a hand-to-hand encounter with a savage. He was promoted first lieutenant in 1858, and was cavalry instructor at the Military Academy in 1859–60.

At the beginning of the Civil War he resigned his commission, and, entering the Confederate army, rose to the rank of colonel. After a short service on the Peninsula, he was appointed brigadier-general of the Texas brigade. He was soon after ordered back to the Peninsula, and while leading his men on foot at Gaines's Mills was shot in the body. In this battle his brigade lost more than half its number, and Hood was breveted major-general on the field. He served in both Maryland campaigns, was engaged in the second battle of Bull Run, and those of Boonesboro', Fredericksburg, and Antietam. His division of Longstreet's corps held the extreme right wing of Lee's army at Gettysburg, "which was really the key to the whole position." In the terrible fighting of the three memorable days he

lost the use of his arm. Two months later he rejoined his command, and was ordered to Tennessee to reinforce General Braxton Bragg. During the second day's fight at Chickamauga, seeing the line of his brigade waver, he rode to the front and demanded the colors. The Texans rallied and charged, and Hood at the head of the column was again shot down. His wound necessitated the loss of his right leg, and while in hospital he was offered a civil appointment, which he refused, saying: "No bomb-proof place for me; I propose to see this fight out in the field."

Six months later he returned to duty, and in the spring of 1864 commanded a corps in General Joe Johnston's army, fighting through the retreat from Dalton to Atlanta. General Johnston was not popular with the "powers" at Richmond, and he was removed on the evidently baseless charge that "he was about to give up Atlanta to the enemy." So General Hood was appointed in his place. With some reinforcements from the Southwest and levies of Georgia militia, he had now under his command an effective force of 41,000 infantry and artillery, and 10,000 cavalry. On the afternoon of July 20 Hood attacked Sherman's army, and after half an hour of deadly work inflicted a loss of about 2000 on the Federal army, while the Confederate loss was about twice as large.

Another attack was made on the 22d, which, like that of the 20th, was "one of the most reckless, massive and headlong charges of the war, where immense prices were paid for momentary successes, and the terrible recoil of numbers gave a

THE ASSAULT OF FORT SANDERS
November 29, 1863

Fort Sanders, Knoxville, Tennessee.—On the 18th of November, 1863, Confederate General James Longstreet had Knoxville completely invested. An almost incessant fire was kept up against the Federal lines till near midnight of the 28th, when a desperate attempt was made to capture Fort Sanders, commanding the Kingston Road. The Confederates were repulsed with a heavy loss. On the 4th of December, Longstreet raised the siege and fell back to Morristown.

lesson to the temerity of the Confederate commander." Concerning the situation that now arose a competent Southern critic says: "We have noticed that Sherman did not have force enough to invest Atlanta completely. This was the great point in Johnston's calculations when they were upset at Richmond; for Sherman, reduced to strategy, would have found his master in the cool and dexterous Johnston, whereas in Hood he had clearly his inferior to deal with—a commander who had indeed abundant courage, but a scant brain with which to balance it. Sherman's army was not large enough to encircle Atlanta completely without making his lines too thin and assailable. He never contemplated an assault upon its strong works. It was his great object to get possession of the Macon road, and thus sever Atlanta entirely from its supplies. It was not sufficient to cut the road by raids; it must be kept broken, and to accomplish this it was clearly necessary to plant a sufficient force south of Atlanta. While Sherman contemplated such a movement, Hood made the very mistake that would secure and facilitate it, and thrust into the hands of his adversary the opportunity he had waited for." Hood sent off his entire cavalry towards Chattanooga, to raid on the enemy's line of communication, and almost instantly Sherman's cavalry were on the Macon road. With his flanks easily protected, the Federal commander quickly followed with his main army, and Hood had now no alternative but to fight and settle the fate of Atlanta. He determined to make the attack near Jonesboro', and the corps of Lee and Hardee were moved out to attempt to dislodge the enemy from the intrenched position he held across Flint River. The attack failed, with the loss of more than 2000 men. Finding his line of supply cut off and the sum of his disasters complete, Hood resolved to abandon Atlanta. He blew up his magazines, destroyed all his supplies that he could not remove, consisting of seven locomotives and 81 cars loaded with ammunition, and left the place by the turnpike roads. He moved swiftly across the country towards Macon, whither Sherman followed; but at Lovejoy's, two miles beyond Jonesboro', he found Hood strongly intrenched, and, abandoning the pursuit, returned to Atlanta.

The fall of Atlanta was a terrible blow to the Southern Confederacy. President Davis had declared, when he removed General Joe Johnston, that "Atlanta must be held at all hazards." It was the most important manufacturing centre in the Confederacy; it was a key to a vast network of railroads, and it was the "Gate City" from the north and west to the southeast. The catastrophe moved President Davis, and mortified the vanity that had so recently proclaimed the security of Atlanta under the command of Hood. He determined to visit his "fighting general's" new lines, to plan with him a new campaign to compensate for the loss of Atlanta, and to take every possible occasion to raise the hopes and confidence of the people. "Mr. Davis," says a Southern writer, "never spoke of military matters without a certain ludicrous boastfulness, which he maintained to the last event of the war. . . . As a military commander or adviser he was weak, fanciful to excess, and much too vain to keep his own counsels. As he traveled towards Hood's lines, he made excited speeches in South Carolina and Georgia. At Macon he declared that Atlanta would be recovered, that Sherman would be brought to grief, and that this Federal commander 'would meet the fate that befell Napoleon in the retreat from Moscow.'"

Referring to this period, General Grant writes: "During this time Jefferson Davis made a speech in Macon, Ga., which was reported in the papers of the South, and soon became known to the whole country, disclosing the plans of the enemy, thus enabling General Sherman to fully meet them. He exhibited the weakness of supposing that an army that had been beaten and fearfully decimated in a vain attempt at the defensive could successfully undertake the offensive against an army that had so often defeated it."

The new offensive movement of General Hood, advised by President Davis, was soon known to the country. Not satisfied with the revelation of Macon, President Davis addressed the army and more plainly announced the direction of the new campaign. Turning to Cheatham's division of Ten-

JOHN B. HOOD

TO THE CITIZENS OF MACON.

HEAD QUARTERS.
Macon. July 30, 1864.

The enemy is now in sight of your houses. We lack force. I appeal to every man. Citizen or Refugee, who has a gun of any kind, or can get one, to report at the Court House with the least possible delay, that you may be thrown into Companies and aid in the defense of the city. A prompt response is expected from every patriot.

JOSEPH E. BROWN.

Report to Col. Cary W. Styles, who will forward an organization as rapidly as possible.

University of Georgia Library

nesseeans, he said: "Be of good cheer; for within a short while your faces will be turned homeward, and your feet pressing Tennessee soil."

On September 24 Hood commenced the new movement to pass to Sherman's rear. The Federal commander was instantly on the alert, sending his spare forces, wagons and guns to the rear under General Thomas. Sherman waited some time at Gaylesville, until he became fully asssured of the direction taken by Hood, and then abruptly prepared to abandon the pursuit, return to Atlanta, and mobilize his army for a march across the State of Georgia to the sea.

On November 20 General Hood began to move his army from Northern Alabama to Tennessee. The battle of Spring Hill followed. There was some bungling and misunderstandings among the Confederate division commanders, and nothing was absolutely gained by Hood. Much of the disaster which subsequently resulted to the Confederate commander's campaign was attributed to the fact that "some of his generals had failed him at Spring Hill." There was nothing left now for Hood but to pursue the enemy. The battle of Franklin followed. The Confederates attacked with a desperation and disregard of death such as were shown on few battle-fields of the war. The victory rested with Hood, but it was dearly purchased; his loss in killed, wounded and prisoners was 4500. Among the killed were Major-general P. R. Cleburne, Brigadier-generals John Adams, Strahl, and Granbury; while Major-general Brown, Brigadier-generals Carter, Manigault, Quarles, Cockrell, and Scott were wounded, and Brigadier-general Gordon was captured.

On December 1 General Hood advanced upon Nashville and laid siege to the town, closely investing it for a fortnight. The opinion long prevailed in the Confederacy that in this pause Hood made the cardinal mistake of the campaign. "If he had taken another course and struck boldly across the Cumberland, and settled himself in the enemy's communications, he would have forced Thomas to evacuate Nashville and fall back towards Kentucky." This was the great fear of General Grant. In

his report of the operations of 1864 Grant has written: "Before the battle of Nashville I grew very impatient over, as it appeared to me, the unnecessary delay. This impatience was increased upon learning that the enemy had sent a force of cavalry across the Cumberland into Kentucky. I feared Hood would cross his whole army and give us great trouble. After urging upon General Thomas the necessity of immediately assuming the offensive, I started West to superintend matters there in person. Reaching Washington City, I received General Thomas's dispatch announcing his attack upon the enemy, and the result as far as the battle had progressed. I was delighted. All my fears and apprehensions were dispelled."

On the night of December 14 General Thomas decided upon a plan of battle, which was to make a feint upon Hood's right flank, while he massed his main force to crush in Hood's left, which rested on the Cumberland, and where the cover of the Federal gunboats might be available. The brunt of the action did not fall till the evening, when the Confederate infantry outposts on the left flank were driven in. Under cover of the night, Hood re-formed his line, and in the morning was found in position along the Overton Hills, some two miles or so to the rear of his original line. The new position was a strong one, running along the wooded crests of closely connected hills. Heavy columns were thrown by General Thomas against Hood's left and centre. Every attack was promptly repulsed. As the day advanced the battle grew louder and louder, and the smoke thicker and thicker, until the whole valley was filled with the haze. It got to be four o'clock in the evening, and "the day was thought to be decided for the Confederates, when there occurred one of the most extraordinary incidents of the war. It is said that General Hood was about to publish a victory along his line, when Finney's Florida brigade in Bates's division, which was to the left of the Confederate centre, gave way before the skirmish line of the Federals. Instantly Bates's whole division took the panic and broke in disorder." "The hill-side in front, dotted with the boys in blue swarming up the slope, the dark background of high hills beyond, the waving

THE BATTLE OF OLUSTEE, OR OCEAN POND
February 20, 1864

flags, the smoke, the wonderful outburst of musketry, the cheers, the multitude racing for life into the valley below," writes a Federal officer—"so exciting was it all that the lookers-on instinctively clapped their hands, as at a brilliant and successful transformation scene; for in those few minutes an army was changed into a mob, and the whole structure of the rebellion in the Southwest, with all its possibilities, was utterly overthrown." Fifty pieces of artillery and nearly all of Hood's wagons were left on the field. After this fiasco he was relieved of command and succeeded by General Richard Taylor.

When the war ended he engaged in business as a commission merchant in New Orleans. During the yellow fever epidemic of 1879 his wife and eldest child died within a few hours of each other, and Hood also succumbed to the disease.

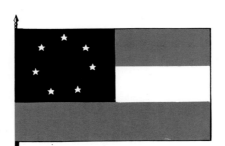

Confederate Flag
Adopted March 4, 1861

Confederate Battle Flag
Adopted 1861

Confederate Flag
Adopted May 1, 1863

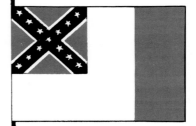

Confederate Flag
Adopted March 8, 1865

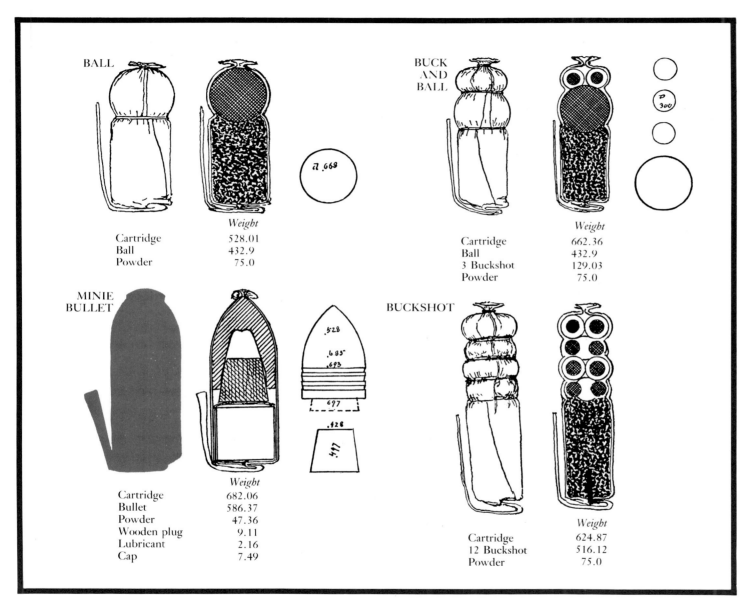

BALL

	Weight
Cartridge	528.01
Ball	432.9
Powder	75.0

BUCK AND BALL

	Weight
Cartridge	662.36
Ball	432.9
3 Buckshot	129.03
Powder	75.0

MINIE BULLET

	Weight
Cartridge	682.06
Bullet	586.37
Powder	47.36
Wooden plug	9.11
Lubricant	2.16
Cap	7.49

BUCKSHOT

	Weight
Cartridge	624.87
12 Buckshot	516.12
Powder	75.0

CIVIL WAR CARTRIDGES

THOMAS JONATHAN JACKSON, C.S.A., 1824–1863

The figure of "Stonewall" Jackson stands forth with an entirely unique individuality among Southern leaders. He was a man in many respects *sui generis*, with a leaven of something resembling Cromwell's "Roundheads" in his composition. There was the same deep devotion, the same fiery onslaught, the same unquailing courage; but the puritanical cant in his case had become a sweet, unassuming sincerity and simple faith. He came of English parentage, his great-grandfather having emigrated from London to Maryland in 1743. Here he married Elizabeth Cummins, and shortly after removed to West Virginia, where he founded a large family. His father was an engineer and died before his son's recollection. His mother died when he was ten years old, and her saintly death is said to have made a profound impression on the lad. A bachelor uncle, Cummins Jackson, assumed the responsibility of bringing him up. He was a very delicate child, but the rough life of a Virginia farm strengthened his constitution. He became a constable for the county while a mere stripling, and at the age of eighteen he was appointed cadet at West Point. The class register placed his birthplace at Clarksburg, West Virginia; the date January 21, 1824. His academical preparation had been imperfect, and he did not attain a high grade. On his graduation in 1846 he was ordered to Mexico, and became a lieutenant in Magruder's battery, taking part in General Scott's campaign from Vera Cruz to the City of Mexico. He was twice breveted for good conduct at Churubusco and Chapultepec. When the United States

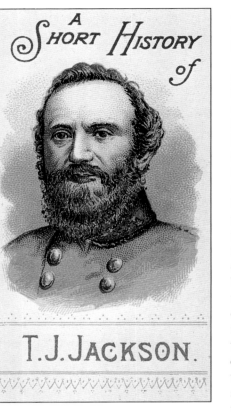

A Short History of T. J. Jackson.

Army was withdrawn from Mexico, he was for a time on duty at Fort Hamilton in New York harbor.

In 1851, on his election as professor of philosophy and artillery tactics at Virginia Military Institute, he resigned from the army. His appearance and manner at this time have been sympathetically described by the lady who subsequently became his sister-in-law: "He was of a tall, very erect figure, with a military precision about him which made us girls all account him stiff; but he was one of the most polite and courteous of men. He had a handsome, animated face, flashing blue eyes, and the most mobile of mouths. He was voted eccentric in our little professional society, because he did not walk in the same conventional grooves as other men. It was only when we came to know him with the intimacy of hourly converse that we found that much that passed under the name of eccentricity was the result of the deepest underlying principle, and compelled a respect which we dared not withhold. He was an extremely modest man, and not until he asked the hand of my sister Elinor in marriage, and the records of his army life were placed before my father (the Rev. Dr. Junkin, President of Washington College), did we know that he had so distinguished himself in the Mexican War."

Then, as ever after, Jackson weighed his lightest utterances in "the balances of the sanctuary," and so ruled his life, we are told, that "he never even inadvertently fell into the use of the common expressions involving the wish that any event or circumstance were different from what it was. To do so would, n his opinion, have been to arraign Providence."

"Don't you wish it would stop raining?" was the careless remark put to him by his wife after a week of wet weather. "Yes," was his smiling reply, "if the Maker of the weather thinks it best." "He never posted a letter," his sister-in-law tells us, "without calculating whether it would have to travel on Sunday to reach its destination, and if so he would not mail it till Monday morning." He took much interest in the improvement of slaves, and conducted a Sunday school for their benefit which continued in operation a generation after his death.

A few days after the secession of Virginia, but before any active hostilities had commenced, Jackson was ordered to Harper's Ferry to drill the military bands that were gathering there from all quarters. When Virginia joined the Confederacy a few weeks later, he was relieved by General Joseph E. Johnston, and then became commander of a brigade in Johnston's army, which rank he held at the battle of Bull Run. In that action the left of the Confederate line had been turned and the troops holding it driven back some distance. Disaster was imminent, and Johnston was hurrying up troops to support his left. Jackson's brigade was the first to get into position, and checked the progress of the Federal forces. The broken troops rallied upon his line; other reinforcements reached the threatened point; the Confederates assumed the aggressive, and wrenched a victory from the very jaws of defeat. In the crisis of the struggle General Bernard E. Bee, in rallying his men, said: "See, there is Jackson standing like a stone wall; rally on the Virginians!" Bee fell almost immediately after, but his exclamation conferred upon the Confederate brigadier-general a baptism that became immortal.

Early in March, 1862, he was at Winchester with 5000 men, while General N. P. Banks was advancing against him from the Potomac. Jackson's instructions were to detain as large a hostile force as possible in the valley without risking the destruction of his own troops. The subtlety of his strategy, the rapidity of his marches and the originality of his manœuvres

during this period have found many skilled chroniclers and admiring critics. Silent as a sphinx, brave as a lion, his unexpected disappearances and mysterious descents upon his enemy at the weakest points inspired something akin to terror in the breast of the Federal soldier. On May 25, 1862, he defeated Banks at Winchester, driving him beyond the Potomac, and effecting large captures of prisoners and stores. On June 8, at Cross Keys, he delivered battle to Fremont, and after a long and bloody conflict night found him master of the field. Leaving Ewell's brigade on the ground, he that night marched the rest of his tired but victorious army to Port Republic, reaching the bridge at dark. General Imboden arrived soon after, and found "Stonewall" Jackson in a humble room, "lying on his face across the bed, fully dressed, with sword, sash, and boots all on. The low-burnt tallow candle on the table shed a dim light, yet enough by which to see and recognize his person. 'General,' I said, 'you made a glorious winding up of your four weeks' work yesterday.'—'Yes,' he replied, 'God blessed our army again yesterday, and I hope, with His protection and blessing, we shall do still better to-day.'" Sure enough, that day he routed McDowell's column, and drove it from the battle-field, before Shields or Fremont could get there to render assistance. "The 'Stonewall' brigade never retreats; follow me!" he cried during the engagement, as he placed himself at their head.

The same authority has given us a pen-picture of Jackson on the battle-field. "The fight was just then hot enough to make him feel well. His eyes fairly blazed. He had a way of throwing up his left hand with the open palm towards the person he was addressing." Once he was asked how it was that he could keep so cool, and appear so utterly insensible to danger, in such a storm of shell and bullets. "He instantly became grave and reverential in his manner," writes Imboden, "and answered in a low tone of great earnestness: 'Captain, my religious belief teaches me to feel as safe in battle as in bed. God has fixed the time for my death. I do not concern myself about *that*, but to be always ready, no matter when it overtakes me.'"

After the action at Port Republic the Federal forces retreated to the lower Shenandoah, while "Stonewall" Jackson hastened by forced marches to Richmond, to unite with General Lee in attacking McClellan. On June 27, 1862, at Gaines's Mills, he turned the scale where Fitz-John Porter was overthrown. He also took part in the subsequent operations during McClellan's retreat. During this period there was some social hobnobbing and interchange of civilities at times between the privates of the opposing armies. One lean "Johnny" was loud in his praise of "Stonewall" Jackson, saying: "He's a general, he is. If you uns had some good general like him, I reckon you uns could lick we uns. 'Old Jack' marches we uns most to death."— "Does your general abuse you—swear at you to make you march?" inquired one of his listeners. "Swear!" replied the Confederate, "no, Ewell does the swearing; 'Stonewall' does the praying. When 'Stonewall' wants us to march, he looks at us soberly, just as if he was sorry for we uns, but couldn't help it, and says, 'Men, we've got to make a long march.'"

About the middle of July, 1862, Lee detached Jackson to Gordonsville for the purpose of looking after his old adversaries of the Shenandoah Valley, who were again gathering under General John Pope. On the 9th of August he encountered the Federal army under Pope and McDowell at Cedar Run, and drove it back in disorder. On the 25th of the same month he crossed the Rappahannock at Hinson's Mill, four miles above Waterloo Bridge. When sunset came next day he was many miles in the rear of Pope's army, moving in the direction of Washington. On the afternoon of the 26th Pope's army broke away from its strong position, to meet Jackson's daring and unexpected move. The second battle of Bull Run, fought August 30, 1862, was the result of this manœuvring and these movements. In the Maryland campaign, two weeks later, General Jackson had charge of the operations which resulted in the investment and capture of the post at Harper's Ferry, with 13,000 men and 70 cannon, while Lee held back McClellan at South Mountain and along the Antietam. "Stonewall" Jackson lost little time in contemplating his victory; when night came

he started for Shepherdstown, and on September 17 the fierce battle of Sharpsburg was fought. In this bloody contest Jackson commanded the left wing of the Confederate army, against which in succession McClellan hurled Hooker's, Mansfield's and Sumner's corps. With decimated lines Jackson maintained himself throughout the day near the old Dunker church, while one of his divisions—A. P. Hill's, which had been left at Harper's Ferry—reached the field late in the day, and defeated Burnside's corps, which was making rapid and deadly progress against the Confederate right flank.

In the spring of 1863, when Hooker's movement upon Chancellorsville was fully developed, Lee ordered Jackson's corps to move up to meet him. On the morning of May 1 Jackson met Hooker emerging from the Wilderness that surrounds Chancellorsville, and at once assumed the offensive with such fierce impetuosity that the Federal commander withdrew into the fastnesses of the Wilderness and established lines of defence. At sunrise, May 2, 1863, Jackson was in the saddle and on the march. All the livelong day he pursued his tedious and dreary way through the Wilderness. Between 8 and 9 p.m. Jackson with a small party rode forward beyond his own lines to reconnoitre. He passed the swampy depression and began the ascent of the hill towards Chancellorsville, when he came upon a line of Federal infantry lying on their arms. Fired at by one or two muskets, he turned his horse and came back toward his own line. As he rode back to the Confederate troops, just placed in position, the left company, unaware of his presence in front of them, began firing, and two of his party fell from their saddles dead. Spurring his horse across the road to his right, he was met by a second volley from the right company of Pender's North Carolina Brigade. Under this wild volley the general received three balls almost synchronously; one penetrated the palm of his right hand, and was extracted that night; a second passed circuitously round the wrist of his left arm, and escaped through the hand; a third traversed the left arm half way from shoulder to elbow, and splintered the large bone of the upper arm. His horse darted aside from the line of fire into the thick brush, and the general's forehead was badly scratched. As he lost his hold on the bridle-rein, he reeled from the saddle, and was caught in the arms of Captain Milbourne, of the Signal Corps.

"Oh, general!" cried Pender, who was soon on the scene, "I hope you are not seriously wounded. I will have to retire my troops to re-form them, they are so much broken by this fire." Jackson, rallying his strength, with firm voice said: "You must hold your ground, General Pender; you must hold your ground, sir!" This was the hero's last command on the field. General Lee received the mournful tidings late at night with profound grief. This was his manly note of sympathy:

"GENERAL: I have just received information that you were wounded. I cannot express my regret at the occurrence. Could I have directed events, I should have chosen, for the good of the country, to have been disabled in your stead. I congratulate you upon the victory which is due to your skill and energy.

R. E. LEE, GENERAL."

Pneumonia set in, with some symptoms of pleurisy, and on the quiet Sabbath afternoon of May 10, 1863, he died. A few minutes before his dissolution, he raised himself in bed and said: "No, no, no; let us pass over the river, and rest under the shade of the trees." Peace to his ashes! His remains rest under the trees.

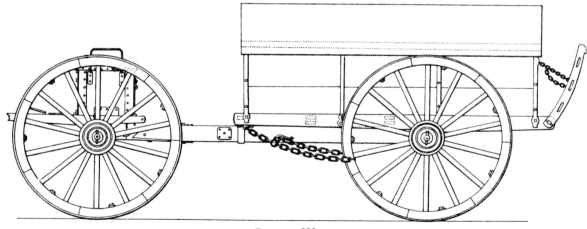

Battery Wagon

THE FORT PILLOW MASSACRE
April 12, 1864

ALBERT SIDNEY JOHNSTON, C.S.A., 1803–1862

It has been said of General Albert Sidney Johnston that "so gifted was he by nature with dignity and with power over men that he seemed born to command." At the close of the Mexican War General Zachary Taylor said of him: "He was the best soldier I ever commanded"; and when in the early part of the Confederate campaign he fell somewhat under the censure of the newspapers, he wrote to a friend: "The test of merit in my profession, with the people, is success. It is a hard rule, but I think it right." A man who was so judged by others, and who so judged himself, was manifestly no ordinary character. He came of New England stock. His father, Dr. John Johnston, was a native of Salisbury, Conn., and at the time of his son's birth was county physician of Nuson County, Kentucky, and resided at Washington. There, on February 3, 1803, Albert Sidney was born. Passing over incidents of his boyhood, we find him, in 1826, graduating from West Point, eighth in his class. Immediately afterwards he was assigned to the 2d infantry, in which he served as adjutant until his resignation, April 24, 1834. He had married Henrietta Preston, and became a widower in August, 1835. After his wife's death he was a farmer for a short time, near St. Louis, Mo., but in August, 1836, joined the Texas patriots, and devoted himself to the service of that republic. Physical characteristics and mental qualities like his naturally brought him into notice. As he rode like a Centaur, he speedily became famed for his brilliant horsemanship. Equally remarkable was he for daring— one of his feats being the slaughter of a puma with his clubbed

rifle. He had entered the Texan ranks as a private, but rapidly rose through all the grades until he was named for the command of the army. He was not permitted to asssume this position, however, until he had met his rival and competitor, General Felix Huston, in a duel, in which he received a dangerous wound.

In 1838 President Mirabeau B. Lamar made him Secretary of War, "in which office he provided for the defense of the border against Mexican invasion. During 1839 he conducted a campaign against the intruding U.S. Indians in Northern Texas, and in two battles at the Salines of the Neches expelled them from the country."

When the Mexican War began he joined the army under General Zachary Taylor on the Rio Grande. His regiment, the 1st Texas rifles, was soon disbanded, but he continued in the service, and was inspector-general of Butler's division at the battle of Monterey. All his superiors recommended him as a brigadier-general, but he was set aside by the president for political reasons, and retired to his farm.

General Johnston "remained on his plantation in poverty and neglect until, without solicitation, he was appointed a paymaster in the U.S. army by President Pierce in 1849." He served as paymaster more than five years, "making him six tours and traveling more than 4000 miles, usually on the Indian frontier of Texas. In 1851 President Pierce appointed him colonel of the 2d cavalry. Robert E. Lee was lieutenant-colonel, and George H. Thomas and William J. Hardee were the majors. General Scott designated Colonel Johnston's appointment

West Point, 1826

General, August, 1861

COMMANDED
Western Department

BATTLES:
Mexican War
Belmont
Mill Springs
Fort Henry
Fort Donelson
Shiloh (Killed)

"a god-send to the army and the country." He remained in command of his regiment and the Department of Texas until ordered in 1857 to command "the expedition to restore order among the Mormons in Utah, who were in open revolt against the National government." In his conduct of affairs there he won great reputation for energy and wisdom. By a forced march of 920 miles in 27 days he reached his little army of 1100 men, to find it lost in the defiles of the Rocky Mountains. By a remarkable exhibition of vigor and prudence, he got his men safely into winter quarters, and before spring had virtually put an end to the rebellion by diplomatic tact. Colonel Johnston was breveted brigadier-general, and was retained in command in Utah until February 29, 1860. After spending about a year in Kentucky, he sailed for California to take command of the Department of the Pacific.

General Johnston witnessed the evolution of the secession movement with unmixed grief. He was a Union man both from principle and policy, for he could not fail to see that the highest offices in the Union were open to his ambition. "He believed that the South had a grievance, but he did not believe that secession was the remedy." Still his heart pulsated in sympathy with his native State, and on April 9, 1861, he resigned his commission. "The Federal authorities," says a Southern writer, "had taken measures to arrest him, or at least to intercept his passage by sea; but he eluded their vigilance by taking the overland route. With three or four companions, increased afterwards to one hundred, on mules, he proceeded by way of Arizona, passed through Texas, and arrived in New Orleans in safety." This was early in September, and, immediately proceeding to Richmond, he was at once appointed commander of the Department of the Mississippi.

When General Johnston arrived at Nashville, September 14, 1861, he found only 21,000 available troops east of the Mississippi. General Leonidas Polk had 11,000 at Columbus, Kentucky; General Felix K. Zollicoffer had about 4000 raw levies at Cumberland Gap, and there were 4000 armed men in camps of instruction in Middle Tennessee. As Tennessee was open to an advance by the National forces, General Johnston took a bold course and occupied Bowling Green, Kentucky, with his 4000 available troops, under General Simon B. Buckner. "This was an admirably selected position," says a military authority, "with Green River along his front, and railway connection to Nashville and the whole South." This place he strongly fortified, and vainly appealed to the Confederate government for troops and arms. Grant had command of the Federal forces of the Cumberland and Tennessee Rivers, while Buell, the other Federal commander, was prepared to attack in front. General Johnston was enabled to hold the National forces in check until January, 1862, during which time a single engagement of note occurred—the battle of Belmont—in which General Grant suffered a reverse by the Confederates under Generals Polk and Pillow.

On January 19, 1862, General Crittenden, commanding the small army defending East Tennessee, contrary to his instructions, attacked the Federal forces under General G. H. Thomas at Fishing Creek. Zollicoffer's brigade pushed ahead and drove the Federals some distance through the woods. He was ascending the hill where the battle raged and sent for reinforcements; the brigade of General Carroll was ordered up; in another moment it was announced that he was killed. A sudden gloom pervaded the field and depressed the army. The repulse that then ensued was converted into a rout, and Johnston's right flank was thus turned. The battle of Fishing Creek was not remarkable for lists of killed and wounded, but it practically surrendered to the Federals the whole of Eastern Kentucky.

General Johnston wrote to his government: "To suppose, with the facilities of movement by water which the well-filled rivers of the Ohio, Cumberland and Tennessee give for active operations, that they (the Federal forces) will suspend them in Tennessee and Kentucky during the winter months, is a delusion. All the resources of the Confederacy are now needed for the defense of Tennessee."

General Grant commenced his ascent of the Tennessee River early in February, 1862, with a mixed force of gunboats and infantry columns, the latter making parallel movements along the banks. On the 4th of February the expedition arrived at Fort Henry, on the east bank of the river, near the lines of Kentucky and Tennessee. The fort was defended by General Tilghman and 2500 Confederate troops, and, as it was quite untenable, his only chance was to delay the enemy every possible moment, and retire his command to Fort Donelson. To this end it was necessary to fight the 11 guns of Fort Henry against an armament of 54 guns and an army nearly 20,000 strong. Tilghman "engaged the enemy for two hours and ten minutes, disabled one of his gunboats, and inflicted upon him a loss of 73 killed and wounded. The Confederate commander and the small garrison of 40 were taken prisoners, after having sustained a loss of about 20 killed and wounded." The fall of Fort Henry was unimportant in itself, but it opened up an avenue of danger to Fort Donelson, which General Johnston had used the greater part of his available force to defend.

Grant approached Fort Donelson with immense columns of infantry and with his fleet of gunboats under command of Commodore Foote. Meantime General Johnston had sent to its defense General Pillow, with a body of Tennessee troops; General Floyd, with his brigade of Virginians; and General Buckner, with most of the troops that had composed the central army of Kentucky. There was a great deal of misunderstanding, delay and lack of harmony among the three generals. Suffice it to say that, after three days' hard fighting and much bloodshed, "General Buckner"—to whom the two ranking generals turned over the command—"called for pen, ink, paper and a bugler, and prepared to open communication with the Federal commander. General Grant had demanded 'unconditional surrender,' and Buckner felt himself compelled to accept what he termed 'ungenerous and unchivalrous terms.'"

General Johnston had awaited the result of the engagement opposite at Nashville. At dawn of the 16th of February he received the news of a defeat. Orders were at once issued to push the army forward across the river. The city papers were issuing "extras" announcing a "glorious victory." The city was in a condition of frenzied hilarity; but "about the time the people were assembling at the churches, it was everywhere announced that "Donelson had fallen." The general said that "Nashville was utterly indefensible; that the army would pass right out of the city." He therefore retreated towards Murfreesboro, "leaving behind him a scene of panic and dismay."

By April 1, 1862, General Johnston had managed to collect at Murfreesboro an army of 17,000 men. He had now been joined by the forces under Beauregard, and his object was to defend the Valley of the Mississippi on a line of operations south of Nashville. The total effective force at his command was now some 40,000 men, or a trifle over. "General Johnston had determined to strike a sudden blow at the enemy, in position under General Grant on the west bank of the Tennessee River, before he was reinforced by General Buell. On April 5, 1862, an informal council of war was held, at which General Beauregard protested against the proposed attack and urged a retreat to Corinth. General Johnston listened and replied: "Gentlemen, we will attack at daylight." Turning to his staff officers, he said: "I would fight them if they were a million!" Beauregard twice renewed his protests, but Johnston was not to be moved.

In the early dawn of Sunday, April 6, the magnificent array moved forward. As General Johnston was mounting his horse to ride forward, he said to Beauregard: "The battle has opened. It is now too late to change our dispositions." To a soldier friend, early in the battle, he said: "We must this day conquer or perish"; and to all about him: "To-night we will water our horses in the Tennessee River."

The battle of Shiloh has been described by many competent pens. It is not necessary to rehash their efforts here; suffice it to say that about two o'clock a minie ball pierced the calf of General Johnston's right leg. He supposed it to be a flesh wound and paid no attention to it. But the ball had cut an artery, and as the doomed commander was riding victoriously forward he was bleeding to death. Becoming faint from loss of blood, he turned to one of his aides and said: "I fear I am

IMPORTANT REBEL NEWS,

Extracts from the Richmond Papers of Yesterday.

The Siege Operations Against Charleston Progressing.

A CONTINUOUS BOMBARDMENT.

The Evacuation of Jackson by the National Forces.

Departure of McPherson's Corps from Vicksburgh up the Mississippi.

Gen. Rosecrans Organizing an Expedition Against Atlanta, Ga.

Jeff. Davis Appoints the 21st of August for Humiliation and Prayer.

New York Times
July 28, 1863

mortally wounded." The next instant he reeled in his saddle and fainted. He was taken to a ravine by strong, loving arms, and stimulants were administered. In vain! No sign or reply came, and soon he breathed his last. Information of the fall of the commander was not communicated to the army. It was still pressing on in its career of victory, his last command ringing along the line: "Forward! Let every order be forward!"

No more touching tribute could be paid to the memory of the departed hero than that made by Jefferson Davis himself when he announced the death in a special message to the Confederate Congress. He said: "Without doing injustice to the living, it may safely be said that our loss is irreparable. Among the shining hosts of the great and good who now cluster around the banner of our country, there exists no purer spirit, no more heroic soul, than that of the illustrious man I join you in lamenting. In his death he has illustrated the character for which through life he was conspicuous—that of singleness of purpose and devotion to duty with his whole energies."

Surgeon's Field Companion

JOSEPH EGGLESTON JOHNSTON, C.S.A., 1807–1891

There was no Confederate commander so remarkable for long foresight and for the exact fulfilment of prophetic words as the general who forms the subject of this notice. "He was more profound than Lee," writes an eminent Southern authority; "his mind could range over larger fields; at all times of the war his cool, sedate judgments were so in opposition to the intoxicated senses of the Confederate people that he was rather unpopular than otherwise, and rested his reputation on the appreciative and intelligent, who steadily marked him as the military genius of the Confederacy." He was the son of Peter Johnston, a jurist, and his mother was a niece of Patrick Henry. His birthplace was Longwood, near Farmville, Va.; the date February 3, 1809. He graduated from West Point, in the same class with General Lee, in 1829, and received his first commission as second lieutenant of the 4th artillery. He was aide-de-camp to General Scott in the Seminole War, 1836–38; and resigned May, 1837. He was a practising civil engineer in 1837–38, and was then appointed first lieutenant in the corps of topographical engineers, and breveted captain for gallantry in the war with the Florida Indians.

He afterwards served in the Florida and Mexican Wars. In the latter he participated in the siege of Vera Cruz, and in nearly all the other battles of that campaign. He was breveted major, lieutenant-colonel, and colonel, April 12, 1847, for gallant and meritorious conduct. He led a detachment of the storming party at Chapultepec, and General Scott reported that he was the first to plant a regimental color on the ramparts of the fortress. He resigned April 22, 1861, to join the Confederate service. He was commissioned major-general of volunteers in the Army of Virginia, and with Lee organized the volunteers who were pouring into Richmond. On being summoned to Montgomery, then the Confederate capital, he was appointed one of four brigadier-generals and was assigned to command at Harper's Ferry. When Beauregard was attacked at Manassas or Bull Run by the National army under McDowell, July 18, 1861, Johnston assumed command, and, as he himself said, "the battle as fought was made by me. Bee's and Jackson's brigades were transferred to the left," and when Kirby Smith, with a portion of Johnston's army left in the Shenandoah Valley, arrived on the field, the Confederate victory was assured. Fugitive thousands rushed across Bull Run by the various fords, and horse, foot, artillery, wagons and ambulances belonging to McDowell's army were entangled in inextricable confusion. "Soldiers in every style of costume, ladies who had come with opera glasses to survey the battle, members of congress and governors of States who had come with champagne and after-dinner speeches to celebrate a great Federal victory, editors, correspondents, telegraph operators, surgeons, paymasters, parsons—all were running for dear life—disordered, dusty, powder-blackened, screaming, or breathless in the almost mortal agonies of terror."

With an entire loss in killed and wounded of 1852 men, the

West Point, 1829

Brigadier General, May, 1861
General, August, 1861

COMMANDED
Armies in Northern Virginia, 1861
Department of the Southwest, 1862
Department of the Mississippi
Army of Tennessee

Confederates had inflicted a loss upon the Federals estimated at 4500 in killed, wounded and prisoners. They had captured 28 pieces of artillery and 5000 small arms; but they showed little capacity to understand the extent of their fortunes.

General Johnston remained in command of the consolidated forces till the spring of 1862, when, finding McClellan about to advance, he withdrew to the Rappahannock, whence he moved to meet the Federal commander. The opposing forces met May 31, 1862, at Seven Pines and joined battle. General Johnston's plan of battle was to embrace an attack at three points by the respective divisions of D. H. Hill, Huger, and Smith. "The greater part of the day was lost in vain expectation of Huger's movement—the most important part of the design. At a late hour of the afternoon Longstreet moved upon the Federal army, while General Johnston remained with Smith on the left to observe the field." Line after line of the National works were carried, and as night fell the Federal army had been driven about two miles, and "had left a track of retreat through swamp and water red with carnage." On the left, where Johnston commanded in person, the Federals held their position until dark. On this part of the field Johnston was disabled by a severe wound in the shoulder, which incapacitated him for duty till the following autumn.

On August 31, 1861, Johnston had been appointed full general, with four others.

When General Johnston was ordered to the Peninsula to oppose McClellan, he asked to be reinforced with troops from the seacoast, to enable him to crush the Federal army. The request was treated with indifference. On March 24, 1863, he was assigned to the command of the Southwest, including the troops of Generals Bragg, Kirby Smith and Pemberton. He at once addressed a letter to the Secretary of War, Mr. Randolph, urging that General Holmes's army of 55,000 men, then at Little Rock, should be ordered to join him, so that he might be able to defeat Grant. Randolph refused to issue such an order, but President Davis countermanded his Secretary's denial, and the indignant official resigned.

In May, 1863, Grant crossed the Mississippi to attack Vicksburg in the rear, and Johnston was ordered to take command of all the Confederate forces in the Mississippi department. Proceeding there at once, he endeavored to withdraw Pemberton from Vicksburg, urging on him the importance of re-establishing communications, and ordering him to come up, if practicable, on Sherman's rear at once, adding: "To beat such a detachment would be of immense value. The troops here could co-operate. All the strength you can quickly assemble should be brought. Time is all-important." On May 14 Grant advanced by the Raymond and Clinton roads upon Jackson. General Johnston did not propose to defend the town—he had no sufficient force to do so. He therefore ordered Gregg and Walker to fall back slowly, offering such resistance to the march of the Federal columns as to allow time to remove or destroy the stores accumulated in Jackson. This work accomplished, General Johnston retreated by the Canton road, from which he alone could form a junction with Pemberton; but the latter appears to have been blind to the possibilities of the position. In disobedience to the orders of his superior, and in opposition to the views of a majority of the council of war, composed of all his generals present, before whom he placed the subject, he decided to make a movement by which the union with Johnston would be impossible. "It was a fatal error," says a competent authority. The delay and aberration of Pemberton left Jackson at the mercy of the enemy, and opened the way to Vicksburg, which was taken by Grant.

President Davis transferred General Johnston, on December 18, 1863, from the Department of the Mississippi to the command of the Army of Tennessee, with headquarters at Dalton, Ga. General Lee had moved from the Rapidan to Richmond, with an increase of reputation at each stage of retreat. Yet when General Johnston moved from the northern frontier of Georgia to Atlanta even with greater success, he should have experienced similar tokens of approbation. "The fact was," says a reliable southern writer, "Johnston was the subject of a deep intrigue in Richmond, to displace him from the command of an army whose affections and confidence he had never ceased to enjoy; and even while he was moving on the march from Dalton, his removal from command was secretly entertained in Richmond." There is a delicate evidence of this. While the march from Dalton was in progress, a letter, written by General J. B. Hood to one who was supposed to have more than ordinary concern in his career, declared then his confident anticipation of being soon elevated from the position of corps commander to the head of the Army of Tennessee. There was other evidence of the intrigue in Richmond. General Bragg, the "military adviser" of President Davis, visited Johnston in his lines around Atlanta, "never apprised him that his visit was of an official nature, put together everything he could to make a case against Johnston, and returned to Richmond with the alarming report that he was to give up Atlanta to the enemy!" Of this pernicious nonsense General Johnston has written: "The proofs that I intended to hold Atlanta are the fact that under my orders the work of strengthening its defenses was going on vigorously, the communication on the subject made by me to General Hood, and the fact that my family was in the town. That the public workshops were removed, and no large supplies deposited in the town, as alleged by General Bragg, were measures of common prudence, and no more indicated the intention to abandon the place than the sending the wagons of an army to the rear on a day of battle proves a foregone determination to abandon the field."

However, on July 17 the bolt fell, and he was relieved of his command, which he was instructed to "turn over immediately to General Hood." Next morning he replied to the Secretary of War, and among other things said: "As to the alleged cause of my removal, I assert that Sherman's army is much stronger compared with that of Tennessee than Grant's compared with that of Northern Virginia. Yet the enemy has been compelled to advance more slowly to the vicinity of Atlanta than to that of Richmond and Petersburg, and penetrated much deeper into Virginia than into Georgia. Confident language by a military commander is not usually regarded as evidence of competence."

On February 23, 1865, Johnston was ordered by General Lee—now Commander-in-chief of the Confederate forces—to assume command of the Army of the Tennessee, and all troops in South Carolina, Georgia and Florida, "to concentrate all available forces and drive back Sherman." The available forces were 5000 of the Army of Tennessee and 11,000 scattered, while Sherman had 60,000 men. "Difficulty of collecting provisions was added to the other difficulties of his position." At this period General Johnston urged Lee to withdraw from Richmond, unite with him, and defeat Sherman before Grant could join him. Lee refused, because he said it was impossible for him to leave Virginia. Collecting, therefore, such troops as he could, he threw himself before Sherman, and on March 19–21 attacked the head of his column at Bentonville, south of Goldsboro. Lieutenant-general Wade Hampton had previously determined the positions of the Federal forces, and with 14,000 men the Confederate commander engaged the 14th and 20th corps of the National army and Kilpatrick's cavalry—an aggregate of 40,000 men. The Confederates were compelled to hold their ground on the 19th and 20th, to cover the operation of carrying off their wounded. Sherman's whole army was now before them, and made many partial attacks, all of which were repulsed. The fighting on the evening of the 21st was close and bloody. General Johnston says of it in his report: "The Confederates passed over 300 yards of the space between the two lines in quick time and in excellent order, and the remaining distance in double-quick, without pausing to fire until their near approach had driven the enemy from the shelter of their intrenchments, in full retreat, to their second line. After firing a few rounds, the Confederates again pressed forward, and when they were near the second intrenchment, now manned by both lines of Federal troops, Lieutenant-general Hardee, after commanding the double-quick, led the charge, and with his knightly gallantry dashed over the enemy's breastworks on horseback in front of his men. . . . Four pieces of artillery and 900 prisoners were taken. . . . The impossibility of concentrating the Confederate forces in time to attack the

THE BATTLE OF ATLANTA
"A general advance was ordered. Schofield's head of column, which Sherman accompanied, came in full view of Atlanta, the fortifications of which were on the opposite hills just across the deep valley, which was thick with men digging away for life, making fresh intrenchments against the Union advance. Sherman rode forward to reconnoiter until his escort drew the fire of the batteries. He determined to try the effect of heavy ordnance, with such successful results that the Confederates were forced to evacuate the town."
Jacob D. Cox, Major General, U.S.A.

Federal left wing while in column on the march made complete success also impossible, from the enemy's great numerical superiority.''

Before daybreak on the 22nd General Johnston moved toward Smithfield, leaving a few wounded, who were too much injured to bear removal. His loss in three days was 224 killed, 1499 wounded, and more than 300 prisoners.

The junction of Sherman's and Schofield's forces was effected at Goldsboro next day. It made an army of more than 100,000 men within 150 miles of the lines in Virginia.

Meantime Richmond had been evacuated and Lee had surrendered to Grant. Johnston therefore assumed the responsibility of advising Davis, whom he found at Greensboro, to summarily end the war. Davis agreed, and the military convention with Sherman followed.

After the war General Johnston was successively president of a railroad in Arkansas, president of an express company, and agent of a fire insurance company in Savannah, Ga. In 1877 he was elected to represent Richmond in congress. In 1887 he was commissioner of railroads, appointed by President Cleveland.

He married early in life a Lydia McLane. She died in 1886.

(General Johnston died on March 21, 1891.)

Interior of Improvised Hospital Car

EDMUND KIRBY SMITH, C.S.A., 1824–1893

General Kirby Smith belonged to a family of brave soldiers. His grandfather, Elnathan Smith, was an officer in the French War and the Revolution. Kirby Smith's father, Joseph Lee Smith, was born at New Britain, Conn., in May, 1776; was educated at Yale College, and studied law at Hartford. He served honorably through the war of 1812, and was promoted through various ranks to colonel, which position he held in 1818. He then resigned his commission and moved to Florida.

From 1823–37 he was U.S. Judge of the Superior Court. He married a daughter of Ephraim Kirby, after whom he named his three sons—Ephraim Kirby Smith, Edmund Kirby Smith, and Joseph Lee Kirby Smith. The sons were all of them trained and educated for a military life, the first and the third losing their lives in their country's service.

General Edmund Kirby Smith was born in St. Augustine, Fla., May 16, 1824, and after completing his school education entered the United States Military Academy at the early age of seventeen, graduating in 1845. He was immediately breveted second lieutenant, and a few months later was sent to Mexico to serve with the army which was commanded by General Scott. The grand march of General Scott against Mexico was begun in March, 1847. He had been a short time before that assigned to the command of the troops in Mexico, and on March 9 he assembled a force of about 12,000 men at Lobos Island and advanced against Vera Cruz, which capitulated on the 26th, after a four days' siege, and nearly 7000 missiles had been fired. With the city the castle

of San Juan d'Ulloa yielded, and the garrison of 5000 men surrendered their arms. This was the first blow to Mexico, but it was only the beginning of a series of victories equally decisive. Scott's army advanced towards Jalapa, and on April 17 reached the Mexican army under General Santa Anna in the mountain pass of Cerro Gordo. General Scott had lost a number of his men, and the army was reduced to about 8500, while the Mexican army exceeded 12,000. By surprising the latter at sunrise, however, a most signal victory was won by the American army. General Scott succeeded in scattering the Mexicans throughout the mountains, "capturing five generals, 3000 men, 4500 stand of arms and 43 cannon; and killing and wounding more than 1000, with a loss of less than 500."

Kirby Smith participated prominently in this battle, and was highly commended for his service. After the total defeat of his army, Santa Anna collected a small remnant and retreated to the City of Mexico, where he organized an army to defend the capital against the advancing American forces. If Scott had been able to follow up his advantage rapidly, this movement on the part of Santa Anna would have been rendered impossible; but, unfortunately, after advancing and capturing successively Jalapa, Perote and Puebla, Scott was forced to wait a long time at the latter place until he could receive reinforcements for his depleted force. When the new troops arrived they were found to be the rawest recruits, and a still longer delay became necessary while these men were being organized and properly trained. It was therefore nearly

West Point, 1845

*Brigadier General,
    June, 1861
Major General,
    October, 1861
Lieutenant General,
    October, 1862
General, May, 1864*

*COMMANDED
Department of Eastern
    Tennessee, Kentucky,
    Northern Georgia, and
    Western North Carolina
Trans-Mississippi Department,
    February, 1863*

239

the middle of August before Scott was able to resume his march; but from that time forward he scored victory after victory. Santa Anna had collected in the capital a force of about 20,000 men; in addition to this there was a smaller army under General Valencia at Contreras, and another under General Rincon at Churubusco. Scott turned from his path towards the capital and captured successively Contreras and Churubusco. In both of these engagements Kirby Smith led his men with the utmost credit, and won for himself the warmest and most complimentary expressions of praise. He was twice breveted for gallantry at Cerro Gordo and Contreras, and was commended by his superiors in command.

There was an armistice agreed upon shortly after the battle of Churubusco, while the peace commissioner endeavored to arrange terms; but this endeavor proved futile, and operations were resumed on September 7 by General Worth against Molino del Rey, on the southwest of the city. This place was defended by 14,000 Mexicans; but Worth, charging it on September 8 with only 3500 men, gallantly carried it, capturing much material and many prisoners. It was, however, at a terrible loss to his own force, including altogether almost one-fourth of his command. Amongst the brave officers killed in this engagement was Kirby Smith's older brother, Ephraim, who was mortally wounded in leading the light infantry battalion under his command against one of the enemy's batteries. The capture of Chapultepec on the 13th, and the triumphant entrance into the City of Mexico on the 14th, therefore brought little pleasure to Kirby Smith, who had lost a brother in the terrible fight of Molino del Rey.

After the close of the Mexican War Kirby Smith gave up active service for a time, and occupied the position of assistant professor of mathematics at West Point during the years 1849–52. He then served for some time on the frontier as captain of the 2d artillery, and was wounded in a battle with the Comanche Indians near Fort Atchison, Texas, in May, 1859. In January, 1861, he was promoted to major; but on the opening of the Civil War he resigned his commission and accepted the appointment of lieutenant-colonel in the cavalry corps of the Confederate army.

Kirby Smith had always possessed warm Southern sympathies. Although his father was a native of Connecticut, Kirby Smith's birth in Florida and early education had imbued him thoroughly with Southern feelings. These had, moreover, been considerably strengthened by his service on the frontier, during which time he had firmly espoused the Confederate cause, and had contracted firm and lasting friendships among the Southern people. He had been formally thanked by the Texas legislature for his services against the Indians, and the Confederate authorities looked upon him as one of their sturdiest defenders. Immediately on the secession of his native State of Florida, therefore, he tendered his resignation to the United States government, and, joining the Confederate army, placed his services at the disposal of the South.

On the 17th of June he was made brigadier-general, and in the battle of Bull Run, which occurred on July 21, 1861, he was severely wounded in the early part of the conflict. The Northern forces, but scarcely trained and almost all of them raw recruits, had been pushed forward hastily by the popular demand in the North for some definite action, and met a most crushing defeat. General McDowell commanded the National troops, and, although he had planned well and, generally speaking, fought well, the battle of Bull Run was decided by a turn of affairs which McDowell could scarcely foresee. General Robert Patterson had been sent ahead from Washington to hold in check the Confederate army in the Shenandoah Valley. Patterson's duty was to prevent that force from joining and reinforcing General Beauregard's army at Bull Run. Fairly considering the Shenandoah Valley as sufficiently guarded, McDowell met the main Confederate army under Beauregard at Bull Run and fought a fierce battle, in which the crest of the hill—the position of advantage—was three times lost and won. McDowell's army, however, held it at about three o'clock in the afternoon, and he counted upon securing the victory, when he was utterly taken back by the appearance of the Confederate force which he had supposed General Patterson was holding in check. This completely reversed the battle, and the National army, tired and disheartened, broke lines and retreated in disorder to Washington. Patterson's excuse for his behavior was that he was awaiting orders from General Scott in Washington, which did not reach him and without which he could not act. However that may be, it was a most fortunate occurrence for the Confederate army; for, as General Johnston has said, whichever army had stood a while longer on that day, the other would have given way.

Kirby Smith's service during the year 1862 was even more able and distinguished, and his position was one of much increased responsibility. He was placed in command of the Department of East Tennessee, Kentucky, North Georgia, and Western North Carolina. During this year General Kirby Smith held his command in direct opposition to an army in which his younger brother, Joseph Lee Kirby Smith, served. The latter, at the opening of the Civil War, acted on the staff of General N. P. Banks for a few weeks, was made colonel of the 43d Ohio volunteers in September, 1861, and commanded a brigade in the capture of New Madrid, Mo., in March, 1862. He was promoted to brevet major, and shared in the expedition to Fort Pillow. In the siege of Corinth, in May, 1862, Joseph succeeded in repelling a Confederate assault, and in other ways rendered efficient service, for which he was breveted lieutenant-colonel. While he was earning an honorable military record in the service of the Union, he was advancing against the forces under the general direction of his brother, Kirby Smith, who, during the Kentucky campaign, led the advance of General Braxton Bragg's army and defeated the National forces under General William Nelson at Richmond, Ky., on August 30, 1862. During September and October Joseph Smith commanded a regiment in the operations in Northern Mississippi and shared in the battle of Iuka, where he displayed great bravery and military tact. In October, while leading a charge to repel a fierce Confederate attack on Battery Robinett at Corinth, Joseph was mortally wounded, and Kirby Smith lost his only remaining

brother under the saddest circumstances: fighting in an opposing army, and killed while repulsing operations which his brother was partially instrumental in bringing about. Joseph Smith was breveted colonel for his bravery on this occasion, but it was an honor which he was privileged to enjoy but a few short days; for he died at Corinth on October 12 in behalf of a cause which his brother was striving with even greater military ability to destroy.

In February, 1863, General Kirby Smith was transferred to the command of the Trans-Mississippi Department, including Texas, Louisiana, Arkansas and Indian Territory. General Kirby Smith excelled the majority of the Confederate officers in mental ability. While many of them were illiterate—and even those who were of marked military capacity and brave officers were, many of them, wanting in education—Kirby Smith had educated himself thoroughly at school, at the military academy and in practical field-service, so that he held intellectually a position far superior to the large number of officers in both the Confederate and the National armies. This characteristic of his had especially inspired the Confederate authorities with feelings of confidence in him, and while he was in command of the Trans-Mississippi Department he was intrusted with the organization of a government, which he effected. His service here is briefly summed up as follows: "He made his communications with Richmond by running the blockade at Galveston, Texas, and Wilmington, N.C.; sent large quantities of cotton to Confederate agents abroad, and, introducing machinery from Europe, established factories and furnaces, opened mines, made powder and castings, and had made the district self-supporting when the war closed, at which time his forces were the last to surrender. In 1864 he opposed and defeated General Nathaniel P. Banks in his Red River campaign."

Immediately on the close of the war General Smith entered into business life, choosing the position, which was offered him, of the presidency of the Atlantic and Pacific Telegraph Company. This office he filled during the years 1866–68; but,

C.S. ARMY
CAPS

General

Col. Cavalry

Capt. Infantry

Lieut. Artillery

feeling a tendency towards professional pursuits, and especially interested in the cause of higher education, he accepted the office of the chancellorship of the University of Nashville in 1870, and remained in the performance of his functions there for five years. In 1875 he was called to the professorship of mathematics in the University of the South at Sewanee, Tenn., and finding the chair congenial to his tastes, he accepted it, and has remained in that position ever since.

(General Kirby Smith died on March 28, 1893.)

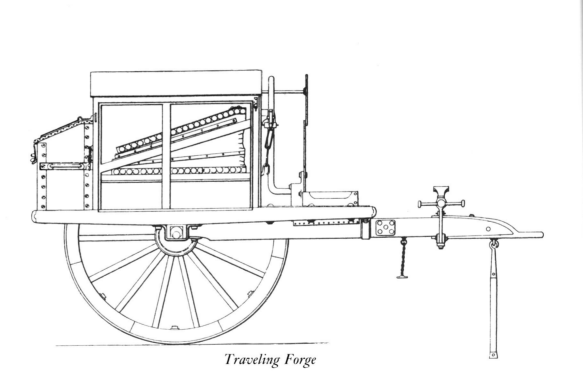

Traveling Forge

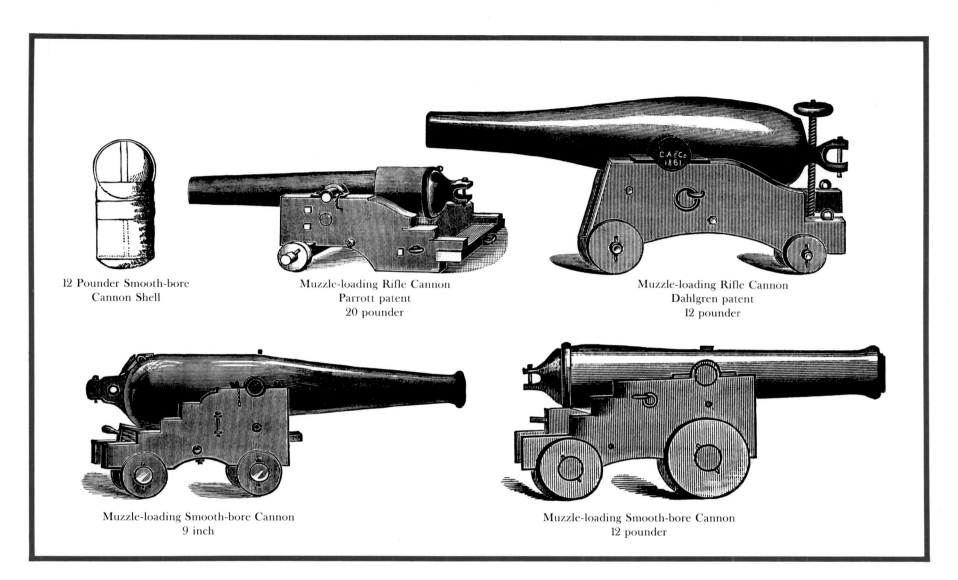

12 Pounder Smooth-bore
Cannon Shell

Muzzle-loading Rifle Cannon
Parrott patent
20 pounder

Muzzle-loading Rifle Cannon
Dahlgren patent
12 pounder

Muzzle-loading Smooth-bore Cannon
9 inch

Muzzle-loading Smooth-bore Cannon
12 pounder

NAVAL CANNON OF THE CIVIL WAR

THE BATTLE OF THE WILDERNESS
May 6, 1864

JAMES LONGSTREET, C.S.A., 1821–1904

Longstreet first saw the light in the Edgefield District of South Carolina, January 8, 1821. He removed with his mother to Alabama in 1831, and was appointed from that State to the United States Military Academy at West Point. As he himself told us, he graduated in the same class with his future antagonist, General Pope, in 1842.

Longstreet was assigned to the 4th infantry. In 1842–44 he served at Jefferson Barracks, Mo.; in 1844–45 in frontier duty at Natchitoches, La.; in 1845–46 in the military occupation of Texas; and subsequently in the war with Mexico, being engaged in the battles of Palo Alto, Resaca de la Palma, Monterey, the siege of Vera Cruz, San Antonio, Churubusco, and Molino del Rey. For gallant and meritorious conduct in the two latter battles he was breveted captain and major. At the storming of Chapultepec, September 8, 1847, he was severely wounded in the assault of the fortified convent. He served as adjutant of the 8th infantry from June 8, 1847, till July 1, 1849; and on frontier and garrison duty, chiefly in Texas, till 1858, being made captain December 7, 1852. He became paymaster July 19, 1858, and resigned June 1, 1861, his sympathies being with the secessionists.

He was commissioned brigadier-general in the Confederate army, and at the first battle of Bull Run commanded a brigade on the right of the Confederate line, where he held a large force of the National army from operating in support of McDowell's flank attack. On General Joseph E. Johnston's retreat before McClellan at Yorktown, Longstreet commanded

the rear guard. He had now been made major-general, and on May 5, 1862, he made a bold stand at Williamsburg, and was at once attacked by Heintzelman, Hooker, and Kearny. He held his ground until his opponents were reinforced by Hancock, when he was driven back into his works.

In a magazine article, written after the war, General Longstreet gives the following picture of the "pinched condition" of the Confederacy even as early as 1862:

"The Federals had been using balloons in examining our positions, and we watched with envious eyes their beautiful observations, as they floated high up in the air, and well out of the range of our guns. We longed for the balloons that poverty denied us. A genius arose for the occasion, and suggested that we send out and gather together all the silk dresses in the Confederacy, and make a balloon. It was done, and soon we had a great patch-work ship of many and varied hues. The balloon was ready for use in the seven days' campaign. We had no gas except in Richmond, and it was the custom to inflate the balloon there, tie it securely to an engine, and run it down the York River Railroad to any point at which we desired to send it up. One day it was on a steamer down the James, when the tide went out, and left vessel and balloon high and dry on a bar. The Federals gathered it in, and with it the last silk dress in the Confederacy. This capture was the meanest trick of the war, and one I have never yet forgiven."

At the end of the seven days' fighting around Richmond,

West Point, 1842

Brigadier General, 1861
Major General, 1861
Lieutenant General, 1862

General Pope took command of the newly organized Army of Virginia, and began to move towards Richmond by the Orange and Alexandria Railway. With the double purpose of drawing McClellan away from Westover and of checking the advance of Pope, General Lee sent "Stonewall" Jackson to Gordonsville, while Longstreet remained near Richmond to engage McClellan in case he should attempt an advance upon the Confederate capital. On August 9, 1862, was fought the battle of Cedar Run, and Pope and his army went to the rear. "At that time," says Longstreet, "General Lee was feeling very certain that Richmond was in no immediate danger from an advance by McClellan's forces; he therefore began at once preparations for a vigorous campaign against Pope." On the 13th of August Longstreet's command was ordered to Gordonsville, and General Lee went along with it. This and subsequent manoeuvrings and minor engagements led up to the second battle of Bull Run, concerning which Longstreet writes: "Shortly before nine o'clock on August 30 Pope's artillery began to play a little. We did not understand that as an offer of battle, but merely a display to cover his movements to the rear. Later a considerable force moved out and began to attack us on our left, extending and engaging the whole of Jackson's line. Evidently Pope supposed I was gone, as he was ignoring me entirely." Meantime Longstreet had discovered a favorable opportunity for attack, and in a few minutes "crash after crash of shot and shell were being poured into the thick ranks of the Federals." That night Pope was across Bull Run, and the victorious Confederates lay down to sleep on the battle-field, while all around were strewn thousands of both armies sleeping the last sleep together.

The next morning the National army was in a strong position at Centreville, and Longstreet sent a brigade across the stream under General Pryor. Jackson toward evening encountered at Ox Hill a part of the Federal forces, and, attacking it, had quite a sharp engagement. Longstreet came up to "Stonewall's" relief, and soon after occurred the unfortunate shooting of the gallant Phil. Kearny, the circumstances of which let General

Confederate Officer's Belt Buckle

Longstreet tell:—"Just as we reached the men on picket, General Kearny came along looking for his line, which had gone. It was raining in the woods, and late in the day, so that a Federal was not easily distinguished from a Confederate. Kearny did not seem to know he was in the Confederate line, and our troops did not notice that he was a Federal. He began to inquire about some command, and in a moment or so the troops saw that he was a Federal officer. At the same moment he realized where he was. He was called upon to surrender; but instead of doing so, he wheeled his horse, lay flat on the animal's neck, clapped spurs into his sides, and dashed off. Instantly a half dozen shots rang out, and before he had gone thirty steps poor Kearny fell. He had been in the army all his life, and we all knew and respected him. His body was sent over the lines under a flag of truce."

On the afternoon of September 15 Longstreet's command and Hill's crossed the Antietam Creek and took position in front of Sharpsburg. On the same afternoon McClellan's army of 90,000 men appeared among the trees that crowned the heights of the eastern bank of that creek. A sanguinary battle was fought, concerning which General Longstreet says— "The Confederates were enabled to drive the Federals back, and when night settled down the army of Lee was still in possession of the field; but it was dearly bought, for thousands of brave soldiers were dead, and many gallant commands were torn as a forest in a cyclone. Nearly one-fourth of the troops who went into the battle were killed or wounded that day. . . . The great mistake of the campaign was the division of Lee's army. At Sharpsburg he had hardly 37,000 men, who were in poor condition for battle against McClellan's 90,000, who were fresh and well."

At Sharpsburg, in Longstreet's opinion, was sprung the arch upon which the Confederate cause rested.

One night in the spring of 1863, as Longstreet was sitting in his tent, opposite Suffolk, Va., there entered a slender, wiry fellow, about five feet eight, with hazel eyes, dark hair and complexion, and brown beard. He wore a citizen's suit of dark cloth, and he handed the general a note from Mr. Seddon, Secretary of War. He was the famous scout Harrison, who in his unpretending way passed unmolested through the Federal army, and returned with highly accurate and valuable information from Washington. Before the army left Fredericksburg for the campaign into Maryland and Pennsylvania, General Longstreet called up the scout, and, giving him all the gold he would need, told him to proceed to Washington City, and remain there until he was in possession of information which he knew would be of value to the Confederates. Longstreet's command reached Chambersburg on June 27, and there Harrison straggled into the lines. "He told me," said Longstreet, after the war, "that he had been to Washington and had spent his gold freely, drinking in the saloons and getting upon confidential terms with army officers. In that way, he had gotten a pretty good idea of the general movements of the Federal army, and the preparations to give us battle. . . . His information proved more accurate than we could have expected had we been relying upon our cavalry." The scout, in fact, gave the details of the movements that soon after led up to the three days' desperate fighting at Gettysburg. General Longstreet commanded the left wing on this bloody field. Before the second day's battle, he and General Lee stood on the summit of Seminary Ridge watching the National troops concentrate on the opposite hill. Both men were using their glasses. After a few minutes Longstreet is reported to have advised his commander-in-chief to "throw our army around by their left and interpose between the Federal army and Washington. Finding our object is Washington, they will be sure to attack us, and when they attack us we shall beat them."

"No," said General Lee, "the enemy is there, and I am going to attack him there."

Longstreet was argumentatively persistent; but Lee was immovable. When the battle of the second day was over, Lee pronounced it a success, because the Confederate forces occupied the ground from which the Federals had been driven, while several field-pieces had been captured.

On the morning of the third day General Lee directed Longstreet to renew the attack against Cemetery Hill, which was probably the strongest point of the Union line. In reply the subordinate officer responded in substance that he had been examining the ground over to the right, and was much inclined to think the best thing was to move to the Federal left.

"No," replied Lee, "I am going to take them where they are, on Cemetery Hill. I want you to take Pickett's division and make the attack. I will reinforce you by two divisions of the 3d corps."

"That will give me 15,000 men," Longstreet replied. "I have been a soldier, I may say, from the ranks up to the position I now hold. I have been pretty much in all kinds of skirmishes, from those of two or three soldiers up to an army corps, and I think I can safely say there never was a body of 15,000 men who could make that attack successfully."

Lee seemed a little impatient at his subordinate's remarks, and nothing more was said. Longstreet thereupon went to work to arrange his troops for the attack. Pickett was put in position and received his directions. The world knows of Pickett's memorable charge, and how his noble division was swept away. Lee came up as the Confederate troops were driven back, and encouraged them as well as he could. He begged them to re-form their ranks and reorganize their forces, and assisted the staff officers in bringing them into something like order again. It was then he used the expression that has been mentioned so often:

"It was all my fault; get together, and let us do the best we can toward saving that which is left us."

"Gettysburg," wrote Longstreet, "was one of the saddest days of my life. I foresaw what my men would meet, and would gladly have given up my position rather than share in the responsibilities of that day. It was thus I felt when Pickett, at the head of forty-nine hundred brave men, marched over the crest of Seminary Ridge and began his descent of the slope. As he passed me, he rode gracefully, with his jaunty cap raked well over his right ear, and his long auburn locks, nicely

BATTLES:
Mexican War
Bull Run
Yorktown
Williamsburg
Seven Pines, or Fair Oaks
Seven Days' battles
Cedar Run
Second Bull Run
Ox Hill
Antietam
Gettysburg
Chickamauga
Knoxville
Wilderness

THE BATTLE OF SPOTSYLANIA
May 8 – 18, 1864

Lieutenant General Ulysses S. Grant, in a council of war at Massaponax Church, Virginia, May 21, 1864. During the prior campaign the Union losses were: at the Wilderness, Spotsylvania, North Anna, and Cold Harbor, from May 5th to June 10th, 54,551 men. The battle of Cold Harbor, General Grant acknowledges was a mistake.

dressed, hanging almost to his shoulders."

Longstreet joined Bragg's army at 11 p.m. on the 19th of September, 1863, and the next day Chickamauga, "the great battle of the West," was fought. In that desperate action with Rosecrans's army Longstreet held the left wing of the Confederate army. At 3 p.m. Bragg seems to have thought that the battle was lost, and even at night seems to have been in some doubt about the issue. Writing to General D. H. Hill in July, 1864, Longstreet said: "It did not occur to me on the night of the 20th to send Bragg word of our complete success. I thought that the loud huzzas that spread over the field just at dark were a sufficient assurance and notice to any one within five miles."

Subsequently General Longstreet was detached to capture Knoxville, but found it too strongly fortified to be taken by assault. Early in 1864 he rejoined Lee, and was wounded by the fire of his own troops in the battle of the Wilderness.

After the war General Longstreet established his residence in New Orleans, where he engaged in commercial business in the firm of Longstreet, Owens & Company. He was appointed Surveyor of Customs of New Orleans by President Grant; Supervisor of Internal Revenue in Louisiana, Postmaster of New Orleans, and Minister of the United States to Turkey, by President Hayes; and United States Marshal for the District of Georgia by President Garfield.

(General Longstreet died on January 2, 1904.)

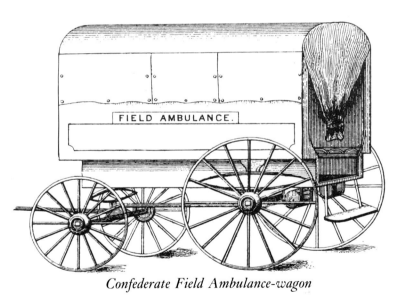

Confederate Field Ambulance-wagon

Battle of Resaca, Georgia.—Shortly after one o'clock, May 14, 1864, Union General Daniel Butterfield's division, supported by those of Generals Geary and Williams, was sent forward to test the enemy's strength, and soon came upon Confederate General John B. Hood's advance under General Carter L. Stevenson, whose guns occupied quite a commanding position. The attack, though promptly met and ably contested by the Confederates, was made so impetuously that Stevenson had no time to withdraw four 12-pounders, which were captured by the Federals, and brought in by the Fifth Ohio. The contest did not cease until midnight. In this engagement the Confederates lost a large number in killed and wounded, besides about 200 prisoners and the battle flags of the Thirty-fifth and Thirty-eighth Alabama Regiments. The Federal loss in front of Resaca was about 2,000; the Confederates report their total loss at 2,200.

JOHN BANKHEAD MAGRUDER, C.S.A., 1810–1871

West Point, 1830

Brigadier General, 1861
Major General, June, 1862

COMMANDED
District of Texas

BATTLES:
Mexican War
Big Bethel
Peninsula campaign
Seven Days' battles
Mechanicsville
Beaver Dam
Savage's Station
Malvern Hill
Galveston

This Virginian was a fine specimen of the dashing, resourceful soldier. Familiarly known in the army as "Prince John," probably no one who ever lived could play off the grand seignior with a more lordly air than he. In the ante-bellum days (so the old army story used to run) Magruder was a lieutenant of artillery at Rouse's Point. There his mess entertained some British officers, two of whom were scions of nobility. "The visit having been unexpected, the mess borrowed, or rented, gold plate and silver plate, cut glassware, rich furniture, and stylish equipages for driving the noble guests around. Prince John assured them that these were but the debris of the former splendor of the regimental mess. 'Only the debris, my lord; the schooner bringing most of the mess plate from Florida was unfortunately wrecked.' One of the dazzled and bewildered noblemen said to Prince John on the second day of the gorgeous festival: 'We do not wish to be impolitely inquisitive, but we have been so much impressed with this magnificence that we are constrained to believe that American officers must be paid enormously. What, may I ask, is your monthly pay?' Assuming an indifferent air, Prince John said: 'Damned if I know'; then turning to his servant, he asked: 'Jim, what is my monthly pay?' The servant was discreetly silent—it may have been from a wink, or it may have been that to remember $65 was too heavy a tax upon Jim's memory as well as his master's."

General Magruder was born at Winchester, Va., August 15, 1810, and graduated at the United States Military Academy in

1830, being assigned to the artillery. He subsequently served in the West, in Maine, and at Fort McHenry, Baltimore. In the Mexican War he commanded the light battery of General Pillow's division, and was breveted major for gallantry at Cerro Gordo, and lieutenant-colonel for Chapultepec, where he was severely wounded. After the Mexican War he served in Maryland, California, and Newport, R. I, where he was in command of Fort Adams.

When Virginia seceded, General Magruder resigned his commission, that of captain of artillery, and entered the Confederate Army. After gaining the battle of Big Bethel, he was made brigadier-general, and placed in command of the Confederate forces on the Peninsula, with headquarters at Yorktown. Large fleets of Federal transports were gathered at the mouth of the Rappahannock. Joe Johnston quickly divined that, while making a show of force along the lower Rappahannock, their object was to transport their force with great celerity to the Peninsula, surprise Magruder at Yorktown and capture Richmond

The sequel proved that General Johnston had guessed rightly. A fearful crisis arose for the new Confederacy. The fate of Richmond hung upon the line held across the Peninsula, from Yorktown on the York River to Mulberry Island on the James River, by General Magruder with about 11,000 men; while McClellan had landed on the Peninsula with 118,000 men, including 10,000 cavalry and a siege train of 103 guns. The commander of this Federal force hesitated before Magruder's line of 11,000 men. Perhaps it was, after all, not so surprising; for

THE BATTLE OF RESACA
May 14 – 15, 1864

"Prince John" was at his best, and his best was something wonderful. No "Colonel Mulberry Sellers" could have made a more prodigious make-believe demonstration with the force at his command. "With admirable adroitness," says one writer, "General Magruder extended his little force over a distance of several miles, placing a regiment in every gap open to observation, to give the appearance of numbers to the enemy." Another author says: "During Lee's absence Richmond was at the mercy of McClellan; but Magruder was there to keep up a 'clatter.' No one was better fitted for such a work. . . . During Lee's absence he made things so lively that each of McClellan's corps commanders was expecting a special visit from the much-plumed cap and the once gaudy attire of the master of ruses and strategy. He put on naturally all those grand and imposing devices which so successfully deceive the military opponent." At all events his ruse succeeded. McClellan took to the spade, and commenced the operation of a regular siege against Yorktown. While he was laboriously constructing his parallels, General Joe Johnston moved down to reinforce the Confederate lines of the Peninsula, in time to save Magruder's little army from the pressure of enveloping forces sufficiently numerous to have devoured it.

In June, 1862, General Magruder, now a major-general, took an important share in the seven days' fighting around Richmond. Before the battles of Mechanicsville and Beaver Dam, Magruder and Huger were ordered "to hold their positions against any assault of the enemy, to observe his movements, and follow him closely should he retreat." The battle of Gaines's Mills had forced McClellan from his original strongholds on the north side of the Chickahominy, and, with his communications cut off on the Pamunkey River, and encountered by the force on the south side of the Chickahominy, it was supposed by the Confederate leaders that he would be unable to extricate himself from the position without capitulation. "But," says a Southern writer, "the enemy had been imperfectly watched at a juncture the most critical in the contest. A great and almost irreparable error had been committed."

Early in the morning of June 29 the pickets at Magruder's and Huger's front were attacked in force; but, instead of giving ground, they drove the enemy down the roads and through the woods into and past their breastworks, and found them deserted. "Far from profiting by this discovery, and commencing the pursuit, these generals allowed the foe to pass across their front, instead of piercing his line of retreat."

As soon as the Federal retreat was discovered, Generals Magruder and Huger were ordered in pursuit—the former by the Williamsburg road, to attack the Federal rear; the latter by the Charles City road, to attack its flank. Late in the afternoon, at Savage Station, General Magruder struck the National rear and attacked it. A severe action ensued, which was only terminated by the darkness of night. The result was not decisive, and the Federals continued their retreat under the cover of night, leaving several hundred prisoners, with their dead and wounded, in the hands of the Confederates.

At the battle of Malvern Hill General Magruder's corps were conspicuous for their *elan* and bravery. "It was four o'clock, and if anything was to be attempted the work must be quick and desperate. An order had been dispatched by General Magruder to bring up from all the batteries 30 rifle pieces, if possible, with which he hoped to shatter the enemy's infantry." It was soon evident that the artillery could not get up in time. Magruder determined to trust to the impetuous valor of his troops, and with 15,000 infantry to storm the hill. "There was a run of more than 600 yards up a rising ground, and an unbroken flat beyond of several hundred yards, 100 pieces of cannon behind breastworks, and heavy masses of infantry in support. The brigades advanced bravely across the open field, raked by the fire of the cannon and the musketry of large bodies of infantry. Some were broken and gave way; others approached close to the guns, driving back the infantry, compelling the advanced batteries to retire to escape capture, and mingling their dead with those of the enemy. To add to the horrors of the scene and the immense slaughter in front of the batteries, the gunboats increased the rapidity of their broadsides, and the immense missiles coursed through the air with great noise, tearing off the tree-tops, and bursting with loud explosions.'' Towards sunset the concussion of artillery was terrific. The hill was clothed in sheets of flame. Shells raced athwart the horizon. The blaze of the setting sun was obscured by the dense canopy of smoke. Darkness shed its merciful mantle on the scene. The attack on Malvern Hill by General Magruder had failed—failed, it was said, because there had been ''a want of concert among the attacking columns.''

On October 16, 1862, General Magruder was placed in command of the Confederate forces in Texas. Arriving there, he found the harbors of this State in possession of the Federals from the Sabine River to Corpus Christi, while the line of the Rio Grande was virtually abandoned. He resolved to gain the harbor, if possible, and to occupy the Valley of the Rio Grande in force. ''The first step of his enterprise contemplated the expulsion of the Federal vessels from the harbor of Galveston and the repossession of that town.'' Having assembled all the available artillery, he occupied in force the works erected opposite the island on which the city of Galveston stands. He also fitted up as gunboats two steamers—the *Bayou City* and the *Neptune*—making them shot-proof by means of bulwarks of cotton bales. ''The Federal fleet, then lying in the waters of Galveston, consisted of the *Harriet Lane*, carrying four heavy guns and two 24-pounder howitzers, commanded by Captain Wainwright; the *Westfield*, flagship of Commodore Renshaw; a large propeller, mounting eight heavy guns; the *Owasco*, a similar ship to the *Westfield*, mounting also eight heavy guns; the *Clifton*, a steam propeller, four heavy guns; the *Sachem*, a steam propeller, four heavy guns; two armed transports, two large barges, and an armed schooner.''

The Federal land forces—a few hundred men—were stationed at the end of a long wharf, and were crowded into large buildings immediately under the guns of the steamships. The approaches landward to this position were impeded by two lines of strong barricades, and communication with the shore was destroyed by the removal of portions of the wharf in front of the barricades. It thus became necessary for the storming parties to advance by wading through the water, and to mount the end of the wharf by scaling ladders.

It was arranged by General Magruder that the naval and military operations should be simultaneous, and should commence before daybreak on January 1, 1863. ''The co-operation of the cotton-boats with the land forces was extremely difficult to obtain—the distance the former had to run being thirty miles.'' The attack was opened a little past midnight by a shot from the Confederate land batteries. The moon had gone down, but the Federal ships were visible by the light of the stars. Leading the centre assault, General Magruder approached to within two squares of the wharves, where the Federal forces were stationed. While the general engaged the vessels with artillery, ''the storming party advanced to the assault. A severe conflict took place at this point, the Confederates being exposed to a fire of grape, canister and shell, and at last being compelled to seek the shelter of the buildings near the wharf.'' As the morning advanced the Confederate fire still continued, while the long-expected cotton-boats came plunging down the harbor and engaged the *Harriet Lane* in gallant style, running into her, one on each side, and pouring on her deck a deadly cross-fire of rifles and shotguns. ''The gallant Captain Wainwright fought his ship admirably. He succeeded in disabling the *Neptune*, and attempted to run down the *Bayou City*. The Confederate boat adroitly evaded the deadly stroke, although, as the vessels passed each other, she lost her larboard wheel-house in the shock. Again the *Bayou City*, while receiving several broadsides almost at the cannon's mouth, poured into the *Harriet Lane* a destructive fire of small arms. Turning once more, she drove her prow into the iron wheel of the *Harriet Lane*, thus locking the two vessels together.'' Almost immediately the *Harriet Lane* was boarded by the Confederates, and after a slight resistance surrendered.

Commodore Smith then sent a flag to Commodore Renshaw—whose ship, the *Westfield*, had in the meantime been run aground—demanding the surrender of the whole fleet,

University of Georgia Library

THE BATTLE OF COLD HARBOR
June 3, 1864

three hours' time being given him to consider. The Confederate propositions were accepted. General Magruder afterwards sent another message by two Confederate officers to Commodore Renshaw; but while they were on their way the Federal commodore blew up his ship, and was himself accidentally blown up with it. Meanwhile, the first period of truce having expired, the Federal commanders, perceiving that the Confederate vessels were too seriously damaged to pursue, gradually crept off. "The small Federal force which held the wharf, discovering that they were abandoned by the fleet, surrendered as prisoners." Galveston thus was captured by General Magruder.

He remained in command in Texas until the close of the war, when he entered the army of Maximilian in Mexico, with the rank of major-general, and was appointed chief of the land office of colonization. He stuck to the unfortunate Emperor's fortunes to the last melancholy scene of all—the execution.

General Magruder then returned to the United States, and lectured in Baltimore and other cities on Mexico. In 1869 he settled in Houston, Texas, where he remained till his death, which occurred February 19, 1871.

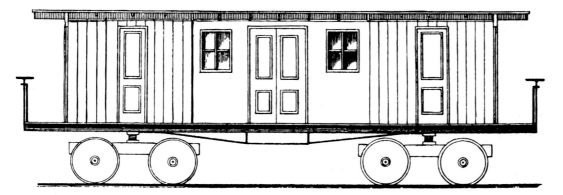

Baggage and Commissary Car of the Army of the Cumberland

JOHN HUNT MORGAN, C.S.A., 1825–1864

Brigadier General, 1861
Major General, 1862

COMMANDED
Department of
Southwest Virginia, 1864

BATTLES:
Kentucky campaign
Columbia
Lebanon
Bradensburg
Corydon
Salem
Lexington
Versailles
Harrison
Cynthiana
Greenville (Killed)

This dashing and intrepid cavalryman was born at Huntsville, Ala., June 1, 1826. He served in the war with Mexico as first lieutenant in a cavalry regiment, and at the beginning of the Civil War he entered the Confederate army as captain of the Kentucky volunteers, and joined General Simon B. Buckner at the head of the Lexington rifles.

During the winter of 1862–63 he commanded a cavalry force in General Braxton Bragg's army, and greatly annoyed General Rosecrans's outposts and communications. He soon began a series of raids in Kentucky, in which he destroyed many million dollars' worth of military stores. He captured and burned railroad trains filled with supplies; he tore up railroad tracks, burned bridges and destroyed culverts in the rear of the Federal army, and made it necessary to garrison every important town in the State. Moving with the utmost celerity, and taking a telegraph operator with him, he misled his foes and at the same time acquainted himself with their movements. In 1862 he was appointed major-general.

As a part of the general plan of action in the West, and an important contribution to the success of General Bragg's retreat, General Morgan's raid in the summer of 1863 occupies a prominent place in the Confederate operations of that time. It not only created an important diversion of Burnside's army, large detachments of which were drawn after Morgan into and through Kentucky, but it prevented the Federal commander from getting in rear of Bragg's army at the time it was men-

aced in front of Shelbyville by General Rosecrans. In the latter part of the month of June the command of General Morgan approached the banks of the Cumberland. "The passage of the river," says a Southern historian, "was weakly contested by three Ohio regiments, which had advanced from Somerset, Ky. General Morgan was obliged to build a number of boats, and commenced crossing the river on July 1. By ten o'clock next morning his whole regiment was over the river; the advance proceeding to Columbia, where, after a brief engagement, the enemy was driven from the town." On the 4th of July General Morgan descended like a flash upon Lebanon. The Federal commander here, Colonel Hanson, was a brave man, who made a fierce and desperate resistance; and only surrendered after the Confederates had applied the incendiary torch to the houses in which Colonel Hanson's small force had sought protection. Morgan captured about 600 prisoners, and a sufficient quantity of fire-arms to equip all his men that were unarmed. Never permitting the grass to grow beneath his feet, the dashing Confederate commander reached Bradensburg on the 7th of July. Next day he crossed the Ohio River, "keeping in check two gunboats and dispersing a force of militia posted with artillery on the Indiana shore." The Federal pursuing column had now increased to seven regiments and two pieces of artillery, and it dashed along in his rear with a determined impetuosity, rivaling his own. When this force reached the banks of the river, the disgust of its commander may be imagined to find that the

THE BATTLE OF KENNESAW MOUNTAIN
June 27, 1864

passenger-boat on which the daring Confederate raider had effected a crossing in flames, and to see his force rapidly disappearing in the distance.

"On the 9th of July," to use the language of a Southern chronicler, "General Morgan marched on to Corydon, fighting near 4000 State militia, capturing three-fourths of them, and dispersing the remainder." Practically "without drawing bridle," he rushed along through Salisbury and Palmyra to Salem, ruining the railroad bridge and the track, and demolishing a vast quantity of valuable stores. Then taking the train to Lexington, after riding all night, he reached that point at daylight, capturing great quantities of supplies, and destroying the railroad depot and track at Vienna, on the Jeffersonville and Indianapolis Railroad. Leaving Lexington, he passed on to the Ohio and Mississippi Railroad, near Vernon, where, finding General Manson with a heavy force of infantry, "he skirmished with him two hours as a feint, while the main command moved around the town to Dupont, where squads were sent out to cut the roads between Vernon and Seymour on the west, Vernon and Lawrenceburg on the east, Vernon and Madison on the south, and Vernon and Columbus on the north."

From Vernon General Morgan proceeded to Versailles, capturing 500 militia there, and gathering together more prisoners on the road, while increasing his own force. From Versailles he moved across to Harrison, Ohio, destroying the track and burning many small bridges on the Lawrenceburg and Indianapolis Railroad. Reaching Harrison, Morgan burned a fine bridge; leaving the town at dusk and moving abound Cincinnati, passing between that city and Hamilton, destroying the railroad, and, a scout running the Federal pickets into the city, the whole command marched within seven miles of it. Daylight of the 14th found him 18 miles east of Cincinnati.

The bold cavalryman had now accomplished a marvelous circuit. He had penetrated the enemy's country, destroying property probably to the extent of ten or twelve millions of dollars; he had cut and partly obliterated an entire network of railroads; he had paroled nearly 6000 prisoners, and plunged several millions of people into a state of hysterical consternation. They say all is fair in love and in war; the proverb needs revision. Be this as it may, General Morgan had done his work.

"After passing Cincinnati," says the historian we have been indebted to principally for the foregoing particulars, "the jaded command of Confederates proceeded towards Dennison, and, making a feint there, struck out for Ohio. Daily were they delayed by the annoying cry of 'Axes to the front!'—a cry that warned them of bushwhackers, ambuscades and blockaded roads. It appeared that every hillside contained an enemy and every ravine a blockade." It was not until the evening of July 19 that the command, dispirited and worn out, reached the river at a ford above Pomeroy. Promptly at four o'clock in the afternoon two companies were thrown across the river, where their foes awaited them and poured a deadly fire in their midst. "A scout of 300 men were sent down the river half a mile, who reported back that they had found a small force behind rifle-pits, and asked permission to charge. The rifle-pits were charged and 150 prisoners captured. A courier, arriving about the same time, reported that a gunboat had approached near our battery, and, upon being fired upon, had retired precipitately." General Morgan, finding this report correct, and believing that he had sufficient time to cross his command, was using every exertion to accomplish the task, when simultaneously could be heard the discharge of artillery from down the river—"a heavy drumming sound of small arms in the rear and right; and soon from the banks of the river came up three black columns of infantry, firing upon our men, who were in close column, preparing to cross." Seeing that the Federals had every advantage of position, an overwhelming force of infantry and cavalry, and that his men were being completely environed, General Morgan gave the command to move up the river "double-quick." But his force was not in such a condition that he could take them all away. Some were on foot, many were sick, others were wounded. He probably left 200 of these as Federal prisoners. Meantime the able-bodied men of his command pressed rapidly to Belleville, about 14 miles, on a running irregular fight, and took the water like sea-lions at that point. Three hundred and thirty men had effected a crossing when again the Federal gunboats were upon them. The chances were fearfully against Morgan and his men. It looked like hopeless desperation to attempt to cross the river under such fearfully adverse conditions. But even then, under the raking fire, a party of officers, headed by Colonel Adam R. Johnson, plunged into the stream, and boldly began the dire struggle for life or death. Of the fearful scene which ensued one of the party subsequently wrote: "The colonel's noble mare falters, strikes out again and boldly makes the shore. Woodson follows. My poor mare, being too weak to carry me, turned over and commenced going down; encumbered by clothing, sabre and pistols, I made but poor progress in the turbid stream. An inherent love of life actuated me to continue swimming. Behind me I heard the piercing call of young Rogers for help; on my right, Captain Helm was appealing to me for aid, and in the rear my friend, Captain McClain, was sinking. Gradually the gunboat was nearing me. Should I be able to hold up until it came, and would I then be saved to again undergo the horrors of a Federal bastile! But I hear something behind me snorting; I feel it passing! Thank God, I am saved! A riderless horse dashes by; I grasp his tail; onward he bears me, and the shore is reached. Colonel Johnson, on reaching the shore, seizes a 10-inch piece of board, jumps into a leaky skiff, and starts back to aid the drowning. He reaches Captain Helm, but Captain McClain and young Rogers are gone."

General Morgan was not one of those fortunate individuals who escaped across the river. With 200 of his men he broke through the Federal lines on the north side of the Ohio and continued his flight in the direction of New Lisbon, with the design of reaching and crossing the river higher up. Forces were dispatched to head him off, and the brave cavalier, who had so often given occasion for surprise and mystery and fear to his foes, was at last brought to bay at a point on the river where there was no escape, "except by fighting his way through, or leaping from a lofty and almost perpendicular precipice." Here

he surrendered himself and the remnant of his command.

How a prisoner of this type should be treated will depend on the side from which his acts and antecedents are viewed. The Southern people thought that the North treated General Morgan "infamously." The following memorandum, made in the War Department at Richmond, and signed by Lieutenant-colonel Alston, voices the Confederate sentiment at the time: "They were carried to Cincinnati, and from thence he (General Morgan) and 28 of his officers were selected and carried to Columbus, Ohio, where they were shaved and their hair cut very close by a negro convict. They were then marched to the bath-room and scrubbed, and from there to their cells, where they were locked up. Seven days later 42 more of General Morgan's officers were conveyed from Johnson's Island to the penitentiary, and subjected to the same indignities."

Some of these so-called "indignities" were no doubt rather acceptable and refreshing from a sanitary point of view. At all events, these outrages did not break the spirit of these brave men. The very officer who made the memorandum quoted partially above wrote in his jail-journal this sentiment of defiance: "There are a hundred thousand men in the South who feel as I do, that they would rather an earthquake should swallow the whole country than yield to our oppressors—men who will retire to the mountains and live on acorns, and crawl on their bellies to shoot an invader wherever they can see one."

Thank heaven, this is not the general sentiment of the South. Abraham Lincoln's speech at Gettysburg—the greatest speech ever spoken by man since the Sermon on the Mount—appeals alike to North and South with ever-increasing eloquence.

Morgan is dead; still we have to pursue his strange, eventful history a page or so further. He dug himself out of the Ohio penitentiary and promptly reported himself for duty to the Confederate forces, ready for another raid. With a force of little more than 2000 cavalry he entered the State of Kentucky, and on June 11 captured Cynthiana with its entire garrison. On the 12th he was overtaken by Burbridge with a largely superior force, and his command effectually dispersed and finally

"I left Knoxville on the fourth day of July, 1863, with about 900 men, and returned on the 28th inst., having been absent just 24 days, during which time I traveled a thousand miles, captured 17 towns, destroyed all the supplies and arms in them, captured and paroled 1,200 regular troops, and lost in killed, wounded and missing only 90 of my men."
John Hunt Morgan,
Major General, C.S.A.

THE BATTLE OF ATLANTA
July 22, 1864

THE BATTLE OF JONESBORO, GEORGIA
September 1, 1864

driven from the State. Bounced from Kentucky, as it were, Morgan attempted a smaller scale of operations in East Tennessee, and was next heard of at Greenville. "The country between Greenville and Bull's Gap is hilly and wild, and very poor." He was staying at the house of a Mrs. Williams, and was betrayed by the woman's daughter-in-law. The Federal officer sent forward his forces. General Morgan's staff, being aroused, were captured one by one. Morgan himself tried to escape by the garden. "He had no weapon," says a Confederate authority; "Captain Rogers having one of his pistols, and one of his clerks the other." Seeing there was no hope of suc-

cessful concealment, he came out from among some grapevines, where he had hidden himself, and surrendered to Captain Wilcox, of the 13th Tennessee cavalry, "who had already both of Morgan's pistols in his possession." A few minutes after there was some shooting done. Northern and Southern authorities are not exactly agreed how it came about to this day. The Northern writers tell how he was trying to escape; the Southern scribes believe that poor Morgan was assassinated.

Be this as it may, Morgan fell, leaving to his countrymen, North or South, a testimony of Kentucky chivalry—"the record of a gallant, dashing life and a fearless death."

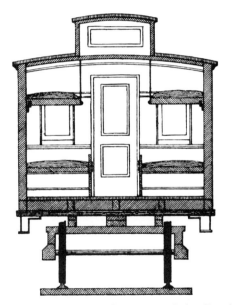

Section of Hospital Car of the Army of the Cumberland

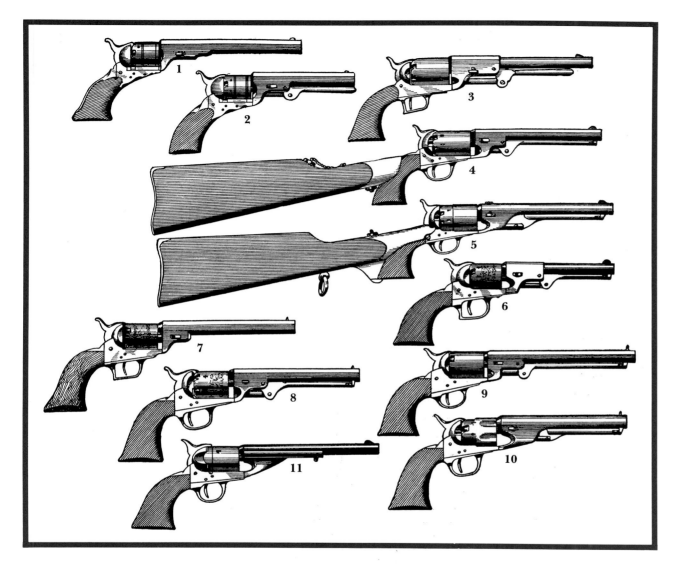

1. Colt's "Texas" Revolver
   Paterson model, 1836
   Calibers .28, .31, .36

2. Colt's "Texas" Revolver
   Model 1840 Caliber .28

3. Colt's Army Revolver
   Model 1847 Caliber .44

4. Colt's Navy Revolver
   Model 1851, with stock
   Caliber .36

5. Colt's Army Revolver
   Model 1860, with stock
   Caliber .44

6. Colt's Army Revolver
   Dragoon model, 1848
   Caliber .44·

7. Colt's First Model Belt Revolver
   Wells-Fargo model, 1848
   Caliber .31

8. Colt's "Old Model" Belt Revolver
   Model 1849 Caliber .31

9. Colt's Navy Revolver
   Model 1857, without stock
   Caliber .36

10. Colt's "New Model" Belt Revolver
    Model 1862 Caliber .36

11. Colt's Army Revolver
    Model 1860
    Caliber .45

COLT REVOLVERS USED IN THE CIVIL WAR

JOHN CLIFFORD PEMBERTON, C.S.A.,1814–1881

West Point, 1837

Brigadier General,
June, 1861
Major General,
February, 1862
Lieutenant General,
October, 1862

COMMANDED
Department of
South Carolina, Georgia,
and Florida, 1862
Department of Tennessee,
Mississippi, and
Eastern Louisiana

BATTLES:
Mexican War
Vicksburg

General Pemberton was of English descent, and belonged to one of the oldest and most respectable of American families. In 1682 Phineas Pemberton, a Quaker, emigrated to this country with his father, and purchased a large tract of land on the Delaware River, naming it Grove Place. He served in a number of public offices in the province under William Penn, and died in March, 1702. After his death Penn wrote of him: "I mourn for poor Phineas Pemberton, the ablest as well as one of the best men in the province." This was the first of the American Pembertons. His son, Israel, and grandson, also named Israel, were both men of great wealth and prominence in the business, political and religious worlds. They were successful merchants in Philadelphia and held responsible civil positions, while standing among the foremost of the Quakers. The younger Israel shared his influence in both church and public affairs with his brother James. The latter was one of the founders and a member of the Board of Managers of the Pennsylvania Hospital, and was chosen president of the Pennsylvania Abolition Society. This last fact is of interest as contrasted with the service of General Pemberton in the *Confederate* army during the Slavery War. James Pemberton was ever interested in the cause of the Indians and Negroes, and favored freedom strongly. Another brother of the younger Israel was John Pemberton, whose interest in his church led him to devote himself to the ministry. He was an active mover in all charitable and benevolent schemes, and traveled extensively through England, Ireland, Scotland, and

A SHORT HISTORY of

J. C. Gen. PEMBERTON.

Holland, preaching Quaker doctrines. On his death, he left his estate—which was very large—to the "several charitable, benevolent and religous organizations with which he had been associated, and for the purpose of aiding in the formation of like organizations."

There was no more prominent nor more highly respected name in Philadelphia than that of Pemberton, and this had been secured by a succession of high-minded, able, and religious men, who had devoted their lives to the noble and unselfish purpose of bettering the condition of their fellow-men; and their own personal success and prosperity in business was but a means to the more thorough accomplishment of that end. They labored to help others, and in the annals of the City of Brotherly Love there can be found no better examples of the pure Quaker character than the Pembertons.

On August 10, 1814, was born in Philadelphia General John Clifford Pemberton, a great-great-grandson of the first Israel Pemberton. John was educated in the schools of his city, and at the age of nineteen, feeling a strong inclination towards military life, he made an application to President Jackson to be admitted to the Military Academy at West Point. This application was successful—chiefly on account of the long-standing friendship between President Jackson and John Pemberton's father—and the boy was admitted to the academy in 1833, graduating with credit four years later. He was then made second lieutenant and assigned to the 4th artillery, his first service being in the Seminole War in Florida

THE BATTLE OF OPEQUON
September 19, 1864

during 1837–39. During this latter year considerable trouble was anticipated in the northern and northeastern part of Maine, where a collision with England seemed imminent. The dispute which gave cause for this apprehension arose out of a difference as to the boundary line between Maine and New Brunswick. Pemberton was in service at the northern frontier during the disturbances of 1840–42. No great outbreak occurred, however, as the dispute was averted chiefly through the wise and judicious management of General Scott, and the whole affair was closed in 1842 by the Webster-Ashburton treaty. From that time until the opening of the Mexican War Pemberton was engaged in garrison duty. He was promoted to first lieutenant during 1842; but until the war in Mexico afforded him an opportunity for distinguished service, his rank remained unchanged. With the first action in that conflict, however, he displayed the military talent which won for him many warm commendations. He was associated with General Worth as aide, and accompanied that gallant commander through the various battles on the approach to and capture of the City of Mexico. General Scott, after the capture of Contreras and Churubusco, advanced on the capital. This was during August, 1847, and Mexico could have been captured at that time; but an armistice was agreed upon, and the peace commissioner, Nicholas P. Trist, endeavored to negotiate agreeable terms with the Mexicans. This lasted until September 7, when it was found necessary to resume operations, and the first movement was made by General Worth on the southwest of the city, attacking Molino del Rey.

Pemberton, who had already been breveted captain for gallant conduct at Monterey, carried himself with much honor through the bloody battle of Molino del Rey, and received promotion to the rank of major in recognition of his able services. As an additional tribute to his valuable and meritorious conduct during this war, he was presented on his return with a sword by the citizens of Philadelphia, and received, together with the other Pennsylvania officers, the formal thanks of the State legislature.

Pemberton was married in the following year (1848) to Miss Martha, daughter of William H. Thompson, of Norfolk, Va. His service from that time until the opening of the Civil War is briefly summed up as follows: "He was promoted captain on September 16, 1850; took part in operations against the Seminole Indians in 1849–50 and 1856–57; and served at Fort Leavenworth during the Kansas troubles, and in the Utah expedition of 1858." He was actively engaged throughout the contest for the possession of Kansas, and manifested at that time considerable sympathy with the cause of the South. Amongst the officers in service in that contest there were many conflicting opinions, varying from the warmest feelings of the secessionist to the equally earnest and decided feelings of the abolitionist. It was a time when many first formed their decided opinions of the great question which rent the country in twain a few years later. Officers were affected by their experience there in widely diverse ways. Pemberton acquired stronger and stronger secessionist tendencies; General Lyon, on the other hand, was affected in an altogether opposite manner; and in 1856, when the troops were ordered to enforce the laws against the abolitionists, he seriously contemplated resigning his commission, that he might not be employed, as he said, "as a tool in the hands of evil rulers for the accomplishment of evil ends"; and it was only his being transferred to another quarter that prevented him from doing so.

When the Civil War opened Pemberton was serving at Fort Ridgely, Minn., and from there he was ordered to Washington, where he made known to a few his purpose to serve the Confederate cause. General Scott used all his influence in vain; and, in spite of all the pressure of personal solicitation from various friends, Pemberton resigned his commission, and, going South, accepted the appointment as lieutenant-colonel of the Virginia State troops, and from that time served faithfully and well the Southern States. His appointment as lieutenant-colonel dated from April 28, 1861, and he was for some time afterward actively employed in organizing and drilling troops. The work of organizing the State artillery and cavalry was the duty assigned him, and on May 8 he was appointed colonel.

Promotion was extremely rapid during the first few weeks of the war—even more so than during the course of the war, except in a few cases; for at the outset many appointments were purely tentative, many rapid changes were made, and often it became necessary to promote an officer of very low rank to a most important and responsible position simply through the lack of a man of long experience to fill the place. Later on an officer's behavior was sufficient indication of his worth, and by estimating his service a deserving rank could be justly assigned. At the opening of the war, the veterans of the Mexican War stood the fairest chance of rapid promotion, possessing records which would recommend them. Of those who served in the Mexican War Pemberton was the equal of any, and his honorable conduct secured him the respect and admiration of the Confederate authorities. It was only, therefore, a little over a month after his appointment as colonel that he was made major of artillery, and two days after that he was made brigadier-general. In the following February he was appointed major-general, and succeeded General Lee as commander of the Department of South Carolina, Georgia and Florida, holding headquarters at Charleston. This latter rank had been given him through the special request of General Lee. He was engaged at that place, strengthening the harbor defenses and placing submarine obstructions, until October, 1862, when he was made lieutenant-general and placed in command of the department that included Mississippi, Tennessee, and Eastern Louisiana, with headquarters at Jackson, Miss.

The objective point of the Northern armies at this time was Vicksburg; and, having advanced to the line of the Memphis and Charleston Railroad, they attempted as a next step the capture of Vicksburg, in order to throw the Mississippi River open to navigation. The city was strongly fortified and garrisoned, and was covered by an army, commanded by General Pemberton, posted behind the Tallahatchie. Grant moved direct from Grand Junction by way of Holly Springs; McPherson, his left from Corinth; and Sherman his right from Memphis to Wyatt,

turning Pemberton's left and forcing him to retreat to Grenada. Grant then sent Sherman back to Memphis, to organize a new force and "to move in boats, escorted by Admiral Porter's gunboat fleet, to Vicksburg, to capture the place, while he (Grant) held Pemberton at Grenada." This expedition, however, failed, owing to natural hindrances, and the capture of Holly Springs by the Confederates. McClernand took command of the Army of the Tennessee at this time, and Vicksburg was left unmolested for a time, while McClernand sent an expedition up the Arkansas River a considerable distance, capturing Fort Hindman, with 5000 prisoners, and clearing the Mississippi from all fear of attack from that quarter. On the return of this expedition, Grant came from Memphis and personally directed the siege of Vicksburg, which resulted in its capture by the combined energies of the National army and navy on July 4, 1863.

With the surrender of the city and 31,000 prisoners, Pemberton returned on parole to Richmond, and remained there until he was exchanged.

This was an unfortunate ending to General Pemberton's military career. From the moment of his entrance into the Confederate service, he had, in spite of some enmity against him as a Northerner, risen rapidly in rank and in the esteem of his fellow officers, until, previous to the capture of Vicksburg, he occupied almost the highest rank in the army. With his defeat and capture by the united skill of Grant and Porter—a combination which it was impossible for him to have withstood under the circumstances—Pemberton's service in the Confederate army was virtually at an end. No command could be given him commensurate with his rank; so he resigned, and, on being appointed inspector of ordnance, served in that capacity till the close of the war.

He then lived on a farm near Warrenton, Va., until 1876, when he returned to Philadelphia, the home of his fathers, and remained there quietly until the spring of 1881. His health failing rapidly at this time, he removed to Penllyn, Pa., hoping that the change would work an improvement in his condition; he grew worse, however, and died at that place on July 13, 1881.

CONFEDERATE BONDS

269

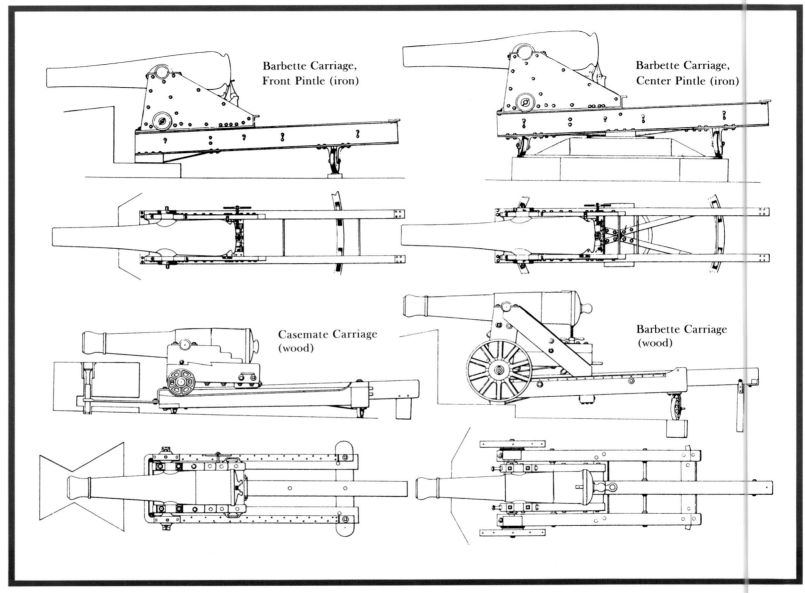

Barbette Carriage,
Front Pintle (iron)

Barbette Carriage,
Center Pintle (iron)

Casemate Carriage
(wood)

Barbette Carriage
(wood)

COASTAL ARTILLERY

GEORGE EDWARD PICKETT, C.S.A., 1825–1875

The Virginian whose name stands at the head of this article was an ideal soldier—the very embodiment and type of a hero born for immortal deeds; and on the memorable summer day to be described further on he made a mark in history to survive as long as the language of glorious emprise is read among men. Pickett was born at Richmond, Va., on January 25, 1825. It was metely the anniversary birthday of Burns, who in his "Scots wa hae wi' Wallace bled" gave the world its noblest battle-song. He also gave mankind that striking image, to be so thrillingly realized by Pickett at Gettysburg, of his Scottish forefathers in the battle-field struggling forward "red wet-shod."

The young Virginian was appointed to the Military Academy from Illinois, and graduated in 1846. He served in Mexico; was made second lieutenant in the 2d infantry March 3, 1847; was at the siege of Vera Cruz; and, in brief, was engaged in all the battles that preceded the assault and capture of the City of Mexico. Duty next took him to Texas, and subsequently he was on garrison duty in the northwestern territory at Puget Sound. At that time the dispute between our government and Great Britain respecting the northwestern boundary was in petulant progress, and Captain Pickett was ordered with 60 men to occupy San Juan Island. This movement excited the gorge of the British governor, who sent three vessels of war to summarily eject Pickett from his position. To use an expressive slang phrase of our day, the Virginian "didn't scare worth a cent." With quiet emphasis he forbade the landing of the

troops from the vessels. "I shall order my men to fire," he said, "if a man of them lands on this island." No doubt there would have been a collision but for the opportune arrival upon the scene of the British admiral, by whose order the issue of force was postponed.

On June 25, 1861, he resigned from the army, feeling that he must, as a man of honor and a Virginian, share the destiny of his State. In February, 1862, Pickett was made brigadier-general in Longstreet's division under Joseph E. Johnston, then called the Army of the Potomac, but which subsequently became the Army of Northern Virginia. He took a prominent part in the work of carnage at Seven Pines. On June 1, 1862, the National forces under McClellan, having thrown across the Chickahominy two additional divisions under command of General Sumner, attacked Pickett's brigade, which was supported by that of General Pryor. The attack was vigorously repelled by these two brigades, "the brunt of the fight falling upon General Pickett." After this his brigade, in the retreat before McClellan up the Peninsula, and in the seven days' battles around Richmond, won such a reputation that it was known as the "Game-Cock Brigade." At the battle of Gaines's Mills, fought June 27, 1862, he took a distinguished part and was severely wounded. The principal part of the Federal army was on the north side of the Chickahominy. Hill's division of the Confederate forces met this large force with impetuous courage. Some of his brigades were broken. The National forces were steadily gaining ground. Jackson had

West Point, 1846

Brigadier General, February, 1862
Major General, October, 1862

BATTLES:
Mexican War
Peninsula campaign
Seven Pines, or Fair Oaks
Seven Days' battles
Gaines's Mills
Fredericksburg
Gettysburg
Five Forks

not arrived. It was a critical moment. Three brigades under Wilcox were ordered forward against the Federal left flank, to make a diversion in favor of the attacking columns. Pickett's brigade, making an independent diversion on the left of these brigades, developed the strong position and force of the Federals in Longstreet's front. The latter at once resolved to change the feint into an attack, and orders for a general advance were issued. At this moment "Stonewall" Jackson arrived, and the air was rent with shouts. Pickett's brigade, supported by part of Anderson's brigade, swept on to the charge with fierce grandeur. Along the whole Confederate line the troops pressed steadily forward, unchecked by the terrible fire from the National forces. In this furious onslaught Pickett fell, severely wounded in the shoulder, and was unable to rejoin his command until after the first Maryland campaign. He was then made major-general, with a division composed entirely of Virginians. At the battle of Fredericksburg his division held the centre of Lee's line and took a conspicuous part in the rout of Burnside that followed.

There is little doubt that General Lee accepted the results of the first and second days' battles at Gettysburg as successes for his army, for he had gained possession of the ground from which he had driven the Union forces, and he had captured a large number of prisoners, and had added a large number of field guns to his artillery corps. On the morning of the third day he had reconnoitred the Federal position from the college cupola, and had come to the conclusion that the left centre was the weakest part in the Union lines. "With that discovery," says a competent military authority, "he determined upon a move the grandest ever conceived by a commanding general, and, as the result proved, the most fatal. One formidable obstacle stood in the way of his hopes—the Federal artillery. By opening an attack along the entire line with his own guns, he hoped to be able to destroy many of the enemy's, besides exhausting his stock of ammunition; so that when the crucial test of the day came—the breaking of the Federal line at the left centre—their heavy guns would be practically useless for defensive purposes. What was to be the next move, was a question in the minds of both armies during the calm which succeeded the cannonading. In the morning Lee had told Longstreet to order Pickett's division, which belonged to his corps, to make an attack in force on the Federal left centre. Pickett had been apprised of the work cut out for him, and, like the brave officer he was, held himself in readiness to perform his duty." His division, consisting of three brigades under the commands of Armistead, Garnett and Kemper, lay in a clump of woods, almost directly opposite the point which they were to attack. The three brigades were made up of 15 Virginia regiments, all tried and true men, who had won many laurels on the battlefields of their native State.

At noon there was a deep calm in the warm air. General Lee determined to mass his artillery in front of Hill's corps, and under cover of this tremendous fire to direct the assault on the National centre. To this end more than a hundred pieces of artillery were placed in position. On the opposite side of the valley might be perceived, by the gradual concentration of the Federals in the woods, the preparations for the mighty contest that was at last to break the ominous silence. At 12:30 p.m. the shrill sound of a Whitworth gun pierced the air. Instantly more than 200 cannon belched forth their thunder at one time. "It was absolutely appalling," an officer writes. "The air was hideous with most discordant noise. The very earth shook beneath our feet, and the hills and rocks seemed to reel like drunken men. For an hour and a half this most terrific fire was continued, during which time the shrieking of shell, the crash of falling timber, the fragments of rocks flying through the air, shattered from the cliffs by solid shot, the heavy mutterings from the valley between the opposing armies, the splash of bursting shrapnell, and the fierce neighing of wounded artillery horses, combined to form a picture terribly grand and sublime."

Part of this time Pickett's division had been lying listening in the woods, but during the last half hour they had been moved into position. The time had now come. The hour was ripe for the fruition of the hopes of the Confederacy. Pickett mounted

THE BATTLE OF CEDAR CREEK
October 19, 1864

"I traveled along the road, but I found it so blocked with wagons and wounded that I was forced to take to the fields. When past the obstructions I again took the road, which I found full of unhurt men. But when they saw me they threw up their hats and faced about, shouting. 'He's got back again!' Getty's division and the cavalry were the only troops resisting the enemy. Gen. Torbert was the first officer to meet me, saying, 'My God, I'm glad you've come.' I rode along the front, the men arose up with cheers of recognition, and soon my whole line, as far as I could see, was driving everything before it."

Philip H. Sheridan, Major General, U.S.A.

his white charger, and, riding up to Longstreet, asked for orders. "Is the time for my advance come?" he asked his general. "He repeated the question," writes Longstreet, "and without opening my lips I bowed in answer."—"Sir," cried Pickett, "I shall lead my division forward."

At the head of his command, he rode gallantly and gracefully down the slope into this thunderous scene of carnage. Longstreet has told how he looked, with his "jaunty cap raked well over his right ear, and his long auburn locks, nicely dressed, hanging almost to his shoulders. He seemed rather a holiday soldier than a general at the head of a column which was about to make one of the grandest and most desperate assaults recorded in the annals of wars." His coolness is illustrated by an incident which occurred shortly after he had given orders to his brigade commanders to prepare for the charge. "He was sitting on his horse," says a Confederate colonel of artillery, "when General Wilcox rode up to him, and, taking a flask of whiskey from his pocket, said: 'Pickett, take a drink with me. In an hour you will be in hell or glory!' 'Be it so, General Wilcox,' returned Pickett, taking the proffered drink; 'whatever my fate, I shall do my duty like a brave man.'"

Down the hill went the 15,000 Virginians with the precision and regularity of a parade. When a short distance from their starting point, they obliqued to the right and then to the left, so as to secure cover in the undulations of the ground over which they were crossing. As they reached the Emmittsburg road, the Confederate guns, which had fired over their heads to cover the movement, ceased, and there stood exposed those devoted troops, as a cloudburst of flame, shot and shell came thundering from the ridge into their devoted ranks. There was no halting, no wavering. Through half a mile of shot and shell pressed Pickett and his devoted men. It was no sudden impetus of excitement that carried them through this terrible ordeal, where every inch of air vibrated and thrilled with the wing of death, and where every footprint was "red-wet" with the dew of destruction. Steadily the heroic 15,000, with rapidly thinning ranks, pressed forward. When within a short distance of the Federal line, their wild yells of defiance were heard above the thundering of the guns. Onward they dashed with a wild disordered rush. Garnett, whose brigade was in advance, fell dead within a hundred yards of the Union front. His men rushed madly upon the 69th and 71st Pennsylvania regiments, who had been awaiting the oncoming attack. General Hancock threw a force on Pickett's flank, and two of Armistead's regiments were frightfully cut up and disorganized by this movement. Armistead, swinging his sword wildly, urged his men forward, and reached the front rank, where he was shot down; but Pickett is unscathed in the storm. His flashing sword has taken the key of the enemy's position, and again and again the Confederate flag is lifted through the smoke. "With what breathless interest we watched the struggle," writes a Confederate officer. "General Lee, from a convenient point, stood calmly looking at the struggle. Not an expression of the face or an action indicated that he had other than hopes of success. He was imperturbable as a rock. What emotions swayed his soul at that supreme moment he and God alone knew."

The first line of the Federals were driven back upon the earthworks near the artillery. There the work of death was renewed with frightful slaughter. Charges of grape shot were fired into Pickett's men with terrible effect. The contestants became mixed in a confused mass, the only way of distinguishing one from the other being the blue and gray uniforms. The fighting became like that of an infuriated mob. "Confederates and Federals faced each other with clubbed muskets, their faces distorted with the fury of madmen. Commands were useless; they could not be heard above the din. A clump of trees just within the angle wall became the objective point of the Confederates. Armistead resolved to take it. Placing his hat on his sword, he rallied about him 150 men, who were willing to follow wherever he would lead. Rushing forward with his gallant band, he reached a Federal gun, and just as he had adjured his followers to 'give them the cold steel, boys!' he fell dead in his tracks, pierced with bullets." The death of this gallant officer marked the complete failure of the Confederate assault, and beaten but undismayed, the remnant of Pickett's men retraced their way across the field now strewn with their dead. Riding up to General Lee, Pickett dismounted, and saluting, said in a voice tremulous with emotion: "General, my noble division has been swept away."—"It was all my fault; get together and let us do the best we can toward saving that which is left us," was Lee's quiet reply.

Thus at Gettysburg the right army of the rebellion was bro-

ken, and it must always stand out in Confederate annals like

Flodden's fatal field,
Where shivered was fair Scotland's spear,
And broken was her shield.

After the war General Pickett returned to Richmond, where he spent the remainder of his days as a life insurance agent, and died at Norfolk, Va., July 30, 1875.

Mountain Artillery Harness

LEONIDAS POLK, C.S.A., 1806–1864

West Point, 1827

*Major General, 1861
Lieutenant General,
October, 1862*

*COMMANDED
Mississippi River Defenses
Army of Kentucky
Army of the Mississippi
Department of Alabama,
Mississippi, and
Eastern Louisiana*

Polk presents an altogether unique figure in the War of the Rebellion. An educated soldier, he had at thirty-two become an ordained bishop of the church. At the first blast of the war-trumpet the Bible and mitre are laid aside for the sword and charger, and he yields up his hearth in the bloody conflict, a martyr to what he considered duty. Regarded either as a soldier of the cross or of the Confederacy, he was a man of essentially practical mind, consulting facts at every step just as the mariner consults the face of the heavens, seeking success above all things, and prudent even to circumspectness.

General Polk was born at Raleigh, N.C., April 10, 1806, and was educated at the University of North Carolina, and afterwards at the West Point Military Academy, where he graduated in 1827, and was breveted second lieutenant of artillery. During his sojourn at the military academy the young man's character and disposition had attracted the attention and sympathy of Rev. (afterwards bishop) Charles P. McIlvaine, then chaplain, and at the suggestion of this reverend gentleman the young lieutenant was induced to study for the purpose of assuming holy orders. He therefore resigned his commission the following December, and was made a deacon in the Protestant Episcopal Church in 1830. His ordination as priest took place the following year, when he was appointed assistant in the Monumental Church, Richmond. He occupied this post for a year, when failing health induced him to go to Europe for the purpose of recuperating. Soon after his return he removed to Tennessee, and became rector of St.

GEN. A SHORT HISTORY OF LEONIDAS POLK

Peter's Church, Columbia. In 1834 he was clerical deputy to the General Convention of the Episcopal Church, and in 1835 a member of the standing committee of the diocese. In 1838 he received the degree of S.T.D. from Columbia, and the same year he was elected and consecrated missionary bishop of Arkansas and the Indian Territory south of the 36th parallel of latitude, with provisional charge of the diocese of Alabama, Mississippi, and Louisiana, and the missions in the republic of Texas. These charges he held till 1841, when he resigned all of them except the diocese of Louisiana, of which he remained bishop till his death, intending to resume Episcopal duties after he had been released from service in the tented field.

In 1856 he initiated the movement to establish the University of the South, and until 1860 was engaged with Bishop Stephen Elliott and other Southern bishops in perfecting plans that resulted in the opening of that institution at Sewanee, Tenn.

At the beginning of the Civil War Bishop Polk was a strong sympathizer with the doctrine of secession. His birth, education and associations were alike Southern; and his property, which was very considerable in land and slaves, aided to identify him with the project of establishing a Southern Confederacy. His familiarity with the Valley of the Mississippi prompted him to urge upon Jefferson Davis and the Confederate authorities the importance of fortifying and holding its strategical points. Amid the excitement of the time and the stirring bustle of war preparation, the influences of his old military training became uppermost in his

THE BATTLE OF FRANKLIN
November 30, 1864

mind. He "smelt the battle from afar," and longed to hear "the thunder of the captains and the shouting." Under these circumstances the offer of a major-generalship by President Davis was not unfavorably regarded. But before assuming "these ill-beseeming arms" he applied for advice to Bishop William Meade, of Virginia, who replied that, his being an exceptional case, he could not advise against the acceptance of the military commission; whereupon the bishop at once translated himself "out of the speech of peace that bears such grace into the harsh and boisterous tongue of war; turning his books to graves, his ink to blood, his pens to lances, and his tongue divine to a loud trumpet and a point of war."—Shakespeare, *Henry IV*.

General Polk's first command extended from the mouth of the Red River on both sides of the Mississippi to Paducah on the Ohio, his headquarters being at Memphis. Under his general directions the extensive works at New Madrid and Fort Pillow, Ky., Island No. 10, Memphis and other points were constructed.

On September 4, 1861, Polk transferred his headquarters to Columbus, where the Confederates had massed a large force of infantry, artillery and cavalry, and three steamboats. Here he strengthened his position and occupied Belmont, a small village on the Missouri shore, so as to command both banks of the stream. With a view of surprising the small Confederate force on the west bank, General Grant collected a fleet of river steamboats, and, embarking at night, steamed down the river unobserved. Within a few miles of Columbus and Belmont the river makes a sudden bend, and at this point Grant disembarked his forces and advanced on Belmont. On the morning of November 7 the action commenced, the Federals making a desperate effort to turn the Confederate right wing. Finally, the Confederate troops running short of ammunition, a retreat was ordered, during which the line was considerably broken up and disorganized. At this critical moment three regiments appeared on the Federal rear, and, finding that Polk himself was crossing and landing troops far up the river on his line of retreat, Grant at once began to fall back. The Federals had not

proceeded far before they were attacked on the flank, while "General Polk in person was pushing the rear vigorously, capturing prisoners and arms." A defeat in the early part of the engagement was thus converted into a victory for the Confederate arms.

General Polk remained at Columbus until March, 1862, when he was ordered to join the army of Johnston and Beauregard at Corinth. He commanded the 1st corps at the battle of Shiloh, and took part in the subsequent operations that ended with the evacuation of Corinth. Being left in command at Bardstown, he was directed by Bragg, if pressed by a force too large to justify his giving battle, to fall back in the direction of Bryantsville, in front of which it was proposed to concentrate for action. "The plan of battle, however, was disarranged: as Polk, after a council with his officers, decided not to risk the attack, but to move, as originally instructed by Bragg, toward Harrodsburg." Proceeding rapidly to that point, Bragg was met there by General Polk on October 6, to whom written orders were given "to move Cheatham's division, now at Harrodsburg, back to Perryville, and to proceed to that point himself; attack the enemy immediately, rout him, and then move rapidly to join Major-general Smith." Polk arrived at Perryville before midnight of the 7th, and at noon next day was fought the battle of that name. When night came, the Confederates had possession of the battle-field, "with thousands of the enemy's killed and wounded, several batteries of artillery and 600 prisoners."

In October, 1862, he was promoted to the rank of lieutenant-general, and during that month and November he was in command of the armies of Kentucky and Mississippi, and conducted the Confederate retreat from the former State. He commanded the right wing of the Army of Tennessee at the indecisive engagement at Stone River. Again at Chickamauga he occupied a distinguished position, although his action there was the subject of much unfavorable criticism by General Bragg.

"On the morning of the 13th September," says General

D. H. Hill, "I was notified that General Polk was to attack Crittenden at Lee & Gordon's Mills." This attack was not made. In his official report Bragg thus speaks of this failure. According to this, his first order to General Polk to attack was dated 6 p.m. of September 12, 1863, and was as follows:

"General: I inclose you a dispatch from General Pegram. This presents you a fine opportunity of striking Crittenden in detail, and I hope you will avail yourself of it at daylight tomorrow. This division crushed, and the others are yours. . . . I shall be delighted to hear of your success."

This order was twice repeated at short intervals. The last dispatch was as follows: "The enemy is approaching from the south, and it is highly important that your attack in the morning be quick and decided; let no time be lost."

When morning came, Bragg was early in the saddle vainly listening for Polk's guns. Chafing with impatience, he sent a messenger, Major Lee, to ascertain the cause of the delay. Major Lee found Polk and his staff seated at a comfortable breakfast, and he so reported to Bragg, whose profanity thereupon was upon a par with that of the British army in Flanders, according to "Uncle Toby."

Bragg had an unfortunate proclivity for finding a scapegoat for every failure and disaster. According to his official report of the Chickamauga campaign, it was only through Polk's disobedience of orders that the Federal army was saved from annihilation. As General Polk was relieved of his command in consequence of this report, it may be well to hear what his son, Captain Polk, who belonged to his father's staff, has to say by way of explanation.

The delay in the attack of the 13th is thus explained: "Polk was told that he would find Crittenden east of the creek about Pea Vine Church, on the Graysville road, and was directed to attack him there at daylight of the 13th. He moved as ordered and found no enemy—Crittenden having crossed to the west of the creek the evening before. General Bragg in his report neglects to take this fact into account, and thus the impression that Crittenden's escape was due to General Polk's tardiness

in moving, rather than to his own tardiness in ordering the movement. It should have been ordered for the morning of the 12th."

Subsequently President Davis, with General Bragg's approval, offered to reinstate General Polk, but he declined. He was then appointed to take charge of the camp of Confederate prisoners that had been paroled at Vicksburg and Port Hudson. In December, 1863, he was assigned to the Department of Alabama, Mississippi, and East Louisiana, in place of General Joe Johnston, who was placed in command of the Army of Tennessee. By skilful dispositions of his troops, he prevented the junction of the Federal cavalry with General Sherman's army in Southern Mississippi. General's Polk's prestige being restored, he was ordered to unite his command (the Army of the Mississippi) with the army of General J. E. Johnston, who was opposing the march of Sherman to Atlanta, and whose headquarters were at Dalton.

Before 10 a.m. of May 13, 1864, the Confederate army moved from Dalton and reached Resaca just as the Federal troops, approaching from Snake Creek Gap, were encountering Loring's division a mile from the station. Their approach was delayed long enough by Loring's opposition to give the Confederate commander time to select the ground to be occupied by his troops; and while they were taking this ground the Federal army was forming in front of them. The left of General Polk's corps occupied the west face of the intrenchment at Resaca. Hardee's corps formed the centre, while Hood's was on the right. On the 14th spirited fighting was maintained by the Federal army all along the front. Sharp fighting was renewed on the 15th, with so much vigor that many of the Federal assailants pressed up to the Confederate intrenchments. In General Sherman's language, "the sounds of musketry and cannon rose all day to the dignity of a battle."

The occupation of Resaca being exceedingly hazardous, General Johnston determined to abandon the place. So the army was ordered to cross the Oostenaula about midnight— Hardee's and Polk's corps by the railroad and trestle bridges

and Hood's by the pontoons. After resting near Calhoun, the army was joined by the cavalry of General Polk's command. In the expectation that a part of the Federal army would follow, it was arranged that Polk's command should engage the column when it should arrive at Kingston. After some manœuvring, General Johnston saw that a battle was inevitable. "The enemy," he says, "got into position soon after our troops were formed, and skirmished until dark. During the evening Lieutenant-generals Polk and Hood asserted that a part of the line of each would be so enfiladed next morning by the Federal batteries that they would be unable to hold their ground an hour. They therefore urged me to abandon the position at once. After the matter was discussed an hour, I yielded." The Con-

federate army abandoned the ground, and some further skirmishing ensued up to June 13. Next day was to be General Polk's last. General Johnston thus simply narrates the last incident of all in the singular career:

"In the morning of the 14th General Hardee and I rode to the summit of Pine Mountain, to decide if the outpost there should be maintained. General Polk accompanied us. After we had concluded our examination, and the abandonment of the hill had been decided on, a few shots were fired at us from a battery of Parrott guns a quarter of a mile in our front; the third of these passed through General Polk's chest, killing him instantly. The event produced deep sorrow in the army, in every battle of which he had been distinguished."

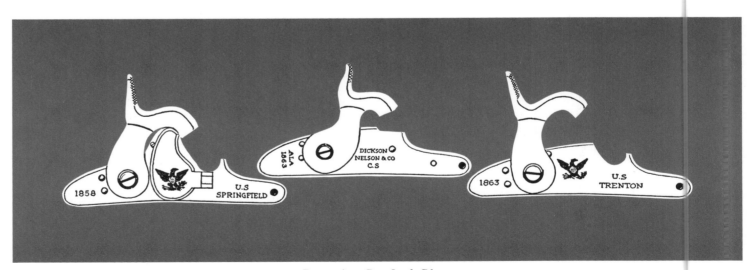

Percussion Cap Lock Plates

STERLING PRICE, C.S.A., 1809–1867

Price has been aptly termed the true "Hero of Missouri." He started into his famous campaign in the West without a dollar, without a wagon or team, without a cartridge or a bayonet-gun. When he commenced his retreat he had about 8000 bayonet-guns, 50 pieces of cannon, 400 tents, and many other articles needful in an army, for which his men were almost exclusively indebted to their own strong arms in battle.

Price managed to subsist an army without governmental resources. He seldom complained of want of transportation. His men were never demoralized by hunger. "They would go into the cornfield, shuck the corn, shell it, take it to the mill, and bring it into camp ground into meal. Or, if they had no flour, they took wheat from the stack, threshed it themselves, and asked the aid of the nearest miller to reduce it to flour. He demonstrated that such an army could go where they pleased in an agricultural country." His men were always cheerful. Frequently, on the eve of an engagement, they danced around their campfires with bare feet and in rag costumes, of which it was declared "Billy Barlow's dress at a circus would be decent in comparison." Price himself wore nothing on his shoulders but a brown linen duster; and this and his long streaming white hair made him a singular figure on the battle-field.

General Sterling Price was born in Prince Edward County, Virginia, September 11, 1809. He was a student at Hampden Sidney College, and read law. In 1831 he moved to Chariton County, Missouri, and was speaker in the Missouri House of

Representatives in 1840–44. He was elected to congress in the latter year as a Democrat, but resigned in 1846, and raised the 2d Missouri cavalry regiment for the Mexican War, becoming its colonel. He moved his regiment, with that of Colonel Doniphan—both under command of General Stephen W. Kearny—from Fort Leavenworth to Santa Fé, more than 1000 miles. Colonel Price, with about 2000 men, was left in charge of New Mexico.

An insurrection eventuated in Santa Fé, to which Governor Brent and several of his officers fell victims during their absence from the town. Colonel Price now attacked the Mexicans, completed the conquest of the province in several brilliant actions, and after his promotion to brigadier-general of volunteers marched to Chihuahua July 20, 1847, of which he was made military governor. He defeated the Mexicans at Santa Cruz de Rosales, March 16, 1848.

General Price was Governor of Missouri from 1853 till 1857; bank commissioner of the State from 1857 to 1861, and president of the State Convention, March 4, 1861. About this time he was commissioned by Governor Jackson as major-general, and authorized to consult with General Harney, of the Federal forces, as to the best mode of "restoring peace and good order to the people of the State, in subordination to the laws of the general and State governments." In view of the riotous demonstrations at St. Louis, Price, having "full authority over the militia of the State," undertook, with the sanction of the governor, to maintain order; and General Harney declared that he had no intention of using the military at his

command to cause disturbance. Soon after this General Harney was removed by orders from Washington, and General Price continued to busy himself with the duties of his command. On June 4, 1861, he issued an address, in which he declared that the people of Missouri should exercise the right to choose their own position in any contest which might be forced upon them, unaided by any military force whatever. In the conclusion of his address he wrote: "The people of Missouri cannot be forced, under the terrors of a military invasion, into a position not of their own free choice. A million of such people as the citizens of Missouri were never yet subjugated, and, if attempted, let no apprehension be entertained of the result."

On June 13, 1861, Governor Jackson issued his proclamation calling for 50,000 volunteers. Price appointed nine brigadier-generals, but the brigadiers had no force at their command; and even if men were not lacking, arms and ammunition were. As for military training and discipline, there had been for years no military organization and not even a militia muster in Missouri. The first development of the campaign was General Price's order to his brigadiers to organize their forces as rapidly as possible, and push them forward to Booneville and Lexington. "No serious thought was entertained of giving battle at Booneville. About 1800 Missourians were assembled in camp near there, and not more than one-third of them were armed." On June 20, General Lyon, with a Federal force 3000 strong debarked near Booneville. There was a skirmish, and the Missourians scattered in flight, leaving three men killed and 25 or 30 wounded.

Governor Jackson took the field in person after this affray, and during the skirmishing that followed General Price was on the sick list. He joined the governor's forces at Carthage in the early part of July. Next day the forces at Carthage, under their respective commands, took up their line of march for Cowskin Prairie, near the boundary of the Indian Nation. Here they remained for several days organizing and drilling. General Price continued to receive reinforcements, and the whole numerical strength of the command was now rated about 10,000.

With this imperfectly armed force it was decided to assume the offensive; and it having been ascertained that the Federal commanders, Lee, Sturgis, Sweeny and Sigel, were about to form a junction at Springfield, it was determined by Price, McCulloch and Pearce to march upon that place and attack the enemy.

When the army reached Crane Creek, about 30 miles from Springfield, a consultation was held as to their future course. General Price earnestly advocated an advance. General McCulloch doubted its prudence. "He looked with great concern on the large proportion of undisciplined men in Price's command, while he regarded the unarmed men as encumbrances." Hence he suggested the manifest wisdom of avoiding battle with the disciplined enemy upon his own ground, and in greatly superior numbers. "General Price resented the idea of the nature of the materials under his command, and assured McCulloch that when the time of battle came these untaught and headstrong men would fight together, and with a resolution which would spurn defeat."

In the midst of this hesitation General McCulloch received a general order from General Polk to advance upon the enemy in Missouri. Another council was thereupon called. "McCulloch exhibited the order he had received, and offered to march at once upon Springfield, upon condition that he should have the chief command of the army. The question of rank was one of no little embarrassment. Price was a major-general in the State service; McCulloch was a brigadier-general in the Confederate service." The question was solved by Price in a noble and patriotic spirit. He relinquished his post to McCulloch, expressing himself in substance as follows: "I seek not distinction. I am not fighting for that, but in the defense of the liberties of my countrymen. It matters little *what* position I hold. I am ready to surrender not only my command, but my life, as a sacrifice to the cause." That his services and his presence among the men should not be lost, he took a subordinate position in the pending contest. McCulloch assumed chief command, and Price was a division general under him.

On the morning of August 10 McCulloch was "quietly taking breakfast," when he was apprised by his couriers that the enemy was in sight, and in great force, and had gained both sides of his camp. In the action that followed the Federal forces were completely defeated, and General Lyon was killed. The Federal loss was about 2000 in killed and wounded; 300 prisoners were taken, and six pieces of artillery. "McCulloch officially stated his loss as 265 killed and 800 wounded. More than half of this loss was among the Missourians commanded by General Price."

After this rather brilliant victory of Oak Hill, or Wilson's Creek, McCulloch and Price could not agree upon a plan of campaign. The former, therefore, took the responsibility of withdrawing the Confederate forces, and retired with his army to the frontiers of Arkansas. In August Price took his troops towards the Missouri River, and pressed onward towards Lexington, which was feebly defended. As Price approached the town a sharp encounter occurred with the Union outposts. When the forces of Price attacked the breastworks they were met by a deadly fire. "Finding that a surprise was hopeless, and that the Federals were assembling a large part of their artillery at the threatened point, the column of attack was withdrawn. Discovering at the close of the day that his ammunition was nearly exhausted, and that his men, most of whom had not eaten anything in thirty-six hours, required rest and food, General Price withdrew from the town and encamped. On the 20th the attack was renewed. Colonel Mulligan, the brave defender of the place, received two wounds, and was finally compelled to surrender. Immediately General Price issued an order that the forces under Colonel Mulligan, having stacked their arms, "were not to be insulted by word or act, for they had fought like brave men." Mulligan, having given up his sword, had it immediately returned to him by General Price, who said he "could not see a man of his valor without his sword."

Finding himself in front of overwhelming forces, General Price commenced his retreat in the latter part of September. It was admirably executed. His army had given an exhibition of spirit and resource almost unparalleled. His ragged heroes had marched over 800 miles, and had fought the Federals wherever found. The campaign was little less than a puzzle to military critics. He now took up quarters at Springfield, to forage his army and obtain supplies. He took up a strong position and fortified it, expecting that McCulloch would move to his assistance. Meantime Major-general Van Dorn had been appointed to the trans-Mississippi command by President Davis. At the battle of Elk Horn, which followed, Van Dorn commanded the united forces of Price and McCulloch. There was little advantage gained by either side in this engagement.

Van Dorn was now ordered to Tennessee, and General Price accompanied him, and took part in the engagements around Corinth. He retreated under Beauregard to Tupelo, was assigned to the command of the Army of the West in March, 1862, and then to the District of Tennessee. He moved towards Nashville, and met and fought General Rosecrans, in command of Grant's right wing, at Iuka, September 19, 1862. He participated in Van Dorn's disastrous attack upon Corinth, and in the operations of General John C. Pemberton in Northern Mississippi during the winter of 1862-63. He was then ordered to the trans-Mississippi department, and took part in the unsuccessful attack upon Helena, July 21, 1863.

General Price was now assigned to the command of the District of Arkansas. He was driven from Little Rock by General Frederic Steele, but successfully resisted Steele's advance toward Red River in March, 1864, and forced him to retreat.

About the middle of September, 1864, General Price entered Missouri, crossing the State line from Arkansas by way of Pocahontas and Poplar Bluff. He had about 10,000 men, under the command of Generals Shelby, Marmaduke and Fagan. His force advanced, driving before him the various outpost garrisons. General Rosecrans was largely superior in force to Price; but he appears to have been unable to concentrate his troops, and the country was surprised to find Price moving almost without molestation, and doing incalculable mischief.

Poor deluded Miss-Souri takes a Secession bath, and finds it much hotter than she expected!

On October 23 General Price was brought to battle by General Curtis, with four brigades of Federal cavalry. Price was defeated, and Generals Marmaduke and Cabell were taken prisoners, while the Confederates lost nearly all their artillery. On the following day Price was again attacked, near Fort Scott, and obliged hurriedly to retreat into Kansas. He then turned into the Indian Territory, and subsequently went into winter quarters in the south of Arkansas. His men were in a worse plight than when they started from that State, and the conclusion of his campaign was an undoubted failure. "The fault is," says a Confederate chronicler, "that General Price had retreated from Missouri, not so much under the stress of the enemy's arm as from inherent faults in his own enterprise. He had declared that his invasion was not a raid—that he came to possess Missouri; but the breadth of the excursion, its indefiniteness and the failure to concentrate on important points ruined him. While his command roamed through the State, his men, brought to the vicinity of their old homes, which they had not seen for several years, were exposed to unusual temptations to desert; and instead of being reinforced, his command was diminished by desertions at every step of the march."

After the surrender of the Confederate armies, General Price went to Mexico, but returned to Missouri in 1866, and died suddenly in St. Louis, September 29, 1867.

RAPHAEL SEMMES, C.S.N.,1809–1877

This distinguished naval officer was born in Charles County, Maryland, on September 27, 1809. President John Quincy Adams appointed him a midshipman in the United States Navy in 1826. In 1834, after returning from his first cruise, he was admitted to the bar, but decided to remain a seaman. In 1837 he was made a lieutenant, and in 1842 he removed to Alabama.

At the beginning of the war with Mexico he was made flag-lieutenant under Commodore Conner, commanding the squadron in the Gulf; and in the siege of Vera Cruz he was in charge of one of the naval batteries on shore.

Lieutenant Semmes served for several years as inspector of light-houses on the Gulf coast. On the secession of Alabama, February 15, 1861, he resigned his commission in the United States Navy and reported to Jefferson Davis at Montgomery. The President of the Confederacy instructed him to return to the North and endeavor to procure mechanics skilled in the manufacture of ordnance and rifle machinery, and the preparation of fixed ammunition and percussion caps. He was also to buy war material on a large scale. In Washington he examined the machinery of the arsenal, and conferred with mechanics whom he desired to go South. Within the next three weeks he made a tour through the principal workshops of New York, Connecticut, and Massachusetts, and purchased large quantities of percussion caps in New York, which were sent to Montgomery without any disguise. Furthermore he made contracts for light artillery, powder, and other munitions of war, and shipped thousands of pounds

of powder to the South. He returned to Montgomery on April 4, to find that he had been commissioned commander in the Confederate navy and placed in charge of the light-house bureau. He relinquished this position within two weeks, to go to New Orleans to fit out the *Sumter*, with which he captured eighteen merchantmen. After the blockade of that ship at Tangiers by the United States men-of-war, he sold her and went to England, having been promoted meantime to the rank of captain. There the *Alabama* was built for him by the Lairds, of Birkenhead. In the House of Commons the senior partner of the constructors stated "that she left Liverpool a perfectly legitimate transaction." Captain James D. Bullock, as agent for the Confederacy, superintended her construction. As a "ruse," she was sent on a trial trip with a large party of ladies and gentlemen. A tug met the ship in the Channel and took off the guests, while the 290th ship built in the Laird yard proceeded on her voyage to the Island of Terceira, in the Azores, whither a transport had preceded her with war material. Captain Semmes and his officers, carried by the *Bahama*, met her there. Under the lee of the island, the ships were lashed together, and the transfer of armament and stores was accomplished on August 20, 1862, and on Sunday morning, under a cloudless sky, the *Alabama* was put in commission. The *Alabama* was built for speed rather than for battle. Her lines were symmetrical and fine; her material of the best. In fifteen minutes her propeller could be hoisted, and she could go through every evolution under sail without any impediment.

Rear Admiral, 1865

COMMANDED
CSS *Sumter*, 1861–62
CSS *Alabama*, 1862–64
James River Squadron

BATTLES:
Mexican War
vs. USS *Hatteras*
vs. USS *Vanderbilt*
vs. USS *Kearsarge*

In less time her propeller could be lowered; with sails furled and yards braced within two points of a head-wind, she was a perfect steamer. "Her speed, independent, was from ten to twelve knots; combined, and under favorable circumstances, she could make fifteen knots." When ready for sea, she drew fifteen feet of water. She was brigantine rigged, with long lower masts, which enabled her to carry an immense spread of lower canvas and to lay close to the wind. Her engines were 300 horse-power, with a condensing apparatus. Her armament consisted of eight guns: one Blakely 100-pounder rifled gun, pivoted forward; one eight-inch solid shot gun, pivoted abaft the main-mast; and six 32-pounders in broadside. The crew numbered 120 men and 24 officers.

The eleventh day after going into commission Captain Semmes captured his first prize. After working around the Azores for some weeks with fine breezes, he shaped his course for Sandy Hook. His prizes gave him regularly the mails from the United States, from which he gathered the fitting out of the army under General Banks for the attack on Galveston and the invasion of Texas, and the day on which the fleet would sail; whereupon Captain Semmes calculated about the time they would arrive, and shaped his course accordingly, coaling and refitting his ship at the Arcas Keys. His plan was to take the bearing of the National fleet, and "after the mid-watch was set and all quieted down, we would silently steam among them, pouring in a continuous discharge of shell, to fire and sink as we went; and before the convoys could move, we expected to accomplish our work and be off on another cruise. But instead of sighting General Banks's fleet of transports, we sighted five vessels of war at anchor, and soon after our lookout reported a steamer standing out for us. We were then under topsails only, with a light breeze, heading off shore, and gradually drawing our pursuer from the squadron. About dark he came up with us, and in an action of thirteen minutes we had sunk the *Hatteras*."

After cruising for some time along the coast of Brazil, Captain Semmes steered across to the Cape of Good Hope, where he played "hide and seek" with the United States steamer *Vanderbilt*, whose commander, Captain Baldwin, had generously explained to Sir Baldwin Walker, the English Admiral of the station at Simon's Town, that "he did not intend to fire a gun at the *Alabama*, but to run her down and sink her." But Captain Semmes had no intention of trying "conclusions" with the *Vanderbilt*. He quietly stole away, and shaped his course for the Straits of Java. "Our long stretch across the Indian Ocean," writes Captain Semmes's executive officer, McIntosh Kell, "placed us in the China Sea, where we were least expected, and where we soon fell in with the China trade. In a few weeks we had so paralyzed the enemy's commerce that their ships were absolutely locked up in port, and neutrals doing the carrying trade." The same officer relates some amusing anecdotes. While taking the burning of their ships very philosophically, as among the fortunes of war, some clung to "creature comforts" with ludicrous persistency. "Upon one occasion, going aboard a fine ship, I told the captain, 'he might bring away his personal effects.' He made a sensational scene by earnestly appealing to me to grant him one request. It was that he might be permitted to take with him 'Spurgeon's Sermons and a keg of very fine whisky.' The sermons I granted, but told him the whisky must go overboard."

It was a popular belief on board the *Alabama* that Captain Semmes had been a parson. This fact inspired many curious sailor ditties, such, for instance, as the following:

Oh, our captain said, When my fortune's made
  I'll buy a church to preach in,
And fill it full of toots and horns,
  And have a jolly Methodee screechin'.

And I'll pray the Lord from night to morn
  To weather Old Yankee Doodle;
And I'll run a hinfant Sunday-school
  With part of the Yankee's boodle.

"One pleasant day, on the coast of Brazil," writes the execu tive officer quoted above, "we captured a prize, and Captain Semmes said to me: 'We will make a target of her. Up to this time we have carried out the instructions of the department—destroying the enemy's commerce and driving it away from every sea we have visited, while avoiding their cruisers. Should we now fall in with a cruiser not too heavy for us, we will give her battle.' I at once called all hands to general quarters, and, taking a convenient distance from our prize, practiced principally with shell to see the effect. Many of our fuses proved defective. Upon visiting the target, I found that one of the 100-pound shells had exploded on the quarter-deck, and I counted fifteen marks from its missiles; which justifies me in asserting that, had the 100-pound shell which we placed in the stern-port of the *Kearsarge* exploded, it would have changed the result of the fight."

Captain Semmes now set his course for Europe, and on June 11, 1864, entered the port of Cherbourg, and at once applied for permission to go into dock. There being none but national docks, the Emperor Napoleon III had first to be communicated with before permission could be granted, and he was absent from Paris. It was during this interval of waiting that the Federal steamer *Kearsarge* steamed into port, for the purpose, it was understood, of taking on board the prisoners the *Alabama* had landed from her two last prizes. Captain Semmes, however, objected to this, "on the ground that the *Kearsarge* was adding to her crew in a neutral port." The authorities conceding this objection valid, the *Kearsarge* steamed out of the harbor without anchoring. After she left the harbor, Captain Semmes said to his chief executive officer: "I am going to fight the *Kearsarge*; what do you think of it?" As a result of the discussion that ensued, Captain Semmes communicated through the Confederate agent that, if Captain Winslow would wait outside the harbor, he would fight him as soon as he could coal ship. The next morning, Sunday, June 19, between nine and ten o'clock, the *Alabama* weighed anchor, and stood out of the western entrance of the harbor, the French iron-clad frigate *Couronne* following. The day was bright and beautiful,

with a light breeze blowing. The report of the fight had been noised abroad, and many persons from Paris and the surrounding country had come down to witness the engagement. As the *Alabama* rounded the breakwater, Captain Semmes discovered the *Kearsarge* about seven miles to the northeast. When everything was ready for action on board the *Alabama*, Captain Semmes mounted a gun-carriage and made the following address:

"OFFICERS AND SEAMEN OF THE 'ALABAMA':—You have at length another opportunity of meeting the enemy—the first that has been presented to you since you sunk the *Hatteras*. In the meantime you have been all over the world, and it is not too much to say that you have destroyed and driven for protection under neutral flags one-half of the enemy's commerce, which at the beginning of the war covered every sea. This is an achievement of which you may well be proud, and a grateful country will not be unmindful of it. The name of your ship has become a household word wherever civilization extends. Shall that name be tarnished by defeat? The thing is impossible! Remember that you are in the English Channel—the theatre of so much of the naval glory of our race—and that the eyes of all Europe are at this moment upon you. The flag that floats over you is that of a young republic, which bids defiance to her enemies whenever and wherever found. Show the world that you know how to uphold it. Go to your quarters."

In about forty-five minutes the action began. Both ships approached each other at high speed, firing broadside batteries at 500 yards. To prevent passing, each ship used a strong helm to port. Thus the action was fought round a common centre, gradually becoming less circumscribed. Captain Semmes stood on the horse-block abreast the mizzen-mast, with his glass in his hand. He cried to executive officer Kell: "Use solid shot; our shell strike the enemy's side and fall into the water." The *Kearsarge*'s 11-inch shells began to do severe execution upon the *Alabama*'s quarter-deck section. The Confederate steamer's decks were covered with the dead and the wounded, and the ship was careening heavily to starboard from the

THE BATTLE OF NASHVILLE
December 15–16, 1864

effects of the shot-holes in her water-line. When the firing ceased, Captain Semmes dispatched an officer to the *Kearsarge* to say that the *Alabama* was sinking. The Confederate steamer settled stern foremost, launching her bows high in the air. Simultaneously her unhappy and desperate crew leaped overboard, and the waves were soon churning with drowning men. Happily an English yacht, the *Deerhound*, was upon the scene, and, having been allowed by the *Kearsarge* to go to the rescue, steamed up in the midst of the drowning men and rescued most of them. Captain Semmes was taken by the *Deerhound*'s boat from the water as he was sinking for the last time.

He went to England with the *Deerhound*, and was presented by officers of the British army and navy with a sword to re-

place that which he had cast into the sea from the deck of his sinking ship.

At Greensboro' he participated in the capitulation of General Joe Johnston, and, returning to Mobile, opened a law office. There, on December 15, 1865, he was arrested by order of Secretary Welles as a traitor. He was never tried, but was released under the amnesty proclamation of President Johnson.

He was for a short time editor of the *Memphis Bulletin*, and subsequently was Professor of Moral Philosophy in the State Seminary of Louisiana at Alexandria. At the time of his death, in August, 1877, he was engaged in the practice of law at Mobile.

U.S.S. Kearsarge

THE CAPTURE OF FORT FISHER
January 15, 1865

JAMES EWELL BROWN STUART, C.S.A., 1833–1864

This brilliant cavalry commander has been happily designated the "Prince Rupert" of the Confederate army. His familiar friends and comrades in arms took the three initial letters of his "given" names and made it "Jeb"—to them he was uniformly "Jeb" Stuart. He was born in Patrick County, Virginia, and graduated from the United States Military Academy in 1854. He joined a regiment of mounted riflemen then serving in Texas, and in 1855 he was transferred to the 1st U.S. cavalry, with the rank of second lieutenant. He married Flora, daughter of Colonel Philip St. George Cook, November 14, 1855, and on Dec. 20 of the same year he was promoted first lieutenant. During 1856 his regiment was engaged in Kansas, and in 1857 in Indian warfare. He was wounded in an action with the Cheyennes on Solomon's River, and while in process of recovery went to Washington to negotiate with the War Department concerning the sale of a sabre attachment that he had invented. Soon after he went to Harper's Ferry with General Lee and identified John Brown.

He then rejoined his regiment at Fort Riley; but in March, 1861, obtained leave of absence, being resolved to shape his course by the action of his State. When Virginia seceded he sent in his resignation, and it was accepted May 7—just after he had been notified of his promotion to a captaincy.

Before noticing the principal events in which he actively participated, it may be well to deal somewhat with the character of the man as he is presented to us by writers on the war. Very clearly one of his best-marked traits was his indifference to danger. It would be difficult to imagine a coolness more supreme. Like Admiral Lord Nelson, he seemed unaware of the meaning of the word fear. It was not that he seemed to defy peril—he appeared unconscious of it. At the battle of Ox Hill, in September, 1862, he advanced a piece of artillery down the road to Fairfax Courthouse, and suddenly found himself in the presence of a buzzing hornet's nest of Federal sharpshooters, who rose from the tall weeds a few score yards distant and poured a deadly fire into the cannoniers. Stuart was at the gun directing the firing, and sat on his horse, full front to the fire, with so perfect an air of unconsciousness that it was hard to believe that he realized his danger. When a staff officer said, "This fire is rather peculiar, general," "Jeb" Stuart seemed to wake up, as it were, to whistling bullets, and said indifferently, "It is getting rather warm."

The habitual temper of General Stuart's mind towards his adversaries was cool and soldierly. Federal prisoners were treated by him with uniform courtesy, and often left his headquarters declaring that they would never forget the kindness they had experienced. "I remember," says a Confederate writer, "an appeal once made to him by a prisoner, which amused everybody. One of his escorts spoke roughly to the prisoner, when the latter, seeing the general, exclaimed: 'General Stuart, I did not come here to be black-guarded'; at which Stuart laughed good-humoredly and reprimanded the person who had coarsely addressed the prisoner."

It is not easy to separate Stuart the man from Stuart the

West Point, 1854

Brigadier General, September, 1861
Major General, July, 1862

BATTLES:
Bull Run
Dranesville
Seven Days' battles
Second Bull Run
Catlett's Station
Ox Hill
Antietam
Chambersburg
Raid around McClellan
Fredericksburg
Chancellorsville
Gettysburg campaign
Middleburg
Upperville
Wilderness
Yellow Tavern (Killed)

1. Prescott Navy Revolver
   Model 1860 Caliber .36

2. Remington Army Revolver
   Model 1858 Caliber .44

3. Rogers and Spencer Revolver
   Model 1862 Caliber .44

4. Pettingill Army Revolver
   Model 1856 Caliber .44

5. Whitney Navy Revolver
   Caliber .36

6. Savage Navy Revolver
   Model 1856 Caliber .36

7. LeFaucheux Pin-fire Army Revolver
   Model 1861 Caliber .41

8. Le Mat Revolver
   Model 1856
   Calibers .44 and 12 gauge

9. Freeman Revolver
   Model 1862 Caliber .44

10. Wesson and Leavitt Revolver
    Model 1837 Caliber .40

11. Joslyn Army Revolver
    Model 1858 Caliber .44

12. Adams Army Revolver
    Model 1853 Caliber .44

13. Raphael Revolver
    Model 1861 Caliber .41

14. Perrin Army Revolver
    Model 1861 Caliber .45

15. Warner Revolver
    Model 1856 Caliber .36

16. Butterfield Revolver
    Model 1855 Caliber .36

17. Allen and Wheelock Revolver
    Model 1857 Caliber .44

18. Beal's Patent Revolver
    Model 1858 Caliber .44

19. Allen and Wheelock Revolver
    Navy model Caliber .36

20. Starr Revolver
    Model 1856 Caliber .44

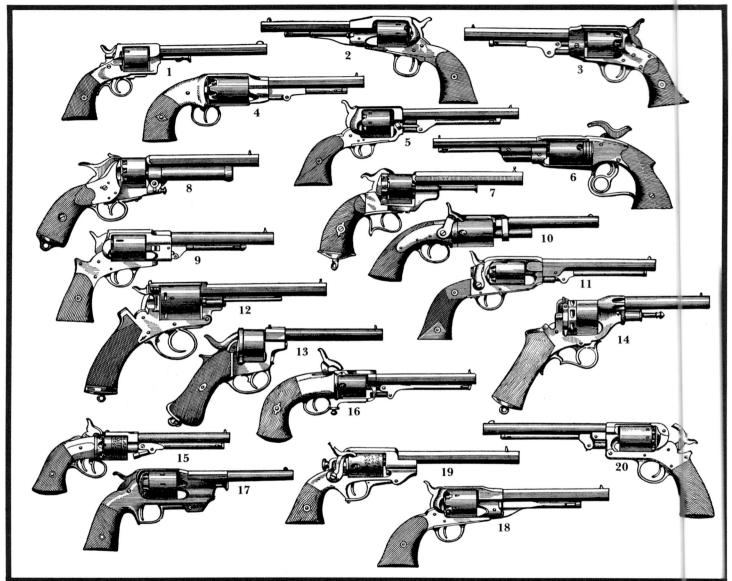

REVOLVERS USED IN THE CIVIL WAR

soldier. He was as ready for a fight as for a frolic. Gifted by nature with a splended physique, he was enabled to defy fatigue. Ambitious, fond of glory, and sensitive to blame or praise, he was yet endowed with a bold, independent spirit, which enabled him to defy all enemies. He was warm-hearted, and loved his friends dearly. There was in him an innate rollicking love of fun, a gallantry towards ladies, a fondness for bright colors, flowing plumes, brilliant spectacles and gay adventure which made him almost a living embodiment of Macaulay's picture of Prince Henry of Navarre. But Stuart's nerve was of stern stuff. Under all that laughter, gayety and cavalierism there was a soul that no peril could touch. That bright blue eye looked into the very face of death without a quiver of the lid, and dared the worst.

Soon after "Stonewall" Jackson's first appearance on the theatre of the war, and while he was holding the Point of Rocks Bridge in the Shenandoah Valley, "Jeb" Stuart was commissioned lieutenant-colonel, and reported to Colonel Jackson for assignment to duty. Jackson ordered the consolidation of all the cavalry companies into a battalion, to be commanded by Stuart, "who appeared then more like a well-grown, manly youth than the matured man he really was." Soon after he performed important services at the battle of Bull Run. He and his "yelling cavalry" swept down upon the rear of the defeated and retreating Union army, and completed its rout and demoralization. During the cessation of operations which followed he perfected his system of pickets and was engaged in several cavalry skirmishes. On September 24, 1861, he was made brigadier-general; and on December 20, 1861, while commanding a large foraging force, consisting of about 2500 men, he fell in with the Union forces near Dranesville. The Federals were in superior force, under General Edward O. C. Ord. A rocket, shot up from Ord's ranks, gave Stuart the first intimation of the presence of his foe. To give his wagon train time to retreat in safety, Stuart prepared for battle. He was exposed to a very severe cannonade, and, finding his men contending at serious disadvantage with a force greatly outnumbering them,

and almost concealed in ambush, after a desultory engagement he drew off his men and fell back two miles. The Federals did not pursue. Stuart's loss in killed and wounded was about 200.

His next notable appearance was in June, 1862, when he was called upon to make an examination of the Federal lines. His famous raid around McClellan's army began on the 13th, by an advance to the South Anna Bridge, on the Richmond and Fredericksburg Railroad. Stuart had with him about 1200 cavalry and a section of the Stuart horse artillery, the principal officers under him being Colonel Fitzhugh Lee and Colonel W. H. F. Lee. Early on Thursday morning they started east, and soon were having a brush with the Union outposts at Hanover Court-house. Thence they moved rapidly east to Old Church, where they had a skirmish and running fight with a detachment of Federal cavalry. There Stuart decided to complete the circuit of the Union army by pushing forward to Tunstall's Station, nine miles further east, and thence to the James. At Garlick's his forces destroyed two transports and a number of wagons. They captured Tunstall's on the York River Railway and tried to obstruct the road, and fired into a train laden with soldiers which dashed past them. After burning a railway bridge and a wagon train, they proceeded by moonlight south to Jones's Bridge on the Chickahominy, the repairing of which delayed their march till 1 p.m. on Friday. Once across, they made their way without difficulty to Charles City Court-house, and reached Richmond by the River Road early Saturday morning, June 16.

General Stuart was incessantly engaged during the seven days' fighting before Richmond. On July 25, 1862, he was commissioned as major-general of cavalry, and on August 22 he crossed the Rappahannock, penetrated General John Pope's camp at Catlett's Station, captured his official correspondence and personal effects, and made prisoners of several officers of his staff. During the night following he made an attack on Manassas Junction, and sent into the town a brigade of infantry, which took many prisoners and carried off stores of great value.

THE FIRST BATTLE OF BULL RUN

"When we regained the crest of the plateau with our guns, the retreat had begun all along the Union line. Gen. J.E.B. Stuart at the head of a body of yelling cavalry was in full pursuit, with drawn sabres. Stuart pursued the fugitives to the Sudley road. The prisoners taken greatly exceeded his own numbers."
*Joseph E. Johnston,
General, C.S.A.*

THE BATTLE OF FIVE FORKS
April 1, 1865

Stuart's cavalry was engaged in the second battle of Bull Run, and led the advance of "Stonewall" Jackson's corps in the ensuing invasion of Maryland. He performed important services at Antietam, guarding with artillery an eminence on Jackson's left that was essential to the security of the Confederate position, and leading the movement that resulted in the repulse of General Edwin V. Sumner's corps. A few weeks later he crossed the Potomac near Williamsport at the head of 1800 picked troopers, gained the rear of the Federal army, rode as far north as Mercersburg and Chambersburg, Pa., returned on the other side of McClellan's position, and recrossed the river below Harper's Ferry.

At the battle of Fredericksburg Stuart's cavalry guarded the extreme right of the Confederate line. Subsequently, in a raid to Dumfries, he ascertained the intended movements of the Union troops by means of a forged telegram that he sent to Washington. At Chancellorsville his cavalry screened "Stonewall" Jackson's march to the right of the Federal army. After General Jackson was mortally wounded and General Ambrose P. Hill was disabled, the command of Jackson's corps devolved temporarily on Stuart, who took command on the night of May 2, and directed its movements during the severe fighting of the following day. He led two charges in person and carried the ridge of Hazel Grove, which was the key to the field. He was sent forward to guard the flanks of the advancing column of Lee's army in the Gettysburg campaign, but was opposed and checked by the Federal cavalry at Fleetwood Hill and Stevensburg, with heavy loss on both sides. At Aldrie he was successful in an encounter with Federal cavalry, but at Middleburg and Upperville he was defeated. He was directed to cross the Potomac in advance of the infantry column, and take position on its right. He held the passes in the Blue Ridge for a while, and then made a raid in the rear of the National army, rejoining the main body at the close of the conflict at Gettysburg.

In the retreat from Gettysburg General Stuart guarded the gaps in the mountains, and while the Confederate army was intrenched on the north bank of the Potomac he engaged in several indecisive engagements with the cavalry of Generals Kilpatrick and John Buford.

During the operations in Virginia which followed the battle of Chickamauga, during the fall of 1863, General Stuart advanced with Hampton's division to protect from observation the flank of the army then moving towards Madison Court-house. On the 11th October the bulk of the Confederate army was at Culpepper; the command of Fitzhugh Lee, uniting with that of Stuart, quickly followed: and Lee had now so manoeuvred that he had actually turned General Meade's flank. But the Federal general had taken timely alarm. He had crossed the Rappahannock, and was rapidly retreating along the railroad line leading to Alexandria. On the 12th Lee arrived on the Rappahannock at Warrenton Springs, and that night General Stuart pushed on to Warrenton. He had guarded the flank of the army, driven off the Federal forces everywhere, and performed invaluable service. With 2000 cavalry he got completely hemmed in between Warrenton Junction and Manassas by the moving masses of the Federal infantry. Nothing remained but to "lay low," in camp parlance, within a distance of the Union troops, where every word of command could be distinctly heard. The body of Confederate cavalry was concealed in a thicket of pines. The accidental discharge of a firearm, the neighing of a horse, the rattling of a chain, would have discovered them to the enemy. The night was passed in fearful suspense. Stuart gave his officers and men to understand that surrender was not to be thought of, but that the foe was to be fought to the last. A council of war having been called, it was resolved, as the best thing that could be done under the circumstances, to desert the nine pieces of horse artillery, and for the cavalry in six columns to endeavor to cut their way through the enemy. But after some reflection Stuart resolved not to do this. At daybreak the rear guard of the Federals were seen in camp cooking their breakfasts, not a quarter of a mile away. Stuart had sent several scouts on foot through the Union lines to announce his situation to General Lee. He ordered them to put on infantry knapsacks, and, shouldering

muskets, to advance in the darkness to the road, fall into the Federal column, and, crossing it, to make their way to Warrenton and say to Lee that he was surrounded, and he "must send some of his people to help him out." Three of the scouts reached Warrenton in safety.

At daylight next morning Stuart knew by the cracking of skirmishers' muskets that Lee had received his message. The Federals were disordered by the unexpected cannonade, and Stuart limbered up his guns, and with cavalry and artillery dashed through the hostile ranks and rejoined General Lee.

On May 10, 1864, a portion of Sheridan's command, under Custer and Merrill, were encountered in the Wilderness by Stuart's cavalry near Ashland, at a place called Yellow Tavern. An engagement took place, and in a desperate charge at the head of a column General Stuart fell, terribly wounded. He was immediately taken to Richmond, and every effort made to save his life; but in vain. Towards evening of next day mortification set in. He was told, in answer to his inquiry, that death was fast approaching. He said, "I am resigned if i be God's will; but I would like to see my wife." He died immediately after joining in singing the hymn beginning:

Rock of Ages, cleft for me,
Let me hide myself in Thee.

Away Down South in Dixie

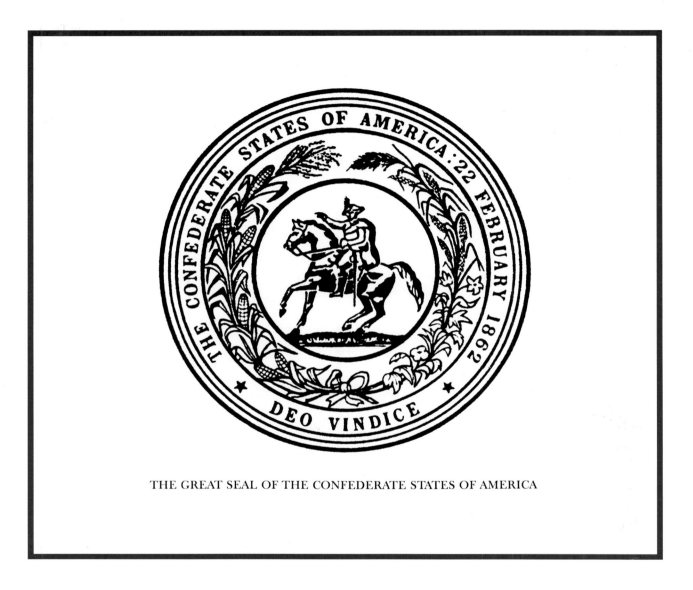

THE GREAT SEAL OF THE CONFEDERATE STATES OF AMERICA

THE FALL OF PETERSBURG
April 2, 1865

THE EVACUATION OF RICHMOND
April 2, 1865

INDEX

(Boldface figures indicate major reference)

ACKNOWLEDGMENTS

First I must thank the great ephemera collector and superb designer Jack Golden for showing me the two rare albums that are the core of this volume and for knowing where to put his hands on illustrations of anything else necessary to the completeness of this project. Next I would like to express my gratitude to Howard Morris for his constant good advice, understanding, and willingness to create the two handsome maps despite a busy schedule. David Arky was very cooperative in photographing the many items in the book, as was Amy Jones in securing some additional pictures. Sharon McIntosh was exceedingly kind to track down some of the most elusive of the Kurz and Allison prints, and Paul Ledman was a good neighbor in making his extensive Civil War collection available. I am also grateful to Mark D. Tomasko, Brian Riba, William Frost Mobley, and High Ridge Books for contributing valuable items to the book. Claire Streeter was indefatigable and ever-cheerful in her research and in the consolidation of far-flung facts. As usual, Robin James was ever-alert to typographical errors and inconsistencies in the manuscript, and Dana Cole was patient and very helpful in the make-up and production of a complex book. I would also like to thank Robert E. Abrams for (once more) taking it pretty much on faith that what I had in mind eventually would result in an attractive and salable book.